READING BATAILLE NOW

READING BATAILLE NOW

Edited by Shannon Winnubst

INDIANA UNIVERSITY PRESS
Bloomington and Indianapolis

Publication of this book is made possible in part with the assistance of a Challenge Grant from the National Endowment for the Humanities, a federal agency that supports research, education, and public programming in the humanities. Any views, findings, conclusions, or recommendations expressed in this publication do not necessarily reflect those of the National Endowment for the Humanities.

This book is a publication of

Indiana University Press
601 North Morton Street
Bloomington, IN 47404-3797 USA

http://iupress.indiana.edu

Telephone orders   800-842-6796
Fax orders   812-855-7931
Orders by e-mail   iuporder@indiana.edu

The paper used in this publication meets the minimum requirements of American National Standard for Information Sciences—Permanence of Paper for Printed Library Materials, ANSI Z39.48-1984.

Manufactured in the United States of America

Library of Congress Cataloging-in-Publication Data

Reading Bataille now / edited by Shannon Winnubst.
p. cm.
Includes bibliographical references and index.
ISBN 0-253-34822-6 (cloth : alk. paper) — ISBN 0-253-21882-9 (pbk. : alk. paper)
1. Bataille, Georges, 1897–1962. I. Winnubst, Shannon.
B2430.B33954R43 2007
194—dc22

2006017102

1 2 3 4 5   12 11 10 09 08 07

CONTENTS

ALPHONSO LINGIS

Foreword: Why Bataille Now?

Philosophy's founding texts, in Greek antiquity, had and have for philosophy a relevance the founding texts of the scientific disciplines do not have; the ultimate issues seem to have been addressed in them from the start. They were long studied with the reverence and hermeneutic sophistication that theologians devoted to Sacred Scripture. With Hegel, philosophy becomes the self-consciousness of history; since Hegel, what is demanded of philosophy is that it give an account of itself. Philosophy moves by turning back on its own texts. The meaning of any text one produces depends on the context; the state of the debate in which it intervenes depends on the prior texts it questions, repudiates, or extends. While research in the scientific disciplines means assemblage of facts and testing of hypotheses, the research required of candidates seeking to enter the academic profession of philosophy means philological, hermeneutic, and critical commentary on texts recognized to exist in the canon of philosophy. Since the meaning of a philosophical text is taken to be multiple, and it multiplies further with each new historical context in which it is read once again, ever more philosophical "research" will be produced. The new information technology promises to aggravate this situation: all the texts will be instantly available on the Internet, but have yet to be assembled, situated in evolving galaxies of interpretive contexts.

In this situation what Georges Bataille meant by philosophy appears singularly unassimilable. For him philosophy arises out of experience, indeed *is* experience. The philosophic wonder is not bent over philosophic texts, but like inquiry in the empirical and social sciences, it is turned upon the outlying environment, the physical and biological world, outer spaces. It crosses the boundaries between disciplines, holds in view what different disciplines uncover and formulate about the same complex entity, situation, or event. For Bataille, to practice philosophy was to scrupulously attend to the empirical researches of physical and cultural anthropology, studying archaic sexual practices and ancient religions, contemporary political science and economics, and the findings of neurology, physical dynamics, and astronomy.

We employ a great deal of cerebral energy in acquiring the relevant information and applying the paradigms to problems, and indeed the information age promises to force us to do so ever more. We also reflect on our experience. And this we consider to be really thinking. For Bataille, philosophical research on philosophical texts was philosophy only in the measure that it is tested by, and that it illuminates, the thinker's experience. But this experience itself is of little interest if it is only the experience of an academic. Experience must go further, deeper, become more intense, must go to extremes if it is to illuminate more than what is commonly known. Bataille withdrew into rural seclusion with his tubercular debility and depression. Pushed to the depths of despair, he gave himself over to psychotropic addiction and pursued the methods of ecstasy of ancient and foreign mystics, engaged his Catholicism to the point of preparing for the priesthood, explored atheism by writing blasphemies, and explored sexuality in thousands of sexual encounters and orgies, making the brothel his temple.

With extraordinary intellectual power, Bataille forged new concepts and tracked down originations, evolutions, confluences, and finalities in outlying regions of empirical observation and experimentation and in depths of inner experience. While biology continues to conceptualize a living organism as open to its environment and driven in its displacements and initiatives by lacks and need, Bataille found in his survey of organisms from the most simple to the most complex a production of energy in excess of what the organism needs, energy that has to be discharged. In his investigations of human economic systems from those of hunter-foragers, nomads, and sedentary agricultural societies to feudal, mercantile, and industrial societies, Bataille found that even societies with the most rudimentary equipment produce luxury products, that all economic systems tend to produce excess beyond what answers to needs or even wants. The disposal of this excess production is an ever more critical problem in the measure that economies acquire more resources and more powerful technological equipment. Bataille linked the devastating wars launched by the technologically advanced societies of the twentieth century to the problem of excess production inherent to their economies. His explanations are of decisive importance today, when the received theory is that the globalized competition of overheated productive economies will force societies to be regulated by democratic institutions and prevent war between them.

Foreword: Why Bataille Now?

It is striking that while anthropologists recognize that for any drive one can think of— belligerence, for example, sexual promiscuity, a touchy sensibility, or a drive for ego-gratification—anthropologists can designate well-documented cultures where this drive has an honored place in the culture, there does not seem to be any culture that has been able to honor all the drives that there are in the human composite. How different in biology and ethology, where for researchers understanding consists in identifying a biological and ecological justification for every anatomical and behavioral trait of each of the 8,000 species of birds and 350,000 species of beetles! Philosophy, on the contrary, has from the beginning promoted an ascesis, honoring certain human drives, discrediting and stigmatizing others. It accompanied and theoretically assisted the conversion of the ancient culture and politics of the passions into the modern culture and politics of emotions and feelings. If there is an ethics in Bataille, it lies in repudiating this ascesis, affirming and honoring base materialism and extreme emotions. He devoted a study to eroticism, domain of the most unbridled imaginative and emotional extravagances. Where philosophy since Greek antiquity had defined itself as a method of consolation in the face of death, Bataille sought in philosophy a joy in dying.

Since the Enlightenment, the philosophy of religions has affirmed only the evolved world religions, the monotheist and providential religions destined to universalization. The philosophy of religion converted religion into philosophy, a metaphorical metaphysics for the usage of the people. Bataille instead initiated himself in the oldest religion, recognized sacrifice to be its core, and devoted himself to particularist religions, elaborated for very restricted hunter-forager or feudal societies. From these ancient and particularist religions, Bataille sought not theoretical explanations, nor, like anthropology, a symbolic representation of the environmental, economic, and political organization of a culture, but sacrificial and ecstatic experiences.

To see clearly the extraordinary accomplishments of his thought, instead of tracking down the antecedents and context of his conceptual tools, we have to do the reverse: we have to disengage his insights from the antecedents and contexts designated by his vocabulary. Bataille works with a concern for the contrast between humans and the other animals that he inherited from the anthropocentrism of philosophy but that he also found anthropology to have discovered in many cultures. Even when, as in *Erotism,* he declared that "animal nature, or sexual exuberance, is that which prevents us from being reduced to mere things. Human nature, on the contrary, geared to specific ends in work, tends to make things of us at the expense of our sexual exuberance" (1986, 158), he identified erotic glamour, exhibitionism, and games to be distinctively human—ignoring the ornamentation of birds of paradise and great-horned sheep; the elaborate and fantastic courtship rituals documented among jewelfish, whitefish, sticklebacks, cichlids, and guppies; among fruit flies, fireflies, cockroaches and spiders; among crabs; among mountain sheep, antelopes, elk, lions, and sea lions; and among emperor penguins, ostriches, argus pheasants, and hummingbirds. He constructed his concept of eroticism as well as of transgression on the human-animal opposition. He equally made toolmaking, language, and laughter to be distinctively human. The early work of Claude Lévi-Strauss similarly sought in the incest taboo the line of demarcation between humans and the other animals, between nature and culture; recent ethologists have been seeking to understand how birds and mammals also avoid incestuous copulations. Today we have to uncover Bataille's insights from his use of the oppositions between human and animal, nature and culture, nature and history, which have been abandoned in the most fruitful studies of evolutionary biology and cognitive ecology—though it is true that the deep sources of this animal-human opposition in many cultures are not being studied today. In general, lacking in Bataille is a detailed knowledge of ethology and ecology now available to us.

There is also a residue of sin and Catholicism in Bataille's theory of transgression. Still, Bataille's intense sense that there is something repugnant in sex, in the spilling of seed and the shedding of blood in sex, is more extensive and far older than Catholicism.

While Bataille forged much of his conceptual vocabulary with the language of surrealism and mysticism, when he set out to formulate a philosophical expression of his insights, he resorted to the language of Hegelianism. To be sure, he wrote only to exceed Hegelianism, constructing a concept of sovereignty in opposition to the Hegelian concept of mastery rising in the master-slave dialectic. Explicitly opposing the telos of Absolute Knowledge in Hegel, he showed all knowledge issuing in knowing nothing, in absurdity and laughter. But it is undeniable that residues of Hegel subsist in Bataille's most original breakthroughs and to some measure deviate from them. The Hegelian notion that the essential work of thought is delimitation and definition, which operate by negation, conflicts with and confused Bataille's own practice. It led him to define sovereignty in relationship with nothingness; in opposition to the worker, the sovereign one aims at nothing; thought is sovereign when its bonds with the real world are broken, when in the break-off of reasonings it is plunged into nothingness, subsisting on its own and by its own force. Sovereignty is thus absolute solitude—which conflicts with Bataille's own conviction that sovereignty is communication. The extraordinary analysis of *Erotism* and *The Accursed Share* is shackled by the dialectic in which historical patterns are forced to be logically successive stages. In fact, today's culture is woven with atavisms as modern art recaptures tribal artifacts, as extreme emotions are driven by the most archaic compulsions. Bataille did realize that art no longer aims to depict beauty that materializes an angelic ideal, as today the religion of a universal and paternal God is giving way to a resurgence of the epiphany of sublime in transitory events.

The editor of this book points out that Bataille's work on political economy, *The Accursed Share,* is the least discussed, but likely the one most relevant to the most urgent theoretical tasks of today. In today's industrialized countries, the problem is not production but distribution. The major powers, driven by their overheated productive forces, are launched into a new Great Game to control not only the energy resources but the globalized market. Industry, increasingly robotized and computerized, reduces ever further its labor costs. Citizens are required, not as producers but as consumers. But with the ever-increasing gap between rich and poor countries, and rich and poor within countries, it remains unresolved how the citizens are to acquire the resources to function as consumers.

The conflict this situation produces is waged in an entirely new form, not with an arms race but with sabotage. The great industrial juggernauts, which require great teams of engineers to assemble, remain vulnerable to small numbers of saboteurs. In the sixties, small commandos hijacked commercial airliners; in the seventies, single individuals injecting arsenic into bottles in out-of-the-way supermarkets brought down giant pharmaceutical companies; in the eighties, high-school dropouts hacked into the supercomputers of the Pentagon; now the greatest military apparatus the planet has ever seen is thwarted by small commandos.

In a world where global economic competition was taken to replace the conflict of political ideologies, religion resurges as the locus of resistance to economic domination. Democratic institutions are promoted, even with military force, to implant the tolerance that would refute the simplifications of religious ideologies. Bataille, however, recaptured the deep compulsions that are institutionalized as religions: the craving for sacrifice that he understood by releasing it in himself.

Bataille is not only a thinker; he is a writer. He wrote literature, but he also forged vigorous and illuminating forms of philosophical expression. To practice conscientiously the craft of writing is an ethical imperative for a thinker. Writing an opaque language designed to demonstrate the sophistication of the writer rather than communicate, clogging one's text with citations to give it authority—these are moral faults in a writer. If one is convinced that philosophy, and one's own insights, are important enough to set aside all the other concerns of life to devote oneself to, one is enjoined to write so as to genuinely communicate with others. In this Bataille is exemplary.

WORKS CITED

Bataille, Georges. 1986. *Erotism.* Trans. Mary Dalwood. San Francisco: City Lights Books.
———. 1991. *The Accursed Share: Volume 1.* Trans. Robert Hurley. New York: Zone Books.

READING BATAILLE NOW

SHANNON WINNUBST

Introduction

Reading Bataille Now—a precocious title, if not a pernicious one, aiming to grasp all readers for all times. But the "Now," as we ironically know from Hegel, is only an empty universal, a meaningless placeholder. While Hegel was confounded by this, insisting that dialectical reason must push forward beyond such empty significations to articulate the Absolute, Bataille thought otherwise. The sheer excess of all those little *nows,* those endless moments proliferating with reckless abandon as the infinity of subjects constitute their particular meanings, became the very object of his thinking, his writing, his experience. And so the title is saved: it is scandalous and luxurious, not totalitarian and arrogant, gesturing to the excess of an endless stream of *nows* that may or may not be subject to further organization.

But, admittedly, the title carries other connotations as well—particularly the problematically moralistic one of stating that now, early in the twenty-first century of the Christian calendar, the time seems to have arrived in which we "Westerners" might want—and even need—to read Bataille. Amidst the transnational circuits of capital, paired with the obfuscating resurgences of nationalist violence, the view of Bataille's general economy may finally begin to make sense: his relentless insistence on the fundamental role of expenditure in all circuits of exchange may finally become a voice we can hear. And so it is not merely Bataille whom we ought to read now, but his three-volume magnum opus on political economy, *The Accursed Share.* (And the title of this book is, once more, certainly precocious—although not necessarily also pernicious.)

But this meaning, too, falls short. To reduce Bataille's text to a kind of

warning that we must now heed is to fail to read him alongside his own courageous thinking—it is to fall back into the restricted economy of useful
morals, demonstrable politics, and anticipated *teloi*. If there is an ethics in
Bataille's texts, it cuts against the grain of such traditional concepts: it
springs from sovereignty, from expenditure, from glorious futility. While
the essays gathered together here speak from the contemporary political
space of transnational capitalism, hyper-moralism, liberalism, and their
more subtle inscriptions in our bodies, desires, pleasures, loves, laughters,
and ecologies, they do so without positing Bataille as The Answer, the salve
for our woes. These essays and this volume struggle not to reduce Bataille to
the restricted economy of utility that he diagnoses so lucidly as the constitutive blind spot of all economies of appropriation. And yet, each of them
also reads him as a voice that speaks quite differently to contemporary experience and all of its contours.

To do this, to read Bataille without reducing him to our prefabricated,
restricted economies of meaning, requires many ways of reading him. Long
taken up in the Anglophone academy primarily by literary theorists and art
historians, Bataille is well known as a literary bad boy—a moniker that has
allowed the disciplines of philosophy, economics, and political theory to dismiss him from their domain. Although French intellectuals of the late
twentieth century—Foucault, Derrida, Lacan, Irigaray, Deleuze and Guattari, Kristeva—widely recognized him as one of the most influential figures
of the early twentieth century, the work of Georges Bataille continues to function as a sort of blind spot in Anglophone scholarship engaging twentieth-
century French philosophy. Associated almost exclusively with his early
work of erotic fiction, *Story of the Eye,* Bataille retains, as Pierre Lamarche
puts it in his essay for this volume, "the simultaneously exotic and scandalous air of the old-fashioned libertine *homme des lettres*—the medievalist, archivist, mystic pornographer who was fascinated by the abject, excessive,
debauched, and diabolical." His name is almost always uttered along with
that other libertine, Sade, ushering them both into the waste bin of literary
erotica, cleanly dismissed from the realm of serious or real "philosophy,"
"political theory," or, most certainly, "economic theory." And yet Bataille
wrote three volumes on political economy, *The Accursed Share.*

The essays of this collection read this omission as an act of willful ignorance. This deliberate omission of Bataille's most systematic work on political economy displays a deeper discomfort with the themes of those
texts: the radical rethinking of the role of expenditure in society. For cultures and philosophical systems so deeply entrenched in the fundamental
value of utility, this is not something easily heard. And for cultures and

philosophical systems so deeply entrenched in instrumental reason as a faculty framed by teleology, this non-teleological rendering of the very act of thinking may not even make sense.

It did not make any sense to Bataille's contemporary culture either. Published in 1949, the first volume of *The Accursed Share* sold so few copies that the second and third volumes were never published during his lifetime. (Bataille died in 1962, and volumes two and three were finally published in Volume 8 of his *Oeuvres Complètes* in 1976.) Written across that intense period of European history that witnessed the close of the Second World War and the emergence of the Cold War, these three volumes attempt to think against the trend of historical thought that would render capitalism or communism the only two alternatives to fascism. Michel Surya describes this as a period of intense production and seriousness for Bataille, a period in which *politics* in its broadest sense took hold of his writing, leaving the Dada and surrealist scandals from the 1930s "a distant and disparate echo" (2002, 372). The struggle not to align himself (despite affinities with communism over capitalism) with either of "the great geo-ideological and soon to be military powers" (2002, 374) apparently pushed Bataille to his "Copernican transformation: a reversal of thinking—and of ethics" (1991a, 25): namely, that *"it is not necessity but its contrary, 'luxury,' that presents living matter and mankind with their fundamental problems"* (1991a, 12, his emphasis).

For Bataille, working to see the general economy and then to change it presents us with a call to ethics. This request of us is evident in the fiction, the early essays, and especially in the systematic work of *The Accursed Share*. But in undertaking this ethical duty, Bataille does not strictly make arguments for and against explicit concepts; he does not disprove the value of utility and then logically prove the desirability of sovereignty. This kind of writing and the epistemology it enacts is precisely the kind of thinking—and living—that Bataille is trying to avoid and undermine. Rather, as Alison Brown puts it, "he exhibits the freedom of sovereignty in his writing: he exhibits the courage to look at the accursed share that many of us refuse out of squeamishness or fear" (personal correspondence).

As the essays in this volume attempt to respond to this ethical call with some of this Bataillean courage, they cross disciplinary boundaries and styles of reading and writing, just as Bataille always did. Locating him explicitly as a kind of missing link between the nineteenth-century Hegel/ Marx lineage and late-twentieth-century French figures, the essays in this collection draw on many disciplines to place Bataille's work in direct conversation with some of the most prevalent contemporary fields of theory: post-Hegelian ethics; Marxist economics and politics; poststructuralist feminism; philosophy of biology; political theory; the discipline of theater; psychoanalysis; queer theory; and economics. Moreover, while many of the essays are written in traditional academic styles of argumentation and speculation, a few respond to Bataille's performativity with their own performative styles, taking up the possibilities offered when we think *with and through* Bataille, rather than only about him. As a whole, the collection aims not only to locate Bataille as a missing historical link, but more provocatively, to argue that he presents an alternative, untaken route.

In Part One, "Situating Bataille," Jesse Goldhammer, Amy Wendling, and Pierre Lamarche place Bataille's work in a variety of historical, political, and philosophical trajectories to begin unfolding what is at stake in his Copernican transformation.

In "Dare to Know, Dare to Sacrifice: Georges Bataille and the Crisis of the Left," Jesse Goldhammer offers an intellectual and political history for Bataille's unique anti-Enlightenment anarchism. Locating Bataille's political thinking in the long trend of French progressivism that reaches back into the eighteenth-century *philosophes* and extends into twentieth-century versions of anarchism, Goldhammer shows how Bataille's early notions of sacrifice and later notions of expenditure break radically from the tradition of leftist politics in France. Goldhammer notes Bataille's participation in several groups—*Contre-Attaque, Acéphale,* and the *Collège de Sociologie*—and draws on his essays from the 1930s, the first volume of *The Accursed Share,* and the work of fiction *Blue of Noon* to argue that Bataille developed a radical form of anarchism fueled by the inability of the left to break from the logics of amelioration and progress embedded in classical liberalism. Following Denis Hollier, Goldhammer develops how Bataille gives anguish, a powerful feeling of torment engendered by the left's tragic circumstances, a political, revolutionary significance—namely, in Bataille's hands, anguish has the power to direct the force of unproductive expenditure. Developing this particularly in *Blue of Noon,* Goldhammer concludes with the provocation that among all the lessons Bataille may have for left-wing political movements —not only in France, but throughout the world—his notions of power may be the most important of all.

Amy Wendling continues to locate Bataille's thinking in its intellectual and historical roots by contrasting his work with that of Marx. In "Sovereign Consumption as a Species of Communist Theory: Reconceptualizing Energy," Wendling shows how Bataille counterposes a profligate nature to the miserly nature characteristic of bourgeois life. While Marx argued that the idea of scarcity is itself historical, determined by the relations of bourgeois economics, Wendling shows how, for Bataille, Marx ultimately falls prey to exactly this naturalized concept, particularly when he valorizes the teleology of revolution. According to Wendling, Bataille's concept of a profligate nature is an exemplar of distinctly non-modern views of nature. To show this, she traces three genealogies of the concept of energy that we find operative in Bataille: the foundation of the discipline of biology (vitalism, mechanism, and organicism); the insights of structuralism; and the doctrine of medieval emanation. She then shows how Marx remains tethered to a narrow concept of energy, which in turn is hampered by a presupposition of scarcity. Because of this, Marx never fully breaks from the nature/culture dichotomy or the bourgeois notion of nature it subtends. Developing this through Marx's theory of labor, which critically lacks any robust Bataillean sense of consumption, Wendling concludes (contra Goldhammer) that all revolutionary political theory is tethered to bourgeois scarcity, which becomes the focus of Bataille's critique in *Sovereignty,* the third volume of *The Accursed Share.*

In "The Use Value of G.A.M.V. Bataille," Pierre Lamarche extends this examination of Bataille's Marxist heritage by placing it in the context of both Bataille's infamous break from the surrealists and his alleged affinity for the Marquis de Sade. Following Wendling's argument regarding the limitations of Marx's theory of labor, Lamarche shows how an attenuated sense of use-value keeps Marxist analyses trapped within the restricted economy of capital. He then traces this analysis of expenditure in *The Accursed Share* back to Bataille's writings from the late 1920s and early 1930s on base materialism and abjection, and particularly his infamous break from Breton. Because this break is precipitated by a different treatment of Sade, Bataille came to be simply identified with a Sadean (and often apolitical) debauchery; however, Lamarche argues that such a reduction occludes the more radical—and political—meaning of transgression at work in Bataille's notions of expenditure and sovereignty. To draw out these politics, he locates Bataille's reappropriation of Sade in Bataille's desire, in the mid/late-1930s, to develop a revolutionary strategy that would provide a meaningful alternative to orthodox Marxism (and its extreme form, Stalinism) and fascism for working-class people—an alternative Breton and the surrealists could not provide. Through an astute analysis of Bataille's meditations on Sade's use-value, Lamarche demonstrates how, for Bataille, Sade's use-value is to subvert the bourgeois morality: through Sade, Bataille shows how we can liberate ourselves from a culture of work—a culture devoted to exchange and accumulation—to a culture that, truly, privileges the satisfaction of real needs and desires—a culture of expenditure. This then gives way to a politics and culture of *enjoyment,* which Lamarche develops through discussions of sovereignty from Volume III of *The Accursed Share,* particularly its break from Hegelian notions of mastery and their implicit counterpart, Marxist bourgeois notions of labor. Lamarche concludes that Bataille's radical politics views the goal of working-class struggle as the liberation *from* work itself.

Part Two, "Pleasures and the Myth of Transgression," then takes up the reading of transgression that Lamarche problematizes. At the heart of the long-standing readings of Bataille as the old-fashioned Sadean libertine lies a notion of transgression as the route to sovereignty, radical expenditure, and all other Bataillean excesses. Drawing out Lamarche's suggestion that such a reading of transgression is limited to a restricted economy, the essays of this section turn to the questions of pleasures and eroticism in Bataille's texts to suggest a reading of transgression from the standpoint of general economy.

In "Bataille's Queer Pleasures: The Universe as Spider or Spit," I place Bataille in the contemporary field of queer theory and its attempts to reorient us radically from the narratives of desire that have grounded concepts of subjectivity in the Western tradition. Situating queer theory through an overview of two of its dominant theoretical frameworks, the Lacanian and the Foucaultian analyses of desire, I show how the texts of Bataille do not fall back into the problematic notions of scarcity that ground not only narratives of desire, but more specifically the politics of capitalism and heteronormative sexuality that they spawn: Bataille's texts operate out of a fundamentally different register that may speak more strongly to the aims of queer theory—the register of pleasure. Locating this political and psychological schema of desire and its scarcity in an epistemology of utility and teleology, I show (through contemporary examples of sodomy laws) how queer politics would benefit from taking up this more general law of utility, if we are to resist heteronormative notions of desire and all of their sociopolitical power. To develop this, I turn to *The History of Eroticism,* Volume II of *The Accursed Share,* to show how Bataille's rich sense of eroticism, "the accursed domain *par excellence*" (1991b, 18), opens a field of pleasures irreducible to the logics of either utility or transgression issued by restricted economies. I contrast Bataillean eroticism with the Hegelian notion of knowledge (and Derrida's reading of Bataille on Hegel) to show how the logic of transgression will never exceed the limited economy from which it is promulgated. I then conclude with that infamous work of pornographic fiction, *Story of the Eye,* to show that it is not a logic of transgression, but of ecstatic pleasures that are gloriously futile, that drives this brilliant story—a story about nothing that may have everything to say to contemporary queer politics.

Zeynep Direk continues this meditation on Bataille's notions of eroticism in her essay, "Erotic Experience and Sexual Difference in Bataille." Developing Bataille's notion of erotic experience in terms of his general economy, Direk shows how erotic experience suspends the world of restricted economy, leading us back to the impersonal ground of our incarnated existence and a way of communicating that takes us beyond our separate identities. Reading this as an invitation to rethink subjectivity by going back to that expenditure of energy in a shared space of incarnated openness, Direk argues that this communication is the very space of sexual difference. For Direk, this raises the question of an ethics of erotic experience, a question that echoes Irigaray's query about an ethics of sexual difference. Facing the apparently misogynist trends in Bataille's fiction and theorizing, Direk boldly argues that his radical reconsideration of embodiment, as both historical and cosmic, undercuts the objectification necessary for such misogyny. Rather, she takes up the masculinized virility of Bataille's writing as a way to place it in the Irigarayan space of sexual difference; and from that space, she then explores the possibility of an ethics of erotic experience in Bataille as a source for rethinking a new cohabitation on earth. Acknowledging the utilitarian civilization in which we live, Bataille invites us to a radical reflection on a new economy that takes seriously the biological nature of our existence. From that point of departure, Direk shows the specific ways in which a Bataillean ethics of eros accommodates negation, violence, and the possibility of harm to the other, enabling it to account for the failures and paradoxes of the eros.

Alison Brown continues these meditations on eroticism, pleasure, desire, sexual difference, and sexuality in her essay, "Malvolio's Revenge." Following Direk's provocative suggestions that erotic experience bespeaks a particular kind of interior communication, Brown takes up the impossible task of writing that experience. She sees quite clearly that Bataille does not use philosophy as a way to prove some arguments over others. He shifts the terrain of philosophy, thinking, and experience radically: he "proves" freedom through the sovereignty he exhibits in his writing. Taking up the possibilities he thereby opens, Brown offers us a fictional gloss on Emily Brontë's *Wuthering Heights,* written from the contemporary hot, sizzling desert of central Arizona. Brown gives us a character, Sadie, who has clearly been killed to the point where she can't even think anymore—literally. It is too painful. Trapped in mere repetition, she has lost all sense of that *extra thing*—that *accursed share*—that never bows down to the yoke of utility. As Brown takes us through the trials and joys of Sadie's transformations out of servility, she shows, once more, how such a transformation can never come from what the restricted economy itself markets as transgressive. The most performative of the essays in this collection, Brown's essay is likely also the most provocative—for those with the patience and ears to hear it.

Part Three, "Bodies and Animality," continues this performative writing as it turns to the reframing of embodied experience that comes through the perspective of general economy. Arguing against several poststructuralist attempts to rethink embodiment, these essays place the body and its animality in Bataille's general economy of expenditure, playfully inviting us to engage such excess through their very writing.

In "The Private Life of Birds: From a Restrictive to a General Economy of Reason," Ladelle McWhorter continues Brown's efforts to think through and with Bataille and the radical possibilities he opens. Taking up the long-standing feminist critiques of phallocentric reason, she shows how the project of countering and dismantling, of moving to rethink the knowing subject as an embodied subject, will not be sufficient to rid epistemology, and the cultures and practices bound up with it, of phallocentrism. Thinking itself must be wholly reconceived, rethought not only as embodied but also as fundamentally a-telic: Bataille's general economy of expenditure invites such a possibility. Meditating on building a birdhouse for her lover, on Darwin's own fascination with bird-watching aboard the *H.M.S. Beagle,* on a possible meeting between Darwin and Frankenstein, and on Irigaray's critiques of mimesis, McWhorter meanders around and through and into and out of this activity of bird-watching—to what end? She insists that I warn you: engagement with this essay may very well amount to a complete waste of time.

In "S/laughter and Anima-lēthē," Lucio Privitello continues the theme of animality in ways that are both more and less systematic than the playfulness of McWhorter. He approaches *The Accursed Share* through animality and laughter, themes that have received less attention in the study of the works of Bataille, especially in reference to his work on political economy. Reading animality and laughter in conjunction (and as a coincidence of opposites), while tracking them through Bataille's *The Accursed Share,* allows the notion of "intimacy" to surface, a notion crucial in the deformations of communication. For Bataille, intimacy is the willingness to be sacrificed and the crowning anti-accomplishment of "project," especially that of the technicalities of professorial philosophical systems. Animality and laughter are the dark heart of Bataille's formulation of a paradoxical philosophy, a philosophy that does not steal away at experimenting outside what is profitably and securely known, which includes the framework of political economy.

Dorothy Holland extends this playful discussion of embodiment through a turn to the discipline of theater. In "Bodies at Play: A General Economy of Performance," Holland argues against the inclination toward an erasure of the material body that often comes in the wake of poststructuralist critiques, particularly those grounded in Judith Butler's concept of performativity. Questioning the use of theatrical metaphors without consideration of actual theatre practices, Holland turns to Bataille to radically reframe our understanding of *bodies at play* from the perspective of general economy. To do so, she follows the more performative styles of Brown and McWhorter, inviting us into the laughter of a bawdy production of *The Taming of the Shrew* and the corporeally challenging and confusing performance of *Mnemonic* by Theatre de Complicite. Her delightfully lengthy descriptions initiate us into a Bataillean sense of play, a play that disrupts the operations of the limited economy by squandering resources, energy, and time. Tracing this Bataillean expenditure in the realm of theater, Holland shows how transgression is not the head-on assault that only reaffirms the strength of the prohibition; rather, it is an oblique movement, a movement toward gloriously wasting the accursed share.

In the final part, "Sovereign Politics," the collection turns to the explicit subject of politics and economics. Drawing on many of the themes in the previous three parts, these essays offer concrete examples of how the shift to the perspective of general economy alters our understandings of economics and politics.

In *"The Accursed Share* and *The Merchant of Venice,"* Andrew Cutrofello uses Shakespeare's play to reflect on Bataille's critique of capitalism. In keeping with the principles of his general economic theory, particularly the question of how to liquidate rather than accumulate excess wealth, Bataille regarded capitalism as completely inept. Instead of enabling individuals to achieve human dignity through shared experiences of sovereign consumption, capitalist relations of production subordinate humanity to the relentless—though doomed—pursuit of unchecked growth. In *The Merchant of Venice,* Shakespeare clearly articulated a critique of nascent capitalism, opposing the pure expenditure of generosity to the calculating logic of usury and investment—an opposition that he frames as that between Christian and Jewish attitudes toward wealth. Bataille, however, took a different view. Not unlike Weber, he regarded capitalism as an extension of Christian asceticism; and accordingly, he looks not to Christ but to Nietzsche for an ethic of shared sovereignty. Bataille also takes pains to show that Nietzsche had nothing but contempt for the inherently servile anti-Semitism that was embraced by his Nazi idolators. Though the anti-Semitism depicted in *The Merchant of Venice* is arguably different in kind from Nazi anti-Semitism, Bataille's critique of fascism and his appeal to a Nietzschean rather than a Christian ethic lend themselves to an alternative construal of the opposition that Shakespeare depicts between the generous Antonio and the calculating Shylock. Cutrofello shows how Shakespeare himself complicates the seemingly clear-cut opposition between Christian and Jew, notably in his treatment of the mysterious melancholy that haunts both Antonio and Shylock's daughter, Jessica. Finally, after comparing Bataille's self-described "Copernican turn" in economics to Kant's Copernican turn in cosmology, Cutrofello explores a number of difficulties that arise in connection with Bataille's view of sacrifice as the only (vanishing) event in which a *pure* act of consumption takes place. After speculating on how Bataille might have liked *The Merchant of Venice* to turn out—with the Christian Portia diabolically claiming a pound of Antonio's *soul*—Cutrofello concludes that when all is said and done, we might still prefer the ending that Shakespeare gave his play.

In "Politics and the Thing: Excess as the Matter of Politics," Richard Lee turns to the most basic category at work in the closed economy of utility: the thing. Musing on childhood experiences of helping his dad with "manly" home improvement projects, Lee traces the question of sovereignty in the closed domain of utility back through Heidegger's meditations on thinghood to show how a more general economy must already be at work in constituting sovereignty—and subsequently thinghood—as such. While Heidegger's phenomenological analysis is, precisely because it is phenomenological, delimited by the sphere that pertains to the mode of being of Dasein, Lee argues that Bataille's shift to the level of general economy necessarily moves beyond that mode of being to the conditions for the possibility of concern at all. Using the function of utility as the link between Heidegger's specific analysis and Bataille's general economic analysis, Lee shows how a Bataillean turn toward practices such as sacrifice and the sacred attune us to those operations that allow for an expenditure without return; consequently, these practices show us how the sphere of utility itself presupposes an entire sphere of expenditure without return that makes possible the sphere of utility in which energy is used for productive purposes. Tracing Bataille's readings of the practices of sacrifice in Aztec societies to the destructive force that the question of wealth poses to us, Lee argues that the issue of politics is not the equitable distribution of things within a closed economy of utility, but the relation of sovereignty to what is the opposite of a thing because it stands outside the realm of ends and means that constitute a thing. It is from this perspective of the sovereign withdrawal from things that Lee argues we must focus our "political" attention on the motivations behind dropping bombs and occupying foreign countries.

Finally, in "Excess and Depletion: Bataille's Surprisingly Ethical Model of Expenditure," Allan Stoekl examines Bataille's theory of expenditure in light of the ecological, as well as the economic, problem of depletion. Is Bataille's theory obsolete? Does it propose, in counterproductive fashion, the need to burn off excess resources—fundamentally, excess energy—when, in fact, we are facing the imminent depletion of those very resources? How does one go about privileging waste in an era in which waste seems to be the root of all evil? Taking up contemporary economic theories of sustainability, particularly those of Stephen A. LeBlanc, Stoekl argues that Bataille's theory is in fact one of both expenditure and depletion. Placing Bataille's insights about the role of expenditure in closed economies in the contemporary context of the global depletion of fossil fuels, Stoekl shows how Bataille's logic may offer a way out of the austerity—and thus the failure—of contemporary theories of conservation. He traces how wealth alters not only according to the productivity of human labor and its technological refinements, but also according to the energy sources burned off: the rise of civilization, Stoekl argues, is tied directly to the type of fuels used to power and feed it. Therefore, the alteration in fuel sources in the last half of the twentieth century presents Bataille's theories of expenditure with a need to think simultaneously about depletion. Showing how Bataille, despite his own theories, opens onto a reconsideration of value in light of its energy sources, Stoekl brings these insights to bear directly on the quandaries facing contemporary "car cultures" and hyper-consumption. By following Bataille's logic, Stoekl argues we will ultimately arrive at another way of thinking about what human survival will mean in the future—how, in other words, sustainability can be conceived in relation to the most fundamental human practices.

As a whole, this collection of essays offers several different ways in which Georges Bataille's three-volume work in political economy, *The Accursed Share,* might radically alter our understandings of the contemporary world. The tone and rhythm and sensibility for such an undertaking is cultivated for us in the Foreword by Alphonso Lingis.

WORKS CITED

Bataille, Georges. 1991a. *The Accursed Share: Volume I.* Trans. Robert Hurley. New York: Zone Books.

———. 1991b. *The Accursed Share: Volumes II and III.* Trans. Robert Hurley. New York: Zone Books.

Surya, Michel. 2002. *Georges Bataille: An Intellectual Biography.* Trans. Krzysztof Fijalkowski and Michael Richardson. London and New York: Verso.

SITUATING BATAILLE

Part One

ONE

JESSE GOLDHAMMER

Dare to Know, Dare to Sacrifice: Georges Bataille and the Crisis of the Left

> *It is a strange paradox: if one perceives the profound lack of a way out, the profound absence of an end and of meaning, then—and only then—can one actually, with a liberated spirit, lucidly tackle practical problems.*
> GEORGES BATAILLE, "POLITIQUE"

Suppose Western leftists conceded that they could no longer judge right from wrong and trust that scientific progress or political power could improve the human condition. What then? Left-wing certainties about justice, progress, and power have strong roots in eighteenth-century France, where ideas circulating among the *philosophes* helped to give birth to the first modern revolution and progressive movement.[1] With their emphasis on natural rights, reason, progress, science, and democracy and their general disdain for any authority other than the rule of law, the French *philosophes* gave radicals on the left-hand side of the 1791 French National Assembly ample justification to retake their sovereignty from aristocratic elites. The Revolution conferred natural rights to brothers, citizens, and workers, safeguarding their freedom and equality; it reveled in practical reason, which illuminated the seemingly uncontrollable causes of human misery, such as superstition, disease, poverty, and ignorance, and paved the way for progress; and it resuscitated the ancient idea of democracy, leaving no safe harbor for monarchism and other tyrannies. Until the early part of the twentieth century, this revolutionary legacy inspired the French left to challenge the exploitation of the many by the few.

By the 1930s, however, the French leftist movement was beginning to show signs of fatigue. Leftists with state power were able neither to convert their theories into effective policy nor to prevent right-wing attacks and cooptation. Similarly, those on the left who challenged the state were ultimately ineffective in mobilizing massive groups of workers. To use a word that held wide currency among French leftists in the 1930s, there was an overwhelming sense of impotence. Though the exhaustion of the left was augured by political events such as the rise of fascism, it was also the product of larger theoretical problems. In the nineteenth century, the French left had often unsuccessfully faced political challenges, but failures such as the revolution of 1848 did not fundamentally weaken core progressive ideas. During the 1930s, however, progressive actions and theories crumbled commensurately in France. Moving to the right, many French progressives abandoned class-based loyalties and parties that had long been the glue of left-wing movements and turned instead toward nationalism. The Soviet Union, wishfully heralded by many in the French left as a model of progressive statecraft, descended into the Great Purge and one-party authoritarianism. Social and economic progress stalled due to the Great Depression, leading many to believe optimistically that capitalism was in mortal danger. One might expect that systemic market failures and unstable parliamentarism would only confirm the left-wing worldview and strengthen its resolve. Instead, political and economic crises drove the French Third Republic to the right. In response to the rise of fascism throughout Europe, the French left rallied to Léon Blum's Popular Front government in 1936, only to discover the radical elements of the Front mollified when its members were actually elected to power. With political authority weakened, economic progress stymied, and social justice undermined by the left's ineffectuality, events of the 1930s revealed that French progressivism was becoming unmoored from its eighteenth-century philosophical anchor.

Georges Bataille's work during the 1930s acknowledges the manifest failure of left-wing political ideas and moves in an altogether different theoretical direction. If the eighteenth-century *philosophes* expressed relative certainty about what was right and good and detailed the politics necessary to bring them about, Bataille doubted that whole enterprise. Bataille was a lifelong leftist in the narrow respect that he wanted to liberate human beings from exploitation, which he broadly defined as reification. In order to overcome the modern institutions and ideas that reduce human beings to servile things, Bataille argued for the adoption of sacrificial practices whose invocation of the sacred would shatter the reifying fictions of modern life. This ambitious project ultimately led him to challenge the founding principles of the French left. For instance, at the very moment when leftists hoped to fight the fascists by emulating their concentration and centralization of authority, Bataille conceived of sovereign power as fragmented, depleted, and purposeless. As Western capitalism sputtered, causing even liberals to cheer state-sponsored production, Bataille theorized a form of useless exchange called unproductive expenditure, a sacrificial practice meant to combat the productive, useful, and accumulative forces that characterize free markets. Bataille placed no credence in the leftist argument that the rational forces of progress would ultimately defeat the emerging violent nostalgia for racial purity and national strength. Instead, thanks to Alexandre Kojève's interpretation of Hegel, Bataille maintained that History had already ended, leaving reason with nothing left to do. Without the dialectical power to expose philosophical contradictions, without any higher truths to reveal, reason and its agents were of little use to the French left. Finally, as French leftists descended into the streets to pit their political ideals against their enemies', Bataille called for an end to the tyranny of idealism because it transformed human beings into the blind servants of abstractions. In short, Bataille recognized the exhaustion of the French left and largely abandoned its progressive idealism without a hint of nostalgia.

In response to left-wing decadence, Bataille began to reformulate the progressive idea of community unfettered by the political fictions of the Enlightenment *philosophes*. His political theory moved in the direction of anarchism, though not of the sort promulgated by European anarchists such as Peter Kropotkin, Mikhail Bakunin, Pierre-Joseph Proudhon, and Georges Sorel. Bataille did not explicitly set out to remake anarchism, nor did he refer to himself as an anarchist. What is more, Bataille cannot easily be classified into either the individualist or collectivist strains of anarchism, because he rejected the superiority of the former and the moralism of the latter. Bataille, however, owes a theoretical debt to late-nineteenth- and early-twentieth-century French anarcho-syndicalism, which harnessed the spirit of mass revolt against capitalism, the state, bourgeois democracy, and authoritarian socialism. Bataille also embraced what one might call the theatrical anarchism of the surrealists, for whom art was a major weapon in their struggle against bourgeois culture. Most importantly, Bataille situated himself within the sphere of anarchism by virtue of his hostility toward human exploitation and unmitigated pursuit of freedom within a social context. Though these commonalities suggest that Bataille maintained a stake in the humanistic promises of the Enlightenment, his anarchism actually calls those very promises into question.

Bataille's version of anarchism rejects accretions of authority—all

authority. Rather than gather due to concentrations, elevations, formaliza-
tions, idealizations, institutionalizations, or centralizations of power, members of Bataillean communities are united by that which repulses them:
abjection generated by sacrificial loss. Although European anarchism was
no stranger to propagandistic violence and the sacrifice of political martyrs,
its adherents never advocated the formation of community around the sublime attractions and repulsions of sacred bloodshed. Kropotkin's mutual
aid, Bakunin's collectivism, and Sorel's syndicates are for Bataille nothing
but facile, idealistic structures of human communality that have unwittingly internalized harmful, reifying notions of individualism and social
justice. With the possible exception of Sorel, European anarchists clung to
a progressive teleology that combined nostalgia for naturalized human beings unburdened by capitalist exploitation with a future golden age of individual freedom. A politics for the end of History, Bataille's anarchism offers
only an unpredictable future stripped of any systemic philosophies that demand human subordination. Headless, Bataille's politics are also completely
unstructured by laws, morals, or ethics. In contrast to the European anarchists, who advocated social justice informed by only the natural moral inclinations inscribed on one's heart, Bataille, following the Marquis de Sade
and Friedrich Nietzsche, rejected such a precious view of morality and,
more radically, the concept of the individual that accompanies it. Contrary
to the ethos of the left, whose idealism has bred a kind of progressive
nostalgia—a longing for what will never be—Bataille crafted a sacrificial,
anarchistic politics that responds to a troubled political world unsupported
by its philosophical foundations.

Bataille's development of counter-Enlightenment anarchism began in
the 1930s and reached maturity after World War II with the publication of
The Accursed Share. During the 1930s, the political events that demonstrated the impotence of socialism, communism, and anarchism also uniquely
framed Bataille's theoretical work. As Bataille began to challenge the assumptions that traditionally supported the left's *Weltanschauung,* he was
both unencumbered and terrified by the fact that the interwar political
chaos prevented the emergence of a hegemonic ideology. Because neither
liberalism, communism, nor fascism could claim victory during this period of massive and unpredictable ideological conflict, Bataille was free to
generate ideas animated by his vertiginous perception of an open political
horizon. This sense of political possibility is best illustrated by his participation in several groups—*Contre-Attaque, Acéphale,* and the *Collège de
Sociologie*[2]—all of which sought in novel ways to actualize elements of Bataille's theory. Supported by these political and intellectual associations,

Bataille prepared for an anarchism fueled by the very weaknesses of the traditional French left.

After World War II, Bataille mostly abandoned political action, choosing instead to promote radical politics through academically minded essays as well as experimental writing. With the powerful rise of American neoliberalism, the onset of the Cold War, and the threat of nuclear annihilation, Bataille's work also assumed a more measured tone. He uncharacteristically synthesized his prewar work into *The Accursed Share*, a treatise on political economy that apparently embarrassed Bataille both because of the "conventional" subject matter and the fact that he found himself in the awkward position of having to explain himself.[3] While it is true that *The Accursed Share* still touts the revolutionary sacrificial ideas that Bataille had first theorized in the 1930s, it also situates those ideas within a landscape of American hegemony, Soviet aggression, and leftist defeat. In the last chapter of the book, Bataille argues that the Marshall Plan is a grand example of unproductive expenditure that safely fosters nonmilitary competition between the United States and the Soviet Union. Gone are Bataille's prewar notions that sacrifice actively undertaken will broadly transform politics and humanity. Gone to some extent is the violence of sacrifice. Instead, Bataille concludes the book with a weak argument about the sacrificial implications of an American policy, which he claims will prevent nuclear war, raise the world's standard of living, and exemplify the revolutionary value of wasting wealth.[4] Compared with his prewar work, these conjectures are indeed modest.

The absurdity of Bataille's position on the Marshall Plan notwithstanding, it does illustrate two key points that also serve as an excellent frame for Bataille's prewar theories. First, in seeking an alternative to nuclear war, Bataille clearly indicates his aversion to nihilism. The value that Bataille places on wasteful sacrifice, violence, or death is not absolute and should not be considered a renunciation of all values. That Bataille relishes the experience of life up until the point of death, that he calls for a life unfettered by abstractions such as humanism, progress, justice, or democracy, is not a denial of existence so much as an affirmation of its potential fullness. Second, as Bataille explains at the end of the Preface to *The Accursed Share*, one intent of the book is to "solve political problems" (1991a, 14). Despite Bataille's theoretical aversion to usefulness and teleology, he imbues his postwar work with a modicum of practicality, direction, and purpose. And though obviously a performative contradiction, Bataille's interest in usefully solving political problems in the postwar period refracts the spirit of his prewar work, which ultimately sought to challenge and reconfigure enervated left-wing ideas.

🏵 *From Anguish to Anarchism*

Scholars generally agree that Bataille's political activities and writings during the 1930s reflect a pessimistic dissatisfaction with modern politics. As Jean Borreil explains in "On Georges Bataille: An Escape from Lameness?": "The point of departure for Bataille's analyses is the 1930s failure known as Stalinism and fascism" (1995, 135). Liberalism belongs on Borreil's list as well. All three forms of politics require the subordination of the working class, whom Bataille championed during the 1930s from an anarcho-syndicalist perspective. Although liberalism is not totalitarian, Bataille maintained that Stalinism, fascism, and liberalism suffer from a similar problem: state hegemony. The first line of his 1933 essay "The Problem of the State" treats this issue succinctly: "In contradiction with the evolution of the nineteenth century, current historical tendencies appear to be propelled toward the state's constraint and hegemony" (1983, 105). It is true that Richard Wolin and Zeev Sternhell have heaped criticism on Bataille for embracing a version of state authoritarianism that Wolin calls "left fascism." But Bataille's blanket disdain for the state and for imperial expressions of authority demonstrates that he cannot easily be accused of adopting fascist means in order to achieve progressive ends.[5]

Horrified by proletarian impotence in the face of growing liberal, socialist, and fascist state power, Bataille looked for novel ways to unleash the revolutionary impulses of the working class. In order to move away from the conventional leftist agenda, which had left the working-class movement (and Bataille) with a profound sense of powerlessness, Bataille began to examine how that experience of powerlessness—that sense of self-loss or feeling of inadequacy, incompleteness, or lack—might radically transform the modern self. Well before fascism became a juggernaut of mass politics, Bataille recognized that its incandescence would be tragic for the left. For Bataille, however, this tragedy was multilayered: it captured the sorrowful state of left-wing ideas, the likely defeat of leftist political organizations by fascism, and, most importantly, the emergence of an identity defined by its being permanently sundered or lacking. Thus, for Bataille, the tragedy of the left is its ontological condition, and as such, the harbinger of an altogether different approach to experience and communality.

Bataille argued that the left's tragic circumstances engendered anguish, a powerful, all-encompassing feeling of torment with important revolutionary potential. Here Bataille describes the significance of anguish:

> Democratic institutions—realizable, and moreover necessary, to the inner workings of a proletarian party—can conversely be an internal limitation. But the principle of democracy, discredited by liberal politics, can therefore

once more become a vibrant force only with the anguish provoked in the working classes by the birth of three all-powerful States. The condition is that this anguish must form as an *autonomous force* based on hatred of the State's authority. It is in this sense that it is currently necessary to say, faced with three servile societies—that not a single human future meriting this name may be achieved absent the liberating anguish of the proletariat. (1983, 107)

In this passage there are hints of Georges Sorel's anarcho-syndicalism as Bataille argues that state hegemony provokes only a salutary proletarian anguish when it crystallizes autonomously, uncorrupted by the cultural servility that characterizes all other modern political systems. Bataille also offers a rare endorsement of democracy. What is noteworthy from a theoretical standpoint is Bataille's argument that proletarian anguish is liberating. This claim is not instrumental: anguish does not provoke revolutionary action, whose goal is to eliminate the causes of that original anguish. Rather, anguish achieves a humanized future by challenging and fragmenting the accumulated, dehumanizing ideas and practices that constitute modern reification. Insofar as the working class experiences its identity as permanently lacking, its anguish is also an enduring emotive condition.

Bataille counterintuitively maintains that the proletariat's anguished feelings of self-loss and impotence are constitutive of a kind of sacred, subversive power, which he calls "sovereignty." According to Bataille, sovereignty actually has two forms: imperative and subversive. *Imperative sovereignty* describes conventional ruling power found in all modern political systems whose legitimacy is constructed on a hierarchical, elevated, and amplified basis. In his postwar writings on sovereignty, Bataille describes its imperative form as belonging to kings, priest, chieftains, and *"all men* who possess and have never entirely lost the value that is attributed to gods and 'dignitaries'" (1991b, 197). Although imperative sovereignty is the preeminent source of state power and is typically associated with mastery, supremacy, and dominion, Bataille argues that it is actually servile because it is instrumental and useful. In contrast, *subversive or revolutionary sovereignty* derives its power from abjection and uselessness. Bataille writes, "Life *beyond utility* is the domain of sovereignty" (1991b, 198). Subversive sovereignty is experienced as unproductive loss and dissolution; rather than authoritatively establish limits (laws), this revolutionary form of power comes into being when limits are transgressed. Subversive sovereignty is the "power" invoked by the tragedy of self-loss, powerlessness, and abjection; it is the revolutionariness of anguish. And, finally, it is the "force" of anarchism because, unlike imperative sovereignty, it tolerates no form of authority.

✺ Sacrificing the Left

From the French Revolution to the mid-1930s, left-wing agitation sought to liberate labor from exploitation because the left has long held that laboring creates human civilization. For the left, human nature is a product of the material conditions under which labor is conducted. Bataille would appear to be sympathetic to this position when he argues that "class struggle has only one possible end: the loss of those who have worked to lose 'human nature'" (1986b, 128). Bataille raises the familiar trope that proletarian liberation requires the elimination of the exploiters, the bourgeoisie. For Bataille, however, the loss of "human nature" is also caused by the liberal principle of classical utility, which leads human beings to value only that which is useful and productive. What modernity has excluded from the realm of meaningful human activities is unproductive expenditure whose goal is to waste sumptuously. Of these practices, which include "luxury, mourning, war, the consumption of sumptuary monuments, games, spectacles, arts, and perverse sexual activity," sacrifice is the most important element (1986b, 118).

Conceived as the useless sacrifice of wealth, unproductive expenditure challenges not only the basic tenets of liberalism; it strikes at the heart of the left's single-minded pursuit of economic justice. Even in the best material circumstances, workers must devote a vast quantity of their labor to the reproduction of life. To paraphrase John Locke, the work of the hands and the labor of the body are productive, useful activities. In contrast, unproductive expenditure denotes frenzied, violent, pleasurable waste. It is true that Karl Marx conceived of economic surpluses as liberating to workers, who, freed from the necessity to work for their own survival, would engage in other nonproductive activities such as philosophy. Yet Marx also famously argued that philosophy was a useful tool for changing the world. Before Bataille, socialists, Marxists, and anarchists would never have argued that humans construct their humanity by producing things in order to destroy them wastefully. For Bataille, however, to expend unproductively that which one fabricates is ultimately a cathartic, liberating experience of de-reification.

It should be noted that Bataille's declaration of war against state power and *homo oeconomicus* was no theoretical novelty in mid-twentieth-century France. In Michèle Richman's description of Bataille's hostility toward capitalism, he sounds utterly Marxist: "Bataille characterizes his enemy as the economizing person whose individualistic ethos is consonant with the pursuit of random ends determined by the criteria of utilitarianism" (1982, 3). It is only when Bataille incorporates a notion of sacrifice into his critiques of power and labor that he departs from these ordinary anarchist and Marxist positions, setting as his goal the fundamental transformation of both politics and its human practitioners. For Bataille, sacrifice describes a wide set of practices—from eroticism to festivals to writing—that challenge the modern modalities of being. As a political practice, sacrifice is a mediated form of self-demolition, which allows its practitioners to unravel violently the tapestry of the modern servile self. Corrosive of conventional forms of power, sacrifice transforms majesty into abjection, the symbol for which is the decapitated Louis XVI during the French Revolution. Sacrifice does not waste power in order to replace it. Instead, sacrifice conjures a subversive sovereign existence, a life beyond utility and reification. Bataille's sacrificial revolution is thus conducted against the supremacy of the head and the labor of the body.

Bataille's concept of sacrifice is a radical departure from the forms typically embraced by modern religions or practiced by non-Western peoples. Simply put, Bataillean sacrifice is an unrecoverable loss. In Bataille's estimation, one doesn't sacrifice with the expectation of a return for one's offering. There is no redemption, vindication, equilibrium, status, power, wealth, or protection that arises from the sacrificial act. Rather, for Bataille, sacrifice is a useless practice; its violence and destructiveness ontologically tear individuals apart, allowing them to forge unique communal bonds with other similarly sundered, anguished human beings. During the 1930s, Bataille discussed sacrifice in erotic, political, mystical, and literary terms. Sacrificial violence occurred either in the brothel, on the street, in the seclusion of the forest, or through the text. Practiced in these loci, sacrifice stands in opposition to the traditional political dreams of the left. If the desire to practice the art of politics were compared to the myth of Icarus, a favorite of Bataille's, then sacrifice would correspond to the sun's blinding, wasted energy, which melted Icarus's wings, demonstrating to all human beings the fragility of their activities and existence. Bataillean sacrifice challenges human beings to confront and test the limits of their communities and being, without ever allowing for the reestablishment of political or ontological order.

🌀 *The Politics of Anguish*

As war raged during the summer of 1940, Bataille wrote a journal entry titled "Misfortunes of the Present Time," a subsection of which he calls "Orphans of the Storm: Exodus." The title and subtitle reflect Bataille's general desire to escape a politics in which an elevated and concentrated authority is focused on the maintenance of servile productive forces. In his journal,

Bataille also nostalgically recalls the Hegelian and Marxian definitions of negation as "action that results in disruption." He concedes, however, that "negativity that's not put to use would destroy whoever lived it—*sacrifice* will illuminate the conclusion of history as it did its dawn." By virtue of its very uselessness, unemployed expenditure—"negativity that's not put to use"—is even more dangerous than Hegel's and Marx's disruptive negativity. Disruptive negativity serves masters: Hegel's cunning of reason and Marx's dialectical materialism. Unemployed expenditure has no higher purpose; it is a lived, tragic experience: "Sacrifice can't be for us what it was at the beginning of 'time.' Our experience is one of impossible appeasement. Lucid holiness recognizes in itself the need to destroy, the necessity for a tragic outcome" (1988, 51). The experience of "impossible appeasement" and the "necessity for a tragic outcome" refer directly to the sense of loss created by the untenable politics of the 1930s. Having arrived at the end of History, the working class could not make use of disruptive negation, which holds the promise of some ideal dialectical resolution. Escape from the storm requires sacrifice on a revolutionary scale or living unemployed negativity, which will liberate the working class by tragically tearing it asunder.

Though Bataille describes himself as an orphan of the storm, he was by no means alone. In 1940, as Walter Benjamin awaited his own exodus from Europe, he composed a series of meditations on History, one of which strikingly evokes Bataille's theoretical dilemma. Unlike Bataille, however, Benjamin remained wedded to a version of the left's idealized view of History. Benjamin's reflections on History are captured in his messianic interpretation of a Paul Klee drawing, *Angelus Novus,* which depicts the angel of History "looking as though he is about to move away from something he is fixedly contemplating." Benjamin continues:

> His face is turned toward the past. Where we perceive a chain of events, he sees one single catastrophe that keeps piling ruin upon ruin and hurls it in front of his feet. The angel would like to stay, awaken the dead, and make whole what has been smashed. But a storm is blowing from Paradise; it has got caught in his wings with such violence that the angel can no longer close them. The storm irresistibly propels him into the future to which his back is turned, while the pile of debris before him grows skyward. This storm is what we call progress. (1968, 257–58)

Along with all of History's detritus, progress propels the angel of History toward an unknowable future. In Benjamin's version of the storm, there is the same inevitable and tragic sense of loss that left Bataille anguished. Unable to close its wings, Benjamin's angel of History is not only immobilized by the lumbering weight of the past; it is also trapped by an ideology of progress, which coercively projects a false image of secular redemption. In keeping with Benjamin's Jewish messianism, the angel wishes to bring History to a redemptive end but cannot. Oriented atheologically, Bataille dismisses the angel's role and the possibility of a postlapsarian wholeness or state of grace. Neither progress nor God can ameliorate the human condition. Left with only History's debris and no possibility of salvation, Bataille turns to revalue his lacerating self-loss into a world-transforming effervescence.

In *Against Architecture,* Denis Hollier observes that Bataille gives anguish political significance:

> Anguish is profoundly historical, but its historical nature is not progressive, it is revolutionary. . . . The revolutionary movement liberates the future from the prisons of science. It faces it head on in its heterogeneity, as something unknown. Bataille speaks rarely of political *action,* but frequently of revolutionary *agitation.* The revolution destroys authorities and imaginary dictatorships that work only because they tap the support of some faith. Including the authority of science. (1992, 55)

Anguish is "profoundly historical" because it is a reaction to uselessness and injustice. Defying fatalism, anguish is also revolutionary because it directs the force of unproductive expenditure. Bataille's political, economic, and philosophical targets are general, overlapping, and mutually reinforcing: concentrations of state power, capitalism, and utilitarianism. In order to liberate themselves, human beings must dare to sacrifice that which enslaves them. Paradoxically, it is the anguish of having nothing left to do that generates this will to sacrifice. Hollier notes that the heterogeneity generated by unproductive expenditure is the essence of this revolt; heterogeneity confronts the quotidian, the powerful, and the productive as something unassimilable, something altogether unknown. This accursed share, as Bataille calls it, is what violently and sacrificially fragments all instantiations of authority, productivity, and utility. Moreover, the revolutionary agitation that challenges the modern forces of servility offers nothing to take their place. It is for this reason that Bataille argues: "Sovereignty is NOTHING" (1991b, 256). Bataille's anguish is perpetually anarchistic, always subverting its superiority and establishment.

Though Bataille carefully read Nietzsche and admired his work, he rejected his claim that the working class was engaged in nothing more than a resentful, nihilistic slave revolt. In Bataille's view, workers wanted liberation from *homo oeconomicus,* not the ability to become economizing creatures on an equal footing. Nietzsche fretted that workers wished only to coronate their morality in order to alleviate their suffering. Although it sometimes appears as if Bataille "celebrates" the pain of anguish for its own sake, he actually takes the Nietzschean view that anguish, like suffering, must be affirmed in certain circumstances. For this reason, Bataille paradoxically argues that liberation requires an ethic of abjectness, which is achieved though a self-abnegating affirmation of anguish. Affirming anguish is an effort to remold the economizing self and its ethical approach to the world:

> If I envisage death gaily, it is not that I too say, in turning away from what is frightening: "it is nothing" or "it is false." On the contrary, gaiety, connected with the work of death, causes me anguish, is accentuated by my anguish, and in return exacerbates that anguish: ultimately, gay anguish, anguished gaiety cause me, in a feverish chill, "absolute dismemberment," where it is my joy that finally tears me apart, but where dejection would follow joy were I not torn all the way to the end, immeasurably. (1999, 25)

Joy before death is one instantiation of the abject ethic that permits Bataille to confront a frightening future shorn of redemptive, left-wing idealism. Bataille describes a heterogeneous experience of immeasurable fragmentation—what Michel Foucault called a "limit experience"—that frees the modern self from its iron cage. There is an element of Nietzsche's *amor fati* in Bataille's practice of joy before death. Bataille, however, not only greets fate joyfully, but he also imagines that encounter as one of fundamental self-transformation. For Bataille, joy in the face of death evokes self-laceration, self-loss, self-annihilation, and ultimately, self-sacrifice. Contrary to those modern thinkers who celebrate the self-sufficient, autonomous, rational individual, and contrary even to those such as Nietzsche who disparage *homo oeconomicus* but nonetheless wish for the appearance of an individual in possession of "higher" values, Bataille suggests that History's end requires "absolute dismemberment." In other words, Bataille's anguish conjures a state of abject loss, which banishes the left-wing fantasies of progress toward a "better" future and renders impossible human enslavement to the ideals upon which these "better" futures depend.

Bataille narrates the politics of anguished, unproductive expenditure in his 1930s fictional works such as *Blue of Noon*. Set in September 1934, *Blue of Noon*'s main character, Troppman, travels to Barcelona, where he witnesses the preparation for and ultimately the failure of the workers' antifascist uprising. With political failure for the left unfolding on the streets below, Troppman finds himself reluctantly engaged in a conversation with Monsieur Melou, a Marxist professor of philosophy. Exhausted and sick, Troppman expresses little interest in the philosophical arguments troubling Melou, who explains that he is particularly bothered by the "dead end into which history is being led by the events that are unfolding before our eyes" (1986a, 60).[6] Having presented Troppman with this "agonizing dilemma," Melou asks, "Should we wrap ourselves in silence? Should we, on the contrary, bestow our help on the workers as they make their last stand, thereby dooming ourselves to an inescapable and fruitless death?" (56–60). Silence or death: such are the dead ends toward which History is driving the working class in their pitched battle against fascism and for political power. Troppman's reaction to all of this: a "long piss" followed by his "thrusting two fingers down [his] throat." After emerging from the bathroom and declaring that he has a fever, Troppman states, "I've considered the problem. But first of all I'm going to ask a question . . . If the working classes are done for, why are you . . . Communists, or socialists, or whatever?" (62–63). Troppman's fever, nausea, and physical disengagement illustrate Bataille's ambivalence toward the working-class movement and anguish that History offers leftists only a dead end.

Troppman's expression of skepticism toward communist and socialist efficacy illuminates the relationship between the end of History and unproductive expenditure. With History over and negativity's having nothing left to do, the left's teleological vision of liberation fundamentally changes. For both Hegel and Marx, whose ideas have profoundly influenced the modern left, work expresses productive negativity and defines the working class. In Hegel's *Phenomenology of Spirit,* work liberates self-consciousness from bondage (1977, 111–9). Critical of Hegel's idealism, Marx argues that the material conditions of work in a capitalist system foster a revolutionary change of consciousness, which in turn precipitates a radical transformation of existing exploitative social relations. Bataille refigures the role of work in the leftist imagination by making the claim that it can no longer drive changes in consciousness or sociopolitical transition. The elements of the socialist revolution that are dependent on work, such as class consciousness, working-class immiserization, and economic crisis, are impossible when negativity no longer possesses creative, productive power. At the end of History, work loses the ability to change human consciousness or inspire political change. Moreover, Bataille argues that the sole purpose of work is banal: the reproduction of life. In this way, the work of work is neither liberating nor able to serve the idealism of the left. Reified by productive negativity or work, human beings can turn only to unproductive expenditure for their true liberation.

Bataille's notion of liberty is untethered by idealism and teleology. He rejects the classical left-wing promise of a multifaceted life free from exploitation because it requires subordination to the rational, productive, and progressive forces of the modern age. Thanks to the Enlightenment, which institutionalized these forces, modern human beings fundamentally experience themselves as slaves, as lacking in themselves. The tragedy of this condition for the left was only exacerbated by what Bataille perceived as the emasculating political events of the 1930s. Bataille, however, departs from the left by embracing tragedy rather than seeking to overcome it. Liberty is not found in a politics that seeks to ameliorate a human condition defined by what it lacks. Instead, liberty occurs when the affective response to servility moves human beings toward excess, to live beyond themselves. The ecstatic self is not a cure for modern servility; it is a tectonic shift in self-definition from lacking to glorious abundance. Augured by anguish, this shift is instantiated by sacrifice, which permits the modern slave to participate in unproductive expenditure and to demolish his/her own reification. Bataille's notion of liberty is thus thoroughly sacrificial, a sacred celebration of the tragedy of self-loss.

Symbolizing the last gasp of traditional left-wing politics, *Blue of Noon* ends sacrificially. Bataille makes no effort to save political cinders. Instead, he relies on Troppman to indicate what politics might look like once the ashes have all blown away. Safely ensconced in a hotel room as the worker insurrection begins, Troppman is politically disengaged and feckless. He is also accompanied by Dorothea, a woman about whom Troppman feels passionately but with whom he is impotent. She taunts him:

> [DOROTHEA:] "You ought to go away. It would be better now if I stayed by myself."
> [TROPPMAN:] "If you'd like it better, I can go out."
> [DOROTHEA:] "You want to get yourself killed . . ."
> [TROPPMAN:] "Why? Rifles don't kill much of anyone. Listen—they never stop firing. That proves fairly conclusively that even the shells leave a large number of survivors."
> [DOROTHEA:] "It would be less dishonest."
> At that point she turned toward me. She gave me an ironic look.
> [DOROTHEA:] "If only you could let yourself go!"
> [TROPPMAN:] "I didn't blink." (1986a, 138–39)

Dorothea and Troppman's exchange reveals the direction in which Bataille drives his own anguish. When she asks Troppman to leave the hotel room, Dorothea opens up the possibility that Troppman would directly face the politics of the coming insurrection. If Troppman were to go outside and to get killed, it would be, as Dorothea puts it, "less dishonest." But Troppman remains inside the hotel and keeps silent about the rising tide of fascism. Speaking through Dorothea, Bataille suggests that silent inaction is unacceptable at the end of History. It is bad faith *tout court.* Dorothea posits an ironic alternative: "If only you could let yourself go!" Dorothea's reference to letting go is a radical alternative to silence, for it invokes the distinctly Bataillean idea that frenzied, self-sundered loss of control—a sexual, political, ontological act—can liberate Troppman from the contradictory alternatives of silence or death.

The political ironies at work in Dorothea's taunting of Troppman help to illuminate the modern left's double bind. When Troppman chooses the safety of a hotel room over the danger of the street, he disengages from mass left-wing politics. Yet for Bataille, such anguished inaction is only a precondition of the total release of energy that will ultimately reengage Troppman in revolutionary agitation. The lesson for the left is clear: break away from traditional left-wing politics and its rivals; the anguish of that break will reveal a path toward subversive sovereign power and sacrificial politics. Given Troppman's unfulfilled (impotent) attraction for Dorothea, letting go also connotes unaccomplished orgasmic release. In "Bataille in the Street," Susan Suleiman translates letting go as "los[ing] your head," which leads her to suggest a Freudian interpretation of decapitation as symbolic castration. Suleiman, however, is not suggesting that Troppman is powerless or emasculated. Instead, she argues that Troppman's losing his head *"restored* his potency, according to that characteristically Bataillian equation which states that a violent loss of control is the precondition of *jouissance,* a radical letting go" (1995, 31). Such "potency as headlessness" points toward a sovereign mode of action, a surge of unproductive negativity generating self-subversive anarchism. Ironically, what letting go means for the left is dissolution: human liberation requires the perpetual sacrifice of the left's foundations so that nothing is established in their place. Lastly, Bataille rejects the alternative to letting go, namely, death. Death's finality offers Bataille none of the benefits generated by expressions of joy in the face of death. In *Blue of Noon,* death befalls the revolutionary intellectual Michael, who lost his head in a more traditional manner: "He went off and got killed" (1986a, 140–41).

While *Blue of Noon* offers a premonition of a postmodern, post-left politics, its distinctiveness rests in the nexus of personal and political emotions that it conveys. In one respect, *Blue of Noon* is a book of mourning for a political tradition that Bataille believes must be sacrificed. Disoriented and nauseous, Troppman laments the inadequacy of the labor movement's confronting of fascism; the fragility of the left's philosophical foundations, which deny those on the street and in government a path toward liberation; and the tragedy of a world soon to be overtaken by fascism. Bataille treats these lamentations as sublime: dangerously attractive and frighteningly repulsive to those searching for human liberation. Most of all, *Blue of Noon* speaks to the individual experience of disorientation when the future is shorn of the possibilities anticipated by the political philosophies meaningful to the left. Bataille himself experienced this feeling when he first confronted Hegelian philosophy, which left him "suffocated, crushed, shattered, killed ten times over" (Noys 2000, 7).

Blue of Noon also celebrates the politics of eroticism and the eroticism of politics. For Bataille, "Eroticism . . . is assenting to life up to the point of death" (1962, 11). It is, in other words, a form of unproductive expenditure that Bataille uses in *Blue of Noon* to highlight the social or collective benefits of sacrifice. Unlike other forms of self-sacrifice such as auto-mutilation, eroticism plays upon the distinctively social elements of self-loss. In *Death and Sensuality,* Bataille writes: "We are discontinuous beings, individuals who perish in isolation in the midst of an incomprehensible adventure, but we yearn for our lost community" (14–15). Though uncharacteristically nostalgic, Bataille claims that "discontinuity" is the modern problem addressed by erotically losing oneself in another to the point of death. By confronting death erotically, human beings create continuity with others: *la petite mort,* the little death, is the French phrase for orgasm. Ecstatic loss of control thus works against modern individualistic discontinuity, thereby forging a connectedness or communication that is altogether outside oneself. As Bataille puts it: "The whole business of eroticism is to destroy the self-contained character of the participators as they are in their normal lives." The goal of eroticism as well as of other social forms of unproductive expenditure is ultimately to dissolve the elements of individualism so that community might form ecstatically.

Written in 1935, the same year as *Blue of Noon,* Bataille's essay "Popular Front in the Street" explores similar themes, but with an analysis that is explicitly political and oriented toward collective experience and action. Describing the significance of the problem that the essay seeks to address, Bataille writes, "One can foresee . . . a serious crisis of the entire Left" (1986b, 166). This crisis was precipitated by the rise of fascism as well as socialist complicity in parliamentary democracy. Often collapsing the distinction between socialism and parliamentarism, Bataille criticizes the political debates, party organizations, and Popular Front leaders for abandoning the "anti-capitalist offensive," the chief aim of the working class. Bataille demonstrates the scope of his radicalism by rejecting the value of political debate, organization, and leadership as well as the efficacy of parties, institutions, and procedures. He also criticizes the fascists when he rails against the "stupid imperialism [that] precisely engendered this fascism" (164). In Bataille's view, no political system suits workers who are merely objects of exploitation, trapped between a "state of prostration and boredom" by the states that claim to represent their interests. Given this situation, Bataille appeals to workers' passions in order to inspire mass revolutionary agitation. He writes that workers "will know how to gather and find together, in this reunion, the burning heat that attracts men from all sides and that will become the basis for an implacable popular domination" (167–68).

Focused on the sovereignty of collective action, Bataille calls for an insurrection in the street, and in doing so, he appears to avoid the very choice made by Troppman in *Blue of Noon.* For Troppman, the experience of impotence did not prevent or impede *jouissance,* letting go or losing his head. In "Popular Front in the Street," Bataille refocuses the locus of impotence from the individual to the masses: "What we have before our eyes is the horror of human impotence" (1986b, 161). In this case, it is the anguished workers who witness the impotence of their leaders. Bataille continues: "We want to confront this horror directly. We address ourselves to the direct and violent drives which, in the minds of those who hear us, can contribute to the surge of power that will liberate men from the absurd swindlers who lead them" (161–62). Bataille's liberating "surge of power" should not be mistaken for the traditional violent uprisings that characterized the revolutions of the modern era. Rather, Bataille describes an explosive "collective exaltation," which frees human beings from the weak political ideals that prevented Western democracies and their leftist critics from rising up against fascism.

Describing the Popular Front demonstrations on February 12, 1934, Bataille signals an inversion of the "surge of power" that is akin to the "potency as headlessness" identified by Suleiman in *Blue of Noon:* "It was no longer a procession, nor anything poorly political; it was the curse of the working people, and not only in its rage, IN ITS IMPOVERISHED MAJESTY, which advanced, made greater by a kind of rending solemnity—by the menace of slaughter still suspended at that moment over all of the crowd" (163). The violent revolt of the workers—their surge of power—is a solar flare, an expression of sovereign power, a great sacrifice of energy whose brightness inspires awe, burns out, and leaves nothing behind. "Impoverished majesty" thus captures the political significance of Bataille's self-subverting, contradictory notion of power that the workers achieve in the street. Power that expends itself, that seeks not to found but to destabilize that which has been founded, is the essence of Bataille's anarchism.

Immanuel Kant audaciously declared, "Dare to know!" Bataille recklessly replied, "Dare to sacrifice!" Such is the origin of Bataille's anarchistic politics, which requires the unproductive expenditure of the political philosophies and fictions that came before. Both previous to and following World War II, Bataille's work responded to the crisis of the left. Detached from its Enlightenment anchor, unable to draw effectively upon its principles in order to battle fascism, the left went adrift. It could no longer articulate convincingly the distinction between right and wrong, no longer trust that the fruits of progress would be sweet, no longer wield political power with the confidence that it would permit human beings to control their destinies. Bataille clearly understood this problem. While his colleagues on the left considered how dialectical materialism would unfold in different political guises, Bataille declared History over and then theorized the meaning of politics in this novel context. Bataille's anarchism shifts the progressive movement's disdain of arbitrary political power, economic exploitation, and social alienation onto terrain that renders human de-reification possible. His anarchism also refigures community as tragic in the sense that its animating effervescence coheres around unproductive, sacrificial self-loss. For Bataille, community is not a moral fiction; it is the connection that forms around the repulsiveness of violent, useless destruction.

Finally, against any authority that declares its superiority, Bataille's anarchism holds out the possibility of headless, decentralized, chthonic power. Of all the lessons for the left, Bataille's view of power may be the most important. Since the age of revolutions began, the left has only challenged concentrations of power with its own alternative distillations. Rather than anticipate the "right" revolution—the one that actually liberates human beings from their modern chains—Bataille calls for ongoing sacrificial fragmentation of the modern self. Bataille does not wish to convert leftist despair into a new vision of wholeness set upon piles of fresh, reifying fictions. Instead, he wants to set the modern self on a pyre built from the trunk of the Enlightenment and its tangled, brittle branches. Bataille will light the match.

NOTES

1. The American Revolution, which preceded the French Revolution by three years, was a rebellion. With the failure of the anti-federalists, who were social radicals in comparison to the federalists, the American rebellion achieved a fundamental change of government without corresponding social or economic transformations. In contrast, the French Revolution precipitated massive social, political, and economic change.

2. Bataille and André Breton founded the anti-fascist political organization *Contre-Attaque* in 1935. When Bataille co-founded the secret society *Acéphale* in 1936, he hoped that it would initiate a sacrificial economy. Finally, between 1937 and 1939, the *Collège* gathered various avant-garde intellectuals in an effort to explore the vast terrain of sacred sociology.

3. Bataille begins his Preface to *The Accursed Share:* "For some years, being obliged on occasion to answer the question 'What are you working on?' I was embarrassed to have to say, 'A book on political economy.' . . . I am still annoyed when I recall the superficial astonishment that greeted my reply; I had to explain myself, and what I was able to say in a few words was neither precise nor intelligible" (1991a, 9).

4. Bataille writes: "*Mankind will move peacefully toward a general resolution of its problems only if this threat causes the U.S. to assign a large share of the excess—deliberately and without return—to raising the global standard of living, economic activity thus giving the surplus energy produced an outlet other than war*" (1991a, 187).

5. See Wolin 2004, and Sternhell and Maisel 1995.

6. *Blue of Noon* was written in 1935 and first published in 1957.

WORKS CITED

Bataille, Georges. 1962. *Death and Sensuality: A Study of Eroticism and Taboo.* New York: Walker and Co.

———. 1973. *Oeuvres Complètes.* Paris: Gallimard.

———. 1983. Le Problème de l'état. *Réimpression de La Critique sociale (1931–1934)* 9: 105–107. Paris: La Différence.

———. 1986a. *Blue of Noon.* Trans. Harry Matthews. New York: Marion Boyars.

———. 1986b. *Visions of Excess: Selected Writings, 1927–1939.* Ed. Allan Stoekl. Trans. Allan Stoekl, Carl R. Lovitt, and Donald M. Leslie Jr. Minneapolis: University of Minnesota Press.

———. 1988. *Guilty.* Trans. Bruce Boone. Venice, Calif.: Lapis Press.

———. 1991a. *The Accursed Share: Volume I.* Trans. Robert Hurley. New York: Zone Books.

———. 1991b. *The Accursed Share: Volumes II and III.* Trans. Robert Hurley. New York: Zone Books.

———. 1999. Hegel, Death and Sacrifice. Trans. Jonathan Strauss. *Yale French Studies* 78: 9–28.

Benjamin, Walter. 1968. *Illuminations.* Ed. Hannah Arendt. New York: Harcourt Brace Jovanovich, Inc.

Besnier, Jean-Michel. 1999. Georges Bataille in the 1930s: A Politics of the Impossible. *Yale French Studies* 78: 169–80.

Borreil, Jean. 1995. On Georges Bataille: An Escape from Lameness? In *On Bataille,* ed. and trans. Leslie Anne Boldt-Irons. Albany: State University of New York Press.

Hegel, G. W. F. 1977. *Phenomenology of Spirit.* Trans. A. V. Miller. Oxford: Oxford University Press.

Hollier, Denis. 1992. *Against Architecture.* Trans. Betsy Wing. Cambridge: MIT Press.

Noys, Benjamin. 2000. *Georges Bataille: A Critical Introduction.* London: Pluto Press.

Richman, Michèle. 1982. *Reading Georges Bataille.* Baltimore: Johns Hopkins University Press.

Sternhell, Zeev, and David Maisel. 1995. *Neither Right nor Left.* Princeton, N.J.: Princeton University Press.

Suleiman, Susan Rubin. 1995. Bataille in the Street: The Search for Virility in the 1930s. In *Bataille: Writing the Sacred,* ed. Carolyn Bailey Gill. London: Routledge.

Wolin, Richard. 2004. *The Seduction of Unreason.* Princeton, N.J.: Princeton University Press.

TWO

AMY E. WENDLING

Sovereign Consumption as a Species of Communist Theory: Reconceptualizing Energy

Recall that Marx tells the history of the bourgeois view of nature. Under bourgeois conditions, the stories told about nature represent a particular economic configuration: capitalism, and its concomitant competitive structure. Here nature is a place where I have to struggle to get what I need, an economy of scarcity. Falsely, the bourgeois class views a miserly and hostile nature as universal, ineluctable, and unavoidable.[1] Bourgeois societies operate as though scarcity is immutable or fixed, and thus natural. Under bourgeois conditions, human societies live out relations of scarcity even in situations of actual plenitude. Spotting this error in judgment, this false universality, Marx diagnoses nature's historicity.

Bataille's merit is to make thought move in economies to which it is unaccustomed. Bataille's concepts operate in grand scales that stretch beyond the circumscribed terrains of the historian, the economist, and the scientist and at the same time link these terrains in a more general field. Using the discoveries of French anthropology as a springboard, Bataille sets Marx's historicized nature into a still more general category: movements of energy on the earth. For this, he draws on the concept of energy particular to late-nineteenth- and early-twentieth-century physics, a topic I will develop in the first section below. The particular set of familial, political, and socioeconomic relations that we recognize as bourgeois are but a tiny subset of these movements, one expression among others. For Bataille, Marx's critique of nature is too limited in scope, since for Bataille, movements of energy are not limited to their significance for human expression. Thus, nature is not the trajectory of human historical development set out in Marx and Hegel; this trajectory makes up but a small subset of the circulation of surplus energy.

Pressing the insights of both Marxism and anthropology beyond the limited economies that produced them, Bataille shows that the earth's energy is superabundant. Not only do relations of scarcity not obtain, but surplus resources are both the reality and the source of strife. Fully continuous with organic life and its superabundant energy, human societies operate in ways not simply foreign to bourgeois political economy, but also unthinkable in its terms. And just as Bataille's nature is not scarce but profligate, his vision of the human being is not that of the embattled bourgeois—or proletarian—struggling for survival. Rather, Bataille's human being does not have self-preservation as his or her most pressing task. We will see in a moment how this critique bears on the most fundamental presuppositions of the philosophy of biology as well as those of political economy.

From the Kant of the third critique and the Hegel who follows him, Marx retains the premise of productive, purposive development in the parallel vectors of history, political economy, and science. The human being and human society are at the apex of all of this culture. Marx also retains a focus on human beings and the forms of human community and agency implied by this teleology. He poeticizes an all-too-human proletariat that develops a political consciousness and gains ascendancy on the technological infrastructure spawned by the bourgeois world. Marx forecasts that the contradictions and collapse of this world will produce the proletarian class as its most essential, progressive product.

Bataille questions the Marxian-Hegelian premise of productive, purposive development, and with it the possibility that the Communist Revolution will be of a different genus than the preceding bourgeois revolutions. Bataille challenges Marx both theoretically and historically. He sees that the theoretical presupposition of scarcity continues to hold in Marx's visions of postrevolutionary life: for Marx, unlike socialist utopian Charles Fourier, people continue to work against a miserly nature even after the revolution. And Bataille's *The Accursed Share* challenges the construct of scarcity as the principle of human societies. Bataille shows scarcity to be merely symptomatic of the bourgeois form by which surplus wealth is accumulated, superfluity being the real principle of organization.

As for Bataille's historical critique of Marxism, volume 3 of *The Accursed*

Share is a commentary on the character of the Russian Communist Revolution. The occasion for Bataille's meditations is Stalin's death in 1953 (1991b, 264–65; 1973, 308–309). Bataille uses this occasion as an opportunity to meditate on the forms of consumption of surplus characteristic of the bourgeois world, under which he classes *both* capitalist and communist societies. He thus continues the historical project of *The Accursed Share* as a whole into his contemporary period, a period in which the dialectic between the accumulation of resources and their use is especially acute. For in the bourgeois world, power and enjoyment are defined by exclusive disjunction (1991b, 352).

🌐 *The Profligacy of Nature*

Bataille focuses on the consumption of surplus rather than production to meet critical needs. His use of consumption as the fundamental term of analysis allows him to trouble neat teleological schemas. Whereas production, or work, is the requirement of an economy of scarcity, consumption is the requirement of an economy of plenitude. The seemingly small shift in emphasis from production to consumption has vast reverberations. In *The Accursed Share* as a whole, Bataille analyzes how copious resources have been accommodated in consumption, or use—and how they continue to be thus accommodated.

To the miserly nature characteristic of bourgeois life, Bataille counterposes a profligate nature. All organic life is conditioned by the pressure to consume the energy from the sun and the matter to which it gives rise. This vast leap in perspective sets human life in continuity not only with animal life, or simply with organic life, but also with all movements of energy. This makes Bataille, especially the Bataille of *The Accursed Share,* an exemplar of distinctly non-modern views of nature. The following paragraphs sketch three genealogies of the concept of energy that we find operative in Bataille: the foundation of the discipline of biology, the insights of structuralism, and the doctrine of medieval emanation.

Part of the romantic critique of mechanist accounts of nature, and also of the unmodified application of physical laws to self-regulating phenomena, the discipline of biology staked out its disciplinary terrain in the late nineteenth and early twentieth centuries.[2] In order to accomplish this, early thinkers in the discipline carved out a new epistemology of nature. Donna Haraway's dissertation and first book, *Crystals, Fabrics, and Fields: Metaphors of Organicism in Twentieth-Century Developmental Biology* (1976), explains this epistemology. Haraway shows how the dueling vitalism and mechanist accounts of nature give way in the late nineteenth and early twentieth centuries to an organicism that integrates features of both earlier accounts.

Organicism reflects our contemporary views of nature, philosophical and otherwise, more aptly than vitalism or mechanism, the antinomic paradigms of modernity. Organicism integrates the view of matter that came to be adopted subsequent to the discovery and use of the concept of energy in modern physics. As a paradigm, organicism deeply troubles classical philosophical categories, and especially matter and form. Contra the classical schema, matter is not simply inert, animated by forces from outside. Views of nature consequent upon this changed view of matter, then, do not have to integrate an occult animating force as an explanatory principle. Both mechanism and vitalism fall away as explanatory schemas once the nature they describe has been thus reconceptualized.

The changed account of form peculiar to organicism integrates a material notion of genetic development. Forms of the organic world develop dialectically and historically with the environment: Darwin is the most familiar example. Organisms operate as wholes and not as units of parts, and the elements out of which a given organism or species builds itself are subordinate to the organism or species as a whole. Form is functional (designed to do or act) and flexible (self-modifying in design when its functionality is challenged). Thus in organicism, the concept of form expands to contain historical, environmental, and material content (Haraway 1976, 39–40).

Material content, in turn, is discovered to be shockingly orderly: it can no longer be defined by form's absence. The discoveries of chemistry have mapped out the structure of the molecule and reduced the materials out of which it is made to a periodic table of elements. Chemistry also discovers that all organic life is carbon-based. Organic life is therefore very much of a piece across its levels of complexity, and it is also not so different from the matter that composes the rocks, wood, and dirt of any particular environment. This, plus the beginnings of the physicist's notion of energy as a sort of matter in motion, suggests a limitless convertibility of objects, forces, and forms in spheres once thought categorically separate.

While matter and form are perhaps the most classical categories troubled by the organicist paradigm, they are not the only categories in trouble. In the absence of a God to serve as guarantor for human separation from and domination of nature, the thinkers of late modernity looked to new categories: rationality in Kant, spirit in Hegel, revolutionary agency in Marx. These categories too are deeply troubled, since the function of the new paradigm of organicism is to situate the human being and his or her environment in unbroken continuity, to be unable to explain organism without environment and vice versa.

It is against this backdrop that Bataille's economic insight about surplus energy—the accursed share—and the requirement that it be wasted can be cited as a characteristic of the earth and all of the species that take their energy from the sun. The human species' participation in the accursed share serves, not as a marker of our species' distinction from and mastery over nature, but rather, as a marker of its immersion in it. Humans remain in and of nature even when the spending of the accursed share takes the forms of "high culture": jewels or art. Bataille shows these expressions to be of a piece with human sacrifice, destruction of wealth in the potlatch; the fruitless sexuality of flowering plants to be of a piece with the repetitive erotic displays of animals like us. The limitless convertibility of energy also explains how the accursed share can take such divergent forms. Against this backdrop, the nineteenth century's most precious categorical distinction, that between nature and culture, simply has no meaning—or at best appears as the vague residue of a theological fiction.

Marx was conversant with the natural science current in his time, but unlike Bataille remained caught in the nature/culture dichotomy, known to him as the contest between materialism and spirit. His historical materialism reflects the changed view of nature prevalent among the eighteenth- and nineteenth-century German physicists and mechanistic materialists. Both prior to and following the later Kant and Hegel, these thinkers paved the way for organicism as a paradigm and for biology as a discipline. They were known as the *Entwicklungsmechaniker,* and among them we find both Hermann von Helmholz and Ludwig Feuerbach. The former became better known for his contributions to the first law of thermodynamics and influence on Robert Boyle; the latter, for the metaphysical commitments that were so to influence Karl Marx.

However, as historian David Cahan (1993) reminds us, the physician von Helmholtz was not without famous mechanistic metaphysical commitments, and his is the physics that subtends both Feuerbach's and Marx's analysis. So while Marx crumbles the exclusivity of the categories of nature and culture and renders them dialectical, these categories are still intact in crucial ways in his text. His insistence on the natural, mechanistic inevitability of the Communist Revolution duels with his notion of spirit-filled revolutionary subjects overcoming their lack of a political education to found a just world.[3]

The second and related path by which we might trace the connections between developments in the concept of energy employed by Bataille is structuralism. *The Accursed Share* is, in many ways, Bataille's response to the anthropological writings of Claude Lévi-Strauss. Structuralism does in linguistics, psychology, philosophy, and anthropology what organicism is doing in biology: insisting upon the rule of the whole as regulatory of the meanings of individual parts.[4] This method holds whether the subject in question is a child's linguistic development as in Piaget, the mutual inter-relation of signifiers as in Saussure, or the discovery of kinship's many possible configurations as in Lévi-Strauss.

Bataille applies the structuralist method in political economy, searching for the transhistorical expression of surplus energy in many human cultures. Structuralism as a method is at once deeply ahistorical and deeply historical: the former, in that it argues methodically for one or two axes of analysis; the latter, in that the range of culturally specific forms that phenomena like language, the incest prohibition, or surplus can take necessarily broadens the range of these axes of analysis. Applying the structuralist method, Bataille expands the notion of energy to encompass a wide variety of both human and non-human expression.

Bataille and contemporary philosophy of biology share some concerns and some fundamental questions because of their common roots in the intellectual trends of nineteenth-century Germany and early-twentieth-century France—romanticism, biology, and structuralism. The shared concerns are especially apparent in the debates surrounding function, development, human nature, and altruism.[5] But Bataille is uncommitted to the teleological premises that the traditional philosophy of biology absorbs from a political economy that has scarce resources as its most fundamental presupposition. Such a philosophy of biology inevitably emphasizes competition and aggression across all levels of organization: in its most contemporary instantiation, genes struggle for mastery across the terrain of generations. Another example is the philosophy of biology's constant emphasis on self-preservation in the life of the individual or the species. Because he questions this presupposition, Bataille is able to offer a vision of life not reliant on the modern view of nature as an economy of scarcity. And this vision of life looks very different.

But from where does Bataille derive this ability to question the miserly nature of the moderns? To answer this, we must give yet a third genealogy of his philosophy, and emphasize his familiarity with premodern and medieval epistemologies. This familiarity gives Bataille access to an earlier view of nature as a plenitude, for in at least some of the medieval conceptions, God's emanation provided for a wealth of resources. As Hans Blumenburg argues, the teleological underpinnings of modern science are a symptom of a changed relationship between the human and the natural world in which the former is juxtaposed against the hostility of the latter rather than seen as a part of its plenitude (1983, 137–143). A medievalist by training, Bataille has access to the premodern vision of the human-nature interface that sets the two in continuity rather than juxtaposing them. In this way, Bataille's organicism is a revised classical philosophical vitalism.

In the register of political economy, Bataille offers a theory of consumption as a critique of Marx's teleological theory of production. He offers a theory of destruction as a critique of the philosophy of biology's default thesis of the self-preservation of the individual or species, or even of the gene. Revisiting the medieval continuity between the human being and nature, Bataille reflects the organicist transformation of the view of the natural world, which is woven of a newly monistic fabric: energy, the energy from the sun or from the atom that replaces the emanation of God.

Everything is composed of energy and will pass in and out of existence as an entity more or less quickly. Everything consumes and is consumed; everything is living, once what it means to live is expressed as consuming and being consumed. Distinctly non-modern, Bataille's human being does not stand over against a hostile nature. That the insights Bataille offers us are so broadly philosophical shows how his work exceeds the boundaries characteristic of most other twentieth-century French thought.

Bataille recognizes the pressure to consume as bourgeois cultures express this pressure. In such cultures, consumption is often coercive. For example, I always have to attend the boss's party whether or not I feel festive, drink her liquor whether or not I am thirsty, and take the suit that I am going to wear to the dry cleaners the day before, even if just for a press. But for Bataille, this pressure to consume is not *simply* ideological, nor limited to the human realm.[6] Consumption conditions all life and, given a long enough time scale, all being. Even a rock accrues sediment. When we do look back at the human realm from such an evolutionary or even geological perspective, it looks different to us.

This pressure to consume as a condition of life is the pressure to convert matter into form and form into matter from the perspective of consumption rather than production, in which matter and form are converted on a human scale through work. It explains the title of Bataille's three-volume work: *The Accursed Share*. The accursed share is the resource that must get consumed, that will get consumed one way or another. It is the food remaining on the plate that must be eaten by someone, be put down the garbage disposal, or putresce into the microorganisms of the air. Bataille offers us the philosophical implications of the law of the conservation of energy as much as a cultural critique of the bourgeois world.

Nature's profligacy means that the resources to be conserved are vast. In bourgeois cultures, wealth has been accumulated and stockpiled over centuries. The law of energy's conservation therefore expresses itself in periodic outbursts of energy-expensive violence. Bataille diagnoses the scientific and economic truth of surplus resources. He then formulates the preeminent contemporary ethical challenge as that of finding ways of "exhausting the surplus *without war*." He writes, "The problem I speak of . . . is that of a world of production that would escape the control of [bourgeois] subjectivity. We must seek exhaustion through rational means as against the subjective means of the pursuit of rank and war" (1991b, 428–29, his emphasis).

Bataille dismisses revolution as an emotionally charged word. Instead, he calls on the bourgeois states, both capitalist and communist, to consider the redistribution of energy and resources in a rational manner in order to avoid this violence. His book is a warning, and in it he appeals explicitly to our rationality.

🌼 *Consumption and Hoarding*

Better than Hegel or Kant, Marx heralds Bataille's account of consumption. Marx distinguishes two types of consumption: productive and individual. In *productive consumption,* I consume resources while making other things that are my real aim. The wood of the boat I build and sell for money is consumed productively. Ultimately, productive consumption has an abstraction as its telos: money or exchange, the promise of something else. *Individual consumption* is when I use resources that then exit the sphere of exchange, when I use them up, as with the wood I burn for warmth or whittle for pleasure. Marx's distinction between productive and individual consumption loosely parallels his distinction between the exchange value and the use-value of any given commodity. But although Marx does discuss consumption, in his analysis he emphasizes production, or work. He inherits this theme from the political economists of whom he is critical, but whose conceptual apparatus he nonetheless shares.

Marx's emphasis on productive consumption is also inevitable, given his view of nature as an artifact of human society. Productive consumption leaves a much greater mark on nature than does individual consumption—and a far more calculable one. Through it a human agent works up the world. And Marx first illuminates this deliberate human productive force as the operative in the Hegelian schema of nature.

Hegel retains some of the early modern vision of a fixed universe expressing itself, albeit slowly, over a vast temporal expanse. Hegel's nature is implicitly rational and waits to be expressed in the human world.[7] Marx shows us the strokes by which this world has been deliberately produced, giving human agency a much broader berth. In his later texts, especially the *Grundrisse* and *Capital,* Marx glimpses the importance of individual consumption, equating it with use-value and with the paradoxes that attend use-value.[8] Having thus illuminated production for the first time in the history of modern thought, Marx is in no position to become consumption's theorist, as Bataille will be.

In section one of the introduction to the *Grundrisse,* Marx gives a four-termed analysis: production, consumption, distribution, and exchange. Marx emphasizes the levels of identity that obtain between production and consumption (1973, 90–94), including their *immediate* identity. He then locates his economic critique in the process of capitalist production and not simply in inequalities of distribution and exchange.

This is known as Marx's labor theory of value. According to this theory, I mix my labor with a naturally given or otherwise unowned thing, and the thing becomes my property. Philosophically, Marx's labor theory of value differs little from those of John Locke and Thomas More. However, in capitalist production, the worker mixes his or her labor with raw materials owned by the capitalist, using tools or machines also owned by the capitalist, and gives up the product to the capitalist market in exchange for a wage. Marx's critique of surplus value claims that the worker gives up more energy in production than he or she is returned in the form of the wage, which allows for only minimally subsistent consumption. Furthermore, he claims that the system as a whole obfuscates this fundamental inequality of production and consumption.

Scientifically, this insight reflects the discovery of nineteenth-century physics that transformations and interchanges between form and matter are possible in the form of energy—or in Marx's vernacular, labor or work. Socially, it leads to more advanced examples about the way *modes* of production and *modes* of consumption condition one another. That is, a certain way of working necessitates a certain mode of living: just as office workers today know the happy hour and the television set. But in the Marxist analysis as a whole, consumption is the missing term, the term that until Bataille lacks crucial development.

Bataille understands and further extrapolates the significance of the immediate identity of consumption and production. For of the four terms with which the *Grundrisse* begins, consumption receives the least attention both in Marx's texts and in subsequent analyses that draw upon his work. While in *Capital* Marx does list the reports of doctors investigating nutritional deficiencies among the working class, he fails to generalize philosophically about the import of these statistics. And though he does understand some of the rudiments of world economics, he does not yet theorize about what Bataille, oriented from consumption rather than production, will call the general economy. Anthropologists, including the Mauss from whom Bataille's work in volume 1 takes its cue, orient their analyses from exchange, as do the critical theorists. Distribution of products remains a merely practical question, though the question of the distribution of the *means* of production, and not simply its spoils, has also been neglected.

Bataille's discussion of bourgeois life in volume 3 therefore focuses on bourgeois consumption, and this allows us to see new things about bourgeois life, production, reproduction, and the resultant political economy. Consumption is a radical principle of analysis in the first place because, in bourgeois thinkers as in bourgeois cultures, the emphasis is always on production, on work.

Bourgeois cultures work from a perceived scarcity of resources, psychologically and socially. We who belong to them cannot see the resources we have accumulated and have long ago forgotten how to use them, to consume them individually. We value our resources not as objects but as signs of our position in social networks. As Fred Schrader writes in his history of the formation of bourgeois society, the bourgeois invention of table manners was not because of a love of beautiful, elaborately carved cutlery, nor a desire for exquisitely prepared food, but because the demonstration of taste showed one's membership in a cultural elite and furthered one's business interests (1996, 102). As such, bourgeois cultures become hopelessly ideal.

As for our resources, bourgeois culture requires us to fear for their loss or their insufficiency. If we are accepted in the ranks of the cultural elite, we fear that our membership will be sullied or cancelled by material inadequacies that cause us, unwittingly, not to circulate the right sort of behavioral signs. If we are marginal to these ranks, bourgeois culture requires us to affect these signs until we possess the means of joining the ranks. Either way, in the wake of postfeudal democratic life, the still-present narratives of class are subject to a leveling mechanism.

Additionally, because the waste prohibition is so strong in bourgeois cultures, arbitrary destruction is fetishized, and especially the arbitrary destruction of the means of production, of which we may take technophobia, hating one's employment, and the desire to wage war as examples. But this sort of destruction is neither use nor enjoyment. Rather, it is the sign and symptom of a rampant productivity run amok. This productivity has amassed and accumulated beyond the wildest expectations of most of human history. It is the perception of scarcity rather than actual scarcity that is at issue in bourgeois cultures. But the cultural fear instilled in such cultures only acts as fur-

ther impetus to even more work and greater accumulation. Wealth and plenitude wear the mask of scarcity and lead to vast stockpiles of accumulated
resources.

The bourgeois is a developed incarnation of Marx's hoarder who "makes
a sacrifice of the lusts of the flesh to his gold fetish" (1887, 133). In the terms
of technical Marxism, the bourgeois does not hoard but accumulates.
Hoarding proper belongs to the historical era of manufacture, prior to the
era of capital. The hoarder proper gathers gold. Bourgeois accumulation is
of the means of production; the bourgeois "hoard" is one of the tools to further productive life, largely things that enable the bourgeois to work more,
faster, or at higher levels. However, accumulation and hoarding share the
same schematics of deferred enjoyment, and Marx uses the terms inter-
changeably in volume 2 of *Capital.* The injunction not to spill on the sofa in
the living room in which I receive the boss from whom I expect a promotion
is of a piece with the gold stashed under the bed.

The accumulation of resources with which to remit payment on one's
infinite debts is the staple of bourgeois psychology. Bourgeois cultures are
therefore predicated on a logic of exhaustive work and a psychology of fear.
According to the Nietzschean schema in *The Genealogy of Morals,* the establishment of memory and the ability to keep promises in the otherwise
flighty human animal required corporeal torment (1967, Essay 2). This torment became historically and psychologically sedimented: we call it conscience. Bourgeois culture lives in and from the fears of conscience; at its
economic origins, the memory of the fealty and other painful exactions of
paternalistic feudal life lay smoldering; at its social and cultural origins, the
memory of revolution's losses are not yet distant. Were it not for this form
of bad conscience, the urge to hoard would be nonsensical among those for
whom resources are plentiful.

Bataille draws the link between accumulation and cruelty explicitly.
He suggests that Stalin's forced industrialization of feudal Russia partook
of the same structure that Marx claims was characteristic of England's bru-
tal primitive accumulation, an accumulation known better to us as the Industrial Revolution and dramatized by Charles Dickens and Emile Zola. In
a section entitled "Communism limited to the destruction of feudal
forms," Bataille writes:

> [A]ll accumulation is cruel; all renunciation of the present for the sake of the
> future is cruel. The Russian bourgeoisie not having accumulated, the Rus-
> sian proletariat had to do it. And the Chinese proletariat will have to do like-
> wise. We shall see that the accumulation of resources with a view to industry

falls upon the proletariat whenever the bourgeoisie is not able to do anything, and that the new role of the proletariat calls for changes that Marx
couldn't have foreseen, changes that seem not to be easy ones, but whose extraordinary consequences ought to again determine the relations of force.
(1991b, 273)

The problem of consumption, expressed in a perception of scarcity
where none exists and in the cruelty of all accumulation, foreshadows the
critique Bataille will level at Marx in the next few pages. Like the bourgeoisie—in fact, exactly like the bourgeoisie—the proletariat will be forced to
accumulate and will bear the same psychological, cultural, and political
scars of the first revolutionary class. Marx's demand that the proletariat
overcome its material conditioning in a revolution that differs in kind from
the preceding bourgeois revolution is a demand for spirit to triumph over
nature. The demand shows Marx's immersion in the modern logic of the na-
ture/culture binary.[9] From Bataille's perspective, he must give up his materialism, find reasons from within this materialism to justify the possibility
of a revolution that does not collapse into the continuation of class privilege,
or give up the doctrine of proletarian revolution altogether.

Sovereignty and the Revolutionary Subject

Bataille's discussion of "sovereignty" occupies the entire third volume
of *The Accursed Share.* This volume explains the final two chapters of volume
1, in which Bataille sketches the forms of consumption characteristic of Soviet industrialization as a modality of the forms of consumption characteristic of the *bourgeois* world, as a cruel accumulation.

In *sovereign consumption,* consumption is not subjected to an end outside
of itself. In the terms of classical Marxism, to act sovereignly is to privilege
use over exchange value, or individual over productive consumption. In a
temporal schema, to act sovereignly is to privilege the present over the past
or future. We might recognize sovereign consumption as noncoercive pleasure or play, consumption that exceeds a productive, work-driven economy.
A sovereign world would have the vision—and the language—to accommodate such a recognition and to accommodate it in a mode other than dub-
bing it irresponsible, irrational, childlike, or mad.

Let me offer an example of sovereign consumption from the realm of
sexuality, a realm that Bataille also highlights in both his fiction and his
philosophy. The compulsory productive heterosexuality characteristic of
bourgeois cultures is also part of the coercion to production. Bataille's por-

nography, all of which describes nonreproductive if mostly heterosexual sex, fits into his project for this reason. Nonreproductive sex—sex for sex's sake, queer sex, or sex for pleasure—are all modes of nonproductive, or sovereign consumption: consumption that does no work, produces no new workers, and uses energy without recompense. All bourgeois cultural taboos about sexuality are rooted in the coercion to production.

For Bataille, the sovereign individual, a version of the Nietzschean noble or Hegelian master (1991b, 219; 1973, 267), "consumes and doesn't labor" (1991b, 198; 1973, 248). Like Nietzsche, Bataille argues that bourgeois societies—we readily recognize them as our own—have made this sort of consumption *impossible* for us by inverting the values attached to it.

Accumulation eclipses the character of the sovereign: we stockpile, hoard, and hold in reserve rather than use or enjoy. Our deepest pleasures derive from the hoarding itself: from the security of knowing it is there, should we want it. Because of this our pleasures remain vicarious, theoretical, indefinitely deferred and abstract. In an inversion of economic values, the pressure to accumulate eclipses Bataille's sovereign consumption. Similarly, in Nietzsche, the priest's inversion of moral values eclipses the goodness of nobility.

For Bataille, the bourgeois class is the first—and ultimately only— revolutionary class: an ascetic class that revolts specifically against the sovereign nobility in favor of accumulation. The bourgeois revolution over against sovereignty conditions and inescapably schematizes all subsequent revolution and appeals to revolution. The very idea and practice of revolution is itself bourgeois. Revolution is a bourgeois concept, and the world in which Bataille finds himself continues to be the world of a *feudal* order that is breaking down. Bataille writes:

> I cannot help but insist on these aspects: I wish to stress, against both classical and present-day Marxism, the connection of *all* the great modern revolutions, from the English and the French onward, with a feudal order that is breaking down. There have never been any great revolutions that have struck down an established bourgeois domination. All those that overthrew a regime started with a revolt *motivated* by the sovereignty that is implied in feudal society. (1991b, 279; 1973, 321)

Conceptually, revolution demarcates the transition from sovereignty to accumulation. Revolution will always be connected with the dissolution of a feudal order and the privileges emblematized by such an order: access to nonproductive consumption, enjoyment, or use-value itself, by right of birth.

But why not, rather, a conception of plenitude and entitlement for all, also by right of birth, instead of competition and struggle for survival? Such a view is impossible when Nietzschean *ressentiment* is the impetus for liberation, because postrevolutionary subjects have learned to demonize the very things that they most desire.

This point goes some distance toward explaining why revolutionary class hatred is insufficiently analytic and confuses the aristocracy with the bourgeoisie. It also explains why the revolution attempted in 1848 was a disaster. Bataille writes:

> The days of June, the Commune, and Spartakus are the only violent convulsions of the working masses struggling against the bourgeoisie, but these movements occurred with the help of a misunderstanding. The workers were misled by the lack of obstacles encountered a little earlier when the bourgeoisie, in concert with them, rose up against men born of that feudality which irritated everybody. (1991b, 289)

Under this historical error, born of the precipitous mixing of classes, the particularity of the bourgeoisie is misunderstood. The bourgeois is no lord or lady waited upon, but a money-grubbing, guilt-ridden, obsessive worker, too cheap to hire help, self-righteously confirmed in his or her work ethic and ascetic way of life. I am not suggesting that the bourgeois does not have privileges. He or she does, but not in the same way as the feudal lord or lady. The bourgeois goal is always further accumulation, never consumption, and therefore never sovereignty.

Bataille writes, "The masses have *never* united except in a radical hostility to the principle of sovereignty" (1991b, 288; 1973, 329). The masses do not unite against accumulation, except when that accumulation is expressed as sovereignty, and therefore not as accumulation at all, but as consumption. The proletarian worker perceives an excessive consumption as the necessary result of the bourgeois accumulation of property. But this is a misperception, for the bourgeois does not enjoy but accumulates.

When the proletarian worker comes to power, a bourgeois revolution recurs because this mass worker, the slave ascendant, forever operates in an economy of scarcity: hoarding resources from the memory of being deprived. The problem of accumulation begins again. The structure is of actual scarcity, followed by perceived scarcity and hoarding that holds on as a historical remainder. Never fully overcome, this remainder becomes part of the historically sedimented fear through which bourgeois cultures function.

The problem is that a resentful revolutionary subject is unfit and unable to enjoy wealth and, by extension, political sovereignty. In *The German Ideol-*

ogy, Marx answers this criticism by claiming that through the process of revolutionary action, the proletariat is able to overcome accumulated habit and conditioning, learn to consume well, and thus become fit for rule (1978, 193). Only an upsurge of violent revolutionary action will be a sufficient lesson in consumption, a trial by violence that returns the bondsman back to the scene of the struggle to the death. For Marx, the emergent subject, baptized by fire, is transformed into a being capable of sovereignty—or dead—at the end of the process. But we have seen that the process of revolutionary action instills not liberation but a fearful repetition of servitude, now internal.

In short, transformation is never so neat as Marx would have it. The problem of how subjects who have lived through oppression wield power has been notoriously sticky, reappearing in all thoughtful considerations of postrevolutionary subjects. In volume 3 of *The Accursed Share,* the problem appears in Bataille's characterization of Stalin as a serf's son come to power, who deliberately carries out a revolutionary program that he knows will not extend beyond the reformations of the bourgeois democracies to the West. In his own list of the tasks of the Provisional Revolutionary Government, Stalin wrote that "none of them would go beyond the limits of bourgeois democracy" (Bataille 1991b, 266–67). The problem appears in Frantz Fanon's *The Wretched of the Earth* (1968) when he considers the Algerian Revolution and the subsequent fitness to rule of those whose political and psychological sensibilities have been shaped by oppression.

The problem also appears in the strains of contemporary feminism that deal with transgendered persons, persons who live out a socially determined gender identity other than the one into which they were born. In Judith Halberstam's *Female Masculinity,* she describes the female to male transgendered person who has seized a prized and structurally privileged position. Halberstam writes, "Gender transition from female to male allows biological women access to male privilege within their reassigned genders" (1998, 143).[10] Such "postrevolutionary" subjects struggle against inhabiting a masculinity that reinscribes the dominant model by which they themselves were oppressed. They must also struggle against being perceived as "class traitors" to women and feminism (Califia 2000; Halberstam 1998, 144).

Having gone through this transition, Patrick Califia considers what he calls "the transformation of manhood and masculinity" (2002, 394). Fully aware of the ambivalence of his postrevolutionary subjectivity, he writes:

> My gender dysphoria [came from the] feeling that there is something wrong when other people perceived or treated me as if I were a girl. Not wanting to be female, but not having much enthusiasm for the only other option our

society offers. . . . Still, I keep thinking there must be something unique about being a man, something fit to be celebrated in ritual and mythology, the stuff of a spiritual mystery teaching. Or is this desire the root of the oppression of women—the need to cordon off certain activities or experiences and say, only we can do this and women may not, because we must have a source of pride and uniqueness in order to have meaningful lives? . . . I wonder if I can talk about what I like about being a man and disliked about being a woman without being attacked for being sexist? . . . Being a fag or third-gender person is a way for me to salvage the good that I saw in my father, the virtues that I see in ordinary men, without being damaged by the ugliness, the unbridled rage, the hatred of homosexuals, the racism, the arrogance that made me wary of my dad. (2002, 394–400)

🌀 *Conclusion*

I remain hopeful about postrevolutionary subjects and the abilities of such subjects to occupy positions of power in critical and self-aware ways. I also remain hopeful about a notion of sovereignty partially liberated from the context of oppression in which it was forged and about consumption as enjoyment that somehow exceeds a context of production, or work. In seeking to keep sovereignty alive, Bataille too does not envision a return to the oppressive sovereignty characteristic of a feudal system. Sovereignty operates for Bataille more as a conceptual, methodological, and *practical* postulate rather than as a historical nostalgia. But it is precisely because of this that sovereignty can stage its insurgency anywhere. Bataille suggests that *enjoyment itself* is the upsurge of sovereignty: "The enjoyment of production is in opposition to accumulation (that is, [in opposition] to the production of the means of production) . . . [Sovereignty is] neither anachronistic nor insignificant [because it is the general] condition *of each human being*" (1991b, 281; 1973, 322, my emphasis).

Sovereignty is the overcoming of the urge to hoard; the overcoming of bourgeois subjectivity; the refusal of the historical sedimentation of cruelty, accumulation, and the bad conscience. Acting sovereignly, I leave behind fear, and I stop living in expectation of death. I fear the loss of enjoyment more than death. Bataille's sovereignty anticipates the existentialist refrain of freedom at any cost. But unlike in existentialism, Bataille's sovereignty preserves corporeality: I live sovereignly, not despite my fears of death, but because of my enjoyment of life. For according to Bataille, "if we live sovereignly, the representation of death is impossible, for the present is not subject to the demands of the future. That is why, in a fundamental sense, living sovereignly is to escape, if not death, at least the anguish of death. Not that dying is hateful—but living servilely is hateful" (1991b, 219).

Nor has Bataille given up on communism: "Sovereignty is no longer alive except in the perspectives of communism" (1991b, 261; 1973, 305). For communism is the only kind of thinking and practice that tries to restore individual consumption, to restore use-value and with it enjoyment as the general condition of life. Bataille knows that the jury is out on communism: its historical moment is too near to take a clear view of its implications as a whole. Because of its historical proximity, communism has fallen between the cracks of dogmatic and politicized positions. Bataille writes that "the lack of interest in understanding communism evinced by practically all noncommunists and the involvement of militants in a cohort acting almost without debate—according to directives in which the whole game is not known—have made communism a reality that is foreign, as it were, to the world of reflection" (1991b, 264). Bataille's comments on communism in volume 3 of *The Accursed Share* seek to redress this gap, forcing the owl of Minerva to take her customary flight earlier than usual.

Cleansed of teleology, communist revolution becomes the theoretical and practical pursuit of such enjoyment, of a different kind of liberation. And in contemporary thinkers as diverse as Jacques Derrida, Donna Haraway, and Antonio Negri, we find sketches of non-teleological liberations, which are no longer revolutions that reinstate repressive subjectivities. Derrida speaks of ongoing, underground practices of resistance (1994, 99). Haraway insists on the non-innocence and impurity of all positions of resistance that appear alongside hegemonic cultural ideals (1991, 1997). Addressing the temporal deferral of communism itself, Negri writes, "Communism does not come in a 'subsequent period,' it springs up contemporaneously as a process constituting an enormous power of antagonism and of real supersession" (1991, 181).

Anticipating these thinkers, Bataille situates the real interest of communism in its vision of a human being whose general condition is to play without labor in an economy of plenty. No price must be exacted for enjoyment, and there is no question of entitlement. The eclipse of this assertion, in favor of the accumulating and stockpiling of the means of production for future use, is communism missing its own best point.

NOTES

1. A possible exception is Locke, who sees nature as a plenitude, an abundance. He is thinking of the land expropriations of imperialism, and later colonialism, as the source of

this abundance. However, one earns the right to nature's abundance in Locke by farming without waste. The waste prohibition is itself predicated on the logic of natural scarcity, a residue in Locke of the more typical view of nature that we see in Hobbes and Bacon.

2. See Keller 2000, especially pp. 45 and 77–182. See also Donna Haraway (1976, 17), who periodizes biology's disciplinary birth in the "years of crisis" from 1850 to 1930.

3. Recall Italian Marxist Antonio Gramsci's notion of an "organic intellectual" (1971). Unlike the traditional intellectual, whose faculties are cultivated by an upper-class education, transmitted unsullied through time and operating according to a classical model, the organic intellectual's faculties are cultivated by the everyday ideological environment and demonstrate the innate human potential for epistemological development. The organic intellectual is part of Gramsci's solution to the Marxist problem of human agency among those conditioned by their material environments for its opposite. It also shows how the language of organicism cross-pollinated with twentieth-century Marxism.

4. See Haraway for a discussion of organicism's relation to structuralism (1976, 16).

5. See Hull and Ruse 1998.

6. This differentiates Bataille's Marxism from the more traditional strain of Marxism that we find expressed in the critical theorists.

7. As Hegel puts it in his *Philosophy of Nature:* "The determination and the purpose [*Zweck*] of the philosophy of nature is therefore that spirit should find its own essence, its counterpart [*Gegenbild*], i.e., the Notion [*Begriff*], within nature. The study of nature is therefore the liberation of what belongs to spirit within nature, for spirit is in nature in so far as it relates to itself [*sich bezieht*] not to another, but to itself. This is likewise the liberation of nature, which in itself is reason [*Vernunft*]; it is only [*erst*] through spirit however, that reason as such comes forth from nature into existence" (1970a, 204; 1970b, 23).

8. In *Capital* Marx writes: "The circuit Commodity-Money-Commodity starts with one commodity, and finishes with another, which falls out of circulation and into consumption. Consumption, the satisfaction of wants, in one word, use-value, is its end and aim. The circuit Money-Commodity-Money, on the contrary, commences with money and ends with money. Its leading motive, and the goal that attracts it, is therefore mere exchange value" (1887, 148). On the paradox of use-value and its fundamental importance for Marxism, see Derrida 1994.

9. Subsequent to the failure of the 1848 revolutions in Paris, the character of Marx's writing changes, becomes less polemical and more historical.

10. Female-to-male transgendered persons have far fewer social and psychological problems subsequent to their transition than do male-to-female transgendered persons, a fact that attests to the continued sexism of contemporary societies.

WORKS CITED

Bataille, Georges. 1973. *Oeuvres Complètes.* Paris: Gallimard.
———. 1991a. *The Accursed Share: Volume I.* Trans. Robert Hurley. New York: Zone Books.
———. 1991b. *The Accursed Share: Volumes II and III.* Trans. Robert Hurley. New York: Zone Books.
Blumenburg, Hans. 1983. *The Legitimacy of the Modern Age.* Cambridge: MIT Press.

Cahan, David, ed. 1993. *Hermann von Helmholtz and the Foundations of Nineteenth-Century Science.* Berkeley: University of California Press.

Califia, Pat. 2000. *Public Sex: The Culture of Radical Sex,* 2nd ed. San Francisco: Cleis Press.

————. 2002. *Speaking Sex to Power: The Politics of Queer Sex.* San Francisco: Cleis Press.

Deleuze, Giles, and Félix Guattari. 1983. *Anti-Oedipus: Capitalism and Schizophrenia.* Trans. Robert Hurley, Mark Seem, and Helen R. Lane. Minneapolis: University of Minnesota Press.

Derrida, Jacques. 1994. *Spectres of Marx.* Trans. Peggy Kanuf. New York: Routledge.

Fanon, Franz. 1968. *The Wretched of the Earth.* Trans. Constance Farrington. New York: Grove Press.

Gramsci, Antonio. 1971. *Selections from the Prison Notebooks.* Trans. Quintin Hoare and Geoffrey Nowell Smith. New York: International Publishers.

Halberstam, Judith. 1998. *Female Masculinity.* Durham, N.C.: Duke University Press.

Haraway, Donna. 1976. *Crystals, Fabrics, and Fields: Metaphors of Organicism in Twentieth-Century Developmental Biology.* New Haven, Conn.: Yale University Press.

————. 1991. *Simians, Cyborgs, and Women: The Reinvention of Nature.* New York: Routledge.

————. 1997. *Modest Witness @ Second Millennium. Femaleman Meets Oncomouse: Feminism and Technoscience.* New York: Routledge.

Hegel, G. W. F. 1970a. *Hegel's Philosophy of Nature.* Trans. M. J. Petry. London: Allen & Unwin.

————. 1970b. *Encyclopädie der philosophischen Wissenschaften im Grundrisse* (1830). Frankfurt: Suhrkamp.

————. 1977. *Phenomenology of Spirit.* Trans. A. V. Miller. Oxford: Oxford University Press.

Hull, David L., and Michael Ruse, eds. 1998. *The Philosophy of Biology.* Oxford: Oxford University Press.

Keller, Evelyn Fox. 2000. *The Century of the Gene.* Cambridge, Mass.: Harvard University Press.

Marx, Karl. 1887. *Capital,* Vol. 1. Trans. Samuel Moore and Edward Aveling. Moscow: Progress Publishers.

————. 1973. *The Grundrisse: Foundations of the Critique of Political Economy (Rough Draft).* Trans. Martin Nicolaus. London: Penguin Books.

————. 1978. The German Ideology. In *The Marx-Engels Reader,* ed. Robert C. Tucker. New York: W. W. Norton.

Mauss, Marcel. 1967. *The Gift: Forms and Functions of Exchange in Archaic Societies.* Trans. Ian Cunnison. New York: W. W. Norton.

Negri, Antonio. 1991. *Marx Beyond Marx: Lessons on the Grundrisse.* Trans. Harry Cleaver, Michael Ryan, and Maurizio Viano. Brooklyn: Autonomedia, Inc.

Nietzsche, Friedrich. 1967. *On the Genealogy of Morals.* Trans. Walter Kaufmann and R. J. Hollingdale. New York: Vintage Books.

Schrader, Fred E. 1996. *Die Formierung der bürgerlichen Gesellshaft, 1550–1850.* Frankfurt: Fischer Taschenbuch.

Wolin, Richard. 1996. Left Fascism: Georges Bataille and the German Ideology. *Constellations* 2 (3): 397–428.

THREE

PIERRE LAMARCHE

The Use Value of G. A. M. V. Bataille

*In the final analysis it is clear that a worker works in order to obtain
the violent pleasures of coitus (in other words, he accumulates in order
to spend). On the other hand, the conception according to which the
worker must have coitus in order to provide for the future necessities of
work is linked with the unconscious identification of worker with
slave. . . . As soon as one attacks the accursed exploitation of man by
man, it becomes time to leave to the exploiters this abominable
appropriative morality.*

BATAILLE, "THE USE VALUE OF D. A. F. DE SADE"

*And down with the denigrators of "immediate human interest," down
with all the scribblers with their spiritual elevation and sanctimonious
disgust for material needs!*

BATAILLE, "THE 'OLD MOLE,' AND THE PREFIX SUR"

The profound enmity that existed between Bataille and Breton for most
of their productive lives is legendary. Its putative theoretical basis is expressed in the skirmish—ca. 1929–30—centering around Breton's denunciation of Bataille in the *Second Surrealist Manifesto* and Bataille's response in
missives collected into the *Dossier de la polémique avec André Breton.*[1] Bataille
is a fraud, attempting to pass off his odious and deranged obsessions as some
kind of perverse social critique, Breton declares. Bataille counters that Breton and his fellow travelers of the second manifesto are sanctimonious hypo-
crites—*poseurs,* whose alleged subversiveness amounts, in actuality, to so
much naive tomfoolery. The height of surrealist, and particularly Bretonian,
hypocrisy is attained by means of their attempt to appropriate the figure and
works of Sade. This gesture strikes two, in particular, of Bataille's very raw

nerves. First, it betrays the bourgeois moralistic idealism that permeates Breton's surrealist circle, an idealism that the delusional Breton refuses to acknowledge and that incenses Bataille, who confronts it with his base materialism. Second, it constitutes another example of the tendency within what Bataille will later refer to as limited economy to eschew use value in favor of exchange value: to overturn the primacy of expenditure over production and accumulation, to sacrifice the satisfaction of immediate needs for deferred project (the "future necessities of work").[2] Why, precisely, does Bataille propose an examination of Sade's "use value" in response to surrealist provocation? Why is Marx's concept helpful in explicating what Bataille views as the vacuousness, indeed, the bourgeois reactionary nature of surrealist "revolt"? In the late 1920s and early 1930s, during the time of his flirtation with the surrealist movement and subsequent confrontation with Breton, Bataille became involved first with the journal *Documents,* a review ostensibly devoted to art and ethnography that lasted only two years and fifteen issues, and then with Boris Souvarine's anti-Stalinist, Marxist review *La Critique sociale.*[3] A brief review of these literary associations will help to ground an analysis of his recourse to the category of use value in articulating his critique of Breton.

Bataille's contributions to *Documents* elaborate his vision of a base materialism. In the sixth issue, we find Bataille's ode to the big toe, which he identifies as the most human part of the human body, reminding us that our filthy, disgusting feet—and in particular, the big toe that provides balance and stability—make possible our literal elevation above our nearest relatives, the apes. In the next issue, Bataille argues that the mythical conception of the sun as symbolizing illumination, edification, the *pinnacle* of truth, is only half the story of the symbolic function of that concept. A more complete ethnographic record shows us that the sun also represents ritualistic slaughter and ex-sanguination by means of the slitting of the throat, the vulture feasting on Prometheus's liver, auto-decapitation symbolized by a man slashing his own throat—that is to say, in general, both the ascent to Icarian heights, and the illusion of Icarian elevation that is confirmed by the inevitable catastrophic fall back to earth. In the third issue of its second and final year (1930), we find Bataille's vehement condemnation of those who, idealistically, misunderstand the revolutionary force of Picasso and Dali in terms of some kind of heroic elevation above regnant aesthetic forms. On the contrary, Dali, for example in his "Lugubrious Game," proposes that liberation and revolution—actual, as opposed to idealist—can only be obtained by wallowing in the ignominy of soiling oneself, "as a pig who rummages in manure and mud uprooting everything with his snout" (1985, 24).

Numerous other articles articulate a similar vision of the ways in which abject, base matter functions to destabilize the hierarchical schematism inherent within all idealist value systems. Bataille's meditations on shit smears in a painting of Dali; on the big toe; the rotten sun; the "hideous," hairy sexual organs concealed within the petals of a flower are not intended to simply reverse a particular hierarchical schema of ideals or values by elevating what had been considered base, lowly, disgusting, above that which is venerated. Again, the point is to show how that which is abjected as inferior and repugnant in any hierarchical system continuously subverts and destabilizes the hierarchy the system is intended to establish, through the need, which the system itself generates, to continuously expel this base matter. The value of what is elevated cannot be maintained without a constant reappropriation of the base—a perpetual return of the repressed, the expulsion of which forms the basis of the process of elevation. *Pace* Breton, excrement, filth, monstrosity, hideousness are not the new ideals that Bataille seeks to elevate to a privileged position, in keeping with his own sordid obsessions. Rather, they are the sorts of things that make possible any attempt to elevate and order ideals and values into a hierarchy. Thus, the point of Bataille's articulation of a theory of base matter is to end this senile fixation on idealist hierarchies— which accomplish nothing anyway, save their own perpetuation—altogether. Reveling in the lowly and repugnant is one way of demonstrating, quite simply, that all matter is what it is; all things are what they are. The attempt to idealize and hierarchically order the matter of the universe is a fool's game, and those who play it are bound to suffer Icarus's fate.

Having earned Breton's wrath through his examinations of base matter in *Documents,* Bataille engages in a vigorous response in the pieces arranged in the aforementioned *Dossier.* Around this time, Bataille is also initiating his involvement with *La Critique sociale.* The explicitly political nature of his contributions to Souvarine's review, which focus in particular on the issue of class struggle in the context of the contemporary historical crisis and prefigure the robust theory of general economy elaborated in the late 1940s, makes it clear that Bataille's problem with Breton is not limited to the latter's idealism, to the sanctimonious moralism that shines through in his denunciation of Bataille in the *Second Manifesto.* To put it another way, it's not just that Breton is a prude, whose finger wagging at Bataille's thoroughgoing debauchery and fascination with all things foul and nauseating invites Bataille's vitriol. It's not just the hypocrisy of an alleged revolt against bourgeois morality that meticulously seeks to maintain standards of propriety and hygiene against the filth Bataille insists upon wallowing in. It is, again, the very real, practical, political impotence of the surrealist's alleged subversion—Bataille's growing realization that surrealist antics will be utterly ineffectual against the rising tide of fascism—that is at the core of the schism.[4] And for Bataille, the moralism and the political impotence are very much intertwined.

It is to the relationship between the need for an actual Sadean—as opposed to Bretonian/symbolic—rejection of bourgeois morality, and the project of building a truly effective revolutionary movement as an alternative to Stalinism, fascism, and the largely discredited liberal democracies of Western Europe, that Bataille turns his attention in his meditations on Sade's use value.

✤ *Use Value*

We all recall the famous first sentence of *Capital,* wherein Marx quotes himself: "The wealth of those societies in which the capitalist mode of production prevails, presents itself as 'an immense accumulation of commodities,' its unit being a single commodity" (1967, 1:35). "Wealth," the collective product of all social labor, takes one single form within capital, that of commodities—*things* bought and sold. Within capital, all of the "wealth" that may be used to satisfy needs and desires *must* take the form of commodities. This imperative is achieved as a result of capitalist ownership of all means of production, a situation that forces the wage laborer to satisfy all of her needs by means of commodities purchased through her wage.

For something to be the sort of thing that can be bought and sold, for a commodity to be a commodity, it must have two characteristics. First, it must have properties that are useful in satisfying some human need, and this usefulness or utility constitutes its use value. Second, it must be able to be bought and sold, to be exchanged for other commodities. As such, there must be some abstract, quantitative form of equivalence that can mediate the exchange between any two commodities with qualitatively different use values. This abstract form of equivalence that must belong to two commodities in order to allow for their exchange—their exchange value—is read by Marx as the quantity of homogeneous, socially necessary labor-time for their production, and is ultimately measured by money as price. According to this labor theory of value, value is created by labor power alone, and within capital, labor is always social labor.

Within capital, the worker possesses one commodity alone, her labor power, which she must sell in order to procure all of the other commodities, things she needs to survive: shelter, food, clothing, and so forth. From the perspective of the worker, commodities are use values; they are things she makes use of in order to satisfy all of her needs, beginning with the need to reproduce her own labor power, to get up the next morning and go back to work. This is her primary need, since, under the regime of the commodity form continuously reimposed by capital, all her other needs can only be satisfied by purchasing commodities with her wage. Bataille expresses this when he remarks that the worker "accumulates in order to spend"; that is, she works and accumulates a wage only in order to spend it in satisfying her needs. From the perspective of the capitalist, however, commodities are exchange values. They are things that can be sold in order to facilitate the accumulation of profit (the realization of "surplus" value, or that portion of the price beyond the cost necessary to produce the commodity), which is then (in part, at least) reinvested in more labor power, which creates more exchange value and more profit, and so on. Thus, within this cycle of profit and reinvestment that is the core of capital—capitalist *expansion*—it is exchange value that makes it possible for the capitalist to continue to put the worker to work, which is the only way the capitalist can create value and profit. And the worker cooperates, since her only access to the things necessary for her survival are commodities she must buy, and her sole means of buying commodities is the wage she garners in continuing to sell herself to the capitalist. Use value satisfies workers' needs and desires. Exchange value perpetuates capital and the commodity form within which all wealth takes the form of commodities, and thus it perpetuates the imposition of work, of waged labor, as the sole means of securing the necessities of the worker's life.

These points must be emphasized to help us to understand the stakes of Bataille's invocation of use value, contra the surrealist's appropriation of Sade. Within capital, human beings encounter the objects that both maintain us and mediate our relations with others paradigmatically under the guise of commodities. From the perspective of the ordinary person—the *worker*—commodities are use values: things accumulated in order to expend them in the satisfaction of needs. From the perspective of the capitalist, these things are exchange values: things accumulated in order for the capitalist to be able to continue to impose the commodity form, and with it the endless regime of work, on the workers, that is, things accumulated in order to perpetuate the process of accumulation. These differing perspectives on the commodity, the differing values a commodity expresses, are incommensurate with one another. A commodity expresses its exchange value only insofar as it is not being used, only as it sits idle, unused, in a warehouse, or on a shelf. A commodity can only express its use value at the expense of its exchange value, as anyone who has ever driven a new car home from the dealership very well knows. To express exchange value is to defer use value, to postpone the satisfaction of real human needs and desires. To express exchange value is to inscribe things within a regime that functions to continuously reimpose the *work* that perpetually defers the *life* of the wage laborer.

So, how did the surrealist appropriation of Sade constitute an instance of privileging exchange value over use value, and why is this politically significant? What was the project of surrealist revolt, and how was it betrayed by this act of appropriation?

🌀 *"The Use Value of D. A. F. de Sade"*

To say that European culture, post-1918, was in crisis is a truism. The intellectual explosion that crisis provoked, from art and aesthetics to literature, psychoanalysis, philosophy, and the sciences, is still reverberating nearly a century later. The war was particularly catastrophic for the nation that was the site of almost all of the major engagements on the Western front, namely, France. The war cost France a generation. It suffered over 6 million casualties, of which 1.3 million died, with countless others horrifically mutilated.[5] Within French intellectual circles the issue of where responsibility lay for this utterly unprecedented disaster became urgent.[6] For the surrealists, following the Dadaists, it was church and state, and in particular, the early-twentieth-century, middle-class, bourgeois morality of the Third Republic, combining the woolly liberalism of republicanism with conservative Catholicism, that had led the way into the trenches. For the surrealists, the pope was a dog, and the millions of rotting corpses fertilizing France's northern frontier had given the lie to the values of bourgeois liberalism that the Republic allegedly stood for and defended. Despite what was supposed to be an all-out assault against these prevailing values and norms, the surrealists who remained within Breton's circle after the schism with Masson and company in the mid-1920s retained a core of traditional values, as I have already noted. Monogamy and fidelity, sobriety, heterosexuality, health, cleanliness, and a general propriety were all *de rigueur*. The sort of libertinism engaged by Bataille and others who had broken with Breton was absolutely anathema. And yet, within Breton's circle, the greatest libertine of all times, the only one who could put even Bataille's notorious debauchery to shame, Donatien Alphonse François le Marquis de Sade, was revered as a heroic god—the great martyr to all those who carry on the labor of moral subversion that Sade himself had initiated. Breton and his circle were the latest to take up this noble struggle, not as a violent spasm of deranged, anarchic drives *à la* Bataille, but on behalf of an *edifying* eroticism. They would inaugurate a resuscitation of those fecund, subconscious, creative impulses—

released, for example, through the practice of automatic writing—which had suffocated under the yoke of both a rigorous intellectual rationalism and a bourgeois moral order that ultimately revealed themselves to be complicit with the technologies and practices of mass murder. As Surya has pointed out, through Breton's appropriation, Sade became no longer a (perverted, odious, deranged) man, nor a body of (perverted, odious, deranged) works, but rather, he had been sublimated, spiritualized as the very ideal of subversion against a system of values whose only purpose was to stifle all creativity and to facilitate complete servitude to a social order bent, ultimately, on self-destruction: "Nothing in [Sade], no matter how *odious* he may have been . . . was not sublimated by his intemperate violence in overcoming *all* servitude. In Breton's eyes, no doubt, the overwhelming nature of this servitude justified him in behaving in whatever way he saw fit, given that this was seen *a priori* as subversive." Thus Breton makes of Sade "an (oneiric) idea; more dubiously, an idol; entirely tragically, a primitive god, praised and hated, adored and execrated" (Surya 2002, 136).

And so Bataille reads this process of sublimation and idealization as a transformation from use value to exchange value. Breton seeks to sublimate and thus subdue the libidinal drives and desires that Sade's body and works set into play. Instead of inciting a movement aimed at achieving gratification in the expenditure of drives and the satisfaction of immediate desires and needs through the overcoming of all moral fetters, Sade is sublimated into an ideal of subversion, which may be circulated hygienically through a literati thus made safe from the base matter that actual subversion would have forced them to confront.[7] *Since we genuflect before the name of, the very word Sade, we show, therefore, by that very gesture, that we have escaped, entirely, the chains of all bourgeois morality.* Sade became the currency of a movement of pseudo-subversion, whose members refused to sully themselves with the real deal, and he could be bought and sold, as the symbol of moral revolt, in bookstores and magazine stands festooned with pamphlets and reviews extolling his genius. The ultimate result—the maintenance of the system that was allegedly subverted.

Breton claims to carry out a revolt against a system of bourgeois values that quashed creativity and freedom and that nurtured subservience to a social order that had demonstrated its pathological perversity in the meat grinder that was four years of trench warfare. Instead, he reinscribes a hierarchy of bourgeois values, abjects what is lowly and repulsive—like the millions of corpses rotting in mass graves—and grants his only concession to the base matter he expels through his elevation of Sade to the status of idol, and thus fashionable currency, of a putatively subversive aesthetic movement. The impotence of surrealist subversion, the vacuousness of the sur-realist's "license to shock" laid bare by the rise of fascism as bourgeois Europe's true shock experience, betrays its function in dutifully reproduc-ing the system it farcically raged against.

Breton's devotion to the *idea* of Sade, while rejecting Sade's actual being, demonstrates his "sanctimonious disgust for material needs" (Bataille 1985, 43). Bataille is not suggesting that the only real material needs are the ones he and Sade have the courage to express and gratify; he is not equating revo-lution with the satisfaction of the most violent of libidinal drives, with utter and complete debauchery. What he expresses in his attack on the surrealist's appropriation of Sade is his violent opposition to all edifying, elevating *mo-ralities of improvement* that demand the repression and sublimation of base drives, desires, and needs and continue to prescribe the decorum necessary to maintain order and propriety. Clean and sober must the worker be to return to the factory each morning, while her liberation from the morality that con-strains her to this order and decorum appears under the guise of a commodity whose exchange value is regulated via the commerce of art galleries and bookstores, and whose use value has been sublimated as an aesthetic experi-ence. Thus, the surrealist appropriation of Sade thwarts any realization of his use value, instead sublimating the revolutionary force of his work into lumpen, abstract, ideal pseudo-subversion, deflecting the actual movement of the complete violation and overturning of bourgeois values into the aes-thetic *shock experience* of the consumer of surrealist provocation/"art"—a shock purchased at the magazine stand, briefly registered, then dissipated as the reader closes the review and returns to the assembly line for the afternoon shift. Bataille wants to take Sade out of the orbit of surrealist circulation and exchange, and thus realize his utility. So what is Sade's *use value*?

By means of his denunciation of the surrealist appropriation of Sade, Bataille demonstrates that he would prefer a subversion of bourgeois values that embraces, indeed chooses, the boisterous high spirits of a night of drunken revelry, the impertinence of afternoon sex stolen from the work-day, the luxuriance of time *wasted* lying on the grass in the park or simply staring out of a window, to the fully commodified/aestheticized shock and to the purchasing of sport utility vehicles and the multifarious projects of home improvement—in short, a subversion that consists of resisting and reversing the ineluctable bourgeois slide from use to exchange value, and the perpetual imposition of the commodity form. He prefers a *morality* predicated on the primacy of the satisfaction of immediate material needs to one that always has an excuse for getting the eager, fresh, clearheaded worker back on the job and for demanding that the satisfaction of material needs remain confined within the sphere of the reproduction of labor (home improvement), and the circulation of commodities (SUVs), with all other activity directed toward production and accumulation (work). Reveling in and promoting the satisfaction of immediate material needs and base libidinal desires outside of the sphere of the commodity form do not constitute the construction of a new hierarchy of values within which the drunken orgy becomes elevated to an ideal to be striven for. Rather, it is the only way to actually challenge the perpetuation of a moral system that demands penance for any elision of the commodity form, any shirking of the duty to be productive. Sade's use value is to enact the subversion of bourgeois morality that the surrealists had only meekly gestured toward, and thus to liberate humanity from a culture of work—a culture devoted to exchange and accumulation—to a culture that truly privileges the satisfaction of real needs and desires—a culture of expenditure.[8]

Fascism had offered the working class something that appealed to them from the perspective of the miserable conditions they suffered through between the wars. Not all, or even most, of course, but enough of them to make Mussolini, Hitler, Franco, and appeasement possible. The stifling banality of orthodox Marxism and the childish insolence of the aesthetic provocations of Dadaists, surrealists, and so forth, offered unacceptable alternatives. Bataille sought a revolution that would actually deliver ordinary people something truly useful. Indeed, I suggest that Bataille's overriding concern during and after this time was the issue of what, precisely, the revolution he and others sought for had to offer to ordinary working people. This is in part (in no small part, in Bataille's case) the question of what the use value of an all-out attack against bourgeois values was for the working class. The answer he sought was to be found in the liberation of human beings from an ethos directed toward the perpetual imposition of work, an ethos that demands that the worker sacrifice herself, day in and day out, for the privilege of being called a valuable, productive member of society rather than a lazy, selfish, indolent parasite—an ethos that expresses the "unconscious identification of worker with slave."

Why isn't the satisfaction of "material needs" consistent with the commodity form, and with a culture that privileges production and accumulation as the prerequisite for addressing such needs? Why isn't liberation the product of work, as Hegel had argued so famously and so well? I would like to briefly relate the above analysis to Bataille's categories of expenditure and sovereignty as they are developed paradigmatically in *The Accursed Share* in order to address these issues before concluding with an assessment of the use value of G. A. M. V. Bataille.

The Use Value of G. A. M. V. Bataille

🜲 Expenditure and Sovereignty

> *The true luxury and the real potlatch of our times falls to the poverty-stricken, that is, to the individual who lies down and scoffs. A genuine luxury requires the complete contempt for riches, the somber indifference of the individual who refuses work and makes his life on the one hand an infinitely ruined splendor, and on the other, a silent insult of the laborious lie of the rich.*
>
> THE ACCURSED SHARE: VOLUME I

> *"I am NOTHING": this parody of affirmation is the last word of sovereign subjectivity, freed from the dominion it wanted—or had—to give itself over things. In this world, the man of sovereign art occupies the most common position, that of destitution.*
>
> THE ACCURSED SHARE: VOLUME III

> *. . . no longer that of producing but of spending, no longer that of succeeding but of failing, no longer that of turning out works and speaking usefully but of speaking in vain and reducing himself to worklessness . . . Now we are perhaps more fairly placed to recognize what is at stake in such a situation, and why Georges Bataille has captured it with the thought of sovereignty.*
>
> BLANCHOT, *The Infinite Conversation*

In the Preface to *The Accursed Share,* Bataille distinguishes between two different approaches to the discipline of political economy and to the problems of economic crisis and to the crisis of overproduction in particular: one that is rooted in anxiety and fear, and one that is rooted in "freedom" and exuberance.

> I am . . . postponing, for a short time, the exposition of my analysis of anxiety. And yet, that is the crucial analysis that alone can adequately circumscribe the opposition of two political methods: that of fear and the anxious search for a solution . . . and that of freedom of mind, which issues from the global resources of life, a freedom for which, instantly, *everything is rich* . . . I insist on the fact that, to freedom of mind, the search for a solution is an exuberance, a superfluity; this gives it an incomparable force. To solve political problems becomes difficult for those who allow anxiety alone to pose them. It is necessary for anxiety to pose them. But their solution demands at a certain point the removal of this anxiety. (1991a, 13–14)

The goal of *The Accursed Share* is to remove, or more precisely, to suspend, this fear and anxiety for the purposes of "solving political problems." Of course, the only way to solve a political problem is through the labor of practical transformation,[9] so this suspension of anxiety undergone in *The Accursed*

Share is the labor of practical transformation that will solve the problems anxiety poses but cannot answer. Fear and anxiety in the face of the exigencies of political economy bring to light the problems of poverty, disproportionate distribution of wealth, immanent threat of war, and so on that freedom, the "freedom of mind, which issues from the global resources of life, a freedom for which, instantly, *everything is rich,*" is set to solve.

The general sweep of Bataille's distinction between limited and general economy, as elaborated in *The Accursed Share,* is well known. Limited economy is economy predicated on the notion of a primal scarcity and the necessity to produce and accumulate in order to safeguard against this scarcity that perpetually threatens existence. It corresponds to economy viewed from the perspective of fear and anxiety. General economy, within which limited economy is inscribed, is predicated on a primal plenitude; the superabundance of solar energy bathing the entire planet every day, a source of energy that continuously gives without taking. This is economy from the perspective of freedom and of those global resources of life with regard to which everything is instantly rich;[10] and from this perspective, the problem of political economy is the problem of dealing with primal *excess.* Rather than producing and accumulating in anticipation of the perpetual scarcity that limited economy continuously evokes as its generative principle, expenditure is revealed to be the primal economic exigency; and the central concern of political economy becomes how to consume that *accursed share* which remains after the satisfaction of all immediate needs, as consume it we must.[11]

Volume 3 of *The Accursed Share* elaborates a theory of sovereignty consistent with the primacy of expenditure in a general economy predicated on a primal excess.[12] In limited economy, sovereignty may be measured by mastery, in various ways, over things. Hegel's dialectical movement from master to slave traces the development of the notion of sovereignty within limited economy through the transition from feudal to bourgeois forms. Through this dialectical movement, Hegel charts the metamorphosis of sovereignty from the master, whose *rank* bestows on him the ability to consume the products of labor without laboring himself—to squander the products of another's labor to no productive end other than self-aggrandizement—to the slave, who manifests the *truth* of sovereignty by means of his actual mastery over things, which is achieved through the very productive labor his servitude compels him to. It is, put simply, the movement from sovereignty thought of in terms of consumption and rank, to sovereignty thought of in terms of the power of production and accumulation. From the perspective of general economy, however, both moments of the dialectic betray an abdication of true sovereignty.

The Use Value of G. A. M. V. Bataille

The master's sovereignty, perhaps closer to the sovereignty of general economy, owing to its emphasis on consumption over accumulation, nonetheless remains within the ambit of the general thralldom to things that holds sway within the realm of limited economy. This is so because in its guise as the consumption of resources for nonproductive ends, it remains, of course, dependent on those who win their share of sovereignty through mastery over things—the slaves. In this, Hegel was certainly correct, and he was correct to diagnose the trajectory of this movement toward greater and greater emphasis on mastery over things. In this way, we move toward the contemporary "bourgeois world," in which human beings measure their worth and dignity in relation to their accumulation of things, and hence, within which "the concern for dignity . . . merges with the desire for the thing" (1991b, 345). The thing is elevated to the status of sovereign, in the sense of sovereign value, and human beings abrogate their subjectivity (the measure of sovereignty left to them in their pursuit of things) in making the object the measure of their dignity and worth.

Bataille locates the solution to this crisis in the renunciation of the immense, inescapable thralldom to things that the perspective of limited economy perpetually engenders through its founding myth of scarcity. Such a renunciation would also entail jettisoning the concomitant need to produce, or to consume the production of others condemned to servitude, and it becomes possible by assuming the perspective of general economy, within which everything is *immediately rich,* and hence, within which, the "I am NOTHING" becomes that "parody of affirmation" which is "the last word of sovereign subjectivity, freed from the dominion it wanted—or had—to give itself over things" (1991b, 421). True sovereignty, from the perspective of general economy, is won through the absolute renunciation of things, and its signs are "poverty" and "destitution."[13] This is simply another way of saying that to continue to inscribe the satisfaction of material needs and desires within the commodity form is to remain squarely within the logic of limited economy, of bourgeois/slave sovereignty, of capital—and hence, that the labor of transformation that carries us from the perspective of fear and anxiety to that of freedom and exuberance also requires overcoming that morality of elevation and edification which functions to perpetuate the imposition of work and the commodity form, and the identification of worker with slave.

But this seems a fool's game—a Pyrrhic victory if ever there was one: We come to ourselves, truly, at last, within a sovereign act of renunciation that secures our destitution. But what, precisely, is the nature of this "poverty" and "destitution" we come into, through the sovereign renunciation of things?

Bataille's state of sovereign destitution is a state of freedom from things beyond utility, beyond what is simply necessary to continue to survive: "Let us say that the sovereign (or the sovereign life) begins when, with the necessities ensured, the possibility of life opens up without limits. . . . Life *beyond utility* is the domain of sovereignty" (1991b, 198). It is a state of freedom from dependence upon things, once "necessities" (and let us allow some *rational* leeway in the stipulation of what counts as a "necessity") have been secured. It is *not* to need things beyond what we actually do need. Concomitantly, it is *not* to see scarcity—and hence the primal necessity of work and accumulation—amidst the insane abundance of things that characterizes the contemporary consumer culture of late capital. Still, one might continue to press at this point, by asking what this "possibility of life" that "opens up without limit" *is,* if not a world of things to be consumed and enjoyed at the sovereign's whim?

Within capital, consumption beyond utility is tied to the continuation of work beyond utility, since under capital the social wealth available for consumption takes the form of commodities that must be bought with a wage. To work beyond utility is to employ the present time for the sake of the future and to thus postpone one's life. The fool's game is to consider sovereign expenditure—as opposed to servile production—solely in terms of things and objects—commodities—to be accumulated and periodically consumed, *enjoyed.* What is important is not the *thing* to be enjoyed, it is the enjoyment itself, and it is utterly irrational to observe as a program of life the (again, perpetual) sacrifice and deferral of enjoyment for the pursuit of things to be later enjoyed. What we come into, freed from slavish dependence upon things beyond utility, is the fullness of each moment of our lives. It is our life, fully here, in this moment, not deferred to the interests of production, accumulation, and consumption—this moment, voided of things, which Bataille also calls the *miraculous.* This movement of true sovereignty as an experience of the miraculous is essayed in a remarkable passage in the very first section of volume 3:

> We don't see the sovereign moment arrive, when nothing counts but the moment itself. What is sovereign in fact is to enjoy the present time without having anything else in view but this present time. . . . If I consider the real world, the worker's wage enables him to drink a glass of wine: he may do so, as he says, to give him strength, but he really drinks in the hope of escaping the necessity that is the principle of labor. . . . If the worker treats himself to a drink, this is *essentially* because into the wine he swallows there enters a *miraculous* element of savor, which is precisely the essence of sovereignty. . . . The glass of wine gives him, for a *brief moment,* the *miraculous* sen-

The Use Value of G. A. M. V. Bataille

sation of having the world at his disposal. . . . The *miraculous* element *which delights* us may be simply the brilliance of the sun, which on a spring morning transfigures a desolate street. . . . More generally, this miracle to which the whole of humanity aspires is manifested among us in the form of beauty, of wealth. . . . What is the meaning of art, architecture, music, painting or poetry if not the anticipation of a suspended, wonder-struck moment, a miraculous moment. (199–200)

Things can occasion sovereign moments, but they are neither the form, nor expression of sovereignty itself. Our existence from *moment to moment* is mediated by things—the food we eat, the pillow we lay our head on—but the moments of our lives only emerge as instances of sovereignty, of freedom, insofar as the substance mediating between them is fully renounced, allowing the individual to emerge from his absorption in things. *Things* are only what sustain me from moment to moment, and *nothing else.* In the moment— which is the only place I truly become present to myself (1991b, 360–61)— they are *nothing.* The wine that "the worker" savors, in the instance of the satisfaction it "gives," Bataille says, is nothing. Wine is wine, and it is wholly other to the joy it occasions of the world being at my disposal, and I being at the disposal of nothing—no things. And if there is no wine on this particular occasion, the worker—freed from things—will savor the water, or "the brilliance of the sun" on a spring morning. And need we remind ourselves that this sovereign renunciation of things also clearly coincides with the rejection of commodity fetishism, which functions, as Marx argues so convincingly, to mystify the realm of the production and circulation of commodities by making the actual, concrete social relations that constitute that realm invisible. Sovereign destitution allows me to become present to myself, and present to myself within that set of social relations that constitute the world I live in, a world no longer obscured by my absorption in things. In choosing poverty, beyond utility, I reject the mystified realm of the endless supply of consumer goods that magically appear on store shelves, bearing no trace of the social relations of production and circulation that got them there from China, Pakistan, Honduras, or god knows where, so very cheaply indeed.

Within limited economy, the satisfaction of material needs takes place under the regime of the commodity form and hence remains subordinated to principles of production and accumulation, that is, to things, which thus maintain sovereignty over us. From this perspective, the satisfaction of material needs is merely an instance of *consumption,* which reanimates the grounding myth of scarcity and which is required for the reproduction of our labor power, which in turn allows us to produce and accumulate, which makes possible consumption, which results in scarcity, which . . . , and so on, and so on. Within general economy, the satisfaction of material needs takes place to no other end than the enjoyment of the miraculous moment itself, a Sadean moment of exaltation that all bourgeois morality seeks to infinitely defer. And hence the primacy of expenditure within general economy also requires a Sadean rejection—a real rejection, not one sublimated as a mere aesthetic "shock" experience that is fully inscribed within the commodity form—of all bourgeois morality.

Within the miraculous sovereign moment "nothing counts but the moment itself," so the satisfaction of material needs from the perspective of general economy is an instance of pure expenditure. Again, the wine and the satisfaction of the moment of its drinking are not the same. The latter only takes place when the former is consumed, not as a moment within the cycle of production, but truly reduced to nothing, without a trace, for example, of the nostalgia that would immediately reinscribe the connoisseur of the (scarce) commodity of wine within the regime of limited economy and thralldom to things.

Free yourself from things. Within capital, the social wealth that is the world of things we buy and sell and use takes the form of commodities. The worker possesses only one commodity, her labor power. For the worker, then, free yourself from things also means free yourself from looking upon yourself as a commodity, as labor power, as a *worker*, as a *slave*. Escape from the ethos of work—of hygiene, propriety, decorum, reliability, sacrifice—in a word, *slavishness*—to the exuberance of life.

❦ Conclusions: The Use Value of G. A. M. V. Bataille

No longer to have to work, but to simply live; no longer to feel shame in the face of one's material needs and desires, but to revel in their satisfaction; no longer to be called indolent and indulgent for choosing to live in the miraculous moment—to enjoy the pleasure of a lover's touch, or the warmth of the sun on one's face—rather than to labor in anticipation of future "scarcity"; no longer to live in thralldom to the world of things that capital elevates to the status of an ideal to be pursued at the expense of life, my own, and others—this would be the use value of Bataille's works, set to work as a challenge to radically rethink the nature of "economy" and of the values—indeed, of the moral order supporting and reproducing the system of social relations that constitutes capital.

To this day, Bataille remains a rather marginal figure within the tradition of twentieth-century European philosophy, while retaining the simultaneously exotic and scandalous air of the old-fashioned libertine *homme des lettres*—the medievalist, archivist, mystic pornographer who was fascinated by the abject, excessive, debauched, and diabolical. Nonetheless, Bataille, by the early 1930s, had developed a conception of class struggle that shared a central insight with the anti-orthodox Marxism of the Critical Theorists and, even more closely, with the Italian New Left of the 1960s and 70s and their American counterparts in the Zerowork movement. In stark contrast with more orthodox Marxisms that view the goal of class struggle as the more equitable redistribution of the social wealth generated by living labor, some form of *from each according to her ability, to each according to her needs,* Bataille and others view the goal of working-class struggle as the liberation from work itself.[14]

From this perspective, the central problem of political economy is not the alienation of labor in all its guises, most conspicuously the alienation of the product of labor from the laborer herself, and the capitalist appropriation of the surplus value that is the product of the worker's living labor. The ultimate goal of progressive struggle is not the redistribution of wealth, in the final instance through the reappropriation of the means of production (though redistribution is certainly consistent with Bataille's aims, as his analysis of the Marshall Plan demonstrates). The problem is the fact that the telos of capitalist accumulation is the endless imposition of work, regardless of the amount of "wealth" it produces, or the relative equitability of its distribution. As Bataille argues in 1932, "The bosses' activity is to produce in order to condemn the working producers to a hideous degradation" (1985, 126–27). This degradation that Bataille invokes is not merely, or perhaps most significantly, the degradation of unequal access to social wealth— again, sovereignty is gained through the *renunciation* of that immense accumulation of commodities that is the form social wealth takes under capital. It is rather the degradation of the endless subordination of life to production and accumulation. The goal, then, is the withering of the perspective of limited economy, accomplished through the utter rejection of all moralities of improvement and through the only truly sovereign act, namely, the renunciation of all wealth and power beyond utility, the renunciation of our slavish devotion to objects, including, most significantly, the object that is one's own deferred time. The return on this investment—the *delight* of it—is, purely and simply, "enjoyment of the moment" (1991b, 361).

NOTES

1. This includes both "The Use Value of D. A. F. de Sade," and "The 'Old Mole' and the Prefix *Sur* in the words *Surhomme* and *Surrealist*" (Bataille 1973, vol. 2). The broader context, of course, is the implosion and factionalization of the surrealist movement during

the late 1920s. Apart from the usual personal animosities that contribute to the various schisms, the central theoretical issue at stake is the relationship between surrealism, politics, and communism in particular.

2. In this way, Breton and Bataille's squabble over the figure of Sade is also the occasion of some of the earliest texts within which Bataille begins to articulate his developing insights into political economy that will eventually be elaborated through his theory of general economy.

3. For a fascinating account of Bataille's relationship to *Documents,* see Hollier 1995.

4. Bataille's profound grasp of the danger of fascism and of the nature of its appeal has been noted by many. For example: "More than anyone else, Bataille was aware of the risks fascism made Europe run (Henri Dubief said forcefully that no one taught people so much about fascism as Bataille) and was also more certain than anyone else of where its strength lay" (Surya 2002, 220–21).

As Adorno and Benjamin grew more and more disillusioned, witnessing the impotence of the Weimar avant-gardists and café leftists in the face of the rise of Nazism, so Bataille was, arguably, the earliest to grasp the vacuousness of surrealist provocation in the face of the rise of fascism in general. The surrealists balked at the logical trajectory of their own revolt against bourgeois values. They refused to fully confront the morality of naive bourgeois liberalism in the way Bataille had tried to do. How could they possibly mount an effective attack against bourgeois liberalism's evil changeling, the fanaticism of the hard right? Neither surrealist antics nor their pompous, moralistic name-calling—their vacuous declaration of the purest of surrealist acts notwithstanding—would be any match against a movement the values of which are promulgated through brick, club, and gun barrel.

5. The devastation wrought on France—which suffered the greatest numbers of killed and wounded proportional to population of any of the combative nations—cannot be overstated. The population of France was 39 million in 1914. With a current U.S. population of approximately 280 million, this would translate to 43 million casualties, 9.3 million of them killed, numbers literally unimaginable.

6. As, of course, it did in London, Berlin, Frankfurt, Vienna, etc.

7. Bourgeois morality, like any idealism, sets up a hierarchy, with all things odious and repellent at the base. Any subversion of this hierarchy that does not, in some concrete manner, take up and elevate what is abject and debased within the hierarchy surely leaves that hierarchy fundamentally unchallenged. This elevation of the base does not necessarily entail its elevation as a new ideal—that is, it does not entail simply inverting bourgeois morality and fixing the inverted anti-bourgeois system as a new hierarchy.

8. The ongoing need to carry through with this task of subversion may be gauged by the sanctimonious self-righteousness of those readers who would interpret this analysis as a naive rallying cry/apologia for spoiled brats who just want to slack off and do nothing while cloaking their indolence in the trappings of virtue. Sigh.

9. See, e.g., Karl Marx.

10. It is the perspective which recognizes, for example, the obvious fact that what we call political economy only began when groups—"tribes," what have you—began to produce more food and goods than they could immediately consume. What to do with this excess beyond what was necessary for the satisfaction of immediate needs was the problem that initiated trade, commerce, economics.

It has been argued, of course, that the alleged inexhaustibility of the supply of solar energy to the planet is, in fact, a myth, and that Bataille's general economy is, in fact, limited. This is utterly beside the point. Indeed, one of Bataille's goals was to resuscitate myth for the purpose of working-class struggle against the fascists, who had so successfully employed myth to their own ends. The target of Bataille's *myth* of general economy—the sad tale of that original sin which we call *scarcity*—is itself a myth. Furthermore, as an empirical claim of the primacy of excess and expenditure in the development of political economy, the empirical evidence seems perfectly capable of supporting it at least as much (more, I dare say) as the alternative. Let us say that Bataille employs a reasonably plausible—and, within the context of his theory of general economy, innocuous—myth in order to disarm an utterly implausible one that has done an unspeakable amount of harm.

11. For a cogent analysis of this necessity, see Amy Wendling in this volume.

12. Bataille 1991b; also *La Souveraineté* from 1973, 8: 243–456. I must limit the analysis of Bataille's reading of sovereignty in volume 3 of *The Accursed Share* to a few central claims. In particular, insofar as Bataille's overriding concern in volume 2 of *The Accursed Share* is with the possibility of the sovereignty of the individual subject, I will eschew discussion of sovereignty as it applies to the state, and/or state apparatuses—i.e., sovereignty in the sense of sovereign power.

13. Clearly, Bataille is consciously echoing the elevation of poverty and destitution found in Christian theology, particularly within monasticism and scholasticism. Part of Bataille's goal is to jettison the frugality and asceticism of that theological tradition in favor, I will argue, of the luxuriance of the satisfaction of material needs that coincides with the escape from thralldom to the material object—*things*—within the sovereign moment of satisfaction.

14. However, Bataille offers an important correction to Marxisms associated with Italian Autonomism, Zerowork, etc. Even within these radical, anti-work Marxisms, the "liberation from work" is generally read as the liberation from work conceived as imposed waged labor, to work conceived as self-directed, productive life activity. Bataille would argue that such a "liberation" remains within the logic of limited economy insofar as it still analyzes the goal of revolution as the liberation of productive forces from the limitations of waged labor and the commodity form, an analysis that ignores the primacy of expenditure and thus fails to recognize that the enjoyment of nonproductive activity—the maximization of life activity that is directed toward no particular productive end, but rather is the sheer enjoyment of the moment—is the goal of any truly progressive revolution. This theme is taken up in my "Selling a Revolution: Negri, Bataille, and the Arcana of Production," in *Reading Negri* (Lamarche forthcoming).

WORKS CITED

Bataille, Georges. 1973. *Oeuvres Complètes*. Paris: Gallimard.
———. 1985. *Visions of Excess: Selected Writings, 1927–1939*. Ed. Allan Stoekl. Minneapolis: University of Minnesota Press.
———. 1991a. *The Accursed Share: Volume I*. Trans. Robert Hurley. New York: Zone Books.
———. 1991b. *The Accursed Share: Volumes II & III*. Trans. Robert Hurley. New York: Zone Books.
Hollier, Denis. 1995. The Use-value of the Impossible. In *Bataille: Writing the Sacred*, ed. Carolyn Bailey Gill. London and New York: Routledge.

Lamarche, Pierre. Forthcoming. "Selling a Revolution: Negri, Bataille, and the Arcana of Production," in *Reading Negri,* ed. Pierre Lamarche, Max Rosenkrantz, and David Sherman. Chicago: Open Court.

Marx, Karl. 1967. *Capital,* Vol. 1. Trans. Samuel Moore and Edward Aveling. New York: International Publishers.

Surya, Michel. 2002. *Georges Bataille: An Intellectual Biography.* Trans. Krzysztof Fijalkowski and Michael Richardson. London and New York: Verso.

PLEASURES AND THE MYTH OF TRANSGRESSION

Part Two

FOUR

SHANNON WINNUBST

Bataille's Queer Pleasures: The Universe as Spider or Spit

To modern Western subjects, the world seems full of desire. Repressed, thwarted, and condemned but also incited, commodified, and celebrated: desires haunt us. Inhabiting a sacred space in the psychic and social landscape, desire harbors the innermost secrets not only of ourselves, but also of the world at large. And it never stops swirling all about us. It is the fundamental plane through which we Western moderns decipher our cherished selves and the meanings of our lives. Western culture commands one central thing of us: to know oneself. We answer through our aspirations, our loves, our hopes and goals: we are religious about desire, perhaps even "ferociously religious" (1985, 179), as Bataille might hope.

But this practice of desire is a particularly odd undertaking. It never seems to arrive where it intends: desire both bespeaks our innermost secrets and foils our attempts to solve them. We keep finding ourselves doing something other than what we thought we wanted to do. Undoing us in the very moment when we wish to know ourselves and others most intimately, desire disarms us. We are farther and farther adrift from that which we proclaim as the inner core of our selves and identities—our own desire. We cannot unravel ourselves, and yet this is what we most *want* to do.

Desire thereby turns back upon itself endlessly, landing us in the neverending circle of the ultimate modern Western desire: self-consciousness. Functioning as what Bataille calls a "restricted economy," desire totalizes our subjectivities. It becomes our central fixation, and yet it is always fleeing our grasps of intentionality, rationality, and even consciousness. Not only do we not understand what we do or why we do it, we often do not even intend to arrive in some of the bizarre places that our desires take us. And yet we keep returning to and re-valorizing this oddly out-of-control desire as the seat of our individuality, as the seat of our identity and our very selves.

What is it, then, that we find meaningful in this never-ending quest of desire? How do we find meaning in a dynamic that never offers any clear *telos*?

Questions of desire have been central to the development of queer theory: What is desire? Where does it come from? How does it develop? Should it be policed? How is it socially regulated, managed, and administered? These are, broadly, the sorts of epistemological, ontological, and ethico-political questions that distinguish the field of queer theory from other academic fields. The most interesting work in this field is that which insists that desire, particularly in the specific form of sexual desire, ought to be conceptualized in relation with other salient categories of contemporary social identity in modern liberal cultures—race, nationality, religion, gender, class, and so on. But the focus on desire nonetheless centers and grounds this field of social theory that we have come to call "queer theory": What then is "queer" about desire?

While the field of queer theory has developed far beyond such a simple reduction, its founding theoretical moves still instruct its trajectories, and perhaps its blind spots. It remains largely driven by two theoretical frameworks: the Lacanian approach, which frames desire as a lack that can never be filled; and the Foucaultian approach, which historicizes the emergence of desire as a central structure of the modern bourgeois individual. While the alleged "battle" between psychoanalysis and Foucault continues to develop into a complex narrative across a number of interdisciplinary fields (from feminist and race theory to postcolonial and queer theory), these two frameworks have served as foundations to differing, and most often antagonistic, analyses of a variety of contemporary social questions. Using these allegedly contradictory approaches as the loose frames for this essay, I want to trace how the texts of Georges Bataille operate out of a fundamentally different register, one that may radically reorient our pursuits of meaning itself and revitalize a radical, even "queer" politics—namely, the register of pleasure.

🅢 *Subjectivity of Desire: Lacan and Foucault*

In his classic writings on the pre-Oedipal mirror stage, Lacan places desire as the founding dynamic in the formation of the subject: one becomes a subject through desire, the specific desire for wholeness. Whether the desire for wholeness that the *Gestalt* of the mirror image presents, the Oedipalized nostalgic desire for the mother's womb, or the unrealizable desire for a symbolic that will heal the ontological alienation of language, one becomes a subject through this fundamental *need* for wholeness, completion, return to pure origins. The deepest parts of one's psychic life are structured by this fundamental desire, fueled by a lack that can ontologically never be fulfilled.

While feminist theorists and, increasingly, theorists of race are using this Lacanian model of subjectivity provocatively, queer theorists have largely learned from it as a normative model operative in this heterosexist world and promptly abandoned it. Particularly with the interpolations of feminist theorists, we can see how Lacan's theories of desire remain firmly entrenched, as a constitutive blind spot and site of anxiety, in a model of sexual difference as oppositional—a schema that grounds heterosexism. Despite its astute analysis of the intersections of social and psychic dynamics, Lacan's model appears to frame desire fundamentally as the phallic subject's lack of his pre-birth wholeness; it thereby appears to offer little to those attempting to resist normative models of heterosexuality as the primary frame for understanding human desire.

However, recent (if very few) Lacanian approaches to queer theory have also argued that the dynamic of desire is problematic.[1] In *Before Sexuality,* Tim Dean argues that much of queer theorists' dismissal of Lacan stems from the Anglo-American misconstrual of his schemas as relying too centrally on the phallus and foreclosing the more intriguing registers of the Real and the *objet petit a.* Attempting to restore these figures to Lacan's corpus, Dean argues that Lacan reads desire only as a postsymbolic phenomenon, thereby locating the Real and *objet petit a* as "the lack of lack" or source of abundance that is ontologically prior to desire.

As Lacan sets out his schema of the Real, Imaginary, and Symbolic, he is forced into particularly convoluted manners of speech in his attempts to delineate the register of the Real. The most well-known formulation of the Real is the one he offers via double-negation, "the lack of a lack," indicating the impossibility of rendering the Real directly in speech. Desire thereby stands in a different relation to the Real than that form through which we experience desire. Experience is always already mediated through the Symbolic, which renders desire as a lack that stands before the judgment of the prohibitive, phallicized Law. But the Real, this "lack of a lack," is devoid of signifiers and does not submit to that Law. Functioning as what Dean calls "a limit to the Symbolic order" (2000, 50), the Real stands in as a representation of that which cannot be represented. But rather than taking the Heideggerian, Derridean, or even Levinasian turn of rendering this "unrepresentable" as that which cancels itself out upon articulation, Lacan struggles to trace the *effects* of the Real without positing some conceptual structure as the cause of those effects, a turn that looks more like strategies we associate with thinkers such as Deleuze and Guattari and, notably, Foucault.[2]

Dean's reading of Lacan strikes a clearly cautionary tone regarding the epistemological and political fallout of any frame of subjectivity through desire, and subsequently through lack. Reading Lacan through the role of the Real and *objet petit a* provides a way to articulate the limits of desire through the limits of the order of knowledge: it is no longer that Lacan insists on a lacking desire as the origin of subjectivity; rather, he is attempting to articulate the limits of knowledge and representation as they constitute the limits of our *experiences* of desire. The alleged problem of desire may turn out to be a problem of knowledge and its refusal to accept any limits to its imperialist drive.

We can hear these same kinds of cautions and hesitancies on the other side of this alleged divide between Lacan and Foucault. Many queer theorists (too many to list) have turned to the texts of Foucault for greater resources for such resistance. Volume one of his *History of Sexuality* became a veritable pamphlet or how-to book for gay/lesbian politics in the 1980s.[3] Through historicizing sexual desire, this text persuasively debunks the conservative contemporary terms of the debates around sexual orientation—namely, the nature/nurture divide. It thereby galvanized a more radical politics and, potentially, a more radical thinking about sexuality.[4]

It may actually be in *The Use of Pleasure,* volume 2 of *The History of Sexuality,* that Foucault offers his most radical critique of modern concepts of desire and their ontology of lack. In volume 2, Foucault traces the historical emergence of the dynamic of desire to its economic, political, and philosophical roots in the Socratic-Platonic tradition. Prior to the development of this "subject of desire," sexual acts and behaviors were not submitted to the law of desire to be deciphered. While they were certainly codified as proper and improper, these categories operated strictly as political and economic regulators, not as moral arbiters about the state of one's subjectivity—and certainly not as the arbiters of what *kind* of person or identity one was or was not. Judgments regarding sexual activity did not stake any claim to onto-logical truths prior to the Socratic-Platonic tradition: the order of knowl-edge limited itself to the parameters set forth by the contemporary values of Greek culture.

As a part of his constant efforts to think from one's historical present,[5] this genealogical work in Greek culture springs from Foucault's own con-temporary sets of values and concerns. *The Use of Pleasure* not only works to historicize sexual desire but also raises the epistemological quandary in-volved in any schematic that reads subjectivity primarily through desire. His focus on the Platonic model and its insertion of lack into the origin of desire springs from a larger effort to problematize the epistemological model that leads us in search of the sources of phenomena, whether historical events or psychological desire. When Plato writes the myth of Eros's conception as the rape of *Pena* by the drunken *Poros* in the garden of Aphrodite's birthday party, we can read this as his inserting the classic narrative of the *Ursprung* into the heart of human desire. But it is in Foucault's disabusing us of this myth of the *Ursprung*—that clear, pure, and essential Origin—that Foucault most hopes to follow Nietzsche and his radical questioning of modern Western epistemologies.[6]

Desire thereby misleads us doubly for Foucault: it reads our subjectivity as anchored in an ontological lack and simultaneously locks us into the nos-talgic quest for that pure origin of fullness and plenitude. The lack demands an answer, but the origin forever recedes from our attempted grasps. Para-dise is lost, just as its definition demands that it always must be. And so this doubled logic of desire is, as my opening musings suggest, totalizing. How to exit this stranglehold of desire?

An attempt to problematize the political and epistemological fallout of the schema that reads subjectivity as driven by desire, which is in turn framed as a lack, thus cuts across both the Foucaultian and Lacanian ap-proaches to this thorny question of desire. The doubled grounding of desire as the lack that is the origin of subjectivity unleashes teleology. If a subject is necessarily a subject of desire, and if that desire is fundamentally driven by the subject's lack of that which would fulfill her/him, then political and psychic life must necessarily be understood in teleological terms. Lack de-mands an endpoint: we are what we want, and we want what we do not have; therefore, we must pursue that which will fulfill us, and we must be able to articulate clearly what that is. This becomes the logic of both identity politics and a hermeneutics of the self: to know what one wants provides the basis of cultural legibility and all its myths of agency, control, mastery, and fulfillment. Enacting a logic of scarcity, this endless pursuit of an endpoint grounds both capitalism and heteronormative sexuality.[7]

We can locate this political and psychological schema in the particular ways that we late moderns constitute the order of knowledge. In locking the order of knowledge into the pursuit of pure and essential origins, we place it in the order of teleology as well. As I will argue below, meaning itself begins to connote the grasping of endpoints and purposes, the clear and distinct demarcation of concepts or entities from the surrounding chaos that is not valued. In the order of experience, this teleologically grounded epistemology renders unfocused, dissipated lives meaningless. In the world of desiring subjects, the thought that nothing might fulfill us, that we are ontologically lacking, will only drive us to desire more vehemently, to want more anxiously, and to become enmeshed more and more deeply in the bastion of identity. But the thought that we might never *know* what we want? That is unthinkable.

🌀 *Law of Prohibition*

Both Foucault and Lacan read Bataille.[8]

And they all recognize, albeit differently, how this dynamic of desire emerges primarily through the logic of prohibition and transgression. Whether Lacan's Law of the Father or Foucault's analysis of "the Repressive Hypothesis," prohibition functions as the mechanism through which subjectivity is cathected. Prohibition sequesters specific objects, actions, and behaviors from the acceptable, normal—even "natural"—realm of experience. It prohibits specific things, creating taboos, which in turn incite desire for the forbidden fruits. Prohibitions exacerbate the lack that is at the heart of the modern subject's desire. And in late modernity, these prohibitive laws become increasingly codified through the arms of both clerical and secular authorities. The more codified they become, the more internalized becomes the source of transgression: one must submit to the laws of desire if one is to become a legible subject.

Bataille develops this particularly in volume 2 of *The Accursed Share,* where he shows how objects, subjects, and activities are eroticized via prohibitions. The exemplar for Bataille here (following Lévi-Strauss) is incest. The prohibition against intergenerational sexual contact within biological families eroticizes the familial ties—and, most importantly, the marital tie—

while ensuring the continued flow of erotic energy in this otherwise closed container. Prohibitions thereby function to eroticize particular realms of behavior and culture within human communities. And the sporadic act of transgression, whether physical or psychological, becomes necessary to re-cathect those boundaries and the objects and subjects they constitute as valuable.

For example, in prohibitions in the United States against sodomy, the anxiety enacted in the prohibition is not about the act of sodomy itself, but about the kinds of subjectivities produced through the prohibition. The anxieties attendant to prohibitions against sodomy respond to two possible subjectivities that might emerge on either side of the act: (1) political, and potentially dangerous subjectivities that might be produced by admitting to such an act—for example, subjects not constrained by a sexual ethics of procreation; and (2) docile subjectivities that refuse or even denounce the act—for example, subjects deeply constrained by a sexual ethics of procreation, with its social and religious ramifications, and generally submissive to laws of repression. It may appear, at first glance, that the first of these, the allegedly "transgressive" subjectivities, overturn the law of prohibition; however, they do not decenter or diminish the anxieties enacted through that law. The "transgressive" subjectivity revolves around the same center as the docile subjectivity—namely, sexuality reduced fully to genitalia.

We see here the full-blown logic of identity politics and its perpetuation of the limited economy of scarcity (lack) and teleology: identity is reduced to desire; but now desire finds its expression through the order of sexuality, which is in turn reduced to genitalia. You are what you desire, and your desire is now clearly and physically demarcated by the actions of your genitalia: we can still *recognize* the sexual act and thereby *know* the identity it enacts. The alleged transgression keeps us circling around the same dynamics as those enacted in the prohibition—physically (genitalia), psychosocially (identity and its politics), and epistemologically (demarcated, recognizable meaning). If the transgression (or overturning) of laws against sodomy is to play any role in a radical queer politics, it cannot do so simply through the valorization of one genital act over and against another. Rather, if it is to uproot the limited economy of desire and identity politics, it must resist the orders of scarcity (lack) and teleology in ways that do not reinscribe their mastery of the social-psychic field.

Bataille thereby sees, as this brief example shows, that the endless transgression of limits will never be a way to exceed those limits: limits are formed to be transgressed. As Foucault and Lacan also show, albeit with strikingly different emphases, transgressing limits only reinstates their power, performing exactly as the law expects and demands. Bataille thereby exposes the impossibility of exceeding a consciousness that is primarily framed by lack through transgression. The law of prohibition only exacerbates the lack that is at the heart of subjectivity, locking one into the logic of teleology and its politics of identity: transgression only reasserts the restricted economy of desire. To experience differently and to frame experience differently, Bataille distances himself from this dominant, normative logic of prohibition-transgression, its subjectivity of desire-lack, and its politics of identity-teleology. To do so, he shifts our attention to the closed economy of utility, a value that galvanizes this larger logic of desire-prohibition-teleology in late modernity and locks us into a specific order of knowledge.

🏵 Eroticism, not Sexuality

In volume 2 of *The Accursed Share,* Bataille distinguishes between eroticism and sexuality. Having explored an eclectic variety of experiences (e.g., potlatch rituals, religious sacrifices, ascetic monasticism) that exceed the closed economy of utility in volume 1, he proclaims eroticism as the exemplary field of sovereignty and "the accursed domain *par excellence*" (1991b, 18) in volume 2. But most of his work in this volume involves setting out a meaning of eroticism that is lost to our modern Western ears. He argues that eroticism exceeds the field of sexuality—and the order of knowledge. For Bataille, sexuality is the realm of human experience that is created through the ontological break with animality; that is, through the abhorrence of animality,[9] sexuality is humanized to distance it from simple animal sexuality. But as a field of experience grounded in "contact with animality," sexuality is haunted by the very abhorrence that originally produced it as a human field of experience. And this haunting is the realm of eroticism: eroticism is the persistent *attraction* to that which humans must—ontologically as humans—abhor. Whether animal sexuality, sacrificial deaths, or a squandering uselessness, eroticism enacts the human attraction to the very thing that humans, as humans, must abhor.

What incites this attraction varies across time and space, with a necessity that is only local to the closed economy in which it operates: religious taboos, economic codes, racial barriers, educational systems, and of course, norms of sexuality all eroticize various acts, objects, and thoughts differently at different times and places. The erotic world is, as Bataille puts it in teasingly Kantian language, "imaginary in its form" (1991b, 29); some aspect of culture is arbitrarily delimited as "erotic." Engaging Bataille's thought experiment and recalling that he was a medievalist, we can imagine rather easily an eroticized world in which sexuality is forbidden (see 1991b, 29). What is sexual may be erotic; but what is erotic need not be sexual.

The erotic thus may be historically experienced primarily through the dynamics of prohibition and permission, but a general perspective shows that eroticism is not reducible to this sort of negation. A general view ushers us into the ways that eroticism uses arbitrarily defined prohibitions to historically reenact the ontological break from animality that ensures our very humanity, without reducing the erotic to the limitations and contours of the sexual.

Bataille thereby distances himself considerably from the hyper-rational approaches of psychoanalysis, which might read the attraction to the horror of animality as a "return of the repressed." It seems that psychoanalysis has claimed the field of sexuality, the field of how drives and desires are structured symbolically, psychically, culturally, and individually, as its realm of investigation and analysis. Psychoanalysis has, from Bataille's general perspective, reduced eroticism to sexuality, which is reduced once more to the conceptual apparatuses of reason and its dominant logic of utility. If sexuality is the realm of experience created through the ontological break with animality, it is that which renders the experience in an acceptable form of "contact with" animality. And it is this "contact" that psychoanalysis has rendered reasonable, even if through negation—that is, through mapping how the irrational functions in our human relations to sexuality. But for Bataille, this contact with animality is not one that can be fully reduced to either reason or reason's negation. Rather, the contact with animality in the field of sexuality is constant, haunting sexuality with the very abhorrence that originally produced it as a human field of experience—the abhorrence that originally drove it to distance itself from this contact. The abhorrence is ontologically necessary. And this is what eroticism enacts and expresses. Eroticism thereby exceeds sexuality, as well as the (rational) grasp of psychoanalysis that attempts to reduce it to the field of sexuality.

But we late moderns have lost this distinction between eroticism and sexuality. For us, living under the modern reign of instrumental reason and its specific ordering of knowledge, eroticism has been reduced to sexuality. Sexuality forms the domain of experience in which instrumental reason can gain a firm foothold, driving so deeply into the social psyche that it shapes the very core of the modern self—namely, one's desire. Instrumental reason can demand that sexuality must be *useful,* which translates into the mandate that it must be reproductive. For example, the fundamental principle of Catholic sexual ethics (with which Bataille was well acquainted) is that the sexual act must be natural. And the single criterion to determine this "natural" status is the openness of the act to procreate. Sexual acts must not foreclose reproduction. They must be useful. The consequent reduction of the excessive possibilities of sexuality to the singular act of heterosexual intercourse is merely an obvious aside.

The problem with queer lives, then, is that they categorically foreclose the biological expression of utility—reproduction. Compensation for this disavowal can apparently only be achieved through the metonymic exchange of capital reproduction for the foreclosed biological reproduction. Only through their finesse of the marketplace can gay (notably, white gay male) lives prove their utility—and even hope to access any power. But their perversion of utility's heterosexist coding of the body and its ultimate power in this closed economy of xenophobia will guarantee that any such entrance to power will be, at best, contingent and fleeting. Queer lives are palatable only when serving as fuel for markets. For example, as we see in the popular television show "Queer Eye for the Straight Guy," the United States and Great Britain apparently love gay white men when they are helping straight men to be better lovers, thereby strengthening heterosexuality while marketing it; or, as Jacqui Alexander demonstrates through an analysis of the white gay tourism industry, gay lives are also acceptable when perpetuating racism or nationalism.[10] But if queer lives are not aiding and abetting the particular closed economy of heterosexual, racist, nationalist capitalism, they are unacceptable; and the clear evidence for this is their perversion of its ultimate law, utility.

This fastening on the utility of the sexual act thereby effectively reduces the domain of sexuality to genitalia: sex is about genitalia, about who does what with his or her genitalia. These are precisely the terms at stake in the aforementioned example of sodomy and, more specifically, in the 2002 anti-sodomy ruling of the U.S. Supreme Court in *Lawrence v. Texas*. This landmark decision, which overturned more than a dozen states' sodomy laws, focused on the act of sodomy between two men and turned on the questions of privacy and the limits of the law. However, in the cultural psyche of the United States, where identity is determined through the epistemological order of instrumental reason, the ruling has effectively continued the reduction of g/l/b/t lives to questions of genitalia: it perpetuates the problematizing of queer lives through the singular question of our use of our genitalia, the restricted mode of access to identity. Sexuality is about the proper *use* of genitals. And that is all.

The installation of this fundamental value, utility, allows not only homophobia but also more general forms of xenophobia to emerge: if sexuality is not reproductive, it is perverse (and the person performing it is a pervert);

but, more generally, if an act is not useful, it is not properly human (and the person performing it is a beast or monster).[11] In the United States, where the Protestant work ethic reigns supreme, we can see that the site of our humanizing is not merely the abhorrence of animality, but more generally *the abhorrence of all that is not useful.* This is what finally horrifies us about animality: its useless squandering of life. Why must we, ontologically, distance ourselves from the contact with animality that is at the root of human sexuality? Because it is useless. To abhor squandering uselessness or, at the other end of production, to abhor excessive waste, is to distance oneself from animality: it is to humanize one's self—and to give reason, particularly instrumentality and its expression in utility, its fullest reign over our social and psychic lives.

But this larger distancing movement from animality has also been erased from late modernity's consciousness. Bataille argues that this distancing from animality functions as the primary criterion to separate humankind into social classes, races, tribes, groups—into differences. But we late moderns cannot allow for any such "*horror* [as the horror of animality to] enter into consideration" (1985a, 117, his emphasis). We cannot even recognize its domesticated transposition into the horror of uselessness. Bataille argues that we can only recognize "the right to acquire, to conserve, and to consume rationally, but [we must] exclude in principle *nonproductive expenditure*" (1985, 117). We must jump over the possibility of uselessness.

Consequently, if we want to resist this attenuation of experience and the politics of domination that come in the wake of these multiple erasures (of eroticism, of nonproductive expenditure), we must investigate this fundamental logic of utility at the heart of sexuality. If queer acts of pleasure are to dislodge the totalizing restricted economies of desire-prohibition-teleology, it may be through the valorizing of their very lack of purpose: this particular kind of lack may usher in a general economy of excessive pleasures that are gloriously useless.

🏵 Knowledge as Limits: The Expansive Scope of Utility

In my musings on the traditional narrative of desire as rooted in an ontological lack, I have argued that the logic of such a desire locks us into a teleological ordering of knowledge and experience: we know who/what we are through the purposes we pursue. This teleological ordering narrows in scope in later modern thought, exemplified perhaps in the texts of John Locke, where utility becomes the singular criterion to determine the satisfaction of desire's demands: we know who/what we are through the usefulness that our lives/actions achieve. Across both of these schemas of broad teleology and more narrow utility, knowledge is ordered sequentially as the progressive development of clearer and more useful endpoints. The demarcation of each segment of thinking—of each concept—thereby becomes critical to the forward march of knowledge's ordering of experience and the world.

This seems to make things much worse. It seems to broaden the scope of this limited economy of epistemological utility and its politics of domination. If this construction of meaning through the delimitation of concepts is the necessary structure of knowledge, then we find ourselves embedded not only in a limited economy of the psychosocial world through desire-prohibition-identity, but also in a limited economy of epistemology: our very impulses to find meaning (through teleology broadly, and utility specifically) and the way that we undertake this process (through the delimitation of concepts) may already enact a normative order of knowledge that sufficiently conditions the emergence of utility as our highest value. A crass concept of utility or even of instrumental reason may thereby prove insufficient as a barometer for transformative politics.

When Bataille turns to this kind of sequential ordering of knowledge, he turns to the texts of Hegel: "Hegel saw very well that, were it acquired in a thorough and definitive way, knowledge is never given to us except by *unfolding in time*" (1991b, 202). Despite his resistance against reducing thinking to any singular method, Hegel's texts nonetheless provide some insight into how this demand for sequential demarcation may anchor the broader logic of utility and its apparent vehicle, instrumental reason.

Hegel reads human consciousness as constantly transgressing its own self-made limitations or demarcations. In *The Phenomenology of Spirit,* consciousness moves through the world in an endless act of exceeding its own self-imposed limits. As Reason's negative labors *ad infinitum,* the self becomes richer and more self-conscious through its gathering of these distinguishing moments and marks, these "limits" that it constructs and exceeds as it internalizes them. The kind of limit that Hegel reads consciousness as constantly constructing and subsequently transgressing is thus not, and cannot become, an *absolute* limit. As Derrida develops in his early essay on Hegel and Bataille, "From Restricted to General Economy: A Hegelianism without Reserve," these limits are always internal to human consciousness for Hegel, always those which Hegel can fold back into the dialectical grasp of Reason. They most often function in two ways: immediately, as a limit that initially appears absolute to consciousness, and mediately (often narrated retrospectively), as a distinction that consciousness—lifted into Reason—has grasped, and thereby read in its true shape as a distinguishing mark within consciousness's experience of the world. Or, to write this in the register of desire that shapes Bataille's (and arguably Hegel's) language, limits function immediately as prohibitions and mediately as transgressed prohibitions in Hegel's articulation of human consciousness.

To grasp the limits through which one has passed, epistemically and existentially, is then to grasp how one is placed, how one makes sense. This recognition of limits becomes the very acts of both thinking and experiencing: it becomes the way that we articulate meaning in our lives and worlds. For Hegel, to be delimited means to be thinking well and grasping experience fully, displaying a predilection toward that which is "meaningful" as the *telos* of human consciousness. And that "meaning" is determined by the clear demarcation of one entity from another.

As Hegel develops more explicitly in the *Science of Logic,* the limit functions as the necessary space of negation, which in turn both distinguishes and connects one identity to another identity (Self to Other). As that limit is more deeply internalized, consciousness realizes that it is dialectically both Self and Other.[12] "Every determinate being . . . determines itself as an other," Hegel explains (1969, 118). The limit serves as the fundamental negation upon which one's consciousness as a being rests: it allows for individuation. The function of limits as internalized into constitutive, distinguishing marks of one's identity thus becomes the necessary condition for identity formation itself: recall the critical role of clear and distinct genital acts to identity politics in the example of sodomy.

Consciousness thereby appears to totalize its grasp on experience, reading all moments as limits or negations that it can—and should—internalize as it unfolds in time. Consciousness appears to operate as a closed economy. This totalizing grasp reaches its extremity when it comes up against the negation of being that Hegel sees as absolute: non-being or nothing, the category with which the dialectic of the *Science of Logic* begins. Against this (allegedly) absolute limit, Hegel demonstrates how a being is not-nothing; consequently, this fundamental limit constitutes the basis on which other negations are sublated into identity (see 1969, 119). The *nothing* is sublated into determinate being—domesticated and made meaningful. With this "absolute" limit internalized, the question of each new relation with an Other becomes a matter of how the apparent limit will be overcome—of how the relation will produce another distinction that is then internalized as a part of one's identity, "a moment of experience." The Other is already reduced to that which is delimited; and only that which is delimited can be meaningful, and thus experienced. Or, in Bataille's language, the question of each new relation is how the prohibition will be transgressed. A *particular kind*—that is to say, a limited notion—of limitlessness thus comes to be viewed as internal to the structure of identity.

Another way of spinning this narrative is to say that Hegel submits the question of identity formation to the mastery of Reason. Negations, or limits, are internalized, made meaningful, made *useful* to the I: one engages negations and limits *in order to know them*. Again, Derrida's essay on Hegel and Bataille is helpful. As he describes it, in the Hegelian *Aufhebung,* "from infinite indetermination one passes to infinite determination, and this transition, produced by the anxiety of the infinite, continuously links meaning up to itself" (1978, 275). The "anxiety of the infinite" here can be read as Hegel's deep anxiety of the meaningless, of that which resists all meaning— what Bataille might call the "formless," which thinking cannot think without turning it into some form.[13] Meaninglessness produces anxiety in this meaning-seeking thinker, just as it does in the culture that he articulates and we still inhabit. Meaninglessness demands the construction of limits, of boundaries, even of prohibitions. Thinking or experiencing limitlessly is untenable, useless, and unknowable; it is thereby also undesirable and, perhaps most troubling of all, it resists mastery.

🏵 *Bataille's Queer Pleasures*

The order of knowledge at stake in Bataille's turn toward general economies is thereby more far-reaching than any simple notion of utility or instrumental reason. Broader, more expansive contours of rationality may be at stake in his challenges to go "in the wrong direction on the paths of knowledge—to get off them" and find that "only unknowing is *sovereign*" (1991b, 208). To go in the wrong direction on the paths of knowledge may be to challenge our very demarcation of concepts, our very act of categorization.[14] While the attempts to find routes into general economies are appropriately numberless (and also unpredictable, shifting with historical conditions), those experiences which resist a reduction to a clear and distinct concept need not be read as defective or *lacking* in some fundamental way. Such experiences may challenge the very epistemologies that subtend such judgments, opening onto kinds of living that resist both these epistemologies of mastery and the politics of domination that they spawn.

As Bataille brings the modern reduction of eroticism to sexuality into focus, he demonstrates how sexuality functions as a closed economy. Provoking us to think in general economies, he shows over and over how eroticism is irreducible to sexuality, drawing on its many other possible expressions: religious sacrifice, spectacles, arts; competitive games, war, cults; flowers, jewels; the list goes on and on across his texts.[15] I suggest that, in the contemporary culture of the United States, the queering of sexual pleasures, along with the intense anxiety that it produces, enacts these excessive possibilities that eroticism harbors and thereby exposes the arbitrariness of the laws of utility and knowledge and their multiple erasures. The queering of sexual pleasures exceeds the reductions of sexuality to genitalia, of identity to desire, of pleasure to utility, and of experience to knowledge: it decenters the heteronormative coding of the sexual body, the restriction of consciousness to legible desires and identity, and the attenuation of life that occurs when meaning is reduced to concepts and goals.

Queer pleasures may, in fact, not even be properly "sexual." Bataille's erotic fiction is filled with eggs, eyeballs, fevers, milk, semen, sheets, wind, rain, illnesses, chalices, sunrays, blood, bicycles, and very bizarre physical positions. Simply read *The Story of the Eye*. A hyper-performative text, this short book leads its readers directly to bodies, perhaps even giving readers' bodies back to themselves in ways they do not recognize and therefore have not experienced. The first chapter, "Cat's Eye," already puts one in a world of bodies and pleasures and fluids, and nothing more. Bataille elaborates the intricate acrobatics of these young bodies with great detail, inviting his readers to concoct some impossible physical positions. And this, in addition to some cat's milk, eggs, and urine, is all we get.

There are no characters in this piece of literature. Yes, we get names and genders and ages, but there are no internal conversations or inter-character dialogues that might give us some sense of "what drives these people" or "who these people are." There is no narrative of desire, and consequently no characters have an identity. Proper names function as placeholders for varieties of bodily fluids and physical positions. The characters respond to the energy of the scenes themselves, wholly externalized by the mesmerizing pleasures around them, rather than being driven by deep psychological structures of desire and its endless transgression of prohibitions. It is never entirely clear where one character or act or idea drops off and another begins.

Bataille gives us the effects of behaviors on bodies. Brimming with arms, hands, blood, eyes, heads, urine, dirt, ejaculations, and eggs, these are stories of bodies and fluids and very odd, very queer, pleasures. Bizarre acts seem to multiply possibilities endlessly, exceeding the law of desire and its coding of the body: genitalia, that which the law of utility deems the proper site of sexuality, are merely one more among this onslaught of objects; they are described with an odd matter-of-factness that contrasts sharply with the sumptuousness of eggs and milk. These are not pleasures derived as the teleological satisfaction of desires. They are irreducible to prior determining logics of desire. There is nothing satisfying in these texts—and, certainly, nothing useful (in the scenes themselves or in our acts of reading them). Nothing useful, and perhaps not even anything meaningful or legible or sensible at all. There is no guiding *telos.*

If to queer pleasure de-centers us from the grip of reproductive sexuality and its heteronormative coding of the body, then it may not occur in realms recognizable as "sexual." It may have nothing at all to do with sexual object choices or other transgressions of the prohibitive law of desire. To queer may mean to be involved in acts of pleasure that offer no return to the closed economies of societal meaning that are driven by utility and the mandate of closed, concise, clear endpoints. Rather, to live in the world queerly may mean to live in the world transformatively, with an eye always toward how relations of bodies and pleasures can be multiplied and intensified. If acts of pleasure veer off the rails of utility and reason, these may be some of the best indicators of queering's effects. To be intensely engaged in activities that are *going nowhere* may itself be a criterion of queering in this teleologically obsessed culture.

Allow me to offer a few examples: the slow, iterative time of intellectual work that never produces anything other than its own activity and pleasure comes to mind. Or to confuse the question of genitalia beyond its registers of legibility would also be to queer this culture: the growing movement of M-F and F-M trannies, who identify neither as female nor male but as forever in-transition-between-genders, are turning the question of sex as a question of genitalia into hilarious contortions. To be as explicit as the law of desire demands: if a female-by-birth who identifies as a lesbian straps on a dildo to have anal sex with a male-to-female trannie who has both breasts and a penis, does this somehow make her straight? (Such an act would not be criminalized under recently outlawed anti-sodomy laws of Texas, which pertained only to same-sex couples.) Or, to offer a cultural example: Pedro Almodóvar's film *Talk to Her* offers us many exquisitely queer pleasures in its beautiful, if tragic (and admittedly problematic), depiction of how the law of desire kills those pleasures and loves that are irreducible to genital acts or clear identities. Finally, to speak in that first-person voice that queering apparently evokes, I surely have the queerest of relations with my flamboyantly gorgeous cat, with whom I am so intensely and erotically "involved" that my lesbian lover often realizes she will always be second in my heart.

In the hopes of reinvigorating queer politics, we can cultivate a sense of pleasures irreducible to *teloi.* If pleasure is not subject to the law of desire, then it need not heed the mandate of having an endpoint. This a-telic, or non-teleological framing of experience would de-center several of the normative assumptions that seem to be paralyzing l/g/b/t political movements. Identity politics has no purchase here: to be queer is not to be homosexual. In fact, these queer pleasures are not even properly "sexual" at all. To be queer, then, is not necessarily to be involved in same-sex sex acts: it is to be involved in acts or pleasures that offer no clear or useful meaning. To be queer is not to respond to the law of desire: it is to have no idea who or what you are, or where you're going. In the globalizing of our ethics of utility and identity politics, this refusal of identity may be among our most radical politics.[16]

NOTES

1. In addition to Dean 2000, see Dean and Lane 2001.

2. For a more detailed examination of this reading of Lacan and what it might mean not only vis-à-vis Deleuze and Guattari, but also for our concepts of desire and pleasure in their relation to the Law, see Winnubst 2006b.

3. See Duggan and Hunter 1995, 167; Halperin 1995, 15–16; and McWhorter 1999, xv–xvi, for overviews of these relations.

4. Whether g/l/b/t political movements have lived out that radical potential is, of course, a different question. It seems that, while letting go of the damaging nature/nurture polarity, g/l/b/t political movements have suffered from an inability to articulate our political agency effectively without recourse to the essentializing moves of identity politics, as the political practices and *issues* of the 1990s easily show: did Foucault not warn strongly enough against the inherent conservatism of "coming-out" narratives such that we still have National Coming Out Day celebrated across college campuses? And how could any truly queer politics argue for entrance to that bastion of heterosexist conservatism, the institution of marriage? I develop this issue of identity politics as a domesticating politics that operates in a restricted economy below.

5. Foucault writes of "the historical a priori" in part III, chapter 5, of *The Archaeology of Knowledge* (1972). This theme echoes across virtually all of his writing and is most explicit in his distancing himself from Kantian transcendental idealism.

6. For Foucault's discussion of Nietzsche and the dangers of the myth of the pure origin (*Ursprung*), see "Nietzsche, Genealogy, History" (Foucault 1977).

7. While my focus here is to develop this in the register of heterosexism, see Lamarche in this volume for the argument regarding capitalism.

8. See Roudinesco 1997 and Surya 2002 for discussions of the fraught relationship between Bataille and Lacan, which included marriage to the same woman (albeit not at the same time); Surya implies that, while Lacan read most of everything Bataille wrote, Bataille largely ignored Lacan's work. Although Foucault only wrote one essay on Bataille, "Hommage à Georges Bataille" (translated into English as "A Preface to Transgression" in Foucault 1977), he was clearly influenced by Bataille's sense of general economy, pleasure rather than desire, and nonproductive expenditure. More explicitly, Foucault also assisted in the publication of Bataille's *Oeuvres complètes* (1973) and was a frequent contributor and editorial consultant to *Critique,* a journal founded by Bataille ("A Preface to Transgression," Foucault 1977, note 1).

9. Bataille reads this as the ontological ground of the practices of sacrifice. See Bataille 1992 for more details; and 1991b, 51–56.

10. See Alexander 1998. Showing how gay capitalism is a pawn of heterosexual capital and its racist, nationalist xenophobia, she writes: "Heterosexual capital would make it appear as though the only gay people are consuming people and the only gay consuming people are white and male" (287). While Bataille does not figure in Alexander's discussion, her work expresses how these Bataillean dynamics can lead to excellent diagnoses of the confluence of capitalism, white supremacist racism, and heterosexism through the mandate of reproduction—utility—within a limited economy.

11. For a discussion of how this dominant value of utility lies at the heart of most contemporary forms of xenophobia, see Winnubst 2007.

12. Echoing "Sense Certainty" in the *Phenomenology*, speech itself falls short in this realization, as the naming of "this" fails necessarily to articulate the ways in which the "this" is constituted by its also always being an "other": language fails to capture this role of limitation that constitutes its very ability to name, belying a general economy that exceeds its limited scope of "meaning."

13. See "Formlessness" in Bataille 1985 for a frighteningly concise articulation of the problem of language in attempting to exceed this logic of the limit.

14. Foucault also suggests this in *The Order of Things* and *The Archaeology of Knowledge*; again, I am also suggesting that Bataille's texts often offer ontological arguments for the kinds of historical arguments we find in Foucault's texts.

15. See particularly "The Notion of Expenditure" and "The Language of Flowers" in Bataille 1985 as well as Bataille 1991a.

16. For a prolonged discussion of the general themes of this essay, and particularly its politics and examples, see Winnubst 2006a.

WORKS CITED

Alexander, M. Jacqui. 1998. Imperial Desire/Sexual Utopias: White Gay Capital and Transnational Tourism. In *Talking Visions: Multicultural Feminism in a Transnational Age,* ed. Ella Shohat. Cambridge: MIT Press.

Bataille, Georges. 1973. *Oeuvres Complètes.* Paris: Gallimard.

———. 1985. *Visions of Excess: Selected Writings, 1927–1939.* Ed. Allan Stoekl. Minneapolis: University of Minnesota Press.

———. 1987. *The Story of the Eye.* Trans. Joachim Neugroschel. San Francisco: City Lights Books.

———. 1991a. *The Accursed Share: Volume I.* Trans. Robert Hurley. New York: Zone Books.

———. 1991b. *The Accursed Share: Volumes II and III.* Trans. Robert Hurley. New York: Zone Books.

———. 1992. *Theory of Religion.* Trans. Robert Hurley. New York: Zone Books.

Dean, Tim. 2000. *Beyond Sexuality.* Chicago: University of Chicago Press.

Dean, Tim, and Christopher Lane. 2001. *Homosexuality and Psychoanalysis.* Chicago: University of Chicago Press.

Derrida, Jacques. 1978. *Writing and Difference.* Trans. Alan Bass. Chicago: University of Chicago Press.

Duggan, Lisa, and Nan D. Hunter. 1995. *Sex Wars: Sexual Dissent and Political Culture.* New York: Routledge.

Foucault, Michel. 1970. *The Order of Things: An Archaeology of the Human Sciences.* New York: Vintage.

———. 1972. *The Archaeology of Knowledge and the Discourse on Language.* Trans. A. M. Sheridan Smith. New York: Pantheon.

———. 1977. *Language, Counter-memory, Practice: Selected Essays and Interviews by Michel Foucault.* Ed. Donald F. Bouchard. Ithaca, N.Y.: Cornell University Press.

———. 1978. *The History of Sexuality.* Vol. 1, *An Introduction.* Trans. Robert Hurley. New York: Vintage.

———. 1990. *The History of Sexuality.* Vol. 2, *The Use of Pleasure.* Trans. Robert Hurley. New York: Vintage.

Halperin, David M. 1995. *Saint Foucault: Towards a Gay Hagiography.* New York: Oxford University Press.

Hegel, G. W. F. 1969. *Science of Logic.* Trans. A. V. Miller. New Jersey: Humanities Press International.

———. 1977. *Phenomenology of Spirit.* Trans. A. V. Miller. Oxford: Oxford University Press.

Lacan, Jacques. 1977. *Ecrits: A Selection.* Trans. Alan Sheridan. New York: Norton.

McWhorter, Ladelle. 1999. *Bodies and Pleasures: Foucault and the Politics of Sexual Normalization.* Bloomington: Indiana University Press.

Roudinesco, Elisabeth. 1997. *Jacques Lacan.* New York: Columbia University Press.

Surya, Michel. 2002. *Georges Bataille: An Intellectual Biography.* Trans. Krzysztof Fijalkowski and Michael Richardson. New York: Verso.

Winnubst, Shannon. 2006a. *Queering Freedom.* Bloomington: Indiana University Press.

———. 2006b. What if the law is written in a porno book? Deterritorializing Lacan, De-Oedipalizing Deleuze & Guattari. *Symposium: Canadian Journal of Continental Philosophy,* Special Edition on Deleuze. Spring 2006. Ed. Constantin Boundas and Arnaud Villani.

———. 2007. Make Yourself Useful! In *Etiquette: Reflections on Contemporary Comportment,* ed. Ron Scapp and Brian Seitz. New York: State University of New York Press.

FIVE

ZEYNEP DIREK

Erotic Experience and Sexual Difference in Bataille

What is the place of "erotic experience" in Bataille's own political economy? As *The Accursed Share* makes manifest, the critique of the classical political economy plays a central role in Bataille's reading of diverse historical worlds. In contrast to modern approaches in the philosophy of history, he does not conceive history as a progressive teleology that establishes in one way or another the primacy of European civilization, but reads it as exhibiting the different ways in which civilizations consumed their accursed share. Bataille develops the term "the accursed share" through the distinction between "general economy" and "restricted economy" and their interaction. However, Bataille also considers world history as a unity in terms of "reification of man" or "alienation." These terms, which he borrows from Marx, are then reinterpreted in terms of "abjection." The abjection of life as a condition of possibility of the human world and thus of history accompanies the subjection of human beings to work and utility.[1] Bataille thereby opens the way for reading history, and especially its capitalist era, as a history of abjection, one in which bodies are disciplined, made to fit in rigid borders that facilitate production and growth.

It is well known that Bataille reinterprets the economic laws of history by reading them in terms of consumption rather than of production alone. Without taking into account the phenomenon of consumption, we cannot understand the ways in which the borders between immanence and transcendence are displaced and redrawn. In order to understand what "erotic experience" means as an experience of consumption, we have to look, first, at its philosophical foundations in Bataille's political economy. Second, we have to highlight the economy of corporeal being on which this political economy rests. From this approach, it follows that erotic experience suspends the world of restricted economy, leads us back to the impersonal ground of our incarnated existence, to communication in the life of immanence beyond separate identities. Bataille invites us to think subjectivity by going back to that expenditure of energy in a shared space of incarnated openness.

It is my contention that this communication is the very space of sexual difference or differentiation. Although I will not discuss in detail Luce Irigaray's philosophy of sexual difference here, I will try to address a few questions that can be offered to Bataille from her perspective. The most important of these questions is perhaps the one that concerns the possibility of an ethics of erotic experience. Can eros be a source for rethinking a new cohabitation on earth? Bataille acknowledges that the utilitarian civilization in which we live has insufficient respect for life, and he invites us to a radical reflection on a new economy that takes seriously the biological nature of our existence. He would not deny that that which is biological or material in the body never appears as such but always as embodied in historico-social structures. He nevertheless affirms the body in flesh and blood, and its cosmic time over against the abstract subject and the time of the project. I will argue that Bataille's philosophy makes room for an ethics of eros that accommodates negation, violence, and the possibility of harm to the other—the failures and paradoxes of the eros.

The Economic and the Erotic

In *The Accursed Share* Bataille uses the notion of "general economy" as an economy of energy based on the exuberance of living matter as a whole. Here, "economy" and "existence" are closely related terms because the real problem of the general economy—the excess of resources—becomes visible only from the point of view of general existence (1991a, 39). Precisely because the economic problem is an existential one, the notion of "classical economy" as determined by the pursuit of surplus to be invested in growth is insufficient to capture the general existential, ontological problem of "the essence of the biomass which must constantly destroy (consume) a surplus of energy" (1991a, 182). Although we highlight the notion of "existence" here, we are not reading Bataille as an existentialist: he does not thematize the possibility of the transcendence of a solitary consciousness based on a factically situated individual and personal existence. Instead, he proceeds to conceive existence radically by going beyond all personalisms, existential-isms, and even beyond the Heideggerian *Jemeinichkeit*. Existence is not pri-marily mine: it is limitless, dynamic, and fluid. In other words, subjective existence cannot be limited by me or by the other I's.[2]

At the foundation of general economy seems to lie a notion of general, impersonal existence and its explosive character.[3] This is a radical thinking of subjectivity in its most fundamental energetic dimension. The inner ex-perience of eroticism reveals the fact that the originary ground of our exis-tence is impersonal. The erotic act, whose sacred nature is manifest in the pagan world, suspends the discontinuity of the world of work. It not only transgresses—acknowledges and negates—the sexual prohibitions, the his-torically constructed borders between different sexes, genders, classes, races, cultures, and ages, but it also dissolves personalities. In other words, it makes us return to *il y a* in which no sex can be one.[4] In erotic experience, being calls its own existence into question by losing itself in the very expe-rience.[5] The distortion of the fixed shapes of such constructed differences and the dissolution of personality in the erotic experience are conducive to a return to the continuity of impersonal existence. In my reading, the term "continuity" here contrasts with the absolute discontinuity of the world, and it does not exclude the possibility that that continuity, as the abyss of impersonal existence, may at the same time be a space of constant differen-tiation. Subjectivity, for Bataille, "is never the object of a discursive knowl-edge, except obliquely, but it is communicated from subject to subject through a sensible, emotional contact: it is communicated in this way in laughter, in tears, in the commotion of the festival" (1991b, 242). Without doubt, intersubjective communication presupposes separate personalities; but at the same time, it requires the interruption of the rigid personal boundaries. Subjects can connect and subjectivities are communicated only through the interrupting acts of violence that shatter the illusion of the coincidence of the subject with itself.

The impersonality of existence, which is erotic through and through, provides Bataille with an ontological perspective that affirms the body in its generality as a communicative, non-separate being, embedded in the dy-namic life of the cosmos. The body as a living organism, as an impersonal part of the biomass, is always to be found in a situation determined by the "play of energy on the surface of the globe and ordinarily receives more en-ergy than is necessary for maintaining life" (1991a, 21). Bataille conceives human existence as a space for the interaction between life and the world, in terms of a dwelling in which the cosmic time and the time of the project constantly interrupt each other. Even though Bataille never consistently uses it, the distinction between the "life" and the "world" that Heidegger privileges in his reading of Nietzsche[6] can be of remarkable value in interpreting Bataille. In "On the Truth and Lies in a NonMoral Sense" (1999), Nietzsche argues that we are creatures who, in order to preserve ourselves, construct a world by way of schematizing life according to our practical needs. On the other hand, life is the chaotic energy that surrounds, penetrates, and constantly challenges us through our bodies. As Heidegger describes it, "life lives in that it bodies forth" (1991, 79). The scientific, conceptual, legal, and moral framework that makes up our worldly nest is analogous to a spider's web built on the branches of a tree over the stream of a river.[7] Without our worldly constructions, we cannot survive; yet life always threatens to take them back from us, to swallow them, leaving us bewildered in the midst of chaotic forces.

The modern capitalist world submits man's activity to use for the purpose of the constant development and growth of the economic forces. In the first volume of *The Accursed Share,* Bataille is concerned with the way restricted economy (constant development of economic sources) poses the general problems that are linked to "the movement of energy on the globe" (1991a, 20). Erotic experience in the modern world, the acknowledgment and the transgression of prohibitions at the same time, is an economic play between life's forces and worldly powers that necessarily reach a limit in the investment of surplus in growth and development. Eroticism is the "unproductive glory" of life energy. Bataille makes clear that erotic desire does not originate in a need or a lack in our being in the world, but derives its being from a surplus, luxury, and frivolity in our being. Not only does the erotic belong fundamentally to luxury, but sexuality too is in its very essence luxurious.[8] Bataille emphasizes that "the excess energy (wealth) can be used for the growth of a system (e.g., an organism); if the system can no longer grow, or if the excess cannot be completely absorbed in its growth, it must necessarily be lost without profit; it must be spent, willingly or not, gloriously or catastrophically" (1991a, 21). Restricted economy of the world is self-destructive, and life's energy cannot be captured and domesticated by the schemas and limits of an ever-growing system:

> In a sense, life suffocates within limits that are too close; it aspires in manifold ways to an impossible growth; it releases a steady flow of excess resources, possibly large squandering of energy. The limit of growth being reached, life, without being in a closed container, at least enters into ebullition: Without exploding, its extreme exuberance pours out in a movement always bordering explosion. (1991a, 30)

Erotic activity is not productive; it is one of the fundamental ways of squandering the excess energy of life that challenges us from within the impersonal, general ground of our incarnated existence. Both eros and war are explosions beyond the limit of the development of productive forces. They are a renewed contact with both life and death, with the impersonal existence that bodies forth. The experience of the front in war is another experience of intimacy with the other, in which the enemy may appear beyond his national, ethnic identity, as a face. The war takes place within the disruption of all political and historical communication; yet at the heart of this very break, the line between friend and enemy may always be blurred by immanent communication. Of course, today's wars have technologically annulled the possibility of experiencing the front. My point is that both the erotic experience and the experience of war strip us of our identities and pave the way for communication between incarnated subjects.

In Bataille's view, both war and eros exceed teleology in the sense that they are never means of growth and development, but are ways of squandering the excess that, without an outlet, would explode the whole system of production. This is precisely why erotic experience, for example, is a sovereign interior experience. By "interior experience," Bataille understands the interruption of the world of utility, action, production, and possession. Such an interruption, because it is both the loss of the subject and of the object, is a destruction of the world in which human existence is submitted to projects wherein the temporality of the primacy of the future determines the significance of the present. We tend to believe that we create ourselves by our projects, deeds, and achievements, but we also suffer the loss of the feeling of self and the intimacy with the others. When relations with others are determined by goal-oriented contexts, it can never lead to "communication" in the specific sense Bataille gives to this term. He denies that selfhood is a future project and that true communication between I and the other can be accounted with reference to contexts of utility (1991b, 43). On the contrary, the sense of the self is to be found in "religion" in the sense of being connected, related again to the immanent continuity of Being.

In order to understand how such a possibility of *religare* is opened up by radical or "interior experience," we must first of all remark that Bataille's use of the "interior" and "exterior" is quite extraordinary. What is at stake is not the interiority of an isolated subject, but the outside of the interior/exterior divide that draws the limits of that subject. Inner experience is a relation of communication with the other, and it is for the other. Bataille insists that its temporality is that of the present. We can further elaborate that temporality by taking the erotic experience as exemplary of inner experience: erotic experience breaks the ordinary time of the world submitted to the primacy of the future and productivity, thereby reinstituting the absolute value of the present moment. The time of the erotic is the reevaluation of the present moment, the affirmation of the beyond being-in-the-world in a return to an amplified contact with the immanent energy of the universe. Erotic *ecstasis*—being outside one's self in passion and desire for the other—is *in-stasis*, a stance in the present moment. The instant of *eros* is the moment of sovereignty. The presence of sovereignty is only revealed through "interior communication" (1991b, 245). Sovereignty does not mean "independence" in the sense of not living in a dependency relationship to the other. All this discourse about dependent/independent relationships belongs to a reorganization of the world in terms of individual growth and productivity. For Bataille, such a setting of one's self as a separate, independent being would be the destruction of the erotic, the loss of the sovereignty of the present, the submission to an economy of survival and growth and the primacy of the future.

The release and the dynamic flow of the erotic energy animating our incarnated existence require that one not close off the possibility of risk and loss by taking precautions and setting defense mechanisms to protect one's average emotional stable being-in-the-world. According to Bataille, "desire demands the greatest possibility of loss" (1991b, 141). We restrict our own erotic affects by setting ourselves up as independent things, that is, as objects of seduction, presupposing that the dialectic of eros should be one of conquest, worldly possession, and utility. From Bataille's point of view, this is indeed the reversal of the erotic dynamic into a logic of "extreme poverty." The loss of the previous erotic experiences by their transformation into worldly gains, the past failures to control the logic of desire, and the inability to avoid the harmful consequences of the inversion of love to hate may limit our future capacity to go beyond the erotic beginnings. One may argue that erotic experience as intersubjective communicative denuding is also impeded by heterosexist roles and prejudices, which prevent us from living up to the erotic dynamics in our bodying forth with the others.[9]

Even though the *telos* of the animal sexuality is reproduction, it is still an expenditure of the animal's being. In the human realm, reproduction is not the *telos* of the erotic desire, but one of its possibilities. The movement of erotic desire goes beyond being in the sense of persisting and acquiring more and more power in our worldly survival and self-preservation. Bataille nowhere denies that we desire to preserve ourselves and make every effort to satisfy our needs to that effect. However, he also makes clear that the movement of desire goes beyond being in attempting to open up life possibilities without limit. Despite the fact that life has many possibilities that cannot be realized indefinitely, the concern for survival and self-preservation is not sufficient to account for our being: being must be rethought in terms of sovereignty—that is, the desire to open life possibilities beyond utility, to enjoy the products of the world beyond the necessities of subsistence and labor. This is not to say that sovereignty is a *telos;* on the contrary, it is the denial of all *telos* in wasting and squandering the excess of being. Erotic luxury goes beyond the needs of self-preservation.

Even though erotic desire is consumption, it is never bound to consume the other or the erotic relationship itself; it simply consumes a surplus and hence it is positivity. On the other hand, that positivity of desire seems to relate, in Bataille's discourse, to the history of the loss of our animal intimacy with the world and the gradual separation from the sacred throughout the displacements of the borders between the sacred and the profane worlds. One should raise the question whether the location of self-consciousness and the truth of deep subjectivity in the movement of man's return to the intimacy of his being signal a nostalgic metaphysics. Bataille notes that the desire for intimacy has become more insistent in modernity. Let us pause here for a moment to shed some light on what Bataille understands by "intimacy": "Intimacy is not expressed by a *thing* except on one condition: that this *thing* be essentially the opposite of a *thing,* the opposite of a product, of a commodity—a consumption and a sacrifice. Since intimate feeling is a consumption, it is consumption that expresses it, not a *thing,* which is its negation" (1991a, 132). Our desire is to regain an intimacy that was always *strangely lost,* and that intimacy that we have "the consciousness of having lost" (1991a, 133) is our own *animality.*[10] Indeed, Bataille's discourse may often lend itself to being misinterpreted in terms of the desire to return to an immemorial past. However, we must not forget that what stands as "the immemorial past" here is still in some sense already present: what is at stake is not the recovering of a simple origin at all, but the acquisition of the self-consciousness of belonging together in an original immanence in differentiation. In other words, "return" here means the acquisition of the self-consciousness of what we already are in our historical forgetfulness.[11]

Moreover, the emphasis on the lost intimacy should not obliterate what is most valuable in Bataille's account of erotic experience—his sense of the history of eros as part of the history of sovereignty. Eroticism lends itself to analysis in terms of a general economy, an economy of being that concerns the global movement of energy, an economy that forbids us to isolate world problems such as poverty, sexual and racial discrimination, war, and militarism from one another. It is based on a rationality that takes into account the dynamics of impersonal existence in considering "totality."[12] Today, Bataille is significant for us precisely because cultural, religious, sexual, and racial forms of domination have become our central ethico-political problems, and we want to fight these forms of servility. External differences produced by means of the categories of race, sex, gender, class, culture, ethnicity, and so forth reproduce the discontinuity of our world in which communication between human beings is cut off and replaced by the return of the techno-orgiastic.

Bataille knows well that erotic experience as a limit experience is constantly subject to the assault of the modern world. Its fragility lies in its being prey to perhaps unavoidable schematization and contracts in the encounter of gendered human beings in particular social, cultural, historical, and racialized contexts that are interwoven by oppressive power relationships. The history of sexual repression, inherited structures of power, and various forms of oppression push erotic encounters to turn relationships into arenas of struggle for self-assertion. Bataille is not blind to the fact that sexuality and power cannot be thought of independently from each other, and he is not proposing a nostalgic metaphysics; he points out the necessity of taking the living body into account in considering the ways that eros interacts with power in paradoxical ways. For example, erotic encounters may become contracted relationships and may turn into partnerships of survival, productive growth, and acquisition of power. But sooner or later, life will suffocate in those contracts and schemes that can hardly contain it indefinitely. We may succeed in protecting our partnerships, but such a success is bound to be taken over by anguish.[13]

My reading of the erotic experience in Bataille as the accursed share of the present world, and perhaps of all historical worlds, and as a space of communication between different sexes is inspired by Irigaray's work. Irigaray thinks of the erotic encounter between the sexes as capable of opening a realm of communication, even though for her the terms of such an encounter are still missing insofar as they are determined solely by men. Thinking normatively on the possibility of such a communication, she invokes both "intimacy" and "distance." Encounter requires that there is more than one desire, and these differently sexed desires should be able to go to the other and loop back to the self. Irigaray understands that condition as the possibility of the growth and the development of the sexed subject, his or her becoming himself or herself (1993, 9). This is not to deny that erotic energy consumes, but Irigaray denies that the two sexes in an erotic relationship have to consume one another and the relationship itself—the very space of their subjective development. For Irigaray, we must try to increase love in the intimacy of erotic proximity and the distance that the respect for difference presupposes. One may add to this, in the spirit of Bataille, that erotic generosity for the other rests on a general economy in which reciprocity is exceeded by giving what I do not have: the excess that exceeds all possession. Without doubt, the fears that make us tremble at the face of the possibility of a future abandonment—anxiety about the future provoked by past experiences—may always force us to surrender the light and the glimmer of the present to a restricted economy. However, in a restricted economy, there can only be a semblance of an erotic engagement primarily because the I (mainly because of his/her fears) would not permit himself/herself to go out of his/her self to intimately communicate with the other. What is really restricted here is the sovereign communication by putting at risk one's identity and stability. Erotic communication is a source of worry and fear: what matters for present-day humanity may seem to be more about keeping one's head above the surface of the water, an economy of self-preservation, prosperity, and growth. However, the question of erotic sovereignty is becoming still more pressing as this restricted economy brings life into ebullition.

🌐 *The Question of Sexual Difference*

Today, the problem of eroticism cannot be separated from our differing relations to the law of the heteronormative symbolic order, which takes desire as always male and yet distributes us in terms of heterosexuality. Given the phallocratic symbolic foundations of culture, can sexual difference ever appear beyond the binary division into heterosexual male and female? In *This Sex Which Is Not One* Irigaray argues that there is only one sex; the other sex is not "one" and does not appear in the phallocratic economy of signification that belongs to Western culture and metaphysics. The subject of the symbolic order is always male. It is well known that *Speculum of the Other Woman* had already made reference to the phallocratic economy of signification in reading Freud in "On Femininity" and claiming that feminine sexual difference cannot be represented except as the outside of that economy, except as death and castration. Nevertheless, the phallocratic economy of signification includes a representation of the feminine as the other of man, reduces the feminine sexual difference by deriving it from the masculine, and thinks of the feminine as a defect, lack, or deviation by taking the masculine as exemplary (1985a, 21, 22, 26).

Sexual difference that has been repressed by Western culture and metaphysics has no logos in the sense of a definition, but that does not mean that we cannot question or problematize it. Irigaray's phenomenology of that which does not appear proceeds by deconstructive readings from within the phallocratic economy of signification in order to put its closure into question. The feminine sexual difference that has been systematically repressed may only be brought back to life by following its traces in different discourses. That which does not appear can only show itself after a cultural revolution that accompanies the overcoming of metaphysics. In other words, a culture of difference is the horizon in which sexual difference may appear. Let us note here that the economy of signification that Irigaray is putting in question is a restricted economy in Bataille's sense, and she can be read as pointing out the general economy of being and life that the restricted economy represses and hopelessly attempts to control. If the symptoms of that which is repressed did not already exist in the restricted phallocratic economy of signification, if the latter were not constantly challenged by that which it schematized and excluded, Irigaray's project could not have been possible. Bataille's economy of being provides an ontological ground for talking about the obliterated feminine sexual difference, a difference beyond the specularization of the same, under the economical-ontological term of "the accursed share." Unrepresentable feminine sexual difference in Irigaray's sense is part of the accursed share. It is a differentiation of the body, which is never an isolated thing, but always part of a global play of energy from which it gets its excess. In the general economy of immanent being, no sex can be "one." On the other hand, immanence in Bataille may offer itself to a reading in terms of an unconscious economy of desire, which for Irigaray may include feminine desire (1985b, 123–24). And furthermore, Bataille can enable us to overcome a limitation in Irigaray, because in re-reading immanence as the repressed place of differentiation, we can go beyond the restriction of thinking sexual difference in terms of masculine and feminine.

How important is the question of sexual difference for Bataille in accounting for erotic experience, given that he does not raise the question of sexual difference explicitly? It is true that Bataille does not thematize sexual difference in his discourse on immanence. However, that does not mean that the question cannot be opened and discussed by situating ourselves in his thought in order to continue philosophizing further in a Bataillean spirit. We know that erotic experience gives access to the impersonal ground of our impersonal existence, which we can take to be as a space of communication beyond worldly identities. Erotic experience can be the transgression of the prohibitions that regulate and constitute heterosexual gender identities—perversion. Bataille's overall perspective implies that perversion is not a deviation from an intrinsically heterosexual nature. On the contrary, he understands perversion as the overcoming of the alienation and servility that restrict the possibilities of intimate communication between bodies that are dynamically and communicatively sexed. Bataille's discourse on erotic desire makes the claim that erotic situations are often provoked by separation and distance and that desire aims at overcoming separation. Love would indeed be a desire to obliterate and erase worldly differences, but at the same time, it opens a space for sovereign differentiation. Oneness in the immanence of carnal communication is quite different than the unity of a couple whose characters have merged in a "we" without difference.

Sexual alienation constitutes our worldly factical situation as incarnated beings, and we recognize it as we find ourselves constantly challenged by the ways that our erotic excess energy overflows our sexual identity. We find glory in letting that energy flow in transgression of the social restrictions of our bodily existence in communication with the other. We find the joy of sovereignty in the sharing of the incarnated freedom with the other. By "incarnated freedom," I do not simply understand the letting of one's own and the other's body be alive, expressive, and responsive beyond all forms of oppression exerted by the norms that regulate gender, class, race, sex, age, and stylistic differences. Incarnated freedom is not just freedom from norms but the creation of new norms and their negotiation in the process of our bodying forth as sexed beings. Bataille's fundamental insight here is the idea that the transgression of borders sets us in intimacy with the other. It is in this intimacy that he finds sovereignty, friendship, truth, compassion, and the welcoming of differences. Sexual difference beyond its cultural allocation and erasing caricatures can only be lived and expressed in the intimacy of transgressive erotic communication. When such an intimacy takes place in the world, it suspends gender identities and lets the differences freely express their own excess energy in communication with each other.

This reading of Bataille may sound too positive, given the fact that much of his fiction may be read as misogynistic. A close reading of his literary works may prove that he was not critical enough of his own sexist prejudices that marked his representations of erotic experience. Is not the subject of that experience always masculine or virile? That Bataille writes without hiding his virility is a positive fact, because he does not obliterate sexual difference by hiding himself behind a sexually neutral discourse. Was not the feminine "a dark continent" for him? In the erotic experiences Bataille narrates, the virility of the "I" is put in question as much as the femininity of the specular other. Neither virility nor femininity can be objects of knowledge, for they are contingent, miraculous differences impossible to know or to predict in the immanent experience of communication. Although Bataille does not explicitly contest the heterosexual divide, he is constantly obsessed with creating and sharing queer pleasures. For example, *Story of the Eye* is a fiction about a friendship through the experiences of transgression of gender identities in the invention and sharing of queer pleasures.[14] I am not suggesting that we read Bataille uncritically, but despite all the sexist elements and characterizations in his work, he nonetheless provides us with a philosophically rich account of eros that will enable us to rethink subjectivity as incarnated and sexually differentiated through intimate communication with others. More importantly, Bataille links the question of eros with economy, politics, and history. Only when we miss the philosophical ideas pertaining to his economy of being that sustain his fictions can the eroticism in them appear to be dominated by heterosexual virility and the traditional representation of the feminine.

Bataille is a thinker of the possibility of sexed communication beyond sexual identities. By communication, which is always sexed in erotic experience, he understands the loss of beings in each other, an ecstatic being in the other, an immanence that connects us with all other living creatures, elemental powers, and the cosmos itself. In his narratives, different bodies connect through their shared excessive life energy and give rise to different pleasures that by their very embodiment undermine social hypocrisy and make possible a way of loving that lets desires flourish in their differences, beyond possession. Bataille's characters do not seek to possess each other's desires, and this is precisely what exceeds the discourse and the norms of heterosexual desire. For example, women in Bataille's fiction are not possessed beings—they are independent, disinterested, and free from monogamous heterosexual contracts that would alienate and make them servile. Carnal act does not transform them into possessed objects. Bataille's notion of erotic experience is a refusal of the objectification of the female body by the male gaze. For him, women are impossible to know, possess, and domestically enclose. Indeed, Bataille is fascinated by the possibility of an insubordinate feminine sexual freedom. He does not privilege the moral traditional value of the sacrificial feminine as virgin, wife, and mother. He is interested in the figures of the woman who breaks with the traditional morality and the prostitute insofar as they represent for him that which cannot be possessed and made into an object in the feminine incarnation. He would agree that subordination of women in heterosexual contracts is a socially and historically contingent form of restricted economy. Precisely because heterosexuality in Bataille would always be under the destruction of a liberating communication that differentiates bodies as sexed beings, his writings do not reaffirm heterosexual normativity, but reveal that it is contingent.

Heterosexual desire opens itself up to queer desires through the element of negation that belongs to erotic experience. Such desires are not queer merely because they transgress heterosexual normativity; Bataille pursues the pervertibility of desire without separating the question of sexual difference from the questions of animality and divinity. In contrast to the difference between animality and humanity, the opposition between male and female within the human species constitutes a secondary difference. That which is divine is placed at the top of the hierarchical system of beings as that which transcends the categorizations pertaining to living beings. Bataille questions this logic because, as is clear in *The Theory of Religion,* for example, a transcendent divinity is a dialectical consequence of the separation of humanity from its own animality. The border between the animal and the human appears, then, as the place of the desire of a lost intimacy in our very communicative being—the realm of the putting in question of gender identities and the very revelation of the erotic truth of sexual differences. Irigaray would agree that the question of sexual difference as an immanent difference cannot be separated from the question of transcendence.

In *The Accursed Share,* Bataille talks about the economic value women have as objects of exchange among men. The control and the domestication of carnal communication reveals its significance from the point of view of general economy: human carnal communication is a relationship to the impure, the accursed, the evil, the expenditure of agonizing excess, the confusion and disorder threatening the profane order of things. The erotic relationship is pregnant with the possibilities of an essential communication with the sacred; it can be the mystical experience of the immanent oneness of the human, the divine, and the animal. Madame Edwarda (Bataille 1995) is a prostitute who is experienced as God. She is not just a means of transcendence; she is not just relegated to the domestication of immanence. She is the unique embodiment of God—mad, contaminated, sublime; interrupting all possibilities of possession, including the profane patriarchal possession of her own sex by men; escaping from the logic of production, reproduction, and growth; breaking with the female status of being an object of desire in the male gaze. Bataille depicts female sexual difference in all its erased, prohibited, and queer dimensions. In other words, the queer in Bataille is a pressing of the limits not only of the binary, but also of humanity defined against animality and divinity. Erotic transgression destroys the profane worldly sexual identities, which are always constructed; and it leaves us naked, in dispersion toward each other. Indeed, there is nothing in Bataille that precludes the possibility that all the configurations of erotic relationships are ways of opening up in intimacy our interior queerness as a dynamic play of life's forces. In a Bataillean discourse, this queerness appears as our own lost strangeness, a longing in our very being. This is not to deny that queerness is constantly created in us as we undergo new experiences. Here, sovereign creation and return to the self belong to one and the same immanent movement of differences, and that which is the same here provides a space for the respect for differential manifestation.

⚜ *The Possibility of an Ethics of Eros in Bataille*

As the Introduction to the first volume of *The Accursed Share* shows, ethics is a concern for Bataille. He writes, "The extension of economic growth itself requires the overturning of economic principles—the overturning of the ethics that grounds them. Changing from the perspectives of *restrictive* economy to those of *general* economy actually accomplishes a Copernican transformation: a reversal of thinking—and of ethics" (1991a, 25). If ethics within restricted economies determines a way of dwelling with others, which provides the stability for the producing of a surplus that could in turn be invested in growth, such an ethics will inescapably be suspended and reversed when growth reaches its limit. What does a reversal of ethics mean?

Bataille interprets history in terms of sovereignty and servility as a play between restricted and general economies in various historical worlds. Overall, *The Accursed Share* seems to declare that our civilization is faced with a whole-scale destruction of itself and that all meaningful discourse about ethics must acknowledge that lesser forms of violence are necessary or perhaps unavoidable for its preservation. But on the other hand, Bataille conceives the end of history as the eradication of the inequalities of resources and status that produced it. To prevent the world from completely destroying civilizations, a more fair distribution of the resources must be undertaken. Of course, a world-scale redistribution of the resources will not equal a situation in which growth is no longer possible everywhere in the world. However, what would happen if humanity were to reach that ideal state? Is there an ethics of general economy, of sovereignty, that we can describe in positive terms such as a new form of cohabitation on earth?

Can there be an ethics based on a general economy? If ethics exceeds the logic of survival, development, growth, self-preservation of the same, if it concerns the relation with the other outside the restricted economy of the same, then it has to be understood on the basis of general economy, an economy of excess without return. If we exclude the possibility of an ethics based on general economy, Bataille's ethics would ultimately be nothing more than a calculation of lesser violence in the conditions of vast inequality created by the modern world. If this is the case, then the reversal of ethics amounts to the paradox of an ethics that permits the conditions of human self-preservation of some societies to be undermined for the sake of the self-preservation of others.[15]

Now let us turn to the specific question of the possibility of an ethics of eros on the grounds of the possibility of an ethics of a general economy of existence. Although such an ethics of eros cannot issue rules or laws, it is clear that its ethical content depends on the existence of communicating sexual differences. In other words, no ethics of eros is possible if sexual difference cannot be instituted beyond "one" and "two." What would an ethics of eros pertaining to general economy be like? Bataille's ethics of eros is an ethics of sovereignty that is achieved through the expenditure of excess energy. Eros provides par excellence a domain for that. First of all, an ethics of eros demands a critique of classical political economy on the basis of general economy. Women in classical political economy appear external in relation to the laws of exchange and as objects of exchange. In *This Sex Which Is Not One,* Irigaray notes that such a critique has to be accompanied by an analysis of the impact of discourse on the relations of production (1985b, 85). Bataille's *The Accursed Share* analyses the place of women in classical economy without explicitly thematizing the symbolic foundations of sexual oppression. Nevertheless, he makes visible the way that economy stands in relation to the laws of general economy. As is well known, Irigaray has argued that at the foundation of social injustice lies sexual injustice, the institution of patriarchy, and the submission of the female sex to the male. She tells us that to overcome this we need nothing less than a revolution of culture, which would gear us toward the respect for sexual difference. Holding the structures of inequality intact by temporary reversals of ethics can be of little value from the point of view of a politics of universal emancipation. Bataille submits the question of the erotic to the question of the economic in a larger sense, yet he does not sufficiently account for sexual oppression.

That erotic experience subverts the operations of classical economy is obvious in Bataille's account, but the revolutionary ethical dynamics of erotic experience are still in need of clarification. What can be taken as ethical in erotic experience in Bataille's sense? The possibility of the ethical lies in the fact that sovereignty lived in erotic experience is not domination over the other and does not imply the constitution of a sameness that will not permit the manifestation of sexual differences. Eroticism is a form of communication with other/s. According to Bataille, we do not come into erotic encounters as self-made, self-coinciding subjects who seek to objectify the other through the master/slave dialectic of the struggle for power. Bataille meets with Irigaray in his insight that the erotic relationship opens a new space for subjectivity. However, what is at stake here for Bataille is what he calls "the profound subjectivity," which I take to be the possibility of the immanence of the divine, the human, and the animal.[16] Bataille is not interested in the subject who is an effect of power struggles, experiences of hardships of life, and past traumas; he is interested in our subjective capacity to take the step in an erotic encounter to renounce generously and luxuriously all struggle for power and to refuse being restricted by our own personal history. Erotic communication can be the taking off of all masks or the space of imaginary substitutions; both possibilities imply the free giving of trust by taking the risk of the other's betrayal.

Bataille speaks of the erotic truth in communication, which I take to be nothing else than a dangerous openness to the profound subjectivity of our sexed being experienced in pain and pleasure. The sovereign fragility that erotic communication requires is the opposite of the mastery over the other. However, Bataille also knows that "betrayal" is also included in erotic experience. He writes, "In eroticism there is ordinarily an impulse of aggressive hatred, an urge to betray" (1991b, 178). He does not spell out the logic of betrayal, but he could have accounted for it as the result of our incapacity to persist too long in what we have always longed for, the profound intimacy of the contact with myself and the other. The erotic truth is participation in the unlimited, yet it is essentially finite and comes with an experience of its own overwhelmingness, a longing for separateness and solitude in the world. Bataille never accounts for that desire.

We can also suggest that betrayal, just like violence, can be "transcendent" and "immanent": it can be a way to overcome the other by setting one's self as independent, a way to exert transcendent violence on the other by asserting one's own superiority; hence, it may involve sexism, racism, and orientalism, a way of asserting one's own mastery. However, it can also be "immanent"—just not being capable of closing off the possibilities of other erotic involvements, other desires. Both war and eros draw from the transgressive forces of life that are at play in our embodiment. These forces can only find momentary or short-term expressions in social life and are often restricted, domesticated, and exploited for the accumulation of a capitalist surplus. Not only the society, but also the individual himself/herself is urged to control or repress the erotic forces in the transgressive movement of bodily expression, for they can destroy the conditions of self-preservation for the individual and harm the economic foundations of the society of growth. Stable relationships and marriages in the modern world often start as erotic encounters and turn into partnerships in economies of growth. When growth comes to a limit and the life energy is completely captured by the restricting schemes and structures of the world, the pressure of the excess energy that we cannot squander in other erotic encounters will turn to depression, negativity in the sense of restlessness, unhappiness, irresolvable conflict, and ultimately to the destruction of worldly stability that presently constitutes the emotional and material conditions of self-preservation. At times, people intuitively struggle to hold such stable structures in place precisely by being unfaithful, for that can be a way to make a suffocating marriage or relationship last longer than it otherwise would. In other words, there will always be a moment in which our existence will be torn apart between the necessities of production and the demands that the excess energy makes on us.

Bataille's conception of eros and the ethics it can bring about has the power to account for the paradoxes of the erotic experience and the way its dynamic space can be generative of new norms. Eroticism is expenditure in a domain marked off by the transgression of laws or rules. Nevertheless, as I have noted above, a transgression such as adultery complies with the transgressed law—this is why erotic experience can often be a paradox (1991a, 124), for transgression both violates and reinstitutes the law. The same holds true for the erotic pleasures that result from the queer transgressions of the heteronormative sexual practices. However, this fact does not close off the possibility that the play of transgression may open the possibility for the challenge and the transformation of the laws, thus giving rise to new norms. The world operates with and imposes the heterosexual binary opposition of woman and man, though the erotic life energy subverts these constructions and makes existence queer in its dynamic, subversive pleasures.

The ethics of the dynamic space of eros must take the notion of singularity seriously and be open to negotiation at all moments of an erotic relationship. The imposition of my own borders upon the other is never ethical and is ultimately destructive of the erotic communication. Bodily borders differ in every erotic encounter. Stable and static borders are a part of our public personality, for we fear and need masks to protect ourselves from possible harm from the others in society. Erotic communication aims at the moment of complete nudity via the dropping of all masks, and we thus come to establish a contact with ourselves in the gaze and the naked presence of the other. However, Bataille does not exclude violence from the dynamic space of the erotic. First of all, he thinks that the leading force of this communication is *negation*. Negation does not show itself only in the transgression of the prohibitions that set the norms for acceptability. Erotic communication can only take place through the negation of separation that makes us individual beings. The overcoming of separation is the interruption of artificially constructed borders, and Bataille never seems to take them for granted.

As *Story of the Eye* may suffice to show, nothing in erotic experiences can prevent my own death or the death of the other. However, it is wrong to infer that rape too may be a radical experience of a renewed contact with immanence. Rape is objectification or reification of the body, and as I have pointed out, Bataille's erotic experience aims at destroying the thing in the body. As an inner experience, it aims at the liberation of the body from being a thing. What is at issue is not the experience of an object by a subject, but the communication of two or more in the unlimited impersonal subjectivity of existence. However, the following question remains: If sovereign experience is "the power to rise above the laws of the society," where can erotic experience find the normativity that would enable someone to take the other's refusal seriously? If violence and evil give us momentary access to immanence, how are the other's life, difference, and sexed being to be respected in the erotic experience? People may die in erotic adventures though a transcendent violence—that is, the assertion of one's power over the other, the ignoring of the other who resists is not part of erotic experience in the immanent sense.

The fact is that erotic experiences may not always be pacific and free of violence. An ethics of eros that comes from Bataille can deal better with the questions of harm, destruction, and violence that the desire for the other may lead to in an erotic relationship. We can better answer the question above if we can distinguish Bataille's position from that of Marquis de Sade. The key in distinguishing their position is the difference between "immanent violence" and "transcendent violence." First of all, immanent violence is a condition for the overcoming of the separation that sets the stage for transcendence and hence power struggles. In Bataille, erotic violence is immanent. In *The Accursed Share,* Bataille talks about Sade's system precisely as "the most consistent and the most costly form of erotic activity," whose condition of possibility is moral isolation, denial of solidarity, and freedom from the respect for others. He makes clear that "solidarity keeps man from occupying the place that is indicated by the word 'sovereignty': human beings' respect for one another draws them into a cycle of servitude where subordinate moments are all that remains, and where in the end we betray that respect, since we deprive man in general of his sovereign moments (of his most valuable asset)" (1991b, 178–79). Expenditure of energy is a negation that, as Blanchot says, becomes apathy in the sovereign man (1991b, 179). In Sade, negation becomes the negation of the partner's interests and existence. Bataille does not deny the affections of pity, gratitude and love, true energy. He writes:

"There is no doubt that the way of individual love obliges us to limit ourselves not only to those possibilities that make allowance for the partner's interest, but also those that the partner herself can bear" (1991b, 174). Marquis de Sade passes beyond this obligation of the individual love by denying the partner's interests and very life and thus opens, according to Bataille, "a new domain to eroticism." Bataille seems to support the Sadean move in denying the social link that attaches someone to a fellow human because community limits the manifestation of sexuality in its free reign. Nevertheless, Sade, in setting the crime as the condition of sensual pleasure, lays down the isolation of the individual, which Bataille denies in erotic communication. The negation of the individuality and of communality when it leads to communication sexed beyond sexual identities dissolves "the close connection between criminal destruction and sensual pleasure" (1991b, 176).

Violence involved in the erotic communication beyond identities is not transcendent but immanent: in that realm of communication it has the character of impersonal existence, a destruction of individuality and public personality. Here the connection between sensual pleasure and crime is dissolved, for I do not distinguish the other from myself anymore. Immanent violence does not set me over against the other in a power position and does not make me higher than him or her. Negation in eroticism denies the separate being; however, what is denied here is not denied for the benefit of some transcendent affirmation. I do not achieve a human or godly transcendence by denying the other's individuality. The notion of immanent violence does not preclude the possibility that no one will, after all, be harmed in erotic communication. We can be harmed, and there would be no one to blame for it. In *Story of the Eye,* Bataille's characters do not come together for orgies to go back to their own lives after the carnal confusion is over. Erotic communication connects their lives in an infinite desire and compassion. The violence that they exert against each other is different from the violence they direct to those who pretend to coincide with their social roles. The release of the abject to the effect of overcoming worldly separation and hygienic hypocrisy is never the end of care and friendly compassion for them, but is *religare,* in the sense of being reconnected. The compassion, here, is first of all respect for the way the other bodies forth in his/her erotic pleasures and to support and welcome his/her pleasures. Negation at work in the erotic experience also paves the way for the impossibility of being indifferent to the other from whom I am not absolutely separated.

In this kind of communication, partners become irreplaceable for each other. Bataille's narratives, such as *Story of the Eye* and *Madame Edwarda,* go beyond works of pornographic imagination if it is true that, as Susan Sontag notes, pornographic imagination tends to destroy irreplaceability by making people easily substitutable by others (1969). Bataille's characters are endowed with intelligence, will, and memory, but they strive to suspend the instrumental reason in erotic consciousness. In his erotic narratives, women do not appear as the victims of male fantasies. As Sontag notes, unlike Sade's character Justine, Bataille's female characters are not exposed to experience in which they are expected to learn, suffer, and transform themselves (1969). The aim is not to teach the victim what the real world is like, but to share a state of consciousness with her. This state of incarnated consciousness transcends the world of power struggles. Indeed, Bataille's way of thinking of our incarnated existence is quite different from Sade's. He knows that the body can only be an object or a thing at the limit, and erotic experience negates the thing in the body. Indeed, Sade and Bataille are concerned with quite different things in sexuality. Sontag is right in emphasizing that Sade's orgies consist of an inventory of a great number of different configurations of mechanical bodies and that he neutralizes the sexuality of all personal connections in order to represent an impersonal, pure sexual relationship. Bataille too wants to neutralize the personal, but he does that in order to experience the impersonal fluid ground of our existence. In the erotic experience, life relates to itself by overcoming the separation and distribution in beings and uses its excess energy for going beyond the profane world of intelligence and work. This is why I think the erotic experience in Bataille cannot be a thirst for annihilation but a source of thinking a new cohabitation on earth.

NOTES

1. The question of abjection is inseparably connected to the theme of death insofar as it concerns precisely the stabilization of the boundary between life and death (1991b, 80–81). It is also connected with the question of sexuality by means of the relation between desire and horror (1991b, 96–97). Bataille emphasizes that the erotic practice brings us back from repulsion (the abhorrence of sexuality) to desire. Although the common sense may take the consciousness of death and eroticism as opposed to one another, Bataille argues that the anguish of death is always linked to eroticism: "Our sexual activity finally rivets us to the distressing image of death, and the knowledge of death deepens the abyss of eroticism" (1991b, 84). Although the questions of abjection and death are central to the question of the erotic, this essay will not concentrate on them. I will attempt to read eroticism in terms of immanent life. However, let us note that, in Bataille's use, the term "life" is not the opposite of death and includes the sense in which "life is a product of putrefaction" (1991b, 80).

2. In *Theory of Religion,* Bataille writes explicitly in a footnote: "I cannot in fact ascribe to subjectivity the limit of myself or of human selves; I cannot limit it in any way" (1989, 32).

3. For Bataille, impersonal, indistinct, immanent existence is divine. See, for example, Bataille 1974, 301. And in *Erotism* Bataille characterizes the explosive nature of life as follows: "We refuse to see that life is the trap set for the balanced order, that life is nothing but instability and disequilibrium. Life is a swelling tumult continuously on the verge of explosion. But since the incessant explosion constantly exhausts its resources, it can only proceed under one condition: that beings given life whose explosive force is exhausted shall make room for fresh beings coming into cycle with renewed vigour" (1986, 59).

4. Bataille read Levinas's notion of *il y a* in *Existence and Existents* and *Time and the Other* as well as Blanchot's writings on *il y a.* It can be suggested that his "impersonal existence" as the ground of subjectivity communicates with the discussions of *il y a* in Levinas and Blanchot.

5. In *Erotism* Bataille writes: "Human erotism is that within man which calls his being in question" (1986, 29).

6. See chapters 11–14 in Heidegger 1991.

7. Nietzsche never denies the superiority of the standards of the human architectural genius: "Here one may certainly admire man as a mighty genius of construction, who succeeds in piling up an infinitely complicated dome of concepts upon an unstable foundation, and, as it were, on running water. Of course, in order to be supported by such a foundation, his construction must be like one constructed of spider's webs: delicate enough to be carried along by the waves, strong enough not to be blown apart by every wind" (1999, 85).

8. Bataille writes: "Under present conditions, independently of our consciousness, sexual reproduction is, together with eating and death, one of the great luxurious detours that ensure the intense consumption of energy" (1991a, 35). In animal sexuality, the squandering of sexual energy "goes far beyond what would be sufficient for the growth of the species. It appears to be the most that an individual has the strength to accomplish in a given moment" (1991a, 35).

9. Even though Bataille often uses heterosexist language in accounting for the erotic experience, in my point of view, it is not clear at all that he submits the logic of erotic desire to heterosexism. That question will be addressed in the following section.

10. How can we be conscious of our lost animality? Even though Bataille believes, just like Nietzsche, that intelligence separates us from such a communication, he seems to affirm with Bergson that we can swim in the reverse direction of intelligence, use intelligence against itself to create the erotic possibility of finding an exit to an organic memory—a self-conscious experience of the internal relation of all living beings. Consuming the excess energy enables us to overcome the intellect in not-knowing and touch the profound ground of our existence in life, nurturing and destructive at once. In Bataille's discourse, the materialization of the erotic desire is a way of negating the servile self, and this is why Bataille thinks that it can lead to the sovereign manifestation of the corporeal life.

11. Bataille writes: "The regret that I might have for a time when the obscure intimacy of the animal was scarcely distinguished from the immense flux of the world indicates a power that is truly lost, but it fails to recognize what matters more to me. Even if he has lost the world in leaving animality behind, man has nonetheless become that *consciousness* of having lost it which we are, and which is more, in a sense, than a possession of which the

animal is not conscious. It is *man,* in a word, being that which alone matters to me and which the animal cannot be" (1991a, 133).

12. For Bataille's reading of "totality," see 1991b, 116–19.

13. According to Bataille, "anguish . . . signifies the absence (or weakness) of the pressure exerted by the exuberance of life. Anguish arises when the anxious individual is not himself stretched tight by the feeling of superabundance" (1991a, 38–39). "Anguish is meaningless for someone who overflows with life, and for life as a whole, which is an overflowing by its very nature" (1991a, 39).

14. See Shannon Winnubst's essay in this volume.

15. For example, such an approach will not license us to condemn, on ethical grounds, the U.S. war in Iraq—a war that Bataille could have interpreted as an inevitable consequence of the accumulation of the American surplus.

16. He uses the term "profound subjectivity" in a few places in 1991b, e.g., 234.

WORKS CITED

Bataille, Georges. 1974. *Oeuvres Complètes.* Paris: Gallimard.
———. 1986. *Erotism.* Trans. Mary Dalwood. San Francisco: City Light Books.
———. 1987. *Story of the Eye.* Trans. Joachim Neugroschel. San Francisco: City Lights Books.
———. 1989. *Theory of Religion.* Trans. Robert Hurley. New York: Zone Books.
———. 1991a. *The Accursed Share: Volume I.* Trans. Robert Hurley. New York: Zone Books.
———. 1991b. *The Accursed Share: Volumes II & III.* Trans. Robert Hurley. New York: Zone Books.
———. 1995. *My Mother. Madame Edwarda. The Dead Man.* Trans. Austryn Wainhouse. New York: Marion Boyars.
Heidegger, Martin. 1991. *Nietzsche,* Vols. III and IV. Trans. Joan Stambaugh, David Farell Krell, and Frank A. Capuzzi. San Francisco: Harper.
Irigaray, Luce. 1985a. *Speculum of the Other Woman.* Trans. Gillian C. Gill. Ithaca, N.Y.: Cornell University Press.
———. 1985b. *This Sex Which Is Not One.* Trans. Catherine Porter and Carolyn Burke. Ithaca, N.Y.: Cornell University Press.
———. 1993. *An Ethics of Sexual Difference.* Trans. Carolyn Burke and Gillian C. Gill. Ithaca, N.Y.: Cornell University Press.
Levinas, Emmanuel. 1978. *Existence and Existents.* Trans. Alphonso Lingis. The Hague: Martinus Nijhoff.
———. 1985. *Time and the Other.* Trans. Richard A. Cohen. Pittsburgh: Duquesne University Press.
Nietzsche, Friedrich. 1999. *Philosophy and Truth: Selections from Nietzsche's Notebooks of the Early 1870's.* Trans. Daniel Breazeale. New York: Humanity Books.
Sontag, Susan. 1969. *Styles of Radical Will.* New York: Vintage.

SIX

ALISON LEIGH BROWN

Malvolio's Revenge

Part One: Smile, with Yellow Stockings

If I were going to paint Bataille, I would call my painting *Smile, with Yellow Stockings*.[1] I would start with an unsmiling photograph of his face and go from there. I would be thinking about Emily Brontë's Heathcliff and Cathy; I would be thinking about Malvolio—his painful ineptitudes. I would be thinking about how one man's evil turns out to be another woman's joke on a meddler, and how things resolve themselves even when we don't know who we are. I would be thinking that Bataille, in the accursed time in which he found himself, spoke sovereign communications in spite of there not being worthy interlocutors. I would paint a tongue and an ear and an array of crossed garters until the photograph was smiling. I would be thinking about Bataille thinking about Racine, hanging out at *Tel Quel*. I'd be happy.

One is influenced by one's first glimpse of a writer, and the first thing I knew about Georges Bataille was that he loved the love between Heathcliff and Earnshaw. Let's start there, at *Wuthering Heights*. We know that Georges Bataille loves Emily Brontë. He tells us so in *Literature and Evil*. Georges Bataille thinks that Heathcliff is evil. He *is* evil. He dreams of evil when he imagines a slow vivisection of those he has loved for entertainment. This dreaming is transgressive. All *pace* Bataille. He writes:

> The mere invention of a character so totally devoted to Evil by a moral and inexperienced girl would be a paradox. But the invention of Heathcliff is

particularly worrying for the following reasons: Catherine Earnshaw herself is absolutely moral. She is so moral that she dies of not being able to detach herself from the man she loved when she was a child. But although she knows that Evil is deep within him, she loves him to the point of saying "I am Heathcliff." (1973, 8)

Bataille remains important philosophically if only for what he writes about evil and for what he writes about transgression. Together these concepts indicate something about loss, temporality, and a glimpse toward an economy without reserve. If pressed by a student, say, or a niece, to say why I find Bataille philosophically important, I would say that in his fiction and in his theory he shows us that while it seems as if there is only one thing, this lived life, there is always a pointing toward there being something else too. Transgression is a kind of dream of evil. Evil is a kind of sovereignty. Evil can be evidenced by cruelty with no other aim than itself. That extra, which is no extra, that place or time of more than *this,* should be valued, treasured, made into myth or ritual. Transgression, for Bataille, is positively related to sexual ecstasy, and the experience of transgression is one of the things that points to this extra, the thing that escapes dialectics or general economy. That such experiences should be made valuable through ritual is because ritual is to community as sexual ecstasy is to individuals. This is what I would say: help make rituals.

Emily Brontë wanders from person to person in *Wuthering Heights.* She uses letters, recitations, gossip, and dreams to arrange placeholders for first-person voices to maintain a level of engagement throughout the novel. Philosophers switch from voice to voice as well. One could say that the philosopher is the wandering first person. Who is writing this passage?

> Literature is *communication.* Communication requires loyalty. A rigorous morality results from complicity in the knowledge of Evil, which is the basis of intense communication.
>
> Literature is not innocent. It is guilty and should admit itself so. Action alone has its rights, its prerogatives. I wanted to prove that literature is a return to childhood. But has the childhood that governs it a truth of its own? (1973, i–ii)

And who speaks of this childhood? Is it Nelly? Heathcliff? Brontë? Who is speaking this? Whose truth is governed by it:

> "You needn't have touched me!" he answered, following her eye and snatching away his hand. "I shall be as dirty as I please: and I like to be dirty, and I will be dirty." (Brontë 1997, 50)

Is this the advent of Bataille's Dirty in *Blue of Noon?* How do we go from one text to the next, so busy or unable to enter that space of reflection, so dirty now, so never clear and distinct? How is it that Bataille, a librarian, can write Dirty? How is it that we let him get away with finding it paradoxical that moral Cathy can love evil Heathcliff? (Is he thinking at some level, how can Emily write Heathcliff?)

I love Bataille. It is a truth about me that almost everyone who knows me also knows, but I don't talk about it very much. I feel a little bit strange about it. The goings-on about sacrifice and all. Everyone knows I love Hegel—I feel strange about that too. All that Orientalism. Scarcely anyone knows that I love Emily Brontë, but I do. What an excess of love, none of it able to go anywhere but outside the general economy. When I read *Wuthering Heights,* I think, Where is this book's Malvolio? Why isn't there a foil for love? Could it be the narrator? Which one? What is the importance of the dogs? Of animality? Why is Malvolio so much more our contemporary than either Heathcliff or even Dirty? Cathy Earnshaw is Heathcliff—or so she says. Viola says, I am not who I am. Bataille is Kierkegaard. I am hot.

It is so hot where I live. Those of us who live here—there are a lot of us—we think nothing of 100 degrees. It is when temperatures rise to 105° or higher that we look at each other in amazement and mumble inanities,

"Hot enough for you?"

"Pretty hot huh?"

as we look at each other again wondering,

"Who is this person who chooses to live here?"

The rest of the year we congratulate each other with smug smiles, thinking of those others shoveling snow, wearing scarves, being cold. Shivering and using hankies. We are attorneys and grocery baggers and professors and programmers and landscapers and the makers of stun guns. We are almost in California and almost in Mexico. Still, we don't talk about water very much. We don't talk about fossil fuel. Lately, like everyone else in the country, we have been talking about evil. "Evil Doers." We're uncomfortable. These words make us feel like time travelers. "Evil Doers," we say, as I presume others do across the country. I presume it occasions discomfort, unease, a sense of being in an accursed time.

It is so hot here the rest of the time that it is hard to maintain rigor. Rigor of any sort is difficult. Having regular meals, talking politely and on point, parking between the lines, keeping one's eyes on the road—all these are difficult, arduous undertakings. The relentless sun, the question to self: Should I back out and just straighten up a little? I'm outside of the lines. Should I try to get by with a drink and supplements in place of food? Still, it is specifically rigor of the mind that becomes our special challenge. Our animality is winning out here in the desert, here in the heat. And it is not special. C-Span. Late afternoon. The cats looking at me with wide angry yellow eyes. Can't you turn up the air? They strut and sit and stare. C-Span flickers. The mute button is on. Angela Davis appears on a screen as if an angel. I haven't been noticing. I find and press the remote's volume. She is saying, "We must stop insisting on the extraordinariness of the U.S. experience," or words to that effect. I want to read her new book slowly and carefully. I will.

I look at bodies of water, sitting here loving Bataille, feeling strange about it, being hot and without rigor. I see a bowl set out for the cats and predictably think about Bataille's saucer of milk, all those other things over and above the milk. There—a bubbling hot tub, beckoning to "sweat the heat out." Over there sits a swimming pool, surrounded by the enemy, the evildoers of the plant world. I bear their scars and have since given myself readily over to plant experts, afraid to touch the living things in my own backyard. I read Bataille, and as I read one volume, I watch the volumes I am not reading literally fade in the sun. It is that bright. Things move that slowly. I close a book and make my eyes like a reptile while I think about Bataille. I consider ordering the DVD of *Wuthering Heights,* but it is too damn hot. I blah blah blah on the phone. Constantly, I worry that I love the wrong philosophers for the wrong reasons. It matters which ones we love. I don't want to get it wrong.

I mention to an old friend and old professor on the phone that I have no rigor in my mind. As soon as I say this, I realize, Oh! This is an odd locution. It is not quite what I mean. He responds, always the analytic philosopher and professor, with homework and with a request (a command?) that I express, if only to myself, what exactly do I mean by rigor? In my mind? He is hilarious when he says this. I am laughing because his phrasing is much like Bill Cosby's when he is repeating a question to a child or small animal: "Did you hear me when I asked you to come here?"—all enunciation and bewilderment at the other's lack of wit. My professor wants to know what I mean by "rigor in my mind." I'm not quite sure. It means among other things that I want to write something worthy of Bataille because I love him. I have to read him more, and this is not a task because it gives so much pleasure. Could it be evil? I read him and forget other aims because he writes passages such as:

> The only element without which choice would make no sense is the prior existence of eroticism. I have adduced the reasons why the transition from animal to man can't be considered sensibly unless we imagine eroticism given—virtually—at one go. Consequently, I can picture man as being open

from the start to the possibility of individual love, much as we are today (think of the persistent rarity of love worthy of the name when one considers numerically limited groups; could refinement of sentiments be so banal these days? What prevails is coarseness of the worst kind). (1991b, 159)

It is not evil to read this passage. I have read these things. Now I find myself reading them again, and I find myself able to merely read. I think that this is probably the right way to go about things now. Now that I understand that, I love freedom. I can finally read Bataille, and with this recognition, a certain peace attends me. Now I can read Deleuze saying of Spinoza, "Freedom is always linked to essence and to what follows from it, not to will and to what governs it" (1988, 71).

So as I read and reread with pleasure the work of Georges Bataille, and with interest—he is better than I thought, I think to myself, sweating and drinking gallons of sparkling water, languishing and stupid; he is wonderful and beautiful. I love Bataille. It is a good thing to read him and a good thing to read Emily Brontë, and how lucky am I to be able to spend my summer this way, in front of a body of water, with sparkling water to drink at hand? My fortune seems unprecedented in its property of "good." It is laughable.

My old friend and professor wants to know why I need rigor in my mind. I had stopped listening to him, wandering around in my mind as I do, and there has been a long pause. I tell him that I am working on a paper about Bataille and that I have been accused of taking an anti-philosophical stance vis-à-vis Bataille and that this hurts because I love Bataille. Or rather that I raise an anti-philosophical specter. I cannot follow this. Furthermore—my blah, blah, blah is unstoppable—the cite used to support my anti-philosophical stance is not from the book where I write these words, but from a Web site that posted my words in European fashion, just the words and my name. No citation. No context. Epigraph-like and unconcluding. Fragmentary. My words sit there, contextless, unable to be true or false in anyone's sense—even Hegel's! Perhaps these authors think it is my Web site and that it is the Web site that is anti-philosophical. I can't tell what they think. My face is hot with shame: anti-philosophical! I know that I am philosophical. The Web site is obscure. Their book is not. People might think that I take a cavalier attitude toward Bataille. I don't care that much what people think, but I am a lover of truth. And I have loved Bataille as a philosopher for decades. His novels are pale to me. They are his white underbelly for me. I don't love his novels. I like them. But if it is transgression I'm looking for, I don't think Bataille. Or Brontë. It is his philosophy that I love, the audacity, the power! I love the absurdity of his exclamations of triumph and naughtiness.

Malvolio's Revenge

I don't know why these comments hurt me, but I'm thinking, This time I had better be careful—I'd better speak for myself. No more throwing myself into characters, no more fooling around. Maybe I should just say: Not only do I love Bataille, but I take him seriously—seriously as a philosopher. Macho-like I will assert that I can laugh with him against Hegel as well as anyone. As you have guessed, I do not actually say any of this to my analytic friend and old professor. Because I am so without rigor, I have paused again. My conversation is languid, lulled, sleepy, hot. Two old friends not talking on the phone, no one saying anything, probably both of us surreptitiously reading, knowing how hard it is to formulate responses to philosophical questions—neither of us wanting to rush the process. We have time. We both think hard. We are breathing.

I tell him that I am working on a paper on Bataille concerning three works: an essay on *Wuthering Heights* that is in a book titled *Literature and Evil;* the novel *Wuthering Heights,* which I also love; and *The Accused Share.* I really love Emily Brontë, I say, she is so tough! I say that these three works interest me and that I want to address these issues: death, freedom, and transgression. I say that the interrelationship between these three issues is one of both rigoretics and erotics. I say that what I am interested in is whether one can have sexiness if there is no place for transgression (the answer is clearly no, but why?) and whether the transgressions of Bataille's fiction remain transgressions for us (the answer is clearly no, but why?) and what is the relationship, then, between death and freedom that can give us a transgression toward sexiness again. I'm embarrassed that I'm interested in sexiness. It is unseemly and unphilosophical. Still, I can't help thinking transgression isn't only abjection. There is the sexy part, which one notices instantly when one is treated to a production of *Twelfth Night* that is neither sexy nor uproariously funny, both of which it must be. Viola and Olivia have to exhibit desire. Viola too. Knowing what she knows and loving the Duke as she does. She has to really want Olivia. And the Duke has to want, if not prefer, Cesario.

I don't actually say any of this while conversing on the phone, in part from guilt—Why should I concern myself with these issues now? Is it unseemly to discuss them when other things have reached this level of insanity? I should be working on regime change, I think. And of course I am, but my fortune! My luck! The ease of my work! I am reading for pleasure!

What I tell my old friend, my former professor, is that I am working on a paper on Bataille and that I cannot understand this paragraph because it is too hot. My inner blah blah is always more verbose than my outer discourse. I read the paragraph out loud to him:

But society contrasts the free play of innocence with reason, reason based on the calculations of interest. Society is governed by its will to survive. It could not survive if these childish instincts, which bound the children in a feeling of complicity, were allowed to triumph. Social constraint would have required the young savages to give up their innocent sovereignty; it would have required them to comply with those reasonable adult conventions which are advantageous to the community. (1973, 6)

Only by dying, first one, then the other, could they maintain this love. Literature is guilty. It is a return to childhood. Literature is Philosophy is Literature. Outside of the social constraints, reader and writer can love each other without reserve. There is no car to park; no food to consider. There is only the free exchange of love, a communication so profound that it shuts out every other thing. It is guilty of refusing the act of life.

The subject of the book is the revolt of the man accursed, whom fate has banished from his kingdom and who will stop at nothing to regain it. . . . I am simply going to recall that there is no law or force, no convention or restraining pity which can curb Heathcliff's fury for a single instant—not even death itself, for he is the remorseless and passionate cause of Catherine's disease and death, though he believes her to be his. (1973, 8)

His fury spins out forever. He is accursed, but he is who he is (innocent child). He is who we want to be: "I am Heathcliff." "I am that madman" (1991a, 197, n. 22).[2]

Part Two: Imagining Transgression in the Suburbs

Here in the heat, Sadie is a luxury. This is not true of all of the women in her neighborhood. To be truthful, it is not a neighborhood. It is an environ. A marvelous milieu. An architected space. Look around in the huge expanse and you will see loosely scattered houses dotting the desert. Look closer and you will see that they are homes. In these homes you will find women and scarcely anyone else. Women reading, women phoning, women lounging, women chatting with one another on "resort-style" recliners next to negative edge pools. These women are beautiful and blonde. They have sculpted bodies and surprised, open faces. They are not luxuries, however. They earn their keep. These women in their luxury homes, absent the husbands, absent the children. The children, and there are few enough of them, are out playing soccer and hockey. They are learning to dance and speak Korean. They are learning how to produce their own pasta, taking lessons in table manners at

Sur La Table or The Kitchen Source. Their teachers are master chefs. The men, the husbands and fathers, live elsewhere, working in Detroit or Zurich or Plano, coming home and zipping out again. The men live in airports and conference rooms. They are self-employed. They cut deals.

The other women are not luxuries in the sense that Sadie is a luxury. They are, instead, useful objects. They volunteer at school, doing everything from chaperoning field trips to cleaning up after field days. They teach the many good things they learned at their very few liberal arts colleges to each other's very few children. Holding BFAs and MFAs and MAs, even MBAs, JDs, and MDs, they impart their knowledge to well-groomed, polite children, gently correcting their grammar, genuinely loving them. These children are easy to love, each child beautiful and charming. These women, who can recite Baudelaire or the meaning of the major Elizabethan dramas, who can recognize symphonies and periods and genres—these women have an easy time remembering each child's name and the names of his or her parents. They maintain elaborate households, calling the exterminators, the gardeners, the landscapers, and the window-washers. They decorate the interiors and exteriors of their homes not once every few years but every season. They make gingerbread houses—or rather, they direct said making—and choose ready-made trees. They hang jeweled eggs on little gold twig trees to welcome spring. They call each other, giving advice about children at this age or that age, referring each other to recent child-rearing books. They tell each other what to serve for dinner when one has lazily (!) spent the bulk of the afternoon exercising by the pool with oodles of sunscreen and the newest movement gadget. They make reservations at restaurants, and they keep in shape. They do crunches and go to dermatologists for peels and lifts. Their breasts are in style. Full when required, reduced when appropriate. They suck fat from here and put it there. They know which undergarment completes which look. They are unembarrassed by push-up bras and wonder at women who fail to wear them—when appropriate. They look fantastic and fabulous and luscious too. They wear little makeup, looking beautiful au naturel—a recherché sort of health. Prescriptives. Origins. They are so happy about the new Sephora! Just like LA! Everything about them is subtle and clean. They manage their husbands' considerable incomes, making them larger than they would be. Their husbands give them elaborate diamond necklaces for Mother's Day, and the women wear them to symphonies and theater in other, better cities.

Sadie looks around and notices this utility; she looks, notices, ultimately perceives herself to be not-useful. She is something else. A luxury. An object of a different sort. Her use-value is on the order of "pet cheetah" or "real

Mercedes." She laughs with her girlfriends about the C class, and then feels vaguely guilty. It is no one's fault that they don't know.

John works very hard and always comes home to her. He loves her beauty. He sends her on vacations. When she is at home, he brings her "skinny food." The low-fat Hot and Spicy Beef from Flo's, a spring salad from Café Crew. He has the butcher at the Pinnacle Peak AJ's hold out several lamb chops until he can pick them up. He will grill them with some peppers and eggplant. He will make her a Manhattan. He loves her intelligence. He doesn't want to come home to stories about how hard it is to get the pool guy to come on time. He doesn't want to hear about the latest methods in child rearing. He is not interested in anyone's feelings about the "low minimum wage." He does not want to rear a child. He is happy that his wife is more than a wife, and he is ecstatic that his wife is not a mother. She is like a man with breasts. She does not complain or nag or invade his space. He is generous about wives—don't misunderstand him. He is not some Neanderthal with out-dated views about women. He understands that the so-called "wife" makes the value in the household more than any other thing. There is evidence-based science on this matter. Everyone knows this. Just as everyone knows that there is no such thing as a happy man who has no wife. Those poor souls with no graciousness in their lives, keeling over of heart attack or stroke be-fore their time! It is just common sense that it is much easier to go to work, make some deals, and bring home the cash. John understands how much harder it is to turn that cash into graciousness and beauty and security and charm. Not to mention that fabulous last turn into more cash. He watched his mother turn his father's slightly better-than-average earning potential into great wealth. He knows personally the worth of a well-run household. Not to mention that everything he knows, he knows because of his mother. The major works of art, the great books, what goes with what suit tiewise, when it is appropriate to wear navy shoes—never—where not to wear button-down collars, what not to order on a first date or important interview, when to eat more than you like to make someone feel good and when not to give a damn about this—yes, this indispensable knowledge comes from his lovely mother. And he is grateful. But he wanted more for himself than even this. He thought: What if I could get a woman and I didn't have to make a baby and she didn't care? What if I could "be with" but also just be quiet. Then I might have someone who is like a man but who is not a man. This is the per-son I want. He wonders if this person will have to be a man. He is not averse to this. But he wants most a manlike person who is a woman. He wants the discreet nature only men have. He does not want a leaky personality. He wants a Sadie-function, the term for which postdates Sadie. Of course.

John can't get enough of Sadie's efficiency and beauty. She is amazing how she gets things done in no time. Plus, she is so beautiful that even now, when he sees her walking down the runway from her latest trip, he can't breathe.

He knows it is not appropriate in this day and age to even think "She's mine," but he thinks this, and he doesn't hold it against himself because he loves her so much.

"I love her so much."

He says to himself all of the time.

"She is so perfect."

He says out loud, quietly to himself in his large, quiet office.

"I am a lucky, lucky man."

This he chants silently, silkily taking his two-year-old Lexus down long, lean desert roads. He feels frugal and wholesome. And he is! He just passed a Viper eating up gas at 1.2 miles to the gallon. And now, what's that? Could it be? Yes, it is a brand-new Lamborghini with Scottsdale Lamborghini plates. He didn't know that they were out yet. Well that is a pretty car, but too flashy for him. Too hard to drive in any case—it would cramp his style. Sometimes he drives around just thinking about how beautiful she is. He likes the placeholders she fills. She looks good on him. He is uneasy sometimes that he doesn't seem to hear her talking much. She is so quiet. They go to the movies, and he sees the big faces on the screen, blank and young. He has never seen a face to compare with Sadie's. Her eyes are smaller than beauty requires. Dark and without communication, they stand on her face moistly. He licks the lids of them when she closes them, and she allows this and responds with quick, low moans. She is excited by virtually anything—a huge plus in John's opinion. She will hold her eyes open for him on command. Her nose is large and Roman. Her mouth, angry or sexy, is always ready to make a polite comment, soft and gravely. His voice and her mouth merge for him. Sometimes she makes words without using her mouth—she is that subtle. He has never caught her eating. There is food there on the plate, and then it is gone. He knows she has eaten it, but he did not see the actions. What grace! How lovely she is!

He has never stopped being excited by her in her presence. She laughs out loud at her own thoughts, saving modulated shows of humor appreciation for his funny stories. She loves to have sex and is never tired of it. She does not pester for sex either. She is ready and willing, aggressive but not pushy. He is proud of her—and of himself for winning her. She does not nag; she does not complain. She smiles.

"She is mine."

Sadie works very few hours. She has few friends.

When she is not working—and what does she *do,* he wonders—Sadie spends her days reading, planning trips to cities where there is an especially good play or concert, making herself more beautiful than she already is, and avoiding her neighbors. Sometimes she takes John with her on these trips; sometimes she doesn't. It works for both of them; this is what they tell each other. When she thinks about John, it is vaguely. She loves him. She cares about him. She brings him home presents. Thoughtful, appropriate gifts. A lovely putting glove just before the current one looks worn. A new racquet right before the club tournament begins. A spare piece of modern lingerie. These geometric masterpieces give the suggestion of a blindfold or mid-Mondrian. She is so perfect, so quiet! Her skin is so smooth. She can imagine a subtle appreciation emanating from him as they smoke cigars, looking across the desert, talking of love, of sexual difference. They think that their relationship resembles Viola's and the Duke's before they realized that Viola is a woman in love. They talk about other art too. Installations of glass. An exhibit of posters depicting cars. A play about the blues. Still, her thoughts of him are vague and without representation. She doesn't know what he looks like, but she knows he is handsome. She cannot make his face in her mind. She doesn't know what he does *exactly,* but she knows that it is lucrative and that he is an attorney licensed in Arizona, Nevada, and Delaware. She manages their money.

"It has been six years since I've been loving women," she tells herself at night. A year ago, it was "It has been five years since I've been loving women." She thinks this, walking around her neighborhood so early in the morning that it is still night to her slumbering neighbors. She thinks, "I am a woman who loves women." She is not a lesbian. She likes lesbians. She frequents their bars and dance clubs. She likes them. She likes to touch lesbians and dance with them and go home with them or not. She does not like to go out for coffee with them, although she likes to do lunch and have dinner with them. She does not like to go to their Pride events and buy jewelry that announces a label. She does not like to donate time to their causes, but she is generous with money gifts to the women she sees on occasion and never more than once. If the truth were to be told, as it rarely is in this life, it would have to be said that Sadie prefers straight women. She loves women who will be the least entanglement. She even prefers married lesbians to straight lesbians. She does not want someone calling her with questions about her future. She does not want to be asked to pay someone's rent or car payment. She does not want to meet the tawdry families, hear the monotonous coming-out stories. She is selfish, our Sadie, and somewhat shallow. That breathy sexy way she has begins to tire those persons not John within a little bit of time, and it is a good thing that she is already somewhere else emotionally when the partner realizes there is nothing going on here. The interior life is dry, brittle, then missing. There is no capacity for evil. No place from which to transgress. She cannot see these dances as celebration and ritual; she cannot hear the love in the stories she is beautiful enough to hear.

To some people, it has to be said, it would be false to not acknowledge this, to some people, Sadie's voice sounds like a little tiny baby voice. Squeak, squeak, squeak. To some people, the clean, even features do not look beautiful at all. She looks vapid and blank like the stretched young faces in movies—without a thought in the world. She is beautiful like a photograph—so pleasing, but not pushing us toward thoughts of something else. Sometimes she looks as if she has never had a fantasy even, as if she just takes whatever is coming to her and then does a breathy little thing she mimics from sexiness. She could be a doll if she weren't real.

Something like truth is coming closer to surface: Sadie does not want to be a lesbian, but lesbians do not want her for long! A more alarming truth is bared: Sadie is most like an old-fashioned man when it comes to women. The kind of man who is caricatured endlessly in literature and television. She is that kind of man, covered in a sort of silky package. But she is herself an old-fashioned woman! She loves women, she likes to be with them, but she doesn't really want to take care of them or get to know them. She doesn't want to know about their *real* lives. Sometimes she pretends that she is a lesbian in the richer, fuller sense. She fancies herself a participant in the community of lesbians. She does not know much about this—only what she learned while she was at college. The anthologies stuffed with personal anecdotes and political theories. She imagines this community the best she can—she sees herself hitting up rich lesbians for consultancy deals, going to community dances and potlucks—this is what she imagines, poor thing. Her imagination is so poor that she thinks her daydreams about making friends with younger dykes whose manners and clothing offend her are in what she calls "the imaginary." She sees herself becoming tolerant of the gender-bending boy girls who fail to excite her at clubs. She stops, not being able to get her mind around this space. She does not want it, and she can't work up what she thinks might be normal guilt about it. Shouldn't she feel bad about this? Shouldn't she speak harshly to herself about her use of a community that opens its doors to her?

God, the truth is that even though she is not a child-hater, she is completely averse to hearing about her lovers' children. It is as if she is in love with the category of woman. Abstract woman: no mother, no sister, no daughter in there. None of the baggage, just the shell woman, with moans and sighs and clever conversation, chin in bridged hands, head coquettishly to one side, tongue playing on the inside lower lip. It is as if she views people as things to appreciate abstractly. Can you conjure the manner in which some people enjoy buying but not displaying paintings, or tasting but not swallowing wine? That is the way she enjoys loving women. When she is surrounded by some woman, she is thinking, I am taking a woman in my hand, I am taking a woman in my mouth. She is not, what do you call it, kissy face. She does not play around; she does not have "playful sex." She does not get involved. She is never dishonest.

Except. Except, John doesn't know. She tells herself that he is right in thinking that she is going to find herself on the beaches of the world. He is right about that. She tells herself, "I love him. I don't love the individual women. In fact," she sometimes thinks further, "I don't love him that much. But he is the closest I've come to loving someone. I should have known that you couldn't lie to someone for years and not expect something similar in re-turn. I've done nothing but look for warmth and skin pressing on mine without demands. Without the fear of coming too close." She tells herself these things but comes full circle so quickly that soon she is saying to her-self, "I love him. I am not lying to him because I don't love them. They are fabric, paper."

It was a surprise meeting Maria. No one had ever talked to her about being a part of a group, a part of an age, in a way that made sense to her. When she looked at Maria, she felt as if she were looking at herself. There was something at Maria's core that reminded her of looking in the mirror. She thought, as she did when observing herself, "Who is this woman? What does she want? Is she capable of happiness?" She had never dared to ask these questions of anyone but herself. She has read all these novels about women in women's communities who partner with each other and raise each other's children or who pretend to be men and women when they are both women or who play both roles. She doesn't mean to be judgmental, but the whole thing seems mildly distasteful to her. She does not have a particular dislike of lesbians. It is people who offend her. (So she tells herself.) And yet when Maria tells her to tell her husband and speaks of this new brand of creature, she feels a resonance with this. She imagines that she might be a part of this new kind of woman. She likes the feeling. What Maria has said to her, after Sadie has confided for the first time, on a beach, in Carmel, that she spends most of her spare time in pursuit of women but that she does not like them or theirs, after she has said this to Maria, God knows why she says this now to her, what Maria says is: "You are the most horrid person I have ever met.

It is unbelievable to me that you should do as you do while thinking as you do. At long last have you no shame? You should not lie to a person with whom you live, of course. And you shouldn't profit from the community building and pain of those you don't care for." Maria says this and more; they are on the beach having spent the day laughing and playing. Right before she is to leave, Sadie tells Maria her increasing sense of contradiction. Maria's anger surprises her. That people care. About anything. She remembered this kind of passion from her prepubescent days at church. Once able to make full arguments, she convinced her parents to leave her be. For God's sake. High-minded, they let her go.

Sadie reminds herself that she is alone, that she does not believe in groups. She thinks that almost every group of people is nauseating. She doesn't mean to have these thoughts. She knows that if she were to verbalize them to anyone, she would instantly be less attractive. Just saying them to Maria resulted in all this thinking mess. Maria is not making sense, just talking and making noises. She knew in advance that it was not an attractive quality to disrespect everyone else. Well, when she was an adolescent, other adolescents found this quality attractive, but she hated them with their black lipstick and dirty clothing. She is disdainful of people who take drugs. Most people who met her, if they could see the contents of her mind—they wouldn't like her! They would be disdainful of her. They would think she had backward social policies. That her life was incoherent. She knows this. She suspects that everyone is equally misanthropic but less self-aware.

One day when she was in stages of becoming a real person, she had given a talk on Bataille, expounding what she thought to be his philosophy of excess, his politics of ritual and art. She was very young, a surprise at the conference. A man in the audience showed her how stupid she was. Didn't she know that Bataille was a fascist? Didn't she know that he advocated the sacrifice of women? Literally. She felt as if he were saying: "Don't you know that Bataille hates you? He'd kill you if he had the chance?" That stung! She had read such things, but she didn't know them. She had let her thoughts stop thinking. She thought that Bataille probably meant something else. She thought he was trying to understand commonality in radically different practices, for one thing. And for another, she thought he was trying to figure out a way for things to feel again, really feel, passion-feel. She listened to this man saying that Bataille was a fascist, and she didn't know what to say. To begin the counterargument would take energy from a reserve she could not find. Never having been too, too attached, she fled the rigor of the academy for the embrace of the business world, and there she found John.

In six years of finding the sort of woman with whom she wants to spend an evening or night, she has not met anyone like those women in books giving potlucks, singing songs together. Maria was right. She, Sadie, is a wrong person. How does she find herself on a beach with Maria? When she tells Maria what she has never even articulated to herself until that point: that she loves John, that she is faithful to him, that she is not in any of her ostensible communities, Maria becomes almost blindingly angry. She says a few cold things about profiting from others' hard work and pain that Sadie cannot follow. Is Maria referring to John? To these women that Sadie doesn't know? That Maria does not know? What pain and work have they offered to her? What makes their clubs different from other clubs? They are businesses. Sadie knows what it takes to do that. What is the big deal? She can't see what Maria is getting at. But then Maria blurts this, stunning in her anger:

"You don't believe that women are people do you? You think that it is not real, these bodies, this talking, all these words?"

Sadie is frightened by this outburst because what the truth would be if she could say it, is that she doesn't think anyone is real. Everything for Sadie is already in the other space beyond what is real. She is on the edge of articulation, and what she would say is that she does not make these fine distinctions. There is only her real: John and Sadie and then nothing else. And John has no face. And hasn't she paid a price for this honesty? She knows what happens when you believe in someone and love him or her. She remembers how it felt to love her mother, and she remembers how it felt to be completely disregarded except as an object to be shown. She doesn't remember particulars so much. She is hazy and vague here too. She does not like all these victims excavating their pain. She hates all the therapeutic rigoretics and reads instead books about the fabrication of victims and the end of psychotherapy. Isn't the fact that she doesn't require anyone to sit and listen to her troubles enough? Hasn't she done enough for the world?

Maria is not impressed. It is the first time that Sadie has tried to communicate with someone at this level, and she sees that like any other skill, practice makes perfect. She has made hash of this, sounding spoiled and, oh God, she sounds unintelligent. Maria has contempt for what Sadie is saying: Sadie can see this contempt, noting at once that this contempt includes this thing, her self, the being behind the words. Maria scoffs at her inner experience. This is not fair. Sadie is not like those others. Sadie is responsible with money. She votes for people who espouse fair economic and social policy. It is not her fault that these people haven't been winning lately and that their not winning profits her. Sadie is too well-bred to complain, but she does think that she is most maligned, in part because her breeding requires her to remain silent, so no one can rush in and take care of her.

What Sadie knows is that Maria does not understand how Sadie engenders productivity. She hates the arrogance of that thought. Still, she just wishes everyone would leave her alone. Is that so much to ask? She wonders sometimes if there will ever be a point when she can relax? Be alone? Be left to her own devices. She is so angry with Maria for pointing out to her how shallow her life is—a life where she is lying to John, who, God bless him, only wants the best for her. Because after her days with Maria, she decides that this is true: that she is lying to John. She comes home from her trip; he meets her at the airport; they go home. Once off the plane, she turns to him and tells him everything. She tells him truthfully and without guile, about the, by now, literally hundreds of women. She has passed herself to herself not only as faithful to John but as a kind of virgin to each successive woman. So many women like to be with someone for the first time, so as she had pretended with Maria but not succeeded, she has pretended so many times before! So when she opens up the gates of honesty, she is also becoming honest with herself. She is carried away:

"Really, John," she is saying, not noticing his face becoming haggard and drawn, "It must be in the hundreds. I can't tell how many. Four hundred?"

Having talked about this with Maria, she feels safe. She is not sure how he will react, but knowing that he loves her, she knows that the outcome, although it may be rocky, will not be unbearable. She chatters on and on, shattering the desert heat with her brittle words. She is warming to her subject matter, feeling so good to finally get everything out in the open, to finally be conversing with the man she loves. She turns to this man and tells him, haltingly, and then chatty-like and all speedy, that she has been kissing and hugging and licking and loving women in cities all over the world. She tells him shyly. And then, not getting a sense from him of how he is feeling, she speeds on, with less and less affect. Just talking words. Maybe they aren't really words that she's saying.

By now, they have parked the car and are sitting on one of many leather couches. They have moved from airport, to car, to home. She has not quite finished, she is still garbling. Blah, blah, blahing. Nevertheless, John now decides to get up from the couch. He looks down at her for a second as if he might strike her. She is not frightened, only puzzled. He does not strike her. He just looks at her for a long, long time. He touches her face gently and turns silently into one of the many rooms in their spacious, formal home. He might die; he might stay; they might have dinner tonight or never speak again. Sadie is not surprised to feel that she doesn't care. Not that much.

❁ *Part Three*

"I am no more mad than you are" (*Twelfth Night* 4.2).[3] It is clear that when we are asked to consider the two lovers coming together in *Wuthering Heights,* we are meant to imagine more than mere ghosts. Not only does Heathcliff dig up Catherine's grave to see her face, he gives orders to have his coffin buried with the side facing Catherine pulled out. "And I bribed the sexton to pull it [the side to Cathy's coffin] when I'm laid there, and slide mine out too" (1997, 276). The popular imagination sings, "Don't fear the reaper" (Blue Öyster Cult 1994), while feeding us Cathy and Heathcliff through a soft lens, their children's limbs flitting across the heath. Ethereal floating. The real book is not gentle about anything: not the weather, not love, not animal companions, not one thing. There, in the book, we are invited to imagine the bodies decaying together. We are shown their craggy graves. Their coffins buried side by side. Linton's coffin, next to Cathy's and to Heathcliff's, tightly locked up.

Bataille writes that Heathcliff is evil because Heathcliff does not want anything in addition to that which he is wanting. Heathcliff is unable to desire something for the sake of something else. As such, he cannot help but be already eaten up by death—by that to which transgression opens up. Bataille writes:

> In as far as it expresses an attraction towards death, and in as far as it is a challenge which exists in all forms of eroticism, Evil is always the object of an ambiguous condemnation. It can be glorious, as it is, for all its horrors, in war. But war has imperialism as its consequence. . . . It would be pointless to deny that Evil always contains a potential tendency to become worse, and it is this that justifies anguish and disgust. But is it no less true to say that Evil, seen in the light of a disinterested attraction towards death, differs from the evil based on self-interest? A "foul" criminal deed is contrary to a "passionate" one. The law rejects both of them, but truly humane literature is the high point of passion. Yet passion does not go without a curse: only a "cursed share" is set aside for that part of human life which has the greatest significance. The curse is the necessary path for true blessing. (1973, 16)

What if the object to which transgression points were Death? The ambiguous condemnation allows us to rail against Evil even while we desire it; it makes the grounding of our Being-toward-Death. This sounds right in theory, especially after so many years; still, Bataille's examples paint the picture of an insane freak, yellow-stockings askew, a fascist. War is not glorious, we might think as we read Bataille (bathing in a kind of self-deception that we notice but that we rightly allow to provide us an escape from, e.g., Homeric adulation of heroics in war). We might think something such as the true blessing is not worth our embracing even passionate Evil, let alone foul Evil. But Bataille brings us back to his vision, his wide-eyed sanity. "Literature is not life" flows around his margins. "Philosophy is not the same thing as life," we can imagine him thinking. "Why must everything be contained by language?" Writing is sovereign because it lets us ask questions, try things on, push the boundaries of our senses, change the actions of our lives, but mostly because it puts us in a position of not being subservient to anything. The reader and the writer in love with each other somewhere else. Why not ask the question and mean it when we ask it: Why is Evil compelling? Why is it there, staring at us from all eroticism but not from all sexuality? Why not imagine answers to these questions? The answer, the main thing, is that asking the question, living the asking of the question, gives us the possibility of blessing, of being good. But the whole thing, it, A=A, requires a kind of mysticism. "I AM joy before death" (Bataille 1985, 238).

"The main thing is always the same: sovereignty is NOTHING." So ends volume 3 of Georges Bataille's *The Accursed Share* (1991b, 441). With this, he wants to open up a new perspective. A place (a time?) where we go beyond consumption and production; where we give up art for art's sake; when we are not bound by dialectical thinking; where we know that salvation is neither in communism, nor capitalism, nor the silence with which one gapes at the Marshall and Truman plans; where one maintains thought without restrictive categories of thought, all the while knowing those restrictions; where we know better than to equate the profane with animality—a place and time for transgression and terrible freedom.

A Derridean reading of Bataille with respect to sovereignty requires us to think about Hegel. More precisely, such a reading forces us to see from the context of Hegel. Hegel, to put it crudely and quickly, works at describing the totality of what is. After Hegel, after the A=A is posited and regarded, eagle-eye-like, the spiritual or dialectical being is necessarily temporal. It, A=A, is over. This means that death itself assures the existence of a spiritual or dialectical being. The negativity that moves this existence is violent. One could read Hegel and think that thinking (philosophy) is necessarily toward death. But if one opens up philosophy, if one expands the relentless negativity that allows even the thought that "it is over" to include creative sacrifice, then philosophy is not just toward and of death, it is of work. What Bataille sees, when looking at many of the same religious practices that Hegel delineates, is that sacrifice does not partake of sovereignty, because sacrifice is essentially servitude.

Another way to put this: Bataille sees that in the lord/bondsman relation, the bondsman does not become lord in every single case. There is no sovereignty in sacrifice. What is sovereign cannot serve—this by definition. What cannot serve, by substitution, is Absolute Knowledge. So, Bataille says, let it go. Or more precisely, don't grow up into that world where imagination is not allowed, where one frets about the all-consuming mouth of negativity, where category restrictions will not allow exceptions to be felt and lived. Let it go. Listen:

> In so far as violence casts its shadow on the being and he sees death "face to face," life is purely beneficial. Nothing can destroy it. Death is the condition of its renewal.
>
> In this union of opposites, Evil is no longer as irrevocably opposed to the natural order as it exists within the limitations of reason. Since death is the condition of life, Evil, which is essentially cognate with death, is also, in a somewhat ambiguous manner, a basis of existence. Though the being is not doomed to Evil, he must try to avoid becoming enclosed within the limitations of reason. Since death is the condition of life, Evil, which is essentially cognate with death, is also, in a somewhat ambiguous manner, a basis of existence. (1973, 15–16)

Death assures the existence of a spiritual or dialectical being. Evil is essentially death. Evil assures the existence of a spiritual or dialectical being. One sees that sovereignty is nothing precisely because it exists within the limitations of reason; it is already as dead as whitened bones. Remember from *The Accursed Share* that death is feared and reviled for the decay it brings and not for its finality. There is foul evil and final (passionate) death, lesser forms of absolute evil and decaying death: points of submission in each case, points of sacrifice and not of sovereignty. There is an invitation here to expand reason beyond prohibitive limitations. Bataille is not interested in merely rewriting the terms of a dialectical structure. He is talking at a concrete and practical level, mystic though he may be:

> The natural domain of the prohibitions is not just that of sexuality and filth; it also includes death.
>
> The prohibitions concerning death have two aspects: the first forbids murder, and the second limits contact with corpses. (1991b, 79)

Heathcliff allows the death of the beloved. Heathcliff decays with his beloved. Heathcliff transgresses what is allowed in death. He rages against it with his massive fury and shows, with his love and his fury, a path to acquiring "true blessing." When Bataille asks us to consider creating our meanings without reserve, without tying ourselves into antecedent categories, he wants us to reconsider everything and to imagine beyond what is offered us. Each context into which we can draw ourselves has to be re-imagined and repainted. In my mind's eye, I am still drawing. This time I sketch Malvolio. He looks like Bataille, eyes looking from under jutting brow, eyebrows moving all over the place, a look of being elsewhere, of having escaped. An unbelievable sexiness: how could it be Malvolio, Bataille sexy? That's wrong! Here he is having his laugh, his revenge. His crime, the crime for which he was done "Notorious Wrong" (*Twelfth Night* 5.1) was to imagine being loved against convention. Servant daring to love mistress takes a turn from bathos to pathos in two hundred short years. Writer, shaking philosophical categories, sits smiling, waiting for counterarguments. This is hard to paint. And yet, it all makes death easier to bear. From death as the occasion to rank souls in some next world, to absolute leveler takes time. Bataille argues:

> Death does not come down to the bitter annihilation of being—of all that I am, which expects to be once more, the very meaning of which, rather than to be, is to expect to be (as if we never received *being* authentically, but only the anticipation of being, which will be and is not, as if we were not the presence that we are, but the future that we will be and are not); it is also that shipwreck in the nauseous. I will rejoin abject nature and the purulence of anonymous, infinite life, which stretches forth like the night, which is death. One day this living world will pullulate in my dead mouth. Thus, the inevitable disappointment of the expectation is itself, at the same time, the inevitable horror that I deny, that I should deny at all costs. (1991b, 81)

Thank you Georges Bataille. You take the gamble, the risk of the accursed share, to open up our eyes to the blind spots that bind us away from noticing that our autonomy, our belief in our sovereignty, starts with a closing off of things that make us uncomfortable. Again he argues:

> But this way of looking at things results in an abstract view, where the immediate abhorrence of, and half-physical disgust for nature—that is, nature as putrefaction—are given arbitrarily as the consequence of a calculation, of a presumed politics of autonomy. As a matter of fact, nothing proves that the struggle for autonomy is not, materially, the consequence of disgust. (1991b, 84)

The revenge of the servants, the underpaid, the "Bastards," is upon us. Bataille escaped all easy explanations of the inevitability of this movement, the necessity of that outcome. He escaped it with his eyes wide open. He joins Emily in watching Mr. Lockwood's complacency with a sort of friendly scorn. Mr. Lockwood, classier than Heathcliff, more urbane, shuffles away, enclosing a sovereign in the hand of a servant. What more chilling sound than the ring of that coin hitting the hard, cold floor![4] He shuffles, he gossips, he opines, he grumbles:

> "They are afraid of nothing," I grumbled, watching their approach through the window. "Together they would brave Satan and all his legions."
> As they stepped on to the door-stones, and halted to take a last look at the moon—or, more correctly, at each other by her light—I felt irresistibly impelled to escape them again. (Brontë 1997, 324)

NOTES

1. In the only scene of the fifth act of *Twelfth Night,* Malvolio utters his last words of the play: "I'll be revenged on the whole pack of you." It is hard to know which is stranger, this line and exit or the Duke's continued use of the name Cesario for Viola. The yellow stockings are not strange, since by now we have become so accustomed to them.

2. The entire note reads: The moment would arrive when passion would no longer be an agent of unconsciousness. It will be said that only a madman could perceive such things in the Marshall and Truman plans. I am that madman. In the very precise sense that there is the choice of two things: Either the operation will fail, or the madman will arrive at the *self-consciousness* I speak of, because reason, being consciousness, is fully conscious only if it has for an object that which is not reducible to it. I apologize for introducing considerations here that refer to a precise fact: that in other respects the author of this book on economy is situated (by a part of his work) in the line of mystics of all times (but he is nonetheless far removed from all the presuppositions of the various mysticisms, to which he opposes only the lucidity of *self-consciousness*).

3. *Twelfth Night* 4.2. Spoken by Malvolio from a dark house to a fool.

4. Lockwood hears it differently than I do. He says, "had he not fortunately recognized me for a respectable character by the sweet ring of a sovereign at his feet" (Brontë 1997, 324).

WORKS CITED

Bataille, Georges. 1973. *Literature and Evil.* Trans. Alastair Hamilton. London: Calder & Boyars.

———. 1985. *Visions of Excess: Selected Writings, 1927–1939.* Ed. Allan Stoekl. Minneapolis: University of Minnesota Press.

———. 1986. *Blue of Noon.* Trans. Harry Matthews. New York: Marion Boyars.

———. 1991a. *The Accursed Share: Volume I.* Trans. Robert Hurley. New York: Zone Books.

————. 1991b. *The Accursed Share: Volumes II & III.* Trans. Robert Hurley. New York: Zone Books.

Blue Öyster Cult. 1994. Don't Fear the Reaper. In *Cult Classics.* New York: Herald Records.

Brontë, Emily. [1847] 1997. *Wuthering Heights.* Enriched Classics Series. Intro. by Laurie Langbauer. New York: Simon & Schuster.

Deleuze, Giles. 1988. *Spinoza: Practical Philosophy.* Trans. Robert Hurley. San Francisco: City Lights Books.

Shakespeare, William. *Twelfth Night.* Ed. Jonathan Crewe. New York: Penguin Putman Inc., 2000.

BODIES AND ANIMALITY

Part Three

SEVEN

LADELLE McWHORTER

The Private Life of Birds: From a Restrictive to a General Economy of Reason

> *To think is to slip in the night on the slope of a roof without parapets,*
> *in a wind that nothing appeases.*
> GEORGES BATAILLE, *The Unfinished System of Nonknowledge*

How I Started Thinking about Birds

My partner is an avid bird-watcher, so for Valentine's Day I decided to surprise her with a custom-made bin for her birdseed. I built it out of plywood and old two-by-fours, painted it green to match the shutters of our house, and fitted it with a raccoon-proof latch. But I wanted it to be more than a serviceable cabinet—it was a Valentine's Day surprise, after all. So inside the bin's lid, I decided to paint a Valentine message in a colorful scene of birds gathering around a birdbath. I thought she'd like it—or if not, she'd at least like me for trying so hard. And that's what we aim for on Valentine's Day, after all, right?

Before building the bin, I had rarely watched the birds she liked to watch at the feeders she hung in the front yard, even though they were clearly visible from my chair in front of the computer in my study. I took a mild interest in her excited reports of finches and bluebirds and chickadees, and I entertained the possibility of constructing a martin house, because martins eat insects that damage vegetable gardens. But I wasn't deeply thrilled by the presence of a ladder-backed woodpecker in our spindly pecan trees, and I didn't know the difference between a thrasher and a titmouse. When the cats caught a bird, as they did now and then, and wounded it terminally, it was my job to put the thing out of its misery quickly by breaking its neck with my hoe. One hoe-length is about as close as I ever got to a bird.

All that changed when I started painting the Valentine's Day card inside the lid of the birdseed bin. I had to start looking at the birds. First of all, since I wanted the eight birds in the picture to represent local species, I had to pay attention to what my partner said she was looking at through the binoculars. That meant sometimes I had to look too. And I wanted a nice range of colors, so I had to remember which species were red and which were blue and which were too dull to bother with. I listened when she talked about them to figure out which ones she especially liked. When she wasn't around, I pored over the *Audubon Backyard Birdwatcher* that I'd bought her the year before but had never perused except in the nature aisle at Barnes & Noble. Before long I had selected my eight birds and was making preliminary sketches of the scene.

I think it was looking at the birds in the photographs that really set me thinking. They are so amazingly beautiful. Many of them are in flight or just coming in for a landing. Each feather is perfectly spread or angled to slice or glide through the air. Before I looked at the pictures, birds were hardly any more to me than flecks of color and bouts of chirping. Looking at these photographs gave me a sense of their seemingly ephemeral bodies as weighty solids, as muscle and water and bone, and of how absolutely streamlined they are and how perfectly controlled. No marble statue of a Greek athlete could give a more acute impression of proportion, coordination, and strength. Their colors in the photographs are intense, even the grays and browns, and as precise as the birds' forms. The downy woodpecker, for example, has a series of white spots on each gray feather that look like white bands when it spreads its wings. But what struck me hardest was the way their bodies expressed the movement they were built to execute. Even in perfect stillness, they seemed about to escape the page. My eyes slipped over their sleek feathered muscles without halt, as if I myself were the air they were gliding through. Were these representations of birds or representations of pure, unhampered motion—pure flight?

I dream of flying. These are always beautiful, joyful dreams. I know Freud says such dreams are sexual, but, while they are pleasurable in the extreme, they don't seem sexual to me. I have sexual dreams too; they consist of having sex. Dreams of flying are more intense, more physically dispersed and all-encompassing, and as a result far more simply sensual than that. They just *are* sensual and nothing else, not social, not gendered, not meaningful. In flying dreams, I am bathed in air and light and move in them and with them effortlessly. Desiring to move is motion incarnate; there is no gap between thought and event. I can go in any direction, at any speed, supported and caressed by the nothingness of endless open space. I feel the cool pressure of wind along the muscles of my bare arms as I turn and dive and soar, without hesitation, without destination. Sensation is but waves of friction at the limit between sky and not-sky. I am energy and movement without impediment. Flight is ecstasy. In those photographs of the birds, I thought I saw the feelings from my dreams.

When I began to paint the birds, the sensation of incorporation of their apparent motion intensified. Paint is a fluid, and the motion of painting is a stroke. The very gesture of painting their bodies seemed to impart to my hand and arm and shoulder the feel of wind stroking wing. As the pigment spread in the light, each feather came to life for me; I began to know each of those eight bodies in their mechanical capacity, in their power to move with and through and against the air; I felt dispersed through them, knowing their motive power as if it were my own. I wish I could describe this process, these feelings, more clearly. In it I knew something I do not, cannot, know. There was a kind of becoming that cannot ever be.

Fascinated now, I began to watch the birds through the binoculars even when my partner wasn't home. I became familiar with many more species, learned when to look for which individual, which pair. From my chair in the study, I threw my gaze among them, unbeknownst to them, into their little circle around the feeders. Through the binoculars, the ladder-backed woodpecker actually had a ladder-back, a cross-hatching of black and white the length of its feather shafts. The house finches' heads glowed deep red, and their necks broke into purple beads as if someone had melted crayons on their crowns. As spring returned, the goldfinches' feathers put on layers and layers of brilliant new gold. The bluebirds shimmered an indescribable purple-blue in the sunlight. The birds sailed and dove and perched and sang, and I watched it all through those binoculars. I spied on them.

It isn't nice to spy. There's something lewd about watching others' lives rather than getting on with your own. And of course gazing through a pair of binoculars is hardly a good way to get the class prep or the housework done. But I couldn't help myself. I do it still. I keep the binoculars unsheathed beside my keyboard so I can grab them the instant an opportunity presents itself. I'm spying on a goldfinch even as I write. Just last week, I affixed a small hummingbird feeder to the windowpane. Much of the afternoon a pair of rubythroats have whirred no more than an arm's length from me. I drink them all in as they drink in the sugar water. Now, if I fail to see a bluebird or a Carolina chickadee for more than a couple of days, I feel restless and anxious. I suppose I am addicted. Some intervention may be necessary here.

🌀 *Carno-phallo-logocentrism: One Woman's Struggle*

When I describe all this looking, especially the ways in which it is mediated, I feel a bit uneasy. I am keenly aware that nobody has much good to say philosophically or politically about the kind of behavior I'm engaging in. There are any number of aspects of it that may be suspect. For example, what about this imposition of my own fantasy life and projects on the community of birds? I'm not really looking at those birds, I imagine someone will say; I'm just seeing what my experience and desires lead me to see, exploiting the birds for my own sensual enjoyment. And that's possible because I'm really distanced from the birds, holding myself secure behind walls and windowpanes, not really looking at birds but at images of birds produced by apparatuses like binoculars and cameras and publishing firms. It all seems very tawdry, doesn't it? It reeks of carno-phallocentrism.

First of all, it's predatory. I'm stalking these birds. Of course, I don't intend to eat any of them, but in a sense, my looking is a very carnal act. Hidden in the shadows, am I not taking a deep erotic pleasure in staring at these delicate creatures who cannot stare back? There's an unsavory fleshy dimension to this whole enterprise. One could suggest that I am using them like a Peeping Tom uses the young girls he watches while he masturbates. Which brings us to the phallus.

Isn't it really all about mastery? I've captured the birds with my gaze—technologically enhanced by lenses and chemicals and consumer capitalist conglomerates that own businesses like Nikon and Barnes & Noble. Almost like Adam exercising his dominion, I can name the birds now. I know the difference between a titmouse and a towhee. Everything is carefully identified, and thus my own identity—my unicity, propriety, my uprightness—is assured. I know who is human and who is bird, and who is really on top regardless of how high we can reach. And secure in that hard and upright sense of self, I play at identifying with the birds. What are they going to do about it? Resist? They've got no say. How phallic is that? Ask Luce Irigaray.[1] It's all about phallic oneness, hard ego boundaries, and my ability to penetrate their circle with my level gaze.

Apparently, Charles Darwin made similar mistakes. It's a danger that science always courts and not infrequently succumbs to. Instead of just looking at the natural world, Darwin projected his own desires, assumptions, and fantasies onto it. He failed to remain objective. And people noticed. Just three years after Darwin published *On the Origin of the Species,* Marx wrote to Engels: "It is remarkable how Darwin recognizes among beasts and plants his English society with its division of labor, competition, opening up of new markets, 'invention,' and the Malthusian 'struggle for existence.'" And Engels wrote: "The whole Darwinist teaching of the struggle for existence is simply a transference from society to living nature of Hobbes' doctrine of 'bellum omnium contra omnes' and of the bourgeois-economic doctrine of competition together with Malthus's theory of population."[2] How embarrassing! But later critics are even more derisive, especially concerning the theory of sexual selection.

Like my partner (and now me), Darwin was an avid watcher of birds. Pages and pages of *On the Origin of the Species* and *The Descent of Man* are given to descriptions of birds, especially pigeons, which Darwin took to breeding. And his prose is effusive. Here is an example:

> Compare the English carrier and the short-faced tumbler, and see the wonderful difference in their beaks, entailing corresponding differences in their skulls. The carrier, more especially the male bird, is also remarkable from the wonderful development of the carunculated skin about the head; and this is accompanied by greatly elongated eyelids, very large external orifices to the nostrils, and a wipe gape of mouth. The short-faced tumbler has a beak in outline almost like that of a finch; and the common tumbler has the singular inherited habit of flying at a great height in a compact flock, and tumbling in the air head over heels.[3]

And so on from there at extraordinary length. Moreover, pigeons are not the only bird Darwin seems fascinated with. In the index of *The Descent of Man,* one finds that the entry for "birds" is a full 4.5 inches long; whereas, by way of comparison, the entry for "bees" is scarcely three-quarters of an inch, and the entry for "brain, of man" but one and five-eighths inches. ("Dogs" fare a bit better, with almost two inches.) In addition, there are five separate entries for various bird species, the one for "blackbirds" being almost one inch in length by itself. And there is even a separate entry for "beak." In a book ostensibly about human beings, why so much attention to birds? A catalog such as the one Darwin amasses could only have been compiled by someone who was utterly obsessed.[4]

Darwin's theory of natural selection holds, as we know, that species change over time as the conditions in which they live change. That is, as circumstances shift, rendering resources more difficult to obtain, those that are better able to get at or take advantage of what exists are more likely to propagate, and thus the next generations are more likely to have their heritable

traits than the traits of those members of the species who died prior to reproducing. Over time, this results in intra-species variation's increasing to
the point that a population becomes different enough to warrant designat-
ing it as a species distinct from the one from which it diverged. Environmental change is the primary impetus for species divergence, but even in a
stable environment there are two other ways that species change might
come about, according to Darwin's work.

One way is through mutation, a mechanism Darwin postulated but did
not understand because of his unfamiliarity with cell physiology and genet-
ics. (He simply thought in terms of random variation, which any gardener
or shepherd or pigeon-breeder inevitably runs across.) Most often, mutation
results in characteristics that are either insignificant in relation to the individual's ability to compete for resources or are detrimental to the individual,
resulting in sterility or early death. Occasionally, however, a mutation results in a characteristic that enables an individual to compete more successfully. Over time, that trait is likely to be passed on, and those individuals
without it may be less and less able to compete against their better-adapted
siblings. Therefore, even in a static environment (were there ever to be one),
it is still quite possible for a population to diverge from its ancestors enough
to be considered a separate species.[5]

Yet a third mechanism for species change, according to Darwin, is what
he called sexual selection. He assumed that males of any species—but he was
particularly interested in birds—are eager to compete with other males for
the possession of (i.e., the right to inseminate) females. But females of most
species do not compete with other females for possession of (the right to extract sperm from?) males. Instead, females demurely sit by and watch while
the males make a display of themselves. Then, at a certain point, the ladies
choose whichever male most pleases them—be it with his beautiful song, his
comely tail feathers, or his exhibition of erotic dance. And thus these sex-
specific traits—the ones most obvious are among male birds like the peacock, the American cardinal, the goldfinch, or the ruby-throated hummingbird—are passed along to the next generation, despite the fact that they are
unrelated to the business of survival and the mechanisms of reproduction.

Now according to many critics, Darwin is on really thin ice here. Not
only is he seeing nineteenth-century capitalism in the natural world, but
now he is adding nineteenth-century sexuality to the picture. "Make no mistake," feminist theorist Ruth Hubbard writes, "wherever you look among
animals, eagerly promiscuous males are pursuing females, who peer from behind languidly drooping eyelids to discern the strongest and handsomest.
Does it not sound like the wish-fulfillment dream of a proper Victorian gen-

tleman?" (Hubbard 1983, 55). The theoretical upshot, as Hubbard points out, is that males are supposedly the primary means by which the species adapts. All females will get inseminated, whether they are superior in any way or not. They need only be born without a sterility-producing mutation and survive to puberty; they do not need to compete for sperm. Only males will win or lose the right to reproduce, and so only males with both the best adaptations *and* the most aesthetically pleasing demeanor will pass their traits on to the next generation, Darwin maintains. And he readily generalizes from songbirds to human beings.

> With social animals, the young males have to pass through many a contest before they win a female, and the older males have to retain their females by renewed battles. They have also, in the case of mankind, to defend their females, as well as their young, from enemies of all kinds, and to hunt for their joint subsistence. But to avoid enemies, or to attack them with success, to capture wild animals, and to invent and fashion weapons, requires the aid of the higher mental faculties, namely, observation, reason, invention, or imagination. These various faculties will thus have been continually put to the test, and selected during manhood; they will, moreover, have been strengthened by use during this same period of life. Consequently in accordance with the principle often alluded to, we might expect that they would at least tend to be transmitted chiefly to the male offspring at the corresponding period of manhood. (Darwin 1968?, 873–74)

Just as female birds sit quietly and watch the male display, so female humans select their mates as a result of this kind of competitive spectacle. Women pay attention to men only and do not compete among themselves. "Thus," says Darwin, "man has ultimately become superior to woman. It is, indeed, fortunate that the law of the equal transmission of characters to both sexes has commonly prevailed throughout the whole class of mammals; otherwise it is probable that man would have become as superior in mental endowment to woman, as the peacock is in ornamental plumage to the peahen" (1968?, 874).

"So here it is in a nutshell," Hubbard sums up, "men's mental and physical qualities were constantly improved through competition for women and hunting, while women's minds would have become vestigial were it not for the fortunate circumstances that in each generation daughters inherit brains from their fathers" (1983, 56). It is no coincidence, she contends, that Darwin put forth his theory of sexual selection in the midst of what we now call the First Wave of Feminism, when women in Britain as well as the United States and elsewhere were agitating for the right to enter universities and the professions—that is, to compete with each other and with men for status and resources and to obtain the financial independence to choose to take themselves out of the gene pool altogether if they liked (1983, 61). Charles Darwin was a social conservative anxious to naturalize and thereby preserve his society's status quo.

See what kind of trouble you get into if you start projecting your own ideas and desires and fantasies onto the natural beings you observe? You can make a real ass of yourself without even realizing it. You have to be careful, which is a matter of being scrupulously honest with yourself, painstakingly accurate in your descriptive claims, and attentive and fair to the beings you observe. That's a lot of work, and it's hard.

🌸 *But Then It Gets Worse*

So what should I do if I want to keep looking at the birds? I don't want to exploit them or do them any injustices. The answer seems to be to get hold of myself and withdraw myself, my own peculiarities of attitude and history, from the act of observation. Really knowing the birds and not just projecting my own fantasies onto them seems to demand this. To know the birds as I want to and sometimes feel I do seems to require that I put aside my desires and passions and just look. Good thinking, reasoning, and understanding derive from that.

But everybody knows that this is a losing proposition. Feminists have been critiquing this notion of objectivity as a prerequisite for knowledge and a foundation for rationality for more than twenty years. The whole idea that we even *can* take up a perspective on the world that isn't rooted in our embodied, material experience (including experiences of need and of fear) is a phallocentric fantasy itself. Talk about the valorization of the self-contained subject of knowledge with its hard ego boundaries! In order to set aside my self, I have to be completely sure exactly what is my self and what is not, which presupposes that my self is a definite, self-identical, unitary thing. Then, having boxed my self up and put it in the attic, I have to enter into the world as pure, disembodied, and ahistorical intellect and observe it with disinterest. Sound likely? The truth is, nobody ever manages to achieve that kind of detachment from themselves; if we did, we wouldn't be human anymore. As Bataille says, perhaps anticipating Irigaray, "Man, or self, is actually related to nature, and therefore to what he denies" (1988a, 115). If good thinking, reason, knowledge require a disembodied, ahistorical subject, we might as well give up now and embrace ignorance and skepticism.

Elizabeth Grosz sums up this epistemological problem when she writes, "The crisis of reason is a consequence of the historical privileging of the purely conceptual or mental over the corporeal; that is, it is a consequence of the inability of Western knowledges to conceive their own processes of (material) production, processes that simultaneously rely on and disavow the role of the body" (Grosz 1993, 187). To correct this problem, we have to avow the role of the body in the production of knowledge, to acknowledge the ways in which our material circumstances condition how and what we think and know. That is the only way to de-phallicize reason and the only way to make reason an enterprise in which non-phallic beings, as non-phallic, can engage. For as Genevieve Lloyd pointed out in 1984, historically in Western epistemology as well as in popular culture, femininity has been considered more or less antithetical to reason, and women have been excluded from participation in endeavors wherein reason plays a role: "Rational knowledge has been construed as a transcending, a transformation or control of natural forces; and the feminine has been associated with what rational knowledge transcends, dominates, or simply leaves behind" (Lloyd 1984, 2).[6] Thinking, reason, and knowledge must be re-thought, de-phallicized, both to break down the barriers that we call sexism and to address the crisis of reason that leads to radical skepticism.

Can we conceive of thinking, reasoning, and knowing non-phallicly? Can we conceive of mentality as continuous with, rather than utterly distinct from, materiality, especially the materiality that is our bodies? Feminists like Grosz seem to gesture in such a direction. "Given the prevailing binarized or dichotomized categories governing Western reason and the privilege accorded to one term over the other in binary pairs (mind over body, culture over nature, self over other, reason over passions, and so on)," she writes, "it is necessary to examine the subordinated, negative, or excluded term, *body* as the *unacknowledged condition* of the dominant term, *reason*" (Grosz 1993, 195). The place to begin is with the body. If we can re-think the body as something other than Cartesian matter in motion, a thought-less machine, think of it as thinking being, maybe we can find ways to exist knowingly and yet fairly, respectfully, and nonviolently alongside beings, like birds, who are not us— and even alongside those who are.

All right then, my task is to re-think the body such that thought, reason, and knowledge could arise there. If I do that, then I'll find a way—we hope —to re-think thinking, reasoning, and knowing as embodied activities so that it will be possible to engage in those activities without making an ass of myself by anthropomorphizing non-anthropic things, without projecting myself on the world to the exclusion of the real differences that constitute real things. Then it will be safe to turn my gaze to the birds.

However, as much as I agree with Elizabeth Grosz (and I do, adamantly!), as much as I believe in the necessity and importance of this project of re-thinking, I'm very uneasy about it. *And that is the reason why I'm writing this essay.* I've tried diligently for years to re-think bodies as thinking things, and with some success. I've written about gardening and eating and dirt and dancing and sexuality—and I'm not about to stop. But I'm afraid something is wrong in this approach.

Here's what worries me: Maybe the point isn't, or shouldn't always be, to know—or at least to know as knowing has been understood for the past four hundred years.[7] Maybe in my rush to get better at thinking (after all I *am* a philosopher), to get observation and reason just right, I forget something that my experience with the birds carries within it. I want to try to explain that uneasiness, that suspicion or fear of mine. I want to try to look at it and see if it means anything. I'll begin by looking at one common means that I and others have used to conceive of thinking as essentially embodied.

🜍 *Mr. Darwin's Triumphal Return*

For all his faults, we really think Darwin was right, don't we? Natural selection just makes sense. Species are not fixed, as our predecessors thought. They do change with time, and how they change has to do with which individuals survive to procreate and how many times they succeed. I just don't doubt this. At most, I could be convinced, maybe, that there were factors in addition to environmental pressure and genetic mutation (although I'm too enamored of the theory as it stands to think of any) but not that the theory of natural selection is false. Mentality, then, is just an evolutionary outcome. As Darwin himself wrote in one of his notebooks, "[T]he mind is [a] function of the body" (1996, 80).

I believe that; the mind is a bodily function, a set of processes that persisted in the human gene pool and were amplified with time because they are so very useful, given our structure and physiological needs, for surviving against the odds and procreating successfully. Darwin writes:

> Of the high importance of the intellectual faculties there can be no doubt, for man owes to them his predominant position in the world. We can see that in the rudest state of society, the individuals who were the most sagacious, who invented and used the best weapons or traps, and who were best able to defend themselves, would rear the greatest number of offspring. The tribes, which included the largest number of men thus endowed, would increase in number and supplant other tribes. . . . At the present day civilised nations are everywhere supplanting barbarous nations, excepting where the climate

opposes a deadly barrier; and they succeed mainly, though not exclusively, through their arts, which are the products of the intellect. It is, therefore, highly probable that with mankind the intellectual faculties have been mainly and gradually perfected through natural selection. (1968?, 496–97)

As a side note (is it a side note?), I will point out that in 1878, just seven years after Darwin wrote these words, the British discovered gold in Tierra del Fuego and began employing their allegedly superior intellects in trying systematically to exterminate the native Selk'nam, whom they declared a "dangerous obstacle to settlement." Hunters were paid to kill them at the rate of one pound sterling per pair of ears, more for the ears of a pregnant woman together with the ears of her fetus. They imported mastiffs to run people down, poisoned sheep with strychnine in hopes the Selk'nam would eat them and die, and inoculated children with fatal diseases (Taussig 1993, 87). Darwin had visited Tierra del Fuego while aboard the H.M.S. *Beagle* in 1832 and had commented at that time upon "how entire the difference between savage & civilized man is" (1934, 118). No doubt he saw the empire's genocidal approach to self-enrichment as evidence of its high degree of civility as well as an inevitability in the course of natural selection. But I will pass over Darwin's highly questionable assumption that the people who win wars are smarter and better than the people who lose them in order to grant him his fundamental point: We think, first of all, because our bodies need to think in order to survive. Thinking is a physiological function, an organic capacity that constitutes a heritable trait like taste buds and opposable thumbs. I think; therefore, I live. This means that thinking, reasoning, and knowing developed as bodily possibilities and are contingent upon the types of bodies that we have. Mark L. Johnson has developed that idea at some length:

> Human beings are creatures of the flesh. What we can experience and how we make sense of what we experience depend on the kind of bodies we have and on the ways we interact with the various environments we inhabit. . . .
>   All of this meaningful, occasionally thoughtful, interaction begins for us at birth, or even earlier, and so it comes to us prior to our learning any language. It depends, therefore, not primarily on propositions and words, but rather on forms of understanding and reasoning that are rooted in the patterns of our bodily activity.
>   . . . [O]ur conceptualization and reasoning are grounded in our embodiment, that is, in our bodily orientations, manipulations, and movements as we act in our world. No matter how sophisticated our abstractions become, if they are to be meaningful to us, they must retain their intimate ties to our embodied

modes of conceptualization and reasoning. We can only experience what our embodiment allows us to experience. We can only conceptualize using conceptual systems grounded in our bodily experience. (Johnson 1999, 81)

Darwin makes a related comment in Notebook N: "Our faculties are more fitted to recognize the wonderful structure of a beetle than a Universe" (1996, 81). Our perceptual apparatus is geared to the world at the level where it is most useful for us to pay attention. We see the part of the spectrum wherein our food sources generally appear; we hear sounds at frequencies made by the things that pose a threat to us; we smell molecules no larger than a certain size (generally about ten angstroms in width), because those are the molecules our prehistoric ancestors most needed to consume or avoid.[8] And reasoning, as an extension of that perceptual apparatus, is a way of solving the problems (getting around obstacles to food sources or evading or defeating oncoming enemies) that our perceptual apparatus reveals. As Horkheimer and Adorno put it in *The Dialectic of Enlightenment,* "Reason serves as a universal tool for the fabrication of all other tools, rigidly purpose-directed" (2002, 23).[9] While of course there is play in the system—mutations that do not kill us prior to procreation may remain part of the gene pool even if they serve no useful purpose—the development of our capacity for thought as a whole is the product of the struggle for the continued existence of our species, reproduced in successive generations because of its vital utility.

Thus construed, our limited intelligence seems hardly the laudatory, semi-divine endowment that definitively separates us from the brutes; it is but one adaptation among others, comparable to the claws of the cat and the green coloration of the tomato hornworm—hardly a quality to be multiplied to infinity, projected into the heavens, and worshipped as the source of all that is. Reminding ourselves of the evolutionary facts with some frequency is a good way to keep ourselves humble. I'm all for that. There's way too much arrogance in the world (much of it white, male, and heavily invested in oil and pharmaceuticals).

As I say, I believe ardently in this project of re-thinking thinking bodily. I believe in it as a feminist, as a philosopher, and as an environmentalist. I believe in it in my viscera because I think our species' and our ecosystem's future depends on it. So I really hate to raise any objections at all.

But . . .

If my whole strategy for re-thinking thinking bodily hangs on the idea that we think because thinking enabled us as a species to work more efficiently and defend ourselves and thus survive, well, how am I going to think about the thinking I do while looking at the birds? Utility doesn't have a whole lot to do with what is happening between me and them. After all (I'll say it again), I'm not going to eat them. And they're not going to teach me how to fly. And watching them wastes time and delays grading essays and getting dinner ready. In my involvement with the birds, utility and efficiency don't seem to play a major role. Something else is going on, and that something, I suspect, is very central or basic to human thinking, yet at its heart has nothing to do with self-preservation at all. If I really want to re-think thinking—and I do, because I think the survival of the planet may be at stake (there's a little superhero in all of us)—maybe I'd better start paying some real attention to thinking without imposing the category of utility. Maybe bodies think regardless of whether thinking helps them preserve themselves. Maybe living bodies are not really all about self-preservation after all.

🌀 *Darwin Meets Frankenstein*

Victor Frankenstein's science project was really quite unnecessary. It went beyond any assignment given him by his professors (certainly none of my reasonable, well-adjusted undergraduates would have done more than the minimum to get their grade), and its product was something the world hardly needs: yet one more man. There are more than enough human beings on this planet. Admittedly, there were fewer in the nineteenth century, and they were not distributed over the landmasses in quite the ways that European capitalist expansion demanded (hence the African slave trade), but even then no one thought the total number of people on earth was dangerously low, nor was the sex ratio a problem. More men were not needed, and more means for producing men were not needed either. Victor stitched together his monster-man just because he wanted to see if he could. He was intoxicated with pure-grain possibility. If the whole thing nauseated him after the fact, that is just one more bit of evidence that his work was not work at all, not a productive enterprise but a frenzy of ecstatic expenditure; when he came to himself later, the long night left him exhausted and embarrassed rather than enriched.[10] Victor had the good sense, though, to take the cure, the hair of the dog; he spent the rest of his life in a frenzied chase across the frozen north, driven by a desire to stop what he himself had animated. Victor Frankenstein was the antithesis of Enlightenment rationality.

But Frankenstein did the seemingly impossible; he restored and reanimated putrefied tissue. His fictional work foreshadowed modern-day organ transplants and electrocardial resuscitation. The most irrational thing he did, it seems, was to repudiate his discoveries. Frankenstein was a genius, but he certainly lacked the vision as well as the spirit of the entrepreneur.[11]

Despite the key role of utility in the theory of natural selection, Darwin's Nature is not totally unlike Victor Frankenstein. It, too, can be viewed as a kind of ongoing frenzy without *telos,* without reasoned goal. The order we perceive in the natural world is not the order of rational production and intelligently planned growth. Even equilibrium cannot be said to have any particular value in this ever-shifting give and take. On the contrary, any order the natural world evinces at any given moment is simply the present result of the frenzy—the "system" is whatever elements or entities can coexist at a given millisecond. Thus, alongside the beautiful symbiosis of flowers and pollinators, of humans and the amoebas that live in our guts, there are also three-legged chickens and two-headed calves and every few weeks new viruses waiting to board our sinuses and our intercontinental jet planes. Natural selection isn't the mechanism that produces the things of this world; it is just the law that kills most of them. Darwin may have meant to be explaining how it was that species would, necessarily, change over time. But once you take change seriously, recognize the frequency of mutation, and take account of the astronomical rate of reproduction in microscopic life as well as in insects and plants, his work really only explains why the whole ecosystem doesn't change more rapidly, entirely, overnight.

The excess constantly produced is simply slaughtered. Half the newly hatched praying mantises eat the other half, sibling rivalry taken to a Dionysian extreme; and tons and tons of pine pollen, sperm of gymnosperms, turn the surface of the rivers lime-green and coat our cars and windowsills and clog our bronchial tubes; and fat blackberries in rain-soaked fields fall to the ground to ferment in the heat, and the blue jays, drunk on their wine, fall prey to well-fed house cats hunting for sport. Nature is orgiastic and utterly irresponsible. As Bataille insists, "On the surface of the globe, for *living matter in general,* energy is always in excess; the question is always posed in terms of extravagance. The choice is limited to how the wealth is to be squandered" (1991a, 23). And further on, "I insist on the fact that there is generally no growth but only a luxurious squandering of energy in every form! The history of life on earth is mainly the effect of a wild exuberance; the dominant event is the development of luxury, the production of increasingly burdensome forms of life" (33).

🏵 Reason in a Restrictive Economy: Or, a Mind Is a Terrible Thing to Waste

If we look at the world from the perspective of the puritan or the capitalist—which we very often do—this natural exuberance, luxuriant growth, and wanton sacrifice seems immorally wasteful, or at least shamefully inefficient. There are starving children in Africa (Iraq, North Korea, Palestine, Detroit) who could eat those fat blackberries—and hell, the blue jays too! Waste not, want not. Or, having wasted, want. Energy should be expended to produce in proportion to need (or to whatever desires good marketing can inspire). And thus it *is* in a perfect world, we insist: One ecosystem under God, indivisible. We only have to adjust our theoretical gaze slightly to recoup the waste, to see the drunken blue jays as seed distribution systems, the pollen's scattered molecules as a natural fertilizer. The answer to everything extraneous is the organic compost heap. Nothing is ever really wasted, is it? If there is profit, it is reinvested in the means of production or used to buy political influence or intimidating status symbols. The struggle for existence just continues at a different level, and all our resources are employed.

And thinking about birds? Sure. It's possible to incorporate even my flights of fancy while gazing at the birds into this puritanical, capitalistic, Darwinian vision of the world. Moments of apparently nonproductive thought are probably necessary for brains such as ours. They serve some purpose, either for release of tension or preliminary experimentation in the interest of future productive (or product) development. I'll find a use for that wasted time; I'll write an essay about looking at birds, get it published, and thereby increase my merit pay. Hah! Everything is a resource. . . .

But here, again, is Bataille: "Every time the meaning of a discussion depends on the fundamental value of the word *useful*—in other words, every time the essential question touching on the life of human societies is raised, no matter who intervenes and what opinions are expressed—it is possible to affirm that the debate is necessarily warped and that the fundamental question is eluded" (1985, 116). You can call any object or event useful, just like you can call any human action selfish. A self-serving goal or result can always be found or postulated. My thinking about birds is useful because it gives me pleasure, for example; it is productive of relaxation or delight, which is essential to my future productivity. You can always say that, but if you say that, Bataille maintains, you are simply refusing to entertain any other possibilities. You are attempting to enclose the universe in your calculating puritanism.

Bataille thinks such attempts are bound to fail, ultimately. You can't really plow all your profits back into the company. If you try, the company will explode. Or at least bad things will happen eventually. Says Bataille,

> The tool, the "crude flint tool" used by primitive man was undoubtedly the first positing of the object as such. The objective world is given in the practice introduced by the tool. But in this practice man, who makes use of the tool, becomes a tool himself, he becomes himself an object just as the tool is

an object. The world of practice is a world where man is himself a thing, which animals are not for themselves (which, moreover, in the beginning, animals were not for man). But man is not really a thing. A thing is identical in time, but man dies and decomposes and this man who is dead and decomposes is not the same thing as that man who lived. (1991b, 213)

If you reduce your production costs to a minimum and plow all your profit back into the company, obviously human beings (yourself included) are nothing but tools in the system. Yet humans are not tools. So somebody is going to go postal. It's inevitable. There will be a frenzy and a sacrifice. Happens all the time.

Bataille thinks this kind of thing happens on a grand scale in thoroughly rationalized societies, societies where all human energy is supposed to be expended in work—or at least in the kind of consumption that makes the economy work. (You shouldn't just putter or daydream; or if you daydream, at least contribute to the productive economy by buying a virtual reality suit to do it in.) It is inevitable in such societies that eventually the pressure will build to the point that there will be uncontainable, horrific explosions of one sort or another. I suspect Bataille would view George W. Bush's out-of-control military spending on irrational, destabilizing regional wars as the inevitable, dangerous, and dismaying outcome of too much Yankee good sense. Bush is thus the geopolitical equivalent of a frenzied postal employee screaming crazed accusations while spraying bullets at his co-workers and boss. However, Bush's family and friends are making a killing in the defense and energy industries (e.g., Dad is on the payroll of Halliburton, which has a multibillion-dollar defense contract to "help rebuild" Iraq), so maybe the frenzy is fake— a simulacrum to assuage the enraged postal workers that lurk in the depths of the rest of us, a virtual expenditure for virtual reality junkies.

Anyway, whether Bataille is right about the dire consequences of excluding useless expenditure from our conception of the universe or not, it does seem to me that he is right to point out that a refusal at the theoretical level to explore the uselessness of events and things is suspect. On the face of it, my looking at and thinking about the birds is a real waste of energy and time. And maybe that simple observation deserves some respect. Maybe thinking isn't primarily useful at all; maybe it's primarily expenditure. But if so, what does that do to my project of re-thinking thinking bodily?

🎖 *Reason in a General Economy*

Maybe I should be more careful. (I say that now, having denounced the president of the United States, who, under the Patriot Act, could imprison me indefinitely without indictment or access to an attorney.) What am I actually saying? I think I'm saying that the importance of my experience of thinking while looking at the birds is that it isn't productive at all. Maybe it can be used somehow after the fact; maybe it has consequences that could be used by someone somehow. But the thinking and the looking that initiate it happen regardless of those possibilities and in the teeth of present demands for productive labor and rational use of my time.

So let's start again.

It might be helpful to distinguish three activities—thinking, reasoning, and knowing. These three usually happen together, but they are not exactly the same. Thinking is just mental activity; it can include contemplating, appreciating, wondering, noticing, questioning, and on and on. Reasoning is a particular kind of thinking, directed toward untangling some intellectual knot or solving a problem. It can be useful, and usually is, since we like to have our problems solved, but it can also be just a kind of rule-governed play. I'm unsure what knowing is. In the Anglo-American tradition it has been monopolized by analytic epistemologists and reduced to a psychological state of possessing correct information. In the European tradition, Bataille implies, things are not much better: "To know means: to relate to the known, to grasp that an unknown thing is the same as another thing known. Which supposes either a solid ground upon which everything rests (Descartes) or the circularity of knowledge (Hegel)" (Bataille 1988b, 108). Since Descartes's time the ground has not proven to be especially solid, leaving us with the other option, which is absurdly reductive, a conception of knowing, as Bataille points out, that gets us absolutely nowhere: "Even supposing that I were to attain [absolute knowledge], I know that I would know nothing more than I know now" (1988b, 108).

Between me and the birds, there is a lot of thinking going on—questioning, appreciating, wondering, noticing, etc. There is also a certain amount of reasoning—considering how to attract them, learning to name them so as to be able to talk about them with my partner, and learning more about their habits by looking them up in books, and so forth. What about knowing? I feel like I'm knowing the birds too—not in the analytic epistemological sense, not that I'm in a psychological state in which I possess correct information about them (although I suppose I may), and certainly not in the ultimately circular Hegelian sense either. I don't seem to be assimilating the birds to what I already know, but rather to be having some new kind of experience that I don't know how to name or categorize. What I feel inclined to call *knowing* here is a feeling in my body of a connection with their bodies as if we were physically intermingled somehow, although not united or fused. But I'll return to that idea below.

Bataille seems to embrace nonreasoning thinking—just undirected, nonproductive mental activity—as part of the exuberant squandering that is the general economy. First of all, human beings themselves are surely among the "increasingly burdensome forms of life" that the "wild exuberance" that is the history of life on earth has tended to spew forth (Bataille 1991b, 33). So anything we do is excessive; we're not needed here. But even from the point of view of the human species, thinking is rarely necessary; and when it is, it is necessary only in the form of reason—that is, thinking in the service of solving immediate problems. More often than not, mental activities like questioning and wondering are detrimental to the business of survival. Curiosity doesn't just kill cats. In the most rational of all possible worlds, ambient thinking would probably be disallowed.

Reason, well trimmed, can be quite useful and is rarely detrimental, at least in the short run and if you are not one of those declared a "dangerous obstacle" by an imperial power. Reasoning is a requirement for human survival, given that we humans are naked, fangless, hornless, and as slow as molasses—exposed and vulnerable, in other words. But it has to be kept in strict limits or it gets tangled up in its own knots, because its calculations are always, as Bataille points out, either incomplete or circular: "The scythe is there for the harvest, the harvest for food, the food for labor, the labor for the factory where scythes are made" (1991b, 112). The circle itself has no point. Survival has no point. Ultimately, life doesn't aim for or serve or mean anything; it just is, exceeding all reason. Says Bataille, "Human life, distinct from juridical experience, existing as it does on a globe isolated in celestial space, from night to day and from one country to another—human life cannot in any way be limited to the closed systems assigned to it by reasonable conceptions" (1985, 128). But from the point of view of getting things done, it is best not to let our reasoning take us to those limits where reason wrecks itself; once there, reason is apt to compromise our survival instincts rather than serve them.

Fortunately, reason usually instinctively ignores the meaningless limitlessness of human life and tries not ever to trace its circles to their points of closure. Thus the outcome of sound (not round) reasoning is a state of knowing. If we reason correctly and well, we will very likely end up possessing some information that will probably be useful for future endeavors, and we may want to call that possessed information "knowledge" in either the analytic epistemological or Hegelian sense discussed above. Taken in either of those senses, however, knowledge is not an especially noble thing. Bataille writes, "I think that . . . at the base of all knowledge there is a servility, the acceptation of a way of life wherein each moment has meaning only in relation to another or others that will follow it" (2001, 129). In knowing, thus conceived, *now* is always in the service of *later;* I am always in the service of my future self. Knowledge as accumulated fact is like so many buried acorns stored up for use in the lean times, and the process of gathering those acorns is the servile work of knowing.

Presumably it was just this knowledge that Darwin was aiming for when he was watching his birds. He was accumulating information, producing a theory, devoting himself—his energy, his time—to an epistemic project that would transcend his present and enrich his future. So he tried to get it right. He really worked hard. All good scientists do.

That is not what I'm doing when I watch birds. I'm thinking. At times I'm reasoning, as I've acknowledged, but the reasoning is in service, not to accumulation and systematization of information, but rather to extension and complexification of play. The play, my pointless, time-consuming involvement with the birds, remains paramount. Reason viewed from the perspective of the general economy is merely a way of devising ever more varied means of needless expenditure. And knowing? What is that?

🌼 Knowing and Mimesis

"[T]he only object of my thought is play, and in play my thought, the work of my thought, is annihilated" (Bataille 2001, 129). Bataille's understanding of looking and thinking as play rather than as work probably fits what is going on with me and the birds a lot better than more traditional Darwinian accounts of thinking as a means of self-preservation do.[12] Reasoning, too, makes sense from the perspective of a general economy in that it operates to vary and intensify modes of mental expenditure. But what about the assertion I made earlier that in my being with the birds, however mediated by distance and technology and however antithetical to naïve empiricism and subjective completion, I feel strongly that there is something I *know*? Bataille, it seems, would be suspicious of any such claim. If this looking and thinking is exuberant play, it can't include servile knowing, storing up facts for future reference. What do I mean when I say I know the birds, and, most importantly in relation to my initial feminist question, how is that knowing bodily?

I have this almost perceptible tingling, a phantom sensation you might say, at the bottoms of my shoulder blades and down my triceps when I watch how the birds swoop from feeder to branch and back. I take this sensation to be a mimetic movement of my own phantom wings, a kind of neurological duplicating of the birds' bodies in flight, just as I might clench a fist while watching a brawl on a movie screen. I'm caught up in the action, alert and poised—still, yet not still at all—incorporating in a dampened way the gestures of the others whose movements I gaze upon. I resonate. I am their muted echo.

We know we mime other humans all the time. If you smile, I smile. If you yawn, so do I. Laughter is contagious, so we say.[13] When one baby in a nursery starts to cry, they all cry. We pick up the speech patterns and intonations of our friends and sometimes of our enemies as well. Throughout our lives we imitate the moves, the language, the physiological attitudes of other human beings. That is how we become who we are and take up a place in the world.

Is it so strange to realize that we do the same with other animals too? I play with my partner's dog by holding his nylabone near my mouth, smacking my lips, and growling in mock warning to anyone who might consider taking it away. He whines and crouches and bounds around the room. I give him the nylabone but then whine and crouch and bound around the room while he gnaws and growls. This is a game he understands and enjoys. I am both another dog and not a dog at all but his familiar human friend and occasional caretaker. This kind of mimetic play is familiar and natural to anyone who spends much leisure time around domestic animals.[14]

Usually when we imitate nondomestic animals, we do so for a human audience rather than in the presence of the animals themselves. At zoos, however, it is not unusual to see human beings of all ages gazing into cages and imitating the animals they watch—not just the primates, but oftentimes even the reptiles and water birds—not for the entertainment of other humans but rather as an almost nonconscious direct response to the movements of the animals.

I want to suggest that this practice of mimicking is a kind of embodied coming to know. And when it goes on long enough, when enough energy and attention have been put into it, it constitutes a corporeal knowledge of the other being. Obviously, this is not primarily a propositional knowledge. It is knowledge as physiological repertoire, and it enables whatever communication there is between one living being and another. Human beings are very good at it—"savages," especially, the civilized Mr. Darwin asserts in his observations at Tierra del Fuego: "All savages appear to possess, to an uncommon degree, this power of mimicry" (1934, 119)—but other animals do it as well. Primates in general "ape" human behavior, but so do parrots and starlings and dolphins.[15] After living with my partner and me for five years, my calico cat has developed what can only be called an approximation to a human kiss. She doesn't lick us when she is affectionate; instead, she parts her lips (such as they are) slightly and brushes against our skin with the flat fronts of her front teeth. And of course all sorts of animals imitate the behavior of other animals in various ways. Consider the mockingbird.

The birds that gather at our feeders and illustrate our Audubon book are especially beautiful animals and awe-inspiring in their adroit multidimensional maneuvering and inhuman speed. They are fascinating to me in their corporeal difference from me, and I explore that difference in their presence first of all in the most obvious way that I can, namely, corporeally.

There are two points that I want to stress here though. First, I want to make clear that this knowledge I say I have of birds is not the false sympathy that results from anthropomorphizing. I do not imagine that the birds have human characteristics or feelings, much less conversations or articulate thoughts. I do not assimilate the avian unknown to the human known, moving toward a Hegelian absolute that is nowhere other than where I started from. *Insofar as watching evokes physiological mimicry,* it is not a projection outward of what lies here within. I am not imposing myself on the birds and then claiming knowledge of what is merely myself misrecognized as a bird. The knowledge that I am describing is not dependent upon identification. Second, I want to reiterate that there is a difference between the mimesis I speak of here and the representational or reproductive mimesis that feminists such as Luce Irigaray have critiqued as phallic (or, when done by women, as a means of survival in an oppressive phallocracy). Phallocentric mimesis is an attempt to incorporate in the sense of "to assimilate to oneself."[16] What happens as I watch the birds is not this kind of consumptive incorporation. It is more like another, non-phallic mimetic possibility that Irigaray herself alludes to when she discusses Plato's dialogues. In an interview with Alice Jardine, Irigaray distinguishes between these two mimeses: "There is *mimesis* as production, which would lie more in the realm of music, and there is the *mimesis* that would be already caught up in a process of imitation, specularization, adequation, and reproduction." The second of these is the phallocentric mimesis that has been "privileged throughout the history of philosophy." But the first, which she calls the mimesis of production, is nevertheless a present possibility, despite its long eclipse and even if it "seems always to have been repressed." This first mimesis, as perhaps figured in the repeated performance of a piece of music (like the mockingbird's?), is never adequation or mere reproduction; it is always open to difference, which is why Irigaray points to it as an opening toward non-phallic possibility. She says, "Yet it is doubtless in the direction of, and on the basis of, that first mimesis that the possibility of a woman's writing may come about" (Irigaray 1991, 134). This non-phallic mimesis proliferates rather than unifies.[17]

In "my" mimetic knowing of the birds, "my" corporeal doubling of them (and I place the pronoun in quotation marks here because this is not a gesture I can really own), I neither become a bird nor assimilate the birds to myself in a way that erases our differences. Instead, I compromise my own human identity; I undergo its partial disintegration in order to give myself bodily over to the performance of the movements of the birds. Rather than unification into a phallic completeness, or even a sort of parody that does nothing more than expose phallocentric striving for similitude and assimilation, this bodily knowing issues in and *is* a proliferation of mimetic fragments. As living proliferation, this knowing can never be complete. Its very essence is its incompletability, since it does not accumulate information to store up for the future. (Thus it is also never servile.)

Why call it knowledge then, one might ask, if it is not and never can be complete? After all, says Bataille, "Completeness should be the basis of human knowledge. If it isn't complete, it's not *knowledge*—it's only an inevitable, giddy product of the will to know" (1988a, 24). Maybe that's all my musings about birds will ever be, a kind of playful giddiness, a tingling in the shoulder blades, and the waves of cool air across my naked, featherless skin.

But then again, maybe what I know in knowing the birds is a step toward or a key to a kind of sagacious completion after all. For Bataille goes on to say, "At the limits of reflection, the value of knowledge, it seems, depends on its ability to make any conclusive image of the universe [and I would add of birds and of the miming self] impossible. Knowledge destroys fixed notions and this continuing destruction is its greatness, or more precisely, its truth" (1988a, 25). Knowledge belongs, in the end, not to the restricted economy of acquisition and preservation, but to the general economy of luxury and waste. Insofar as knowledge can be complete affirmation of incompletability, insofar as knowledge shatters identity, it is a grand means of spending the excess—and even what is not viewed as excess—for it forces the sacrifice of everything that human traditions and institutions seek to preserve, up to and including immutable human selves and immortal gods. In its truest operations, knowledge is not in the service of utility and conservation at all but an event of pure expenditure.[18]

And thus I think I can say, without opposing Bataille and without acquiescing to the philosophical traditions that would disembody the knowing subject, that I *know* the birds; I know them non-phallicly, mimetically, incompletely or completely in affirmative incompletability, in the proliferation of corporeal gestures that are my body, my humanity, my reason, my mind. This proliferation is ever open to differing, and knows itself to be completely so. I know the birds within the general economy wherein knowing is open-ended play and servile reason is a tool of expenditure. I know them, and in the knowing, both I and they proliferate in difference.

NOTES

1. Or, if you don't know her well, you can just look at her book *Speculum.* See Irigaray 1985, esp. 133–37.

2. Quoted in Hubbard 1983, 50.

3. My copy of Charles Darwin's *On the Origin of the Species* bears no publication date. The introduction refers to the twentieth century as if it were current, and the book, a hardback volume that also includes *The Descent of Man,* bears a price tag of $3.95 and my grandfather's signature and handwritten date of December 7, 1968. I shall cite it hereafter as Darwin, 1968?, and page number. This quotation comes from page 24.

4. And as Charles Scott reminds us in *The Lives of Things* (2002, 111), "We should beware, I think, of gifts from the obsessed." Perhaps even as we accept it, we should beware of the legacy Darwin leaves us.

5. Random variation or mutation can give rise to divergence in species if some barrier is imposed between the population with the mutation and that without it. An example is the coloring of urban squirrels. In Alexandria, Virginia, there is an area of land wherein squirrels are cut off from the rest of the city by very busy streets without an above-ground system of power lines or suspended traffic lights. The squirrels in that area have become predominately black rather than grayish-brown as are most squirrels along the eastern seaboard. In my own neighborhood in Richmond, Virginia, which is not isolated in any such way, there are a number of white squirrels and brown squirrels with white flanks. Should they become isolated by future urban development, it is possible that their progeny eventually will be all white. Of course, color variation, having nothing to do with reproduction, does not distinguish one species from another; without further mutation, these populations would not diverge enough to be classified as anything other than unusual squirrels.

6. Max Horkheimer and Theodor Adorno also figure reason as phallic in their discussion of Odysseus in *The Dialectic of Enlightenment: Philosophical Fragments.* See Horkheimer and Adorno 2002, 26.

7. Another distinct possibility is that there is something wrong with trying to revalue a devalued term in a binary instead of just ditching the binary altogether. Charles Scott moves to a discussion of physicality as opposed to a revaluation of "the body" in his wonderful book, *The Lives of Things* (2002).

8. See Burr 2002, 104, for width of molecules, and 57 for connection between molecular size and human needs.

9. ". . . and," they continue, "as calamitous as the precisely calculated operations of material production, the results of which for human beings escape all calculation." Later on in the book they assert, "Reason acts as an instrument of adaptation and not as a sedative, as might appear from the use sometimes made of it by individuals. Its ruse consists of making humans into beasts with an ever-wider reach, and not in bringing about the identity of subject and object" (Horkheimer and Adorno 2002, 185).

10. For the description of Victor's obsessive, frenzied pursuit of knowledge and scientific technique, see Mary Shelley's *Frankenstein* (1831), chapters 4 and 5. At the begin-

ning of chapter 5, Victor recoils in horror from his creation and soon resolves to end its life, if only he can catch it.

11. Imagine if he had been invested in pharmaceuticals!

12. Bataille's view doesn't have to conflict with the theory of natural selection if we construe natural selection as acting to eliminate traits rather than to generate them. The capacity to think came into existence as one more form in which the cosmos squanders its energy; it persists because it hasn't killed us yet. But it still could; the jury's still out.

13. Bataille at times speaks of laughter as one of the ways human beings shatter themselves and communicate with others in sacrifice. See Bataille 1988b, 97.

14. A reader of one draft of this essay has asked me to distinguish my descriptions of mimesis here and elsewhere in this paper from Deleuze and Guattari's notion of "becoming animal." First, I will say that I love Deleuze and Guattari's work on becoming animal and would not be unhappy if my work resembled it in some ways. But I do think there are some differences in mimesis as I describe it here and becoming animal, not least of all because they actually say straight off, "Becoming is never imitating" (Deleuze and Guattari 1987, 305). But there are more concrete reasons. In playing with my partner's dog, I am not becoming dog in the sense that the dog and I are not entering into an assemblage together (although you could possibly say each of us in turn enters into an assemblage with the nylabone). Contrast this example with Deleuze and Guattari's example of the wasp and the orchid in *A Thousand Plateaus.* This is a natural symbiotic relationship in which beings that humans conceive of as separate in fact act as each other's organ systems. The wasp is the penis for the orchid. The orchid is the breast for the wasp. Or more accurately, the wasp plays a crucial role in the orchid's reproductive system, and the orchid plays a crucial role in the wasp's digestive system. The apparently two things actually operate as one thing— or at least it can be seen that way; there is no way that it *is.* If an experienced rider rides a well-trained horse, we can speak of becoming horse or the horse's becoming human because again there is an assemblage whose parts operate synchronistically, even though not symbiotically. Deleuze and Guattari often give examples wherein there is reciprocity of becoming. It may seem that my dog example involves reciprocity, even if not simultaneity, but my bird examples do not. The birds are virtually untouched by my activity. Insofar as synchrony, or reciprocity, and assemblage are central aspects of becoming animal for Deleuze and Guattari, then the mimesis that I am trying to describe here is not that; if, however, those characteristics are inessential, perhaps there is more overlap. Our examples are similar in that all insist on difference within the event. There may well be other important similarities. For the discussion of becoming animal, see Deleuze and Guattari 1987, 232–309.

15. For fascinating and humorous accounts of starlings and other birds imitating both human speech and song and humanly produced instrumental music, see Rothenberg 2005. For stories about scientists playing mimicking games with dolphins, see Gray 1979.

16. When women in a phallocracy are forced to imitate the images of woman that masculine subjects have produced, they are in effect trying to incorporate that image and divest themselves of whatever else they might be in order to do it.

17. Naomi Schor suggests that Irigaray actually discusses three types of mimesis in her work—one that is merely masquerade, one that is parody, and then another that is a kind of positivity rooted in the difference of mimesis as difference. She writes: "And, finally, in the third meaning of mimesis I am attempting to tease out of Irigaray's writings, mimesis comes to signify difference as positivity, a joyful reappropriation of the attributes of the

other that is not in any way to be confused with a mere reversal of the existing phallocentric distribution of power" (1989, 48).

18. One cannot help but think of Nietzsche's third essay in *Toward a Genealogy of Morals,* where he points out that, taken to its logical conclusion, theism must kill God—that is, a commitment to ultimate, immutable truth must end by undercutting the illusions that form its own foundation. Knowledge is intrinsically self-overcoming, whether it wills itself so or not. This is Nietzsche's insight, and Bataille is certainly no stranger to it.

WORKS CITED

Bataille, Georges. 1991a. *The Accursed Share, Volume I.* Trans. Robert Hurley. New York: Zone Books.

———. 1991b. *The Accursed Share, Volumes II & III.* Trans. Robert Hurley. New York: Zone Books.

———. 1988a. *Guilty.* Trans. Bruce Boone. Venice, Calif.: Lapis Press.

———. 1988b. *Inner Experience.* Trans. Leslie Anne Boldt. Albany: State University of New York Press.

———. 1985. The Notion of Expenditure. In *Visions of Excess: Selected Writings 1927–1939.* Ed. Allan Stoekl. Trans. Allan Stoekl, Carl Lovitt, and Donald M. Leslie Jr. Minneapolis: University of Minnesota Press.

———. 2001. *The Unfinished System of Nonknowledge.* Trans. Michelle Kendall and Stuart Kendall. Minneapolis: University of Minnesota Press.

Burr, Chandler. 2002. *The Emperor of Scent.* New York: Random House.

Darwin, Charles. 1934. *Charles Darwin's Diary of the Voyage of the H.M.S. Beagle.* Ed. Nora Barrow. Cambridge: Cambridge University Press.

———. 1996. Notebook N. In *On Evolution.* Ed. Thomas F. Glick and David Kohn. Indianapolis: Hackett Publishing Company.

———. 1968? *On the Origin of the Species and The Descent of Man.* New York: The Modern Library.

Deleuze, Gilles, and Felix Guattari. 1987. *A Thousand Plateaus: Capitalism and Schizophrenia.* Trans. Brian Massumi. Minneapolis: University of Minnesota Press.

Gray, Elizabeth Dodson. 1979. *Green Paradise Lost.* Wellesley, Mass.: Roundtable Press.

Grosz, Elizabeth. 1993. Bodies and Knowledges: Feminism and the Crisis of Reason. In *Feminist Epistemologies,* ed. Linda Alcoff and Elizabeth Potter. New York: Routledge.

Horkheimer, Max, and Theodor Adorno. 2002. *The Dialectic of Enlightenment: Philosophical Fragments.* Trans. Edmund Jephcott. Stanford, Calif.: Stanford University Press.

Hubbard, Ruth. 1983. Have Only Men Evolved? In *Discovering Reality: Feminist Perspectives on Epistemology, Metaphysics, Methodology, and Philosophy of Science.* Ed. Sandra Harding and Merrill B. Hintikka. Dordrecht: D. Reidel Publishing Co.

Irigaray, Luce. 1991. *The Irigaray Reader.* Ed. Margaret Whitford. Oxford: Basil Blackwell, Ltd.

———. 1985. *Speculum of the Other Woman.* Trans. Gillian C. Gill. Ithaca, N.Y.: Cornell University Press.

Johnson, Mark L. 1999. Embodied Reason. In *Perspectives on Embodiment: The Intersections of Nature and Culture.* Ed. Gail Weiss and Honi Fern Haber. New York: Routledge.

Lloyd, Genevieve. 1984. *The Man of Reason: "Male" and "Female" in Western Philosophy.* Minneapolis: Minnesota University Press.

Rothenberg, David. 2005. *Why Birds Sing: A Journey into the Mystery of Bird Song.* New York: Basic Books.

Schor, Naomi. 1989. This Essentialism Which Is Not One: Coming to Grips with Irigaray. *Differences: A Journal of Feminist Cultural Studies* (Summer): 38–58.

Scott, Charles. 2002. *The Lives of Things.* Bloomington: Indiana University Press.

Shelley, Mary. [1831] 1994. *Frankenstein.* New York: Dover Publications.

Taussig, Michael. 1993. *Mimesis and Alterity: A Particular History of the Senses.* New York: Routledge.

EIGHT

LUCIO ANGELO PRIVITELLO

S/laughter and Anima-lēthē

> *The truth, whatever it is, be damned. What we need is laughter.*
> FEYERABEND, *For and Against Method*
> *I have come to debase the coinage.*
> DIOGENES

🌺 *Toward the Impossible Restoration of Intimacy*

Bataille's general economy is a myth of the restoration of intimacy.[1] From this perspective, *The Accursed Share,* as a work on political economy, is unrecoverable and satisfies the condition of "the impossible," that is, the awareness of writing to no avail, where content and conclusion unravel instead of providing remedies. *The Accursed Share* claims systemic coherence even though it is not the product of a patient, servile re-reading of systems. The paradox is exacerbating but necessary.[2] It is my claim that the theme of animality and laughter offsets this paradox and endangers prosaic understanding by pitting intimacy against philosophies of "metaphysical scaffolding" and teleologically driven unrest.[3] Animality and laughter are a chase after an insoluble problem: the restoration of intimacy without succumbing to religion, ethics, social planning, or market.[4] Intimacy interrupts the system of debit and credit, suspends work, and cancels the assumptive origins and ends of the production of meaning at all costs, that is, "project." The will-to-system isolates discourse by judgments that set up boundary conditions, reducing one to becoming a specialist (in this case a restricted economist), compromised in the ability to hear questions other than those for which the systematization will provide ready-made answers.

Yet *The Accursed Share* is a strange attempt at bookkeeping.[5] While in search for the shock of the heterogeneous, Bataille's brand of bookkeeping unwillingly presents itself behind the veil of a homogeneous project. There is a type of violence inherent in Bataille's more theoretical texts. Bataille, who seems to border the prescriptive, sees the denial of sensual animality and the denial of the given world as two negations that have misguided humankind.[6] From these denials Bataille seeks experiments of inner experience and communication, what he calls the experience of "the impossible." A sober return (or a historically minded guidebook approach) would already be a utilitarian move, a work of "project," producing a figure of animality that is captured and revealed as a "*sacred character*" of difference.[7] For Bataille, the sacred is a leap into experiments outside of the teleological coordinates of labor, the negation through prohibition, and the awareness of death.[8]

> If there is within us, running through the space we inhabit, a movement of energy that we use, but that is not reducible to its utility . . . we can disregard it, but we can also adapt our activity to its completion outside us. (1991b, 69)
>
> I have so much to say to you that I am not writing—everything that is tormenting both of us: I am not surprised it's this way. If it were otherwise we would be okapis with wings. Now the okapi does not have wings and despite its apocalyptic tongue it has strange and tender hooves which stumble in the shadows. (Laure 1995, 149)
>
> What I feel towards you could never take any recognizable form, or be named, or be something ordinary—Only signs of life are necessary. (Laure 1995, 136)

For Bataille, what is necessary is "real life," an "incomparably splendid place" beyond what registers as productive versus nonproductive expenditure. Necessity is the movement of the "living organism," or animality.[9] Animality entails the exuberance of "multiple destructions," also exemplified as the "unbroken animal" and "wild beast" at the summit of consumptive expenditure.[10] The exuberance of living matter, real life or animal experience, is not reducible to its utility, nor can it be neatly conceptualized within an ontological machination from human aspirations or anguish.[11]

> We need on the one hand to go beyond the narrow limits within which we ordinarily remain, and on the other hand somehow bring our going-beyond back within our limits. The problem posed is that of the expenditure of the surplus. We need to give away, lose or destroy. (1991b, 69)
>
> We need a thinking that does not fall apart in the face of horror, a self-consciousness that does not steal away when it is time to explore possibility to the limit. (1991c, 14)

Animality and laughter make up the poles of self-consciousness that do not steal away at the limits when faced with the restoration of intimacy, which in the same movement is the rejection of "project" and the embrace of nondiscursive experiences. Project absorbs and reinvests the squandering of stabilized meaning, servile to the laborious prose of understanding and the production of meaning.[12] Project is production-writing oriented toward a finished product, a book, a discursive experience that courts a facile communication of experience. Instead, Bataille desired a communication that already gives the "embryo of a degradation of the experience" (2001a, 49), one that is incomplete and cannot overcome the limits of the moment through theoretical costume and makeup.[13] Project encircles writing and is there captured by a collar of its own making, a "minor mode" of communication, in which things are given in narrative and reflected on as things in narrative (see 2001a, 161).[14] Bataille desired another type of writing, a "book [that] might be something else . . . a mixture of the aspiration to silence and that which [spoke in him]" (2001a, 174, 202), instead of accumulating and investing the limits of the moments for a return. In contrast to project, there is animality and laughter, impossibilities of facile assimilation, re-markings of the violence against exegetical prose, and a gamble against the house of discursive experience, or the "burden of design" of the real world of utility expressed in coercive explanations. Bataille succeeded in creating a space for such impossibility of assimilation. Writing on his texts must partake in re-marking the violence that astounded him, which is ultimately a rebellion against exegetical projects and "discursive experience."[15]

Part of Bataille's un-working of the prose of restricted economy and part of this very writing that grapples with the themes of animality and laughter shift traditional tones of argumentation into a contestation where questions postpone the work of consoling conclusions:

> The opposite of project is sacrifice. Sacrifice [or consumption] falls into the forms of project, but only in appearance (or to the extent of its decadence). (1988a, 136–37)

Animality and laughter deny "project" by consuming their very sovereignty. The restoration of intimacy is this consumption. Intimacy is nothing that can be made use of as a thing and has *"nothing as its object"* (1991b, 190). As an aspect of animality, it "bring[s] other objects of thought into contact with [the] depths of the world" (2001a, 90). This is what Bataille called "scissiparity." Intimacy as laughter ultimately clips the abundance of animality, attesting to the "apotheosis of what is perishable" (1985, 237), an example of what Bataille called the "embryo of a degradation of the experience" (2001a, 49).[16]

> The true luxury and the real potlatch of our times falls to the poverty-stricken, that is, to the individual who lies down and scoffs. A genuine luxury requires the complete contempt for riches, the somber indifference of the individual who refuses work and makes his life on the one hand an infinitely ruined splendor, and on the other, a silent insult to the laborious lie of the rich. (1991b, 76–77)

Laughter reveals the inhuman depths of the human animal. Bataille's laughter is not a social corrective force (as was Bergson's), a comical staging, or collateral to entertainment weaned from horror.[17] Laughter is the refusal of discourse.

> It is contradictory to try to be unlimited and limited at the same time, and the result is comedy. (1991b, 70)
>
> . . . thanks to me, the most banal image has taken the form of dream, desire, drama, passion, now that only the sweetest hilarity will relieve you from all that is burdensome. (Laure 1995, 152)

The sweet hilarity of laughter is the experience of "non-knowledge," and "results from every proposition when we are looking to go to the fundamental depths of its contents, and which makes us uneasy" (2001a, 112).[18] Uneasiness is to arrive at a conclusion that will not be treated as a consolation or as a conceptual plateau. Animality is a contestation opening in and from experiential sundering, an obscure intimacy with the flux of the world.

> The regret that I might have for a time when the obscure intimacy of the animal was scarcely distinguished from the immense flux of the world indicates a power that is truly lost, but it fails to recognize what matters more to me. Even if he has lost the world in leaving animality behind, man has nonetheless become that *consciousness* of having lost it which we are, and which is more, in a sense, than a possession of which the animal is not conscious: It is *man,* in a word, being that which alone matters to me and which the animal cannot be. (1991b, 133)
>
> As for me I am beyond words, I have seen too much, known too much, experienced too much for appearance to take on form. (Laure 1995, 152)
>
> The sacred thing externalizes intimacy: It makes visible on the outside that which is really within. (1991b, 189)[19]
>
> [T]he transition from animal to man . . . is a *setting in place* . . . the value of a setting in place of social existence. (1991b, 190)

The setting in place is an opening for "inner experience." This opening is the suspension of personhood in a "realized void [that is] of *Me* . . . that the total improbability of my coming into the world poses in an imperative mode, a total heterogeneity" (1985, "Sacrifices," 130; 1988a, 116). This is the "accursed share" (*part maudite*), and what remains beyond exchange in the artifice of rates of exchange. Somewhere, as an unconscious imperative, an imperative without an ideal realm and outside the rules of a particular game, play reveals this heterogeneity, the joy of profitless operations and the experience of the expenditure of energy for the glory of play.[20] Play can then also be understood as intimacy, and animality is the corporeal joy sundered in and by the inassimilability of its physical existence.[21] Such is how Bataille envisions living matter in general.[22]

This vision replaces humanistic mysticism (discourse) with the mysticism of animality (experience). For Bataille, "experience" is synonymous with experiment. It is a provocation of events outside of what is profitably and securely known at any cost, and from a language of restricted economy. When cases are computed by cost (discourse, logic), experience is remodeled to prevent what tears one apart from the consolation of conclusions. There is no exchange of concepts solvent enough for Bataille to withstand or stabilize the ever-flowing wave of the primacy of experience (or "privileged instance" of animality) with its thousand convergences apprehended at the culmination of a loss of comprehension, or non-knowledge. Animality and laughter emerge, yet are poised at the edges of this culmination as slippage.[23] As examples of such slippage, Bataille unfolds six domains of delirium under the rubric of a "positive atheology"—laughter, tears, sexual excitation, poetic emotion, the sentiment of the sacred, and ecstasy—to which animality is substrate and surface.[24] These domains are nonaccumulative in any sense of "project," squandering profits through deficit processes of the excessive wealth of living nature.[25]

> It is the philosopher's contradiction to be brought to confuse a miserable instrument with the totality of being. This is his contradiction and also his misery. (2001a, 108)[26]
>
> There can be no compromise in integrity, plentitude . . . life. (Laure 1995, 153)

As part of a philosophy founded on the experience of animality and laughter, there is what Bataille calls a "philosophy that can accomplish the rigorous movement that leaves one mute in a consequential way, which dismisses derivatives" (2001a, 122).[27] Animality and laughter are spurs for such a movement. Yet Bataille's circle of friends remained an impossible community of singularities, a community still unable to turn against the servile and prosaic development of thought, teleology, system, and style, which viewed development from underdevelopment.

I think all the things you do in that "little circle of friends" will never amount to more than topics of conversation. (Laure 1995, 133)

Bataille believed that Reason and those with reasonable intentions never return intact from services rendered. For Bataille, "thought is a useful prohibition." The notion of animality attains the force of transgression by its very "incompleteness," as laughter does in its being unsustainable (see 2001a, 253).

It is necessary to contrast the courtesan's carefully arranged beauty with the disheveled animality of the maenads. (1991c, 140)

The incompleteness (and violence) that Bataille envisions in contrast to the work of Reason is that "of the serpent or the spider [Nature] which turns you to stone . . . it does not confound but slips; it dispossesses, it paralyzes, it fascinates before you might oppose anything to it" (2001a, 232).[28] This type of violence is the fulfillment of thought and is as much a part of reason as is rhythm and intensity—all of which are effects of non-knowledge.[29] The burst of laughter, like animality, the uncontrollable laughter of the dance of the flux of the world, corresponds to what Bataille called "full violence," a primacy of experience insubordinate to ends, precarious, entwined by "unavowable accords" and part of a consciousness that displaces the value of its own finality.[30]

In Pursuit of the Value of Intimacy; or, Do All Creatures Economize?

In volume one of *The Accursed Share,* subtitled "Consumption," the "living organism," "living nature," the "biomass," and animals represent luxury and excess, a kind of luxury that is ultimately useless, and a kind of activity that pointlessly dissipates into the universe. This is due to an overgiving of energy. Economic mankind, restricted to the world of utility, has lost the sense of this pursuit of luxury and wild exuberance, a loss that is the product of the fear of non-meaning. In volume one of *The Accursed Share* we are faced first with the "unbroken animal," that is, of untrained and undirected energy that would destroy us. This kind of energy is continually sweeping across and actually is, for Bataille, the very way energy moves upon the earth. The human predicament is that each individual is part of this movement, *nolans volens,* but resists its modes of useless consumption, or finds niches for it, as in aesthetic productions.

Bataille's suggestions entail finding how and where humans may dispose of such excess, either as "growth" or "turbulence." Growth and turbulence belong to Bataille's example of the "gardener's path," the necessity for and waste of fertility plotted within a larger plot, as an intension within "extension." The gardener's path is the microcosm upon which luxury, waste, reproduction, death, and eating are extended in an activity closest to our interactions with the earth. One must think of the animal, both domestic animals and the glorious wild beasts, as a gardener's path in movement. Their trajectories are movements of consumption, carriers of a destruction unencumbered by the signs and space of things used. Man is foreign to this naked glory, and as Bataille states, "is *in search of* [this] *lost intimacy* from the first" (1991b, 57). In such a space, gifts overflow with an animal force, a playful glory stripped of the marks of rank, blind to circulating riches, impossible to pay for, and part of the flux of the world as the "obscure intimacy of the animal" (1991b, 133).

> I insist on the fact that there is generally no growth but only a luxurious squandering of energy in every form! The history of life on earth is mainly the effect of a wild exuberance; the dominant event in the development of luxury, the production of increasingly burdensome forms of life. (1991b, 33)[31]

Through volume one of *The Accursed Share* it is important to envision this wild exuberance as the "network of *exteriority* within." As the feeling of superabundance, animality and laughter make up the network that Bataille describes as "*seeing* 'what is' [as] tissue[s] of consciousness . . . enclosing me in some way in my exteriority" (2001a, 85). The life of "authentic sovereignty" (2001a, 96), cut from the lathe of sensible experience, is the incalculable, indefinite immanence of such a turning (a carving action), and not the structuring exercise of the construction of power.[32] Authentic sovereignty, as Bataille sees it, is a refusal, and is no longer intellectual nor reflectively servile, but capriciously plays in the void that is opened by "luck."[33]

> In animality we can never lose sight of the sovereignty of immanence. (2001a, 241)[34]

Immanence, or the instant, is "the wild beast . . . at the summit" (1991b, 34), and its fallout is the "individual who lies down and scoffs" (1991b, 76). Diogenes embodies the meeting of wild beast and the individual who scoffs, and can be seen as a figure drawn by the coincidence of opposites.

> We are not as hardy, free, or accomplished as animals. (Diogenes)[35]

Diogenes' "pantomimic materialism" (Sloterdijk 1987, 103) is similar to what Bataille calls scissiparity, or the immortality of the lowliest forms of life.[36] Yet nowhere does Bataille develop a link with the figure of Diogenes, afraid perhaps of the accusation of Cynicism, of the laugh (as Sartre noted) that resembles a sickly smile that does not make one laugh, or perhaps afraid of entering into a discourse with the history of philosophy, with the themes of animality and laughter that would weaken their contestation.[37] Yet with the cynicism of Diogenes, Bataille would have found an ally and a way to "give a new twist to the question of how to *say* the truth" toward which his idea of communication and heterogeneity clearly strives.[38] This is what I see as the heart of Bataille's unworking of project.

Within volume one of *The Accursed Share,* and as an example of unworking, Bataille does not give in to describing or defining the term "animality." In the nine mentions of animality contained in the first volume of *The Accursed Share,* one may piece together a view of Bataille's use of the animal and of "animality," which, at first glance, is the lowliest, yet most widespread form of contestation.[39] To begin, the animal is endowed with the "obscure intimacy" of the world's flux, which humans recognize as a power or *consciousness* that they have lost (1991b, 133). This is the governing thought of the description of animality, a central, authoritative, yet negative order allowing for excessive expenditures, receding, dissipating, and pulling consciousness behind it. Because of this, destruction is necessary, the destruction that cancels the rule of utility between humans and animals (1991b, 56). Destruction cancels the *"real* order" and restores the animal to its obscure intimacy with the flux of the world, its "accursed share" (1991b, 57–58). Restoration is the *glory* of "senseless frenzy, [and the] measureless expenditure of energy," and revolt (1991b, 71). Humans participate in excess by the destruction of the wild beast by rivaling the depredations of depredators (1991b, 34), for the unbroken animal cannot be trained; its surplus energy can only be destroyed (1991b, 24). Death (and also growth and sexual reproduction) is thus restored to the flux of the world (1991b, 27), and with it a garden path is left abandoned to the over-rich forms of animal life (1991b, 30). This returns the animal to its timeless place and immortal mode of scissiparity with the world (1991b, 32).[40]

Bataille's view of "animality" is knee-deep in a Cargo Cult Economics, where the quantitative is altogether skirted for a qualitative theory or judgment of existence.[41] Through an excess of income set in motion by excessive consumption, Bataille turns total loss into the superabundant investment of animality. When the animal is returned to its timeless and immortal mode of scissiparity with the world, it is *saved. Saving* is thus increased, and along with it a re-humanized naturalism, where expenditure outstrips production, anthropology overtakes economics, and myth trumps logic.[42] This move is noted by Bennington and is a move that "makes sense only within a closed finite surface [the spherical form of the earth]" (Bennington 1995, 53).

> Writing this book [*The Accursed Share*] in which I was using my energy, my time, working; my research answered in a fundamental way the desire to add to the amount of wealth acquired for mankind. (1991b, 11)[43]

For Bataille, the animal emerges as the luxury and receptivity of profits that are wasted (consumed), receiving and squandering beyond necessary needs.[44] From the mentions of animality in the first volume of *The Accursed Share,* capital is violently saved and begins to accumulate as Bataille's myth of general economy.[45] As the explosion deep within a re-humanized order, animality was the intimacy seen as divine nature, outside the mediated circuit of the mortgage bond of transcendence.[46] Myths and rites are ways to regain this form of intimacy beyond labor, which wastes labors for the splendor of "interior freedom" (1991b, 57–58).

From the Scoff to Sovereign Laughter

In the second volume of *The Accursed Share,* "The History of Eroticism," we find a more sustained engagement with the notion of animality, where Bataille determines a link between the world of eroticism and thought. Animal simplicity is sovereignty not divested of sexualized thought. Bataille determines this link by rethinking the meaning of "animal simplicity," or "indefinite immanence."[47] Animality is representative of a life outside utility, history, and the mechanical order. It is a world left behind, where eroticism remains incommensurate as an object of reflection. What is uncomfortably experienced as loss remains as the "total social fact," where the "whole of life takes form" (1991c, 51). Through laughter (or thought as chance and play), this totality is experienced as the foolishness of knowledge.[48] Faced with the movement of the totality of being, the need of knowledge cannot be satisfied.

Volume two of *The Accursed Share* can be seen as a history of the sensibility to chance, of the effects of consumption beyond the structures of purpose. This applies as equally to what one thinks as to how one feels or is felt, that is, if sovereignty, as Bataille believes, holds sway as eroticism. Thought (as eroticism) defines a field through censure directed at what is useless, filthy, and prohibited. And yet the only communication that would participate in what Bataille called his Copernican turn from *restrictive* economy to *general* economy would be of the sexual relation as festival and potlatch. Bataille stated that the "potlatch is at once a surpassing of calculation and the height of calculation" (1991c, 47). What is called for, then, is that such surpassing and summit be directed toward sexual activity, or animal impulse "destitute of meaning" (1991c, 48). As in the example of the gardener's path of volume one, here any detour will find itself overrun by movements wider and more excessive than those of provisional negations. The "given world" and "animality" are these wider, more excessive movements. For Bataille, any and all transitions are caught up in the example of the gardener's path (even his own writings), and only in its "initial movement [is the gift] contrary to animality" (1991c, 56) as the negation of the idea of Nature as restrictive, conservative, and mindful of what is futural. Children are also an example of the negation of a gift, initially squandering the rule of command for future life, until trained.[49] This drama is ultimately played out as that of *self-consciousness:* what is perhaps Nature's most antithetical prohibition, fought as the boundary of differentiations, yet taking place in the mire of the same field shared with the animal. This drama carries the greatest excitation and the most intimate contestation, for it seeks to hopelessly recalibrate self-consciousness through sexuality, filth, and death, that is, to become another gardener's path in movement, a voracious impulse of consumption.

The destruction of what is held sacred is also present in the event of laughter, or "passionate release." Laughter is the consumption of communication. It marks the limits and faux frontier of *"an external form of intimacy,"* by turning things accepted as product (and meaning) into processes of sacrifice and non-possessive relation of self-consciousness with *"nothing as its object."*[50] This is most clearly experienced by self-consciousness in the event of laughter. Laughter is the "indication of [such a] festival's meaning"— and, according to Bataille, contrary to animality, if, and only if, seen as comic laughter (1991c, 90, 435n3). Comic laughter is a shield against "sacred animality," a protective veil of shame that covers over the "horror of nature [and first animality]" (1991c, 93), whereas "animal life [and the types of laughter emerging in and as such life] is without history" (1991c, 94). Uncontrollable laughter (that of the gods, as Nietzsche reminds us) is mentioned as one such emergence, as is excessive joy, horror, contagious destruction, and the vertigo of the experienced sundering of the "totality of being" (1991c, 118). This is the "embrace" of the "animality that [one] can grasp in the totality which the embrace constitutes" (1991c, 118). In the final account, such an embrace is also veiled, for it is part of the view of natural animality that has lost the intimacy of divine animality and that may only be glimpsed in a sidereal glance as the "disheveled animality of the maenads" (1991c, 140). In that moment, and precisely because of such a moment, is the mark of the sovereign's destruction. There is no doubt as to why the courtesan must watch such a writhing with Sadean apathy.

> There is horror in being: this horror is repugnant animality, whose presence I discover at the very point where the totality of being takes form. But the horror I experience does not repel me, the disgust I feel does not nauseate me. (1991c, 118)

For Bataille, laughter is how incommensurability does not ultimately entail incommunicability but rather allows a glimpse of the natural sovereignty of animality, or the slippage that shifts the terrain of the composition with the world, a composition that regains its rich and excessive quality.[51]

> Man appears to be the only animal to be *ashamed* of that nature whence he comes, and from which he does not cease to have departed. This is a sore point for us. (1991c, 62)

Shame, and the taking leave of animal simplicity (chastity) make up the notion of "prohibition," the setting apart of humans from their animal nature, and the creation of the ongoing drama of (and for) humanization. The animal's place in nature is felt as the thwarted and tormented desire of return to a life marked in its movements but undefined in its form.[52] The leap into this formless space, as the step into the unknown, requires that which is ultimately destitute of meaning, while bathing in an irresistible impulse.[53] Bataille's idea of a starting point is where one may oppose the "elementary forms of the negation of animality" (1991c, 53–54) to the animality of eroticism, which is "a crack in the system [that] secretly and at the deepest level . . . belongs intimately to human sensuality and is the mainspring of pleasure" (1986a, 105; see 1991c, 70).

> There is no communication more profound: two beings are lost in a convulsion that binds them together. But they only communicate when losing a part of themselves. Communication ties them together with wounds, where their unity and integrity dissipates in fever. (1985, 250)

To experience this, philosophy must shift its terrain. Philosophy must draw closer to the "unintelligible caprice" of the animal's bond to the world, to life, and simultaneously estrange itself from what will automatically respond as foreign to non-knowledge. Bataille's mysticism of animality has nothing to do with a sense of responsibility for the world, environmentally and politically speaking. Bataille saw the capricious effects of sovereignty and non-knowledge. The loss of responsibility is due to the shifted terrain that Bataille envisions, one in which systematization is discarded. This loss is due to the following borders:

a)   the erosion of the "world of utility" (1992, 43);
b)   the "return to intimacy" (1992, 44);
c)   the realization of animal sovereignty (1986a, 81); and
d)   the dissolution of the "professorial tradition of philosophy." (2001a, 82)[54]

However, this is not an excuse to grant animals the prerogatives of the human person. Neither is it a recourse to assimilating animals from the outside, where "the human being has [already] determined [what] separates [it] from the animals" (2001a, 291n3). The shifted terrain presents animality as *muthos,* and exposes laughter as what is directed in the face of *logos.* These moments give way to the feeling of the sacred, anguish, ecstasy, terror—and, in rare moments (sovereign moments), poetry or evocations which slip into silence.[55] Silence is at the core of Bataille's disciplined indiscipline, and he is clear in stating that "the sovereign is in the domain of silence" (2001a, 126). He also speaks of fleeing into a sovereign silence, which is "the silence of the glorious, victorious, exalted man," of dissolved efforts (2001a, 200; see also 238). Silence is contestation as perpetual rebellion against itself. The breaking of silence is the coercive giving of meaning that betrays the space of the lack of meaning. Bataille's idea of discipline, and where the sovereign's truth is silence (2001a, 103), calls for the "silent, angelic feeling of divine mockery" (2001a, 108) attained by approaching "maximum silence" (2001a, 122). His writings mask this contestation, and even the partial view that sees nothing but "lacerated screams" throughout his texts is, for Bataille, "also silence," and "resolves itself, becoming silence" (2001a, 214, 235).

> I cannot claim while laughing *to know: to know* insofar as it is a linguistic term is given to me in the discursive articulation of my thought, not in some revelation exterior to language. (2001a, 171)
>
> Poetry . . . is the sacrifice in which words are victim . . . we would in no way have anything of the human about us if language had to be entirely servile with us. (1988a, 135)

Animality is similar to this function of the familiar recognized as a movement where familiarity plunges into the lost depths of the strange, of silence, of the "accidental, natural, perishable," of the intensity of the experience and the instant (1991c, 91). Bataille poses this problem at the very edge, where method loses its detachment and becomes sacrificed for a poetic and passionate life.

> They [the mystically inclined, and lovers] no longer live for the community; they only live for sacrifice. Thus little by little they are possessed by the desire to extend, through contagion, their sacrificial frenzy. Just as eroticism slides without difficulty towards the orgy, sacrifice, becoming an end in itself, lays claim to universal value, beyond the narrowness of the community. (1985, 252; see also 118–20)

🌑 *Dire-delectations*

Between animality and laughter there is an irresolvable tension and a point of contrary movement. Bataille sees the turning away from animal nature, or "animal avidity," in the type of laughter "whose object is comical." Nothing is more contrary to animality than the scoff of comic laughter (or in eroticism, "smutty laughter"), which represents a whitewashing of the dark love (sovereign laughter) that allows a leap into the unknown.[56] Here Bataille returns to Nietzsche's specific type of laughter that kills the spirit of gravity, calling for the invention through laughter of a future of laughter.

> Perhaps this is where we shall still discover the realm of our *invention,* that realm in which we, too, can still be original, say, as parodists of world history and God's buffoons—perhaps, even if nothing else today has any future, our laughter may yet have a future. (Nietzsche *BGE* §223)

For Bataille, laughter contains an infinite capacity for reversal, from disgust and terror to seduction and ecstasy. In this way, laughter reveals its affinity with wisdom, something Bataille aimed at from Nietzsche's influence. Different kinds of laughter have this power, for even in the happiest laughter of the child (1988a, 90), afternoon laughter (1988a, 97), infinite laughter (1988a, 66), convulsive or deadly laughter (1988a, 97), or in the laughter in Turin (2001a, 74), laughter retains itself within the syncopation of discontinuity.[57] Laughter resides within non-knowledge and still breathes. According to Bataille, laughter is the dilections of the body (and perhaps of a text), its movement and its time signature.[58] Perhaps this is where "original laughter" can be thought of as originary power (Lingis 1997), and where originary power is the victory laughter that Bakhtin spoke of as

> a victory over the mystic terror of God . . . and most of all over the oppression and guilt related to all that was consecrated and forbidden . . . which

> clarified man's consciousness and gave him a new outlook on life . . .
> [where] . . . all unearthly objects were transformed into earth, the mother
> which swallows up in order to give birth, and something larger that has
> been improved. (Bakhtin 1984, 90, 91)

However, Bataille would disagree that something larger has been improved.
Siding with Nietzsche, he maintains that although animality is integral to
sacrifice, the "sacrificial animal does not share the spectator's ideas about
sacrifice, [because] one has never let it have its say" (Nietzsche 1974, §220).
The sacrifice remains for nothing. This explains Bataille's position on heterogeneous complicity, which resides at the heart of animality as the heterogeneity that returns in sovereignty (sovereign laughter), reducing activity to a
deafening silence. This abandonment to muteness (speech exasperated) is a
revolt against the servility of conclusions and sets explanatory reconciliation
adrift.

In contrast to this, there is the laughter of comedy, an activity built on
the attitude toward veiling death, loss, shortcomings, and failure, in ex-
claiming and protecting the "I am" from the tumultuous stream of life that
drags the body along, tripping and falling wherever it goes.[59] Comedic
laughter is the last barrier and immunization against the rupture and conta-
gion of animality. It protects the spectacle and denies "compenetration" by a
violence that wounds while consoling. Comedic laughter reveals what it
laughs about, concluding merely a step beyond the threshold of "project":

> Laughter, though, only infrequently corresponds to the outline of compen-
> etration (1988a, 142).[60]

✻ *The S/laughter of Subjectivity*

Laughter is the sound of how the individual loses itself in an earthly
debauchery and of where the earth is experienced as the animality of the
coursing of life bursting forth from subterranean and swampy regions, as
wounds and ruptures, "literally torn away by joy" (1987, 33). Laughter is
the joyful s/laughter of subjectivity.[61] As the summit (excess) and decline
(exhaustion) of thought, laughter moves between the coincidence of sensible
appeals and the work of meaning as a threshold where "project" begins to
degenerate.

The laughter (devoid of the mode of reaching and doing away with) is
what Bataille calls "major laughter," akin to complete sovereignty over the
minor sovereignty of comedic laughter. This can be seen as the risk of the
game, gamble, or sacrifice, where there is no assurance. Major laughter "puts

the equilibrium of life in danger" and ridicules a life if the game is transformed into "project" (2001a, 144, 98).[62] Laughter is a shedding or a slipping out of what was once believed true in relation to the future, which Bataille adopted from Nietzsche's "I love not knowing the future" (*Ich liebe die Unwissenheit um die Zukunft*). Laughter that knows the future, or laughter dissected in the form of a treatise or as part of aesthetics, amounts to nothing more than an interminable preparation of a cathexis.[63] Bataille's move takes us from the outside view of the object of laughter (most commonly seen in comedic humor, the opposite of animality) to the non-knowledge of laughter, its inner experiment, which is indistinguishable from animality. According to Bataille, this space of laughter requires "two conditions: (1) that it's sudden; and (2) that no inhibition is involved" (1988a, 140). Laughter is thus always on the edge of slippage, exposing, in the words of Nietzsche, the "superabundance of means of communication . . . extreme receptivity, stimuli and signs . . . constituting the high point [and for Bataille, the only point] of communication and transmission between living creatures—it is the source of languages" (Nietzsche 1968, §809).[64] But this can only be expressed in a slipping:

> With the least slippage [*glissement*], the movement of life is no longer tolerable. Everything is built on a foundation of slippage. The most timid laughter absorbs infinite slippage. (Bataille 1988a, 98)[65]

What remains overlooked in the attempts at writing about Bataille's notion of laughter are the types and the domains of laughter that make up the power to sacrifice "project." There is a sense in Bataille's texts of a giving way in/to laughter from the silent gravitational center of animality. This aspect of a giving in/to laughter (the joyful silence of rebellion) is present in Bataille's erotic fiction, autobiographical pieces, poetic experiments, and theoretical meditations. In volume three of *The Accursed Share,* there are six types of laughter. These types are coordinates for the wasteful luxuriance that underlines and consumes discursive economy:

1. 1991c, 235—laughing at an imagined tragic situation.
2. 1991c, 233—laughter as objectively conditioned impulse.
3. 1991c, 230—laughter as recognized "classical" sovereignty.
4. 1991c, 204—laughter and/as tears.
5. 1991c, 203—laughter that stops thought.[66]
6. 1991c, 439n3—perfect laughter that does not laugh.

Along with these types of laughter from volume three of *The Accursed Share,* the occurrences of laughter in the works of Bataille belong to three major regions or "domains": the laughter of extreme depths, the laughter of glistening surfaces, and chthonic laughter. The borders between these "domains" are porous and contagious.[67] The borders of the volatile phenomena of laughter are "elements that are impossible to assimilate" (1985, 140–41). While it is difficult to sustain an explanatory thread cast across the void of impossible assimilation (a main thread throughout my approach), the tension of such violence and astonishment must prove unrecoverable (Bataille's very wish), especially in relation to the notion (event) of animality. Laughter is merely the first step across the void, and for Bataille it was Nietzsche that took the step. Nietzsche, as Bataille stated, is the "first to locate [the experience of laughter, but] he didn't give it a sufficient explanation" (2001a, 154) (partly due to Nietzsche's restricted treatment of animality).

Laughter at extreme depths captures the "radiance where foundation is ultimately a collapse," where in laughing one knows that one is sinking, as is seen in *Story of the Eye,* where Simone stands over the tomb of Don Juan.[68] Simone's laughter is sovereign, insubordinate, and far beyond its utility as calculated effect. Its necessity obeys an "animal injunction" that is cast as a sounding lead into the ambiguity of the sacred.[69] Such is what Bataille means by using the expression *"impossible and yet there it is"* (1991c, 206).[70] Perhaps this too is the world where animals are for themselves (naturally sovereign), untrammeled by the difference between what is dead and what is alive, since death, according to Bataille, is merely what "opposes the happy fecundity of practice" (1991c, 217).[71] In sovereignty, Bataille believed that there is a return to animality—a taking part of what the world is as a flux of experiential sundering, but gained from a position of slippage.

> Laughter slips on the surface, the whole length of slight depressions: rupture opens the abyss. (1988a, 91)

The laughter of glistening surfaces, or "laughter's superfluity," reveals the crackling skin of the intensity of experience. Bataille speaks of this as "laughter [at] the explosion point" (1994, 136).[72] Laughter from the chthonic chasms of the earth is the laughter of "time's laceration," the evocation of nothingness, or transcendence contained in a teacup.

> As soon as Proust's teacup is taken for what it is—God's fall (the fall of transcendence) into the ridiculous (into immediacy and immanence)—that teacup becomes impalement. (Bataille 1994, 64)

Chthonic laughter (original laughter) sets the "equilibrium of life in danger" (2001a, 144; Lingis 1997, 81). The happy laugh of the "sovereign operation" *"expiates this authority at the same time"* (2001a, 185, 98).[73] Chthonic laughter is the decapitating laughter of an atheological community.

> When I laugh there is something incomparable in the object of my laughter. Philosophy cannot have any other object. Besides, in my mind, I made the object of this laughter a substitute for God; here I saw nothing less than a principle of the universe. What was revealed to me, with a *violence* that astounded me, was that in the world and in the inconceivable void that it opens up, there is nothing that is not violently laughable. (2001a, 160)

This is where laughter succumbs to a soundless peel of silence.[74] Not a soundlessness from the absence of being, but from what Bataille sees as the "horror in being . . . the repugnant animality whose presence I discover at the very point where the totality of being takes form" (1991c, 118). The domain of silence is that of the sovereign, for the "instant is silence" (2001a, 290n4), a foreignness in familiarity that draws laughter out of the experience of a loosening of personal thought, a bloodletting of joy through hazarding another's word.[75]

> Laughter moves towards immanence, and in that nothingness is the object of laughter—but it is thus an object of a destruction. (1994, 189)
>
> We are carried in the stream of hilarity: laughter is the effect of a rupture in the link of transcendent connections; these comic links with our equals, continually broken and continually retied, are the most fragile, the least heavy. (2001a, 86)

This dimension of the abyss is the experience of the body overtaken from having over-given itself, as was Bataille's experience in his ascent of Mount Etna in 1937 together with Laure (Colette Peignot).[76] The same kind of experience is had in the expending of energy in laughter. Laughter is the sound of language's consumption as we scale and slip on the inclines of meaning. The choice not to be a "prosaic man," but instead be put at risk by his own process of writing (éc-*rire*), was Bataille's touchstone.[77] Such a process of writing partakes in the risk of a philosophy of laughter, "a radiance whose foundation is ultimately a collapse" (2001a, 138; Surya 2002, 491).

The reluctance to define his experience as a "method," which is seen in his text *On Nietzsche,* can also be understood as Bataille's affinity with a position that Baudelaire called "childhood regained at will" (Bataille 2001b, x). Instead of a defeat, this disregard for "project" is seen as unburdening of inner experience.

When questioning fails, we laugh. (1994, 47)

My life (or rather my lack of one) is my method. Less and less do I question to know. That's something that pretty much leaves me indifferent. And I live. And I question in order to live. I live out my quest. (1994, 110)[78]

Nothing is stranger to me than the fashion of personal thinking. I [am put into] play when I bring forth a term, the thought *of others,* that risks my grasp of the human substance that surrounds me. (Bataille in Rey 1988, 29, my translation; Bataille's italics)

Animality as the Throat of Laughter

Laughter is the cut throat of "animal pity."[79]

The lovely human beast always seems to lose its good spirits when it thinks well; it becomes "serious." And "where laughter and gaiety are found, thinking does not amount to anything": that is the prejudice of this serious beast against all "gay science."—Well then, let us prove that this is a prejudice. (Nietzsche *GS* §327)[80]

The condition of "laughter" is *knowing how* to resolve life's ordinary difficulties. Possibly the decisive thing is looking at laughter as a necessity foreign to tragedy. With a tragic attitude, the mind is overcome and is half-Christian (that is, submissive to inevitable misery); it abandons itself to the consequences of its downfall. (Bataille 1988a, 102)

In *The Accursed Share,* volume three, "Sovereignty," Bataille mentions relations between animality and sovereignty. Sovereignty entails not descending into the brutalization of "the other's animality," but instead, of viewing the animal in others as the *"fellow creatures,"* something that hunters once experienced.[81] As part of what Bataille calls "the impossible," or in the breach that produces the sovereign person, there stands the notion of a return to animality, a return that "goes into the composition of the world to which it is opposed . . . [and is part] of the imbroglio of relations that arise from the continual opposition of the most diverse possibilities" (1991c, 342, 341). This opposition, as the return to animality, "has always been . . . and will remain, *in the storm*" (1991c, 343). The storm is due to a suspension of coercive conclusions and theatrically posited origins and is the violence directed against the building of neat exegetical-theoretical stages, chain-linked arguments, and the chatter of intellection:

The return to animality that we perceive in sovereignty—and in eroticism—differs radically from the animal starting point. (1991c, 342)

From this perspective, inner experience awakens from its "animal slumber [and] receives the limited solution of the festival" (1992, 53). A festival by its nature is contagious, and it is in what is contagious that insidious laughter distinguishes the imperceptible difference between the divine world and the asylum. The contagiousness of this laughter belongs to the carnival sense of the world: to existence's superabundance, to the farce of Nature, where nonproductive expenditure and loss converge—raw and primary.

The natural sovereignty of animals is ultimately seen as a limit opening up a void, and against which at the other end is the emergence of the authentically sovereign, that is, a non-knowledge displacing the self-interested servility of knowledge. Sovereignty is not mastery in the Hegelian sense of the term, but a process of de-subjectification, a stripping of the self, unhinging the idea of a self housed by a body that responds to "me." The "me" becomes useless at the point where nakedness serves no end but pure gratuitousness, like the silence savored after a burst of laughter. Sovereignty is not a modification of acquired behavior invested with guarantees.[82] As Bataille sees it, within the "difference between the animal [natural sovereignty] and me [authentic sovereignty] the unknowable intermingles" (2001a, 242).[83]

> The animal opens before me a depth that attracts me and is familiar to me. In a sense, I know this depth: it is my own. (Bataille 1992, 22)

Bataille understands this depth, or void, created by how the unknowable intermingles, as the obscure intimacy experienced in laughter.[84]

🐾 *Anima-lēthē*

Bataille speaks of animal existence as that which is "measured only by the sun and rain, dismissing categories of language" (1988a, 58). Animal existence struggles so that language may be turned back upon itself, not because animality answers the questions at the limits of language, but because the questions are there made superfluous.[85] This is the impossible coin, the "horse-sovereign," that Bataille uses in his bets against the squirrel-game (*écureuil, caisse d'épargne*) of "specialized philosophy."[86] At the summit of philosophy (Hegel), Bataille saw philosophy turn against itself by the realization that "entails at once a discipline and the abandonment of discipline . . . where human effort shows its impotence and relaxes in the feeling of its impotence with no regrets" (1986a, 259). Animality is the internal form where the philosophical familiar is recognized as the form that allows said familiarity to plunge once again into the lost depths of the strange, into an "indefinite immanence which admits superiority nowhere" (2001a, 85).[87] Animality is part of the abandonment, of "sacrifice, laughter, poetry, ecstasy. . . which break closed systems as they *take* possession" (1988a, 136). Like a philosophy of laughter, a philosophy of animality draws from an experience of complicity, and complicity is "less that of bodies [or communication] than that of the void which they embrace" (Surya 2002, 7). Animality is "immediacy or immanence" in the situation where an animal eats another animal.[88] For Bataille, immanence is the giving of "the *fellow* creature" in a situation divested of affirming the difference by the processes of subordination.[89]

> Something tender, secret, and painful draws out the intimacy which keeps vigil in us, extending its glimmer into that animal darkness. (1992, 23)

This drawing out of intimacy culminates in Bataille's understanding of the sacred without religion (theology). Bataille's sacred is the "search for lost intimacy" (1992, 57). In *Theory of Religion,* Bataille is clearest in describing animality as the obscure life of intimacy, beginning as the capriciousness of the animal *"in the world like water in water,"* and ending as the "destructive intimacy" that degrades all that is before it.[90] The search for lost intimacy follows the contestation of silence, aimed against the investment of stages of consciousness. Intimacy dissolves consciousness as mastery and is in the instant as the animal is in the world. For Bataille, "intimacy cannot be expressed discursively" (1992, 50), and it remains as the "immanence that submerges" us in "useless consumption" (1992, 36, 71). Turning away from coerced intellection ("project"), we are faced with the animal's unintelligible caprice: a life lived against the order of guided investments. In sacrifice, intimacy is restored. The space of sacrifice is the absence of individuality, of violence suffused with anguish, where "a person that surrenders to immanence puts humanity in check [allowing] glimpses [of] the unconscious intimacy of animals" (1992, 53) and of sovereign instances.

To re-read *The Accursed Share* through the themes of animality and laughter provides passages across the order of things for sovereign instances. Animality is an example of such intimacy, an intimacy communicated outside the discursive order of the real world of utility, where there is a loss of individuality in a shared life and where anguish, sacred and violent, is where within the sacred and violent anguish humanity is put in check through the "slow action of sacrifice." This is part of what Bataille calls "inner experience" or the inner experiment allowing us "to emerge through project from the realm of project" (1988a, 46). "Project" is the continual recuperation of failed attempts at the anticipation of wholeness, completion, usefulness, and the effort of having foreseen and avoided failure. "Project" is the patient, servile intention of filling in the outlines of a system from beginning to end, subverting and postponing the violent primacy of experience. In opposition to this, there is a writing that seeks chance, "not of the isolated author, but of the anonymous all-living" (1973, 3:69).[91] The abandonment of "project" through the emergence of animality, and the crowing anti-accomplishment of "project" in and as laughter, are the themes and notions that are risked, and ultimately sacrificed, in Bataille's *The Accursed Share.*

One cannot save oneself on paper. (Laure 1995, 197)

NOTES

1. "In connection with intimacy, nothing further can occur" (1991b, 189). For Bataille, labor replaced intimacy. It established "things" by severing the subject by servility. "It is this degradation that man has always tried to escape. In his strange myths, in his cruel rites, man is *in search of a lost intimacy* from the first" (1991b, 57). Bataille's *The Accursed Share* seeks to establish an economy for the world of intimacy, a world that, as he states, "is antithetical to the *real* world . . . [and thus opposed to] *an external form of intimacy* [religion] . . . opposite of a *thing*, the opposite of a product, of a commodity. . . [and of] the full possession of intimacy [the trap of self-consciousness as externalized intimacy]" (see 1991b, 58, 129, 132, 189). Intimacy can be seen as the "stronger mode of love, the festival, and art—communicational unreason" (Goux 1990, 224). Volume one of *The Accursed Share* ends with a return to the paradoxical, where sovereignty is not to be seen as a completion of self-consciousness, but as its ruination through consumption. In volume two of *The Accursed Share*, intimacy is the "embrace" (see 1991c, 114–19). The "embrace" is for Bataille a link that he also calls a "spiritual link" or contact between the mental level and what relates to it as equal. The economic level, that of exchanges, are "soluble in spite of everything," culminating perhaps in nothing more than "intestinal saturation" (2001a, 5). There is much of this intestinal saturation present in *The Accursed Share*, enough so as to have passed for serious economic reflections, but that was not Bataille's aim. Economic ruminations are a mere pretext to how Bataille ascends to the summit of his idea of contact with others (viz., intimacy), and that through animality and laughter, which ultimately is the impossible contacted, and the turning away from the chores of servile labor (the possible). The impossible is where a motive, or subordinate operations, is not determined in the expenditure of surplus.

2. Bataille mentions that his concern from 1914 on was with the "formulation of a paradoxical philosophy" (see Bataille 1986b, 107–10). The "Accursed Share" is this paradox. Its truth, as Bataille states, "is paradoxical . . . contrary to the usual perception" and veiled at its "highest point of exuberance" (1991b, 37; see also 1991c, 111–12).

3. See Bataille 1985, 45; and 1991c, 14.

4. "I wanted to avoid redoing the work of the economists, and I confine myself to

relating the problem that is posed in economic crises to the general problem of nature"
(1991b, 13). *"My method is at the antipodes of elevated ideas, of salvation, of all mysticism"*
(2001a, 99). See also 2001a, 283n5.

5. Animality could be seen as the bookmark left in the tome of sexual life that marks
what is filthy. See 1991c, 70; see also 1988a, 38.

6. The third negation (product of the propensity of human specificity) is the awareness of death (1991c, 53). For Bataille, "Archaic humanity [was] not always sure of being
different from animality" (1991c, 339).

7. However, a "return to animality... differs radically from the animal starting
point" (1991c, 342). See also 1991c, 335.

8. Labor, prohibition, and death are aspects of human specificity. See 1991c, 53, 61–
63, and 76.

9. The movement here intended is the "play of energy." Bataille does admit, and begins with, "a basic fact: the living organism, in a situation determined by the play of energy on the surface of the globe, ordinarily receives more energy on the surface than is
necessary for maintaining life; the excess energy (wealth) can be used for the growth of a
system (e.g., an organism); if the system can no longer grow, or if the excess cannot be completely absorbed in its growth, it must necessarily be lost without profit; it must be spent,
willingly or not, gloriously or catastrophically" (1991b, 21).

10. 1991b, 23, 24, 34; see also 1991c, 14.

11. "There can be anguish only from a personal, *particular* point of view that is radically opposed to the *general* point of view based on the exuberance of living matter as a
whole" (1991b, 39). See also 1985, 51.

12. As William Pawlett (1997) pointed out, commentaries on Bataille's work suffice as
such attempts at "project" (e.g., Derrida, Foucault, Habermas), and most recently Agamben's (2004) end of history–redemptive pietistic theoretics.

13. "What is in some way dispersed in these conditions is traditional philosophy. The
sovereignty (sovereign authority) of the aesthetic ... subordinates philosophy, as Christians subordinated it to theology, but this time it is no longer subordinated to the object
intellectually and dogmatically defined by the experience, but directly to the experience
that is taking place, no longer accepting any limit and always going to the extreme of the
possible. In other words, in these conditions, ethics and knowledge disengage themselves
from every transcendent element" (2001a, 173).

14. "Vanity exists at the level of project" (2001a, 203).

15. Yet one must, even for Bataille, in some degree "work and hold aloof from the possibilities offered by transgression," because philosophy is also a competitive game (1986a,
260; see also 1988a, 59; 2001a, 227–28).

16. "In the kingdom of the instant, the sovereign not only outs other men in the grip
of dangerous and capricious acts, he remains there himself; the sovereign is in this way one
who can in no way bring himself to safety, being unable to live beneath the burden of design" (2001a, 189).

17. "Laughter may not show respect but it does show horror" (1986a, 265–66). Cf.
Bergson 1928. For Bataille, laughter carries one further than thought and is not opposed
to thought. *"Laughter* and *thinking* ... complete each other" and "laughter was tanta-
mount to God ... although raised outside of religion" (see Bataille 2001a, 153).

18. It is interesting to note the use of the concept of "non-knowledge" in Karl Jaspers,
or where "cognition ceases, but not thought. By technically applying my knowledge I can
act outwardly, but non-knowledge makes possible an inner action by which I transform my-

self. This is another and deeper kind of thought; it is not detached from being and oriented toward an object but is a process of my innermost self, in which thought and being become identical" (Jaspers 2003, 127). See Bataille's "Discussion on Sin" (2001a, 66) for Hyppolite's question and mention of Jaspers in relation to Bataille's use of "communication."

19. The festival is as important to animality as it is to the divine, being the excessive show that makes the earth alluring and fascinating as it moves and seduces through horror and the negation of horror. Bataille believed that earliest man attributed divine life to animality (see 1991c, 138). He calls this "sacred animality" (see 1991c, 93, 150).

20. See Root 1989, 224–25.

21. "Glory" is a key concept in Bataille's vision throughout *The Accursed Share*. Glory is "senseless frenzy . . . measureless expenditure of energy . . . the fervor of combat" (1991b, 71).

22. "We can ignore or forget the fact that the ground we live on is little other than a field of multiple destructions" (Bataille 1991b, 23). "A surplus must be dissipated through deficit operations. The final dissipation cannot fail to carry out the movement that animates terrestrial energy" (1991b, 22). Terrestrial energy is also seen as the dance, the "decomposing agility (as if made of the thousand idle futilities and of life's thousand moments of uncontrollable laughter)" (1988a, 127).

23. Animality and laughter can be seen as atomic moments of the "impossibility of [experience's] enduring" (see Bataille 1985, "The Sacred," 241).

24. Each of these domains is an opening into the void, and each is part of what is violently laughable. See 2001a, 106, 160, 217; and 2001a, 94, 182.

25. Bataille speaks of this as "the movement that animates terrestrial energy" (1991b, 22). Animality is what allows a glimpse, *in general,* of such a movement carried outside one's isolated situation (see 1991b, 22–23). See also 2001a, 146, where Bataille specifically states that laughter "opens a sort of general experience."

26. "What does philosophy matter since it is this naïve contestation: the questioning that we can only undertake when we are appeased! How could we be appeased if we did not rely on a whole body of presupposed knowledge? Introducing a metaphysical given at the extreme limit of thought comically reveals its essence: that of every philosophy" (1991a, 40).

27. Yet, "philosophy cannot accomplish this movement while remaining on its own terrain" (2001a, 122). "Insofar as I am doing philosophical work, my philosophy is a philosophy of laughter. It is a philosophy founded on the experience of laughter, and it does not even claim to go further" (2001a, 138). This is intimately connected with a philosophy of play (2001a, 130), of the "useless employment of oneself, of one's possessions" (1991b, 73). "Generally speaking, philosophy is at fault in being divorced from life. The consideration I am introducing is linked with life in the most intimate way" (1986a, 12).

28. "No one bothered to reflect that 'Nature' behaved in a ridiculous way" (1986a, 232).

29. "I mean that violence corresponds to animality, in which consciousness, in some way bound up with it, cannot have any autonomy [and] the domain of violence is that of religion" (2001a, 228, 229). "The most *Christian* time of my life was spent with you" (Laure 1995, 151).

30. In this vein there is also the "laughter of Reason," the laughter that opens a domain to death, and to what, beyond madness, mirrors reason. See 2001a, 231, 160.

31. "I want only chance . . . [w]hich is my goal, my only goal, and my sole means" (1994, 143). See Veblen 1994 [1899], Chapter XI, "The Belief in Luck." What is most interesting is to follow Veblen's view of how the "extra-causal" factor in luck (or chance) is a

noneconomic utility. See Bataille, 2001a, 17, 156–58, 188, 213. "There are only words in the night, exchanged by chance, with a single devotion: luck" (2001a, 68). Perhaps at his clearest, in *Eroticism* Bataille states, "Chance, inescapably the final sentence, without which we are never sovereign beings" (1986a, 250).

32. See 2001a, 96, where Bataille distinguishes major (or complete sovereignty) from minor sovereignty, as well as mentioning the "sovereignty of the burst of laughter" that distorts the classical idea of sovereignty. "Sovereignty is an act of rebellion against every rule" (2001a, 161). See also "Socratic College" (2001a, 5), where Bataille speaks of "authenticity" as what embraces the filth of life, the "foul smell [that] also marks the presence of life." In contrast to "authentic sovereignty," one could place Bataille's mention of "arbitrary sovereignty," or the sovereignty of the theologians (see 2001a, 107). Bataille also saw that what was missing in Heidegger was "sovereignty" (2001a, 161; see also 2001a, 194).

33. In Bataille, lack becomes purpose without ends, and ends put into perpetual play. See 2001a, 172, 198, esp. 283n5, where Bataille notes that "sovereignty differs in no way from the limitless dissipation of 'wealth' of substance." "This sovereign loss of self ruptures the isolation of the unitary subject, and self and other dissolve. In the ceremony of human sacrifice, the victim communicates his anguish to the community, permitting the latter to collectively share the confrontation with death, the ultimate loss" (Root 1989, 220).

34. For Bataille, transcendence is made up of the "world of objects that transcend" him, and that weld his exteriority from the emptiness within. "Nevertheless, I survive this alteration by binding ties of immanence (returning me to indefinite immanence which admits superiority nowhere)" (2001a, 85).

35. "Animals make [nature] a field of slaughter and extend its possibilities in this way: they themselves develop more slowly. In this respect, the wild beast is at the summit: Its continual depredations of depredators represents an immense squandering of energy . . . [I]n the general effervescence of life, the tiger is a point of extreme incandescence. And this incandescence did in fact burn first in the remote depths of the sky, in the sun's consumption" (Bataille 1991b, 34).

36. See 1991b, 32; see 1985, 15–16, 45–52.

37. See Surya 2002, 334; Bataille 2001a, 160, 70–74. Yet, Bataille does engage in what he calls the "idiocy of philosophy" (2001a, 169; see also 205).

38. See Sloterdijk 1987, 104–107, 143–44, 194–95, 531–32.

39. In *The Accursed Share,* volume two, Bataille develops the term in more detail, and also lays the groundwork for what later was taken up by Lacan as "a joy, moreover, that is excessive" [*jouissance*] (see 1991c, 103). Bataille is clear in his idea that a mystical animality is root and soil of everyday life, for even "the lowliest and least cultured human beings have an experience of the possible—the whole of it even—which approaches that of the great mystics in its depths and its intensity. . . . Nothing is more widespread: by chance a human being finds himself in an incomparably splendid place; he is not at all insensitive to it, but he can't say anything about it" (Bataille, *History of Eroticism,* 13).

40. For a view of this, see 1991c, 117, where Bataille seeks to speak of *"the concrete totality of the real,"* free of a theistic frame, whether as God or Nature. Animality is the embrace of the totality, which the embrace (intimacy) constitutes (1991c, 118).

41. The Cargo Cult was noticed in the actions of New Guinea tribesmen just after the Second World War. Many of the American planes that fought had to release their cargo, and the inhabitants prospered because of it. To secure the continuation of such prosperity, the tribesmen replicated the planes and the airstrips (as mock-ups). McCloskey (2002, 46–56) mentions this, and it was Richard Feynman who dubbed mock science as "Cargo Cult Science."

42. See Keynes 1965 [1935], 64. See also Bennington 1995, 46.

43. "Consumption is the sole end and object of all economic activity. The greater the consumption for which we have provided in advance, the more difficult it is to find something further to provide for in advance, and the greater our dependence on present consumption as a source of demand. New capital investment can only take place in excess of current capital-disinvestment if future expenditure on consumption is expected to increase" (Keynes 1965 [1935], 104–105).

44. "Every weakening in the propensity to consume regarded as a permanent habit must weaken the demand for capital as well as the demand for consumption" (Keynes 1965 [1935], 106).

45. See Bennington 1995, 53; Derrida 1992, 34–70.

46. See 1991c, 137. This relation becomes a focus of chapters 3 and 4 of Part Five, "The History of Eroticism," as well as chapters 1 through 3 of Part Six, "The Composite Forms of Eroticism."

47. Indefinite immanence is a loss, a void, or a hole left from what animality seemed to be, and from the impossibility of a return to the, so to speak, filth of such an a-utopia. See 1991c, 23; and 2001a, 85.

48. "The problem with philosophy is the passage from the knowledge of limited objects to the knowledge of the entirety of what is" (2001a, 165).

49. "In theory, we must envisage the transition from animal to man as a drama, which we can take as having lasted and as having had ups and downs, but whose unity we must grant . . . in the sense of a lasting effect [and] still the motive of the activity we pursue" (1991c, 73).

50. From the nine mentions of animality in *The Accursed Share: Volume I,* along with the un-working of the event of laughter, one is granted an order of things consecrated from the upheaval of destruction and the possibility of confronting this order in a sovereign manner. This is where Bataille sees the place of "intimacy." As he writes, "intimacy is not expressed by a *thing* except on one condition: that this *thing* be essentially the opposite of a *thing,* the opposite of a product, of a commodity—a consumption and a sacrifice" (1991b, 132). This also serves as a starting point for self-consciousness, and at the same time where, because of its possession of intimacy, "nothing further can occur" (1991b, 189). See also 1991b, 58, 129. What Bataille is asking for is a fresh "*setting in place*" (1991b, 190), and an "overturning of the ethics that grounds [economic principles]" (1991b, 25). Animality and laughter are the coordinates for this Copernican re-mapping. For an exercise in Bataillean ethics, see the discussion in Connor 2000, 94–104.

51. See 2001a, 189. "Thought is asexual: one will see this limitation—antithetical to sovereignty, to every sovereign attitude—make of the intellectual world the flat and subordinate world that we know, this world of useful and isolated things, in which laborious activity is the rule, in which it is implied that each one of us should keep his place in a mechanical order" (1991c, 24). Animal simplicity, simple animal sexuality, sensual animality, carnal animality, animal excitation, and the undefined life of the beasts are tied to the abhorrence of nature, and the accursed share opposed to the "neutral part" of separate domains (see 1991c, 77–78, 83). Bataille sees this neutral part as the "isolated aspect" that remains embedded in the total social fact, the drama of a perpetual transition of animality-humanity, not to formal states (see 1991c, 52, 73). Animality is the bridge between the various forms of worlds (see 1991c, 21–22). Animality is contrary to the *gift* as it is to a philosophy of expectation (1991c, 56; see 2001a, 166, contra Agamben 2004). Animality is the "lasting effect [of the drama]" (1991c, 73).

52. For thought to join eroticism, its object would need to remain beyond its grasp. "A new domain opens to consciousness from the death of thought; from non-knowledge a new knowledge is possible" (2001a, 124). "There is no philosophical given, no revealed theory, but there is a point where thought resolves itself in something other than thought" (2001a, 166). See also 1991c, 23–24.

53. Here Bataille would cite the distinguishing attitude toward sexual activity, where prohibition-and/as-coveting marks the object's orbit in the order of things. Animality is as much a detour of its negation as it is a new possibility and impetus, and at perhaps a more intimate level (as an exteriority within), it too is coveted. See 1991c, 48, 93.

54. "Generally speaking, philosophy is at fault in being divorced from life. But let me reassure you at once. The consideration I am introducing is linked with life in the most intimate way" (1986a, 12). Bataille sees this dissolution from Nietzsche's perspective. From within the history of thought, "Nietzsche's is the only philosophy that wrenches one away from the servitude inherent in philosophical discourse; the only one that restores sovereignty to the free spirit" (1991c, 401; see also 112). It is sovereignty akin to childlikeness (1991c, 65, 114, 409). Such a position is made clear by what Bataille sees as "having suffered from the non-knowledge of knowledge . . . from the foolishness of knowledge" and from having "made philosophy the experience of this suffering" (2001a, 165).

55. See 2001a, 245. On the concept of "slippage," within *The Accursed Share* Bataille refers to nudity as the slippage toward obscenity (1991c, 149, 151), an escape of the object of desire, as it is the impetus for the chase, seen also in "alcohol, war and holidays" (1991c, 188). Bataille sees sovereignty as a burst of laughter, which is, within the philosophical arena, the sovereignty of foolishness because of how it must be subordinated to thought as a wolf to a collar. See Bataille 2001a, 96, 169, 174.

56. Laughter is related to the notion of "sacred animality," not to "first animality" (or "animal avidity") (1991c, 91). First animality is the delirium of being naked, a procession and the very ecstasy of shame as seen in the figure of Pierre Angélique (see Bataille 1973, 3:22; and 1988c, 95–98. See also 1991c, 48, 90, 91, 93, 435n3; and 1991a, 17). On the difference between Bataille's sense of laughter and comedy (the comedy where individuals lose themselves) and the egocentric scoff, see 1991c, 109. Bataille also mentions a laughter that is roused by indecency, avoiding dark love in his late text, *Eroticism*. There he states, "[f]or it is laughter that justifies a form of condemnation that dishonors us. Laughter takes us along the path that transforms prohibition and inevitable necessary decencies into a blinkered hypocrisy and a lack of understanding of the issues at stake. Extremes of license coupled with joking go hand in hand with the refusal to take erotic truth seriously, I mean tragically" (1986a, 266).

57. Bataille also sees syncopation between "smutty laughter" and "total laughter" (1986a, 267). "What that loud and smutty laughter distracts us from is the oneness of extreme pleasure and extreme pain, the oneness of being and dying, of knowledge finishing with this dazzling prospect and final darkness. No doubt in the long run we might laugh at this truth, but it would be total laughter, not stopping at contempt for something repugnant but overwhelming us with disgust" (1986a, 267).

58. As "literature [it] is *communication* . . . requiring loyalty," communication exposed and willing to be sacrificed (Bataille 2001b, ix). See also 2001b, 27, 188–89.

59. See 1991c, 138.

60. "This is because a 'beyond' begins with a feeling of nakedness. Asexual nakedness is simply stupor taken to the limit. But as it awakens us to an awareness of physical touch (touch of bodies, hands, moist lips), it's gentle, animal, and *sacred* . . . since, once naked, we

each open to more than what we are, and for the first time we obliterate ourselves in the absence of animal limits. We obliterate ourselves, spreading our legs, our legs opening as widely as possible, to what no longer is us but is something impersonal—a swampy existence of the flesh. The communication of two individuals occurs when they lose themselves in sweet, shared slime" (1994, 98). "Two beings communicate with each other through their hidden rents. There is no communication more profound: two beings are lost in a convulsion that binds them together. But they only communicate when losing a part of themselves. Communication ties them together with wounds, where their unity and integrity dissipates in fever" (1985, 250). See also Connor 2000, 52–58.

61. The s/laughter of subjectivity is not the loss of our selves, not the product or dross of the stylistic trickery of writing, or theater, which are mere reactions, as Bataille wrote, to "*the poverty of animal life*" (1991c, 109). These aspects are merely the fall, of which the s/laughter of subjectivity is an unnerving vertigo.

62. Even Bataille took up principles and thus fell into "project," and only by the sporting quality of the hunt for conceptual exercises can his call to "chance" lacerate his books further. In the themes of animality and laughter there is a chance that a new reading of the works of Bataille can commence, eliminating the obstacles of both his mystic ancestors and poststructuralist orphans. "Project" is to make sense, to write over Bataille, and to even rewrite Bataille, and that as his death wish and only chance, is to dismantle projects for the game that laughs at his anguish and distress. Animality and laughter set us upon the path between transgression and work, the only path on which Bataille moved (see 1986a, 261).

63. Nietzsche's principle of future-blindness is exemplified by Zarathustra's "good fortune" to have been laughed at by the crowd, accepting that he has been taken as mouthpiece of the satirical jester. The good fortune is that laughter places one with others, and in the example of Zarathustra, it was such laughter that signals his descent among men. As Bataille would say, "laughing, I'm back again, back with other human beings" (1988a, 60). See Nietzsche 1954, Prologue §8.

64. See Bataille 1988a, 96–98, for an understanding of the movement between outside and inside as "slipping," or the slippage (*le glissement*), found at their borders.

65. See also 1991b, 149, 151, 188; and 2001a, 97.

66. Laughter also frightens, to which Bataille counters the "laughing playfulness" of the child's take on things, opening up to the "infinite laughter" (the gamble), and the relation of dancers, whose "laughter is laughter itself," or that opening of the "unspeakable intimacy" within as mad laughter (see 1988a, 98, 107–108, 119, 139, and 153).

67. They are ultimately where "we communicate with the unlimited world of those who laugh" (1988a, 97). The "domains" that Bataille lists are laughter, tears, sexual excitation, poetic emotion [evocation], the sentiment of the sacred, and ecstasy. See Bataille 2001a, 159–60.

68. Bataille in Surya 2002, 491; see also Bataille 1987, 68.

69. See 1991c, 199–200.

70. "The object of tears or of laughter—and of other effects such as ecstasy, eroticism or poetry—seemed to me to correspond to the very point at which the object of thought vanishes. Up to that point, that object might be an object of knowledge, but only up to that point, so that the effect of knowledge would regularly fail. (Every philosopher knows how exhausting is the impossibility of working out the problem of laughter . . .)" (1991c, 208–209).

71. "The sovereign moment . . . is posed for us, not as a secondary form, but as a need to fill the void of the world of useful works" (1991c, 227; see also 230 and 239).

72. This can be seen as Marcelle within the wardrobe, Simone atop Don Juan's tomb, B's relation to Dianus, "herself animally pleased at [his] folly," and Edwarda's pleasure. See Bataille 1987, 14, 68; 1991a, 22; 1988a, 119; and 1989b, 158.

73. "If I say that my laughter encloses knowledge, it is an intellectual position, it's true, but in this way I realize a sovereign operation in that my judgment is related to an element that is no longer intellectual" (2001a, 172).

74. The "perfect laughter [is] the laughter that doesn't laugh" (1991c, 439n3). Silence or the laughter that does not laugh is akin to the "vacuum of thought" (see 1991c, 203).

75. See 2001a, 177–78. "To destroy transcendence there has to be laughter" (1994, 55). But what is beyond the suture of transcendence if not the swoon calculated in advance by the smile of wanton eyes? (see 1988a, 27). "The longed-for swoon is thus the salient feature not only of man's sensuality but also of the experience of the mystics" (1986a, 240).

76. For an account of the ascent on Mount Etna in Sicily with Laure, see Bataille 1986b, 103–105. See also Surya 2002, 258.

77. This risk is the result of excess, of a consciously incomplete recalibration of all constraints, and as what poetry puts at stake. See Bataille 2001b, 37, 39, 42. In this light, commentary on Bataille's work should not become work, or what writing was for Bataille, mere "concern," or "worry"—a task of building, rather than a construction site in full and endless movement. See also 2001a, 214.

78. This is where Bataille "wants people to laugh, shrug their shoulders, and say, 'He's having fun at our expense, he's alive'" (1994, 7).

79. See Pawlett 1997, 171, 173n24.

80. "It is a laugh, a sob, a silence that has nothing, which hopes for and retains nothing. Because the mania of possession made intelligence the opposite of laughter, a poverty at which those who are enriched by their mad generosity laugh endlessly" (2001a, 200).

81. As fallout of this, there is the "contempt for the other's animality," the brutality and scales of judgment as to a person's place in humanity (see 1991c, 334, 339).

82. Sovereignty belongs to the "necessity of abandoning the project while en route" (2001a, 264).

83. "As soon as human beings give rein to animal nature in someway we enter the world of transgression forming the synthesis between animal nature and humanity through the persistence of the taboo; we enter a sacred world, a world of holy things" (1986a, 84).

84. "The relationship between laughter and the unknown, a relatively measurable element . . . represented as having an effect that will be proportional to the importance that this diminution of the known nature, or this suppression of the known character of nature, makes us laugh" (2001a, 136).

85. See 1986a, 252. ". . . sleep and laughter . . . detach themselves, forgetting" (2001a, 89).

86. Specialized philosophy entails specialized discipline and activity (1986a, 254; see also 1988a, 24, 107).

87. Animality is "that SECRET—that the body abandons" (1991a, 80; 1991c, 119). The necessity of abandon is seen in eroticism and extended to "abandoning the project while en route [where] despair and indifference appear equally unacceptable [as does] the middle solution [of] the squirrel's game" (2001a, 264). As Bataille states, "hopelessness is not a return to animal nature" (1986a, 135), whether it is of the existential or the cynical brand.

88. See 1992, 17.

89. "For the animal, nothing is given through time" but takes place "this side of dura-tion" (1992, 18). "Every problem is in a certain sense a problem of the *use of time*" (2001a, 81).

90. See 1992, 19, 23, 36.

91. See Bataille 1973, 3:496n1.

WORKS CITED

Agamben, Giorgio. 2004. *The Open: Man and Animal.* Trans. Kevin Attell. Stanford, Calif.: Stanford University Press.

Bakhtin, Mikhail. 1984. *Rabelais and His World.* Trans. Hélène Iswolsky. Bloomington: Indiana University Press.

Bataille, Georges. 1973. *Oeuvres Complètes.* Paris: Gallimard.

———. 1985. *Vision of Excess: Selected Writings 1927–1939.* Edited with an Introduction by Allan Stoekl. Trans. Allan Stoekl, with Carl R. Lovitt and Donald M. Leslie Jr. Minneapolis: University of Minnesota Press.

———. 1986a. *Eroticism, Death and Sensuality.* Trans. Mary Dalwood. San Francisco: City Lights Books.

———. 1986b. Writings on Laughter, Sacrifice, Nietzsche, Un-knowing. In *October 36,* 80–102. Cambridge: MIT Press.

———. 1987. *Story of the Eye.* Trans. Joachim Neugruschel. San Francisco: City Lights Books.

———. 1988a. *Guilty.* Trans. Bruce Boone. Venice, Calif.: Lapis Press.

———. 1988b. *Inner Experience.* Translated with an Introduction by Leslie Anne Boldt. Albany: State University of New York Press.

———. 1988c. *L'Abbé C.* Trans. Philip A. Facey. London: Marion Boyars.

———. 1989a. *The Tears of Eros.* Trans. Peter Connors. San Francisco: City Lights Books.

———. 1989b. *My Mother. Madame Edwarda. The Dead Man.* Trans. Austryn Wainhouse. London: Marion Boyars.

———. 1991a. *The Impossible.* Trans. Robert Hurley. San Francisco: City Lights Books.

———. 1991b. *The Accursed Share: Volume I.* Trans. Robert Hurley. New York: Zone Books.

———. 1991c. *The Accursed Share: Volumes II & III.* Trans. Robert Hurley. New York: Zone Books.

———. 1992. *Theory of Religion.* Trans. Robert Hurley. New York: Zone Books.

———. 1994. *On Nietzsche.* Trans. Bruce Boone. New York: Paragon Press.

———. 1995. *Encyclopaedia Acephalica.* Edited by Robert Lebel and Isabelle Waldberg. London: Atlas Press.

———. 2001a. *The Unfinished System of Nonknowledge.* Trans. Michelle Kendall and Stuart Kendall. Minneapolis: University of Minnesota Press.

———. 2001b. *Literature and Evil.* Trans. Alastair Hamilton. London: Mario Books.

Bennington, Geoffrey. 1995. Introduction to Economics I: Because the World Is Round. In *Bataille, Writing the Sacred.* Ed. Carolyn Bailey Gill. London: Routledge.

Bergson, Henri. 1928. *Laughter: An Essay on the Meaning of the Comic.* Trans. C. Brereton and F. Rothwell. New York: Macmillan Company.

Connor, Peter Tracy. 2000. *Georges Bataille and the Mysticism of Sin.* Baltimore: Johns Hopkins University Press.

Connor, Steven. 1992. Absolute Rubbish: Cultural Economics of Loss in Freud, Bataille, and Beckett. In *Theory and Cultural Value.* Cambridge, Mass.: Blackwell.

Derrida, Jacques. 1992. *Given Time: I Counterfeit Money.* Trans. Peggy Kamuf. Chicago: University of Chicago Press.

Goux, Jean-Joseph. 1990. General Economics and Postmodern Capitalism. *Yale French Studies* 78: 206–24.

Jaspers, Karl. 2003. *Way To Wisdom: An Introduction to Philosophy.* Trans. Ralph Manheim. New Haven, Conn.: Yale University Press.

Keynes, John M. 1965 [1935]. *The General Theory of Employment, Interest and Money.* New York: Harcourt, Brace & World.

Lakatos, I., and P. Feyerabend. 1999. *For and Against Method.* Edited with an Introduction by Matteo Motterlini. Chicago: University of Chicago Press.

Laure [Colette Laure Lucienne Peignot]. 1995. *The Collected Writings.* Trans. Jeanine Herman. San Francisco: City Lights Books.

Lingis, Alphonso. 1997. The Misunderstanding. *Parallax* 4: 79–88.

McCloskey, Deirdre. 2002. *The Secret Sins of Economics.* Chicago: Prickly Paradigm Press.

Nietzsche, Friedrich. 1954. *Thus Spoke Zarathustra: A Book for All and None.* Trans. Walter Kaufman. New York: Penguin Books.

———. 1966. *Beyond Good and Evil.* Translated with commentary by Walter Kaufman. New York: Vintage Books.

———. 1968. *The Will To Power.* Trans. Walter Kaufman and R. J. Hollingdale. New York: Vintage Books.

———. 1974. *The Gay Science.* Trans. Walter Kaufman. New York: Vintage Books.

Pawlett, William. 1997. The Use-Value of Georges Bataille: Social Science, Textuality and Being-in-Excess. *Parallax* 4: 167–74.

Rey, Jean-Michel. 1988. Bataille e Nietzsche. In *Georges Bataille: Il politico e il sacro.* Ed. Jacqueline Risset. Naples: Liguori Editore.

Root, Deborah. 1989. Disappearing America: Bataille's Reading of the Aztec Sacrificial Economy. *Social Discourse* 2 (Spring-Summer): 221–28.

Sloterdijk, Peter. 1987. *Critique of Cynical Reason.* Trans. Michael Eldred. Minneapolis: University of Minnesota Press.

Surya, Michel. 2002. *Georges Bataille: An Intellectual Biography.* Trans. K. Fijalkowski and M. Richardson. London: Verso.

Veblen, Thorstein. 1994 [1899]. *The Theory of the Leisure Class.* New York: Penguin Books.

NINE

DOROTHY HOLLAND

Bodies at Play: A General Economy of Performance

Theater is this crucible of fire and of true meat where anatomically, through the stamping down of bones, of members, and of syllables, the bodies are remade, and the mythical act of making a body is presented physically and naked.

JACQUES DERRIDA, *The Secret Art of Antonin Artaud*

Only by canceling, or at least neutralizing every operation of knowledge within ourselves are we in the moment, without fleeing it. . . . The miraculous moment when anticipation dissolves into NOTHING, detaching us from the ground on which we were groveling, in the concatenation of useful activity.

GEORGES BATAILLE, *The Accursed Share: Volumes II and III*

 Bodies Do Not Lie

There is a classic theatre story about Eleonora Duse that demonstrates the notion of the body as a site of a fundamental authenticity and truth. For those who do not know about her legendary acting talent, Duse was famous for a remarkable naturalness: she refused to wear stage makeup; she astounded audiences with her ability to express genuine emotion on stage rather than relying on conventional theatrical representations of emotion; in short, she appeared to be actually living on stage rather than performing. Duse was held up as the antithesis of another equally famous late-nineteenth-century diva, Sarah Bernhardt. While Bernhardt was touted as the exemplar of superb technical virtuosity and theatricality, Duse was the exemplar of an inner truthfulness and spontaneity. When George Bernard Shaw reviewed Duse's performance in the title role of Magda in June of

1895, he was astonished to see a rather shocking physiological occurrence take place during her performance: Duse blushed. Shaw describes the moment in the play where Magda, after many years, unexpectedly meets the father of her child. Shaw notes that Magda handled the awkward occasion fairly well until she actually looked at the child's father:

> Then a terrible thing happened to her. She began to blush; and in another moment she was conscious of it, and the blush was slowly spreading and deepening until, after a few vain efforts to avert her face or to obstruct his view of it without seeming to do so, she gave up and hid the blush in her hands. After that feat of acting I did not need to be told why Duse does not paint an inch thick. I could detect no trick in it: it seemed to me a perfectly genuine effect of the dramatic imagination. (Shaw 1991, 371)[1]

This blush can be seen as a double sign, pointing both to the fictional world of the play and to Duse's own material existence—the facticity and presence of her living body. The jolting intrusion of the latter into the former is what captivated and shocked. The story goes that Shaw even returned to the theatre the next night to see if it would happen again; and amazingly, at the same moment in the play, a blush swept up over Duse's face just as it had in the previous night's performance.

A New York critic observed the same effect in Duse's performance of *Magda* several months later, in February of 1896:

> In the second act, when after many years she comes face to face with her betrayer, you witness something the like of which I am positive has never been seen before. . . . In a moment her whole past history rises up before her, the blood suffuses her neck, her face, her very eyes it seems, and she turns away bowed down with shame. How the actress accomplishes these things passes all understanding. (quoted in Le Gallienne 1965, 138)

How did she do it? If you have never tried to blush, try to do so now. Difficult, isn't it? Impossible, really. As anyone knows, blushing is a function of the autonomic nervous system and is not subject to command. How did Duse repeatedly call up the unsummonable, the involuntary rush of blood that so thrilled and perplexed Shaw and the other spectators? Many critics insisted that Duse must have relied on improvisation and the inspiration of the moment in her playing, for this was no artificial manipulation. This was the real thing, the body's unmediated expression of inner feeling. The body does not lie.

A similar belief in the efficacy of the body as a signifier of nature and truth is evidenced in the Living Theatre's famous production of *Paradise*

Now (1968). The performance began by breaking the traditional spatial division between actor and audience: the actors came down off the stage and into the auditorium to speak directly to audience members. They repeated a litany of oppressions that they suffered: "I'm not allowed to travel without a passport"; "I don't know how to stop the wars"; "I'm not allowed to smoke marijuana." These repetitions, which began quietly, built in volume and urgency as actors enticed audience members to join in, to get involved in their protests. With the final section and the repetition, "I'm not allowed to take off my clothes," the actors began to disrobe and invited spectators to do the same (Neff 1970, 60).[2] As if casting off the chains of oppression with the clothes shed, naked and near naked bodies were offered up as the primary instruments of revolt against an oppressive system—The Establishment. "The nature of the master is to lie," writes Julian Beck (1991, 35). Against the lie, Beck and company countered with the truth of the body. Beginning with the "Rite of Guerilla Theatre" and disrobing of actors and (some) spectator bodies, *Paradise Now* consisted of a series of loosely scripted episodes of rites and visions of revolution. The performance culminated in a march of actors and audience members out of the theatre and onto the street—naked bodies leading the way toward a direct confrontation with the police who invariably waited outside: us against them, the triumph of freedom against oppression. Bodies do not lie.

Whether in times of revolt or conservatism, the theatre has always been associated with a very real potential for transgression. This potential danger lurks not only within the theatres of the avant-garde; it is an ever-present possibility, even in the most hallowed edifices of culture. For example, at the Shakespeare Globe Theater in London in the summer of 2003, a Women's Company took the stage for the first time in history. They mounted two all-female productions: *Richard III* (with the superb British actor Kathryn Hunter as Richard) and *The Taming of the Shrew* (with Kathryn Hunter as Kate and the Tony Award–winning British actor Janet McTeer as Petruchio). Just to clarify, male characters were not changed to female; female actors played the male roles as men; in other words, playing fully cross-gender much as Shakespeare's all-male company would have played female roles in 1593.

Shrew was a particularly apt choice for the Women's Company since it is a play about supposed identities and gender politics. The performance of this play via female bodies yielded delicious contemporary resonance and theatrical delights for the audience; it offered a taste of the ribald kind of public gender play that I imagine Elizabethan audiences might have enjoyed with the performance of *Shrew* by the Shakespeare's own company. To give you a sense of the performance event, let me describe Janet McTeer's entrance as

Petruchio. Admittedly, the audience came to the performance with the knowledge that this would be an all-female company, so the question foremost on our minds was "How are they going to pull it off?" The first scene with the suitors (Lucentio, Gremio, Hortensio, and Baptista and his daughters) confirmed that, through costume, makeup, voice, posture, gesture, and that ineffable theatrical magic that allows the actor to shift her "I am" at will, these highly competent female actors could signify a believable maleness very well indeed. However, the role of Petruchio, that quintessential macho braggart who comes to wive it wealthily in Padua, would require more than adequate technical skill; he must own the stage, command it and us and the wildcat shrew by force of his masculine power. McTeer had the physical attributes to carry it off: she is tall (6'1") and has a powerful stage presence. Those of us who had seen her as Nora in Ibsen's *A Doll's House* (the role for which she won the Tony Award in 1997) would recall her buoyant and flittering femininity as Nora, her soul-wrenching anguish as the profound emptiness and falsehood of her marriage became painfully clear. But Nora was such a thoroughly feminine character. How would this tall, lanky, womanly woman embody the hyper-masculine Petruchio, we might wonder?

Petruchio arrived, riding in a wooden cart that was pulled through the pit, forcing the sea of groundlings to give way as he passed. In the cart with him was a very pregnant wench. Those close to the cart could see his hand caress her bosom as he stood up. Bidding farewell to the wench with "Verona, for a while I take my leave, to see my friends in Padua," he leaps from the cart and up onto the stage, where he struts about taking stock of "Padua" (including all of us in the audience, of course, with special attention to a bevy of attractive young females standing close to the front of the stage). The audience laughs, immediately recognizing the behavior; and Petruchio, acknowledging our approval, puts hands on hips, puffs out his chest, and nods, as if to say, "Yeah, I do this cocky stuff pretty well, don't I?" Another wave of laughter. There is a palpable sense of fun with the multiple layers of signification at play, the quick circuits of meaning and impulse exchanged between audience and actor in this quintessentially theatrical playing space. Then, spotting the column stage left, Petruchio crosses to it, reaches down to undo his fly, deftly mimes the act of relieving himself against a "tree." Howls of laughter, not only at the deftness of the representation, but also at the daring in making that acting choice. So this is how it will be: full-bodied, bawdy, and delightfully theatrical. Standing near the corner of the stage, two women in the audience are straining to get a good look at the floor at the base of the column that Petruchio leans against; another wave of laughter goes up as people realize what the women are looking for, and we delight in the ludicrousness of their response and the great fun of it all.

Not everyone in the audience was delighted, however; one indignant gentleman and his wife were moved to flee the theatre at intermission. I descended the stairs right behind this stylish middle-aged couple. Halfway down the stairs, the gentleman suddenly stopped and turned around. His eyes met mine, and he held out two tickets, "Would you like these?" he asked. He proudly explained that they were the best seats in the house, but they wouldn't need them anymore because they were leaving. They were not going to put up with this kind of nonsense. "This is absolutely ridiculous," he said with great authority. "I'm an actor, and I know. This play was written for a man and a woman!" I didn't have the heart to correct him, to point out that it was actually written for two men. After all, I was an American tourist, this was his country, his Shakespeare, and besides, his wife looked painfully embarrassed as she stood quietly behind him peering over his shoulder. So I let it go, took the tickets, and moved down from my cheap seats to enjoy the rest of the play with unobstructed sight lines and luxurious proximity to the stage.

The best upset of the day, however, was not the indignant exit of the actor and his wife, but a woman in the audience whose sudden shock prompted an involuntary outcry near the end of the performance. It happened when Janet McTeer (as Petruchio) picked up Kathryn Hunter (as Kate) and bellowed out, "Come, kiss me Kate," then did so. As soon as their lips met, this woman in the audience cried out at the top of her voice, "I can't believe it!" Well, of course, that only tickled the rest of us no end, and we all had a fabulous laugh. The actors, too, were clearly delighted and made an even greater flourish of the kiss, which prolonged our waves of laughter. Still, the woman was truly shocked. Evidently, it was all well enough for females to pretend to be men in the play, but for two female bodies to actually move torso-to-torso and press their lips together, that was a transgression not to be endured without public protest. A blush is a blush, and a kiss is a kiss. Bodies do not lie. Or do they?

🌣 *The Act Which Is Not One*

This is not a simple question. Inextricably related are notions of subject, agency, performativity, and the possibility for transgression. In other words, the nature and efficacy of the body is challenged in the aftermath of the poststructuralist critique of presence—a critique that not only dismantles notions of a preexisting, fixed, and transcendent subject with the power to exert (his) free will upon the (natural) world, but also seems to challenge the very materiality of the body itself, as Judith Butler, following Foucault, has argued. Bodies, too, are constructed and not simply rendered "naturally." Therefore, the efficacy of the body as a sign of unmediated truth is called into question.

How might the critique of presence inform our assessment of Duse and whether her blush was real or feigned, whether it expressed true emotion or merely an artificial effect? First, let us consider how her contemporaries explained the phenomenon. We can dismiss those who explained the blush as the effect of sudden improvisation, for the regular reoccurrence of that blush, at precisely the required moment, gave evidence to a more remarkable phenomenon: a craftsmanship so extraordinary that it completely disappears. Shaw attributed the blush to the force of Duse's imagination. A similar explanation was offered by the great American actor and theatre director Eva Le Gallienne, who claimed that Duse's artistry was controlled by "a transcendent imagination . . . and served by a body which had been molded into a flawless instrument" (1965, 156). This notion of the artist exerting the force of her imagination to play the instrument of her body harkens back to the eighteenth century, to Diderot and his pivotal treatise on the paradox of the actor's art.[3] It is a vision of Nature revealed, yet Nature controlled and fashioned by the mind of the artist. The artist is the doer, the body the instrument, and art, by definition, the product of the artist's imaginative, disciplined, and diligent doing. But a poststructuralist critique challenges this notion of the transcendent, controlling artist and her natural, truth-telling body. Instead, Duse appears as a social agent constituted in a discursive social field rife with tensions over the distinctions between the categories of natural and mechanical, of sincerity and deceit. Her blushing body expresses neither truth nor lies; and rather than an instrument *being played,* it instrumentally *plays itself,* or, rather, materializes its instrumentality by way of performative acts selected from the collective social repertoire of possible acts.

As for the unmediated, liberatory, and truthful bodies of the Living Theatre—those supposedly inherent qualities must dissolve under critical scrutiny. The bared flesh was hardly unmediated: no handicapped, no aged, no obese figures appeared; only young, trim bodies found their way onto the stage. Cultural norms and regulatory schemas were tenaciously in force, despite cries of "Freedom Now!" And, for all the castigations against the Establishment, the company performed within the auspices of that Establishment in multimillion-dollar theatres on college campuses for upper-middle-class audiences, offering what might be seen as a commodified taste of revolt, a transgression that reaffirmed the rule against which it nakedly danced head-to-head. And as to truthfulness, one might say that these bodies did lie, if lying is marked by a disparity between stated beliefs and actions, between the talk and the walk. Despite protestations against the oppressions and social injustice, the acts (theatrical and performative) of the Living Theatre wholly conformed to prevailing hetero-normative gender regulations. The "Rite of Universal Intercourse" enacted in *Paradise Now* was exclusively heterosexual, and traditional gender roles prevailed. Although the performance included protests against the war, the state, drug laws, capitalism, and racial bigotry, no protest was enacted against the violent oppression of, and violence toward, homosexuals. But then, historical possibilities are necessarily constrained by historical conventions, as performativity theory claims; the women's movement and gay rights movement had not yet fully emerged on the social horizon. Performativity might suggest that, as social agents, the actors of the Living Theatre were constrained by the repertoire of possible and recognizable acts of their time.

🏵 *The Bifurcation of Act and Recognition*

Recognizable acts. Possible acts. Referring to this dual aspect of the performative, Butler writes that "a phenomenological theory of constitution requires an expansion of the conventional view of acts to mean both that which constitutes meaning and that through which meaning is performed or enacted" (1990, 272). She continues this clarification (via Beauvoir) by noting that the body suffers a certain cultural construction not only through conventions that sanction and proscribe how one acts one's body, the "act" or performance that one's body is, but also in the tacit conventions that structure the way the body is culturally perceived (1990, 274–75). Act and recognition would seem to go hand in hand, and normative and regulatory pressures might tend to ensure their mutuality; yet the unstable nature of the act which is not one—neither wholly self-same in its iterations, nor consciously taken up and performed by a preexisting subject—assures possibilities for variant acts and/or (mis)recognitions. Butler elaborates on the act and recognition components of performativity by way of a theatrical metaphor: a script that "survives the particular actors who make use of it," but requires other actors to actualize and reproduce it "as reality once again." Butler notes that, although the new actors might enact the script "in various ways," their interpretations will necessarily take place within the confines of "already existing directives" (1990, 277). The script metaphor is telling. Actors (and bodies) are posited as narrowly constrained interpreters of pre-existing discursive texts, and legibility is paramount.

Now there is much that I find attractive about the concept of performativity: how it tickles the brain, yielding the pleasure of a good puzzle, the pleasing disorientation of an engaging contradiction, and that rush at suddenly seeing something anew from a startlingly different perspective. You will note that I am pointing to body experiences of theory. Furthermore, the conception of the performative as a process of constitutive acts resonates with my experience as an actor, particularly with regard to the theory of physical actions and certain actor-training programs that approach the work from a strong physical focus, such as the Alexander Technique, Tadashi Suzuki Technique, Lecoq, and Viewpoints. Most importantly, I like the potential for transformation, for self-fashioning and social change inherent in the complex of ideas at play in the field of poststructuralist criticism.

At the same time, I find several aspects troubling: first is the wholesale use of theatre terms and metaphors without a serious consideration of actual theatre practices. As Judith Butler readily admits, "Philosophers rarely think about acting in the theatrical sense" (1990, 270). In the positioning of theatre in contradistinction to "real life," there seems to be a tendency toward the reiteration of a false/true dichotomy that the philosophical discourse elsewhere denies. We might question the extent to which the presupposition of *theatrical* as false (i.e., playacting, not real, a lie) serves as the constitutive outside of a *real* (true) life which it produces, thus rendering theatre the alterity haunting the boundaries of the real as the persistent possibility of its disruption and rearticulation. Theatrical language, within the discourse on performativity, remains just that—language; there is little serious consideration of embodied theatre practices. There is little consideration of bodies at all. Although critical discourse has, in many respects, moved beyond Cartesian dualism, there seems to be a continual inclination toward one side of the old duality—a persistent reenactment of the fundamental devaluation and denial of the material.

At its extreme, the discourse on performativity invokes a pervasive silencing effect in respect to material bodies. Butler briefly addresses this issue in the Introduction to *Bodies That Matter,* where she acknowledges that the radical constructivist position can appear to refute "the reality of bodies" in the refusal to concede certain "facts" of materiality. Butler defends her position, her refusal to make concessions to any appeals, by proclaiming that "there is no reference to a pure body which is not at the same time a further formation of that body," and she requires "the prior limitation of the extra-discursive" (1993, 10–11). Now I can appreciate the tactical restraint and the impulse to protect the extra-discursive by way of non-concession. And I recognize that to call into question is not to deny, that a refusal to concede can simply be a refusal to delimit, a refusal to enact the violence of referentiality that excludes as it produces, constructs only through erasure. It is a compelling argument, but it is an argument whose immediate and primary effect is silence. And bodies need to be considered. A refusal to speak, to write, to refer to "bodies" will not alone free material bodies from the potential violence of normative, regulatory, and injurious effects. Furthermore, this emphasis on the discursive and the disregard of the play of physicality lies at the heart of the problematic bifurcation of act and recognition within performativity.

🌀 *The Bifurcation Problem*

The bifurcated model of act and legibility, of performance and spectator, presents several problematic aspects: the undergirding inclination toward an autonomy of thought; the notion of separate and discrete boundaries; and a misunderstanding of the dynamics of the live performance event. The metaphor of the script surviving (death?) and exerting its inherent directives to future generations of actors valorizes thought over the material, a transcendence of consciousness in perpetuity via the text. In practice, an existing script is not taken up in order to bring *the script* to life; it is taken up by actors, directors, and/or designers because they recognize something appealing in the text, something that they want to explore, to test, to discover, to promote, or simply to enjoy. Furthermore, neither the script nor the directives that adhere to the script (i.e., printed stage directions, character and set descriptions) exert definitive constraints on the live theatre artists and subsequent productions—subsequent productions of existing scripts vary greatly, both from the "original" production and from all other subsequent productions.

As to the performance event itself, it is not an act that can be read objectively at a distance; not a message-sent, message-received exchange, with each component as separate and discrete, discernable and known. The performance event is not a bifurcated doing and recognizing; not separable, but rather mutual interactions, adjustments, and play within a field of living material bodies. As Jerzy Grotowski notes, "The core of theatre is an encounter" (1968, 56, 58). The one-way communication model does not begin to convey the complexity of that encounter. Furthermore, spectators are not passive observers, not simply witnesses to the acts of performers; they are interactive participants in the collective performance event, as Anne Ubersfeld writes in *Reading Theatre:*

> There is no one spectator; rather there is a multiplicity of spectators who react to each other. Not only do we rarely go to the theatre alone, but also

we cannot be alone at the theatre. Any message received by one spectator is refracted (upon fellow spectators), echoed, taken up, and sent off again in a very complex exchange. (1999, 23)

Live performance occurs within a field of heightened energy, where visual, auditory, tactile, discursive, and kinesthetic stimuli abound in a relatively open and multifaceted perceptual field (unlike film, where the camera directs the spectator's gaze). The dynamics of recognition are profoundly grounded in the living matter of physical bodies, in the muscles, bones, cells, and neural pathways. As Charles Scott explains in *The Lives of Things,*

> Bodies are not unities but sites that are composed of a variety of more or less dense elements and of conflicting forces that are ruled, more or less, by parts of the conflict. Bodies compose a fluid constellation of interacting forces in which the rule is always up for grabs at any moment. Within this perspective, a moment is a digestive process that has as its aim the continued movement and activity of the body. (2002, 167)

Physical bodies are not passive receptors or docile instruments. Physical bodies participate, select, resist, resonate, digest, echo, enjoy, and embody directives of their own, both onstage and off. How, one wonders, could they possibly not be included in the consideration of performativity?

✸ *Physical Bodies in a Limited Economy*

On the other hand, bodies are messy. They exceed the cohesive thought that would grasp and hold them tight. They resist attempts to be represented in language. But it is not solely this difficulty of capture that relegates physical bodies to subordinate and marginal situations; the effects of a far more pervasive and fundamental bifurcation are at work—the bifurcation that marks the leap from animal to human, as Bataille explains in *The Accursed Share:*

> Not wanting to depend on anything, abandoning the place of our carnal birth, revolting intimately against the fact of *dying,* generally mistrusting the body, that is, having a deep mistrust of what is accidental, natural, perishable—this appears to be *for each one of us* the sense of the movement that leads us to *represent* man independently of filth, of the sexual functions and of death. (1991b, 91)

In its wake, the world of thought, grown strong in the space carved out by prohibitions, now rules with a Cyclops-like tyranny (able to look in only one direction and from a singular point of view, lacking all depth perception, and missing the whole of which it is but part), yet holding sway over "the flat and subordinated world that we know, this world of useful and isolated things, in which laborious activity is the rule" (1991b, 24).

Bataille argues that, within this limited economy, servile man enslaves himself to production, accumulation, and utility. Man becomes the equivalent of a tool, and "like the tool, he who serves—who works—has the value of that which will be later, not of that which is" (1991b, 218). Man projects himself into an ever-receding future, thus rendering himself blind to the present moment (the only moment there is):

> From the start, the introduction of *labor* into the world replaced intimacy, the depth of desire and its free outbreaks, with rational progression, where what matters is no longer the truth of the present moment, but rather, the subsequent results of *operations*. . . . Once the world of things was posited, man himself became one of the things of this world, at least for the time in which he labored. (1991a, 57)

Thought and calculation rule. Within the limited economy, the physical body is doubly subordinated: it serves as both abject horror and productive tool. Rendered *abject* by the repulsion for that which is accidental and perishable, the physical body serves as the constitutive outside of thought itself. As a *tool,* the physical body is used, controlled, and driven—a primary instrument in the service of production, its behavior governed by prohibitions against idleness and non-(re)productive sexuality. An object of knowledge, its identity is fixed, its directives clear: be productive, be *useful.*

 Undermining Bifurcation: Bataillean Transgression with Sovereignty in Its Wake

> *Play alone uses up the resources produced by labor.*
> GEORGES BATAILLE, *The Accursed Share: Volumes II and III*

> *Work consists of whatever a body is obliged to do, and Play consists of whatever a body is not obliged to do.*
> MARK TWAIN, *Tom Sawyer*

What's to be done? Play. Play can disrupt the operations of the limited economy by consuming, by squandering resources, energy, and time. Play can disrupt the ethos of utility and the enslavement to useful ends. Play as if your life depends on it! Bataille didn't say that, but he might have; for that was his analysis—"living servilely is hateful" (1991b, 219). And there is more at stake than individual fulfillment. As Bataille demonstrates in the first volume of *The Accursed Share,* "energy finally can only be wasted." This is the fundamental law of the universe. Although man tries to deny it, "his denial does not alter the global movement of energy in the least: The latter cannot accumulate limitlessly in the productive forces; eventually, like a river into the sea, it is bound to escape us and be lost to us." The excess, the accursed share, must be wasted, either gloriously or catastrophically (1991a, 11, 23).

Bataillean transgression is not the head-on assault that only reaffirms the strength of the prohibition (e.g., the Living Theatre example); but rather, it is non-engagement, an oblique movement, a movement toward the abject. The pleasures of play that no end limits or justifies. Play that disrupts the would-be autonomy, the tyranny of thought and its bifurcation of subject and object, that tyranny "which aims to reduce its object to the condition of subordinated and managed things" (1991a, 74). Play. Laughter. Tears.

> Deeply rhythmed movements of poetry, of music, of love, of dance, have the power to capture and endlessly recapture the moment that counts, *the moment* of rupture, of fissure. As if we were trying to arrest the moment and freeze it in the constantly renewed gasps of our laughter or our sobs. The miraculous moment when anticipation dissolves into NOTHING, detaching us from the ground on which we were groveling, in the concatenation of useful activity. (1991b, 203)

Now it's time to engage in some play of our own.

The Tiger Is in Space What Sex Is in Time

One of the foremost physical theatre companies in the world is the London-based company, Theatre de Complicite.[4] Complicite is known for innovative interpretations of classics and for devised works created by the actors in the company through a lengthy process of research, collaboration, and exploratory workshops. *Mnemonic* (1999) is one of their devised works. It is devised from multiple sources: material from the actors' own lives; the words of John Berger, Konrad Spindler (*The Man in the Ice*), Anaïs Nin, Hans Magnus Enzenberger, and Benoit Mandelbrot (inventor of fractal geometry); and the collaborative contributions of Complicite's artistic directors and designers. The company is renowned for its unique integration of image, music, media, text, and inventive physicality, and for a mode of playing that invites the audience to engage with complicity in the theatre event. *Mnemonic,* as the title implies, is a play about memory; but at a deeper level, as I hope to demonstrate, it is a play about embodiment. As such, it is also a play about expenditure without return. But enough introduction, let's go to the theatre.

The auditorium is full, the audience abuzz with pre-show chatter and energized anticipation. The stage itself is dark and empty save for a simple wooden folding chair near the front of the stage and a rock lying nearby on the floor. The chair and rock are illuminated slightly by a lighting instrument above. As we take our seats, we find a small plastic bag on our chair like the ones on transatlantic flights; we settle in, place jackets carefully on seat backs, stow personal items on the floor under our seats; the small plastic bags rest in our laps. The house lights dim . . . Simon McBurney enters from the audience carrying a handheld wireless microphone. A follow spot catches him as he climbs the steps up to the stage. This is an unexpected and provocatively informal appearance by the evening's director and star, but not wholly unconventional—it seems to be some kind of director's pre-show speech: "Good evening ladies and gentlemen. Before we start the show I'd like to say one or two words about memory. Yesterday somebody asked me why are you doing a show about memory? And I was trying to remember . . ." The audience laughs. OK, it's more of a stand-up routine than a director's pre-show speech. He continues,

> Perhaps it's because one of the last great mysteries is the one we carry inside our heads. How we remember, why we remember, what we remember. Or maybe it's simply that they say that the human memory starts to degenerate when you are only twenty-eight years old, and as I am now over forty the matter is becoming a little pressing. (1999, 3)

Another laugh. McBurney's opening monologue is charming, playful, provocative. He continues to talk about memory, about how modern theories "revolve around the idea of fragmentation" and that it's not the cells that are important as much as the connections between the cells. Further, that these cells are constantly being remade: "Even as I am talking to you, part of your brain is changing. You are literally developing new connections between the neurons. They are being fabricated even as I speak. It's called sprouting" (3).

He continues talking about shifting contours and chaotic maps and losing your way and the job of memory to put the pieces back together. And about memory not being just an act of retrieval but "a creative thing, it happens in the moment, it's an act, an act . . . of the imagination." And what helps us choose what to remember is the hippocampus "here at the base of the brain," he says, pointing to the back of his head.

And the way it chooses is to fasten upon either something that we already know or what we have an emotional attachment to. So, for example, perhaps I thought about my father because this chair was his. (*Gesturing to the folding chair to his right.*) I *know* it. He sat on it. And so did my grandfather. In fact it's a chair I know very well because I have used it in several of my shows. . . . (5)

McBurney sits down on the chair and goes on to an association about the rock near his foot and a lover who may have tripped over that rock. Suddenly the chair breaks and he falls! "Oh, Jesus," he cries; then he recovers with a joke: he will always remember that mishap because his hippocampus must be squirting lots of chemical juices right now. We laugh. Just as we are wondering whether that really was an accidental mishap or a planned event, McBurney confesses that the chair is not really his father's chair but a fake chair, a joke chair—"a joke to make you laugh . . . I want you to remember this chair." And the rock? To remind him not to go on too long. He takes out a smaller rock from his pocket and says that the smaller rock is to remind him to warn us to turn off our cell phones: "If anybody's mobile phone goes off during the performance, they will be forcibly ejected from the auditorium" (6). More laughter. We see people reaching for their cell phones to make sure they're switched off.

We are now eight minutes into the opening monologue (not that we are aware of the time; Simon has been much too engaging for any clock-watching). Because we cannot take anything for granted, we are attentive and fully engaged in the moment. The monologue will continue for seven more minutes, during which time Simon leads us on an inner journey: "Before we offer you some of our fragments, we would like you to reassemble some fragments of your own" (6).[5] Simon instructs us to open the plastic bags that have been resting in our laps and to take out the sleeping mask and the leaf inside. "Put on the mask." We all do so, laughing at both the oddness of the request and the distinct feeling of silliness that we are experiencing. Now blindfolded, we hear Simon ask us to think back to last Sunday morning: "Where are you? What's the weather like? What do you see?" He leads us further back each time. New Year's Day 1999 . . . Autumn 1991 . . . and further back: "You are six years old. It's summer. Or perhaps your first day of school. . . . Look down at your feet. What shoes are you wearing?" Playing along, I imagine looking down: black patent-leather Mary Janes! Oh, I remember those! Sense memory.

Look behind you to your right, hold up your hand in your imagination. Another hand clasps yours. It is your mother. Look up to your left. Another hand clasps that one. It is your father. And now look back behind your right-hand side. Behind your mother, with a hand on each of her shoulders, are her parents . . . and to the left on your father's side are his parents. His mother. His father. Six people stand behind you. All looking at you. (7)

Simon continues to talk us through the steps of imagining the increasing numbers of relatives standing behind us. By the beginning of the nineteenth century, 256. By the beginning of the eighteenth century, "assuming there are no kinship ties," 4,064. And back and back we go in our imagination, to a thousand years ago when "that line would be longer than all people who have ever been born. Which of course is not possible—but it means that you are related to everyone sitting in this theatre" (7). Some of us laugh, others sit silently calculating that possibility. At last, Simon instructs us to remove the blindfolds. We do so.

We open our eyes to find Simon seated on stage with his own blindfold on, chewing gum, holding his leaf, and listening to the same instructions that we've been listening to: "Now look at the leaf," Simon's voice continues; but the voice is no longer coming from Simon's body. The voice that was live and present to us just a moment ago in the living organism uttering these words is now a recorded facsimile; and Simon McBurney's captivating presence is suddenly gone; he has become someone else (his costume, situation, and physicality all changed). With this abrupt shift in perspective and actor identity, we experience a moment of distressing/pleasing disorientation. Simon, the actor, has assumed a character, not a representation of an absent presence, but a representation of the present bodies—our bodies—sitting in attendance at this very performance. Here and now. Together we are all following the (recorded) instructions to look at the fractal patterns on our leaf and to imagine those lines as the long lines of ancestors leading to us. Then his cell phone rings! We laugh, remembering the injunction against cell phones. Embarrassed and expecting to be thrown out of the auditorium straightaway, he answers it, sotto voce, and mimes working his way apologetically down a row of disgruntled audience members toward the exit.

VIRGIL: Well I was in a theatre, in the middle of a show—
MAN'S VOICE: You were in the theatre? What were you doing in a theatre for God's sake?
VIRGIL: I don't know. Why does anyone go to the theatre?

We laugh.

MAN'S VOICE: I'll call you later. Go back in.
VIRGIL: No, no, I can't, it's much too embarrassing—

> MAN'S VOICE: What were you seeing?
> VIRGIL: I thought I was going to see some dance, or something . . . it's this company that people said were really very physical, apparently they used to be funny . . .

We laugh again.

> MAN'S VOICE: Yes?
> VIRGIL: But what happened was that this guy came on and did this whole rap about memory.
> MAN'S VOICE: A lecture?
> VIRGIL: No, no—a performance and then we all had to put on these blind-folds. (9)

And now Virgil relates the whole experience, or at least the key aspects, in-cluding walking his friend through imagining a line of relatives stretching back in time. This blurring of now and then, of present experience and the replay of memory, we easily recognize: it is what we experience in one way or another every day of our lives—the foundation of our memory resting on the sensory, embodied perceptions, reinscribed, repeated, retold, reworked, remembered.

Virgil suddenly stops talking and looks straight out as though remem-bering his conversation, but the conversation continues; that is, the sound of the conversation continues uninterrupted via yet another seamless shift from live to prerecorded sound. We actually see this second shift from live to recorded sound; but even though we see it, we still get a rush of disorien-tation—a momentary disjunction: What's going on? Where are we? What's happening now and what's a replay? a memory? Clearly, we can't be sure. "This is what he's getting at," Virgil's voice continues, "the further back we go, the more chaotic our inter-relationships become. In other words, we do not know where we come from. . . . We know that we're here but we don't know why" (11).

As Virgil-who-is-one-of-us (remember) arrives at center stage, a bed, small sink, table, and television suddenly slide on and assemble around him. Home. Ah, yes, we recognize it immediately: he's home. And we settle back a little in our seats. Virgil switches on the television, takes off his clothes, and sits, naked, on the bed. Talk about a double sign pointing to both the fictional world and the actor's material existence! Well, that's courageous. My thoughts spin off: he seems comfortable enough. . . . Is that a tattoo?! Oh, my God, Simon McBurney has a tattoo band around his upper arm. Isn't that odd. . . . But just as quickly, my attention is called back:

VIRGIL (on his cell phone): Hi, it's me again.
MAN'S VOICE: Oh, God.
VIRGIL: Listen, I just wanted to explain—
MAN'S VOICE: It's two-thirty in the morning.
VIRGIL: Well, never mind, I was awake anyway. (14)

We laugh. Virgil continues: "The point being, you know, why did she leave?
. . . The point is that Alice is in a state of turbulence . . . our emotions are
essentially fluid. We have . . . hello? . . . hello, oh, shit" (15).
We laugh.

Virgil turns on the answering machine and listens to Alice's last message over and over: "Now you have to wait and follow me." Tossing about,
unable to sleep, he takes his pillow and lies down on the floor downstage, his
head resting on the rock (the rock from the prologue, remember?). Lights
dim. Ah, sleep, at last. Sound of radio static and fragments of a broadcast:

> Who can say what caused a high-level southerly air current between the
> fifth and eighth of March 1991 to transport a Saharan dust which darkened
> the sky and fell over a wide range of the Austrian Alps. . . . It could have
> been a movement of a camel, a mountaineer's sweat. . . . All movements of
> the earth contribute to the chaotic movement of weather. . . . (15–16)

Sound of loud wind, a sudden wash of brilliant blue skylight all across the
back of the stage, and stark white side light as two actors clothed in huge
parkas move in a slow-motion ascent up onto the table and the bed. We are
in the Alps, and simultaneously in Virgil's apartment. The mountaineers
look down where Virgil is lying on the floor. As the mountaineers move
slowly downstage toward Virgil's naked body, we hear "From a distance of
eight to ten meters, we saw something sticking out of the ice. Our first
thought was that it was rubbish. . . . But as we came closer, Erika said, 'But,
it's a man'" (16).

The play unfolds like Virgil's thoughts—fragmented, turbulent, swirling movements as his thoughts turn to Alice and to his other obsession: the
body of the 5,000-year-old Iceman found in the Alps in 1991. Objects trig-
ger memories of Alice and the replaying of fragments of conversations, im-
prints of moments together. In another area of the stage, we see Alice on her
journey, a journey taken suddenly on the heels of her mother's funeral. ("She
died. She never said a thing. . . . It was her sister who told me my father was
alive. Might be alive.") We see Alice on the Eurotrain heading across France;
at the Berlin train station where her wallet is stolen; at her sister-in-law's in
Poland receiving a box of her father's belongings (objects that give witness

to his life—a pair of shoes, a lighter, a fancy shawl). We see Alice on yet another train in a chance encounter with a BBC correspondent who speculates on the meaning of her father's objects: a smoker (obvious), a piano player (only the right shoe heel worn down), and a Jew (the shawl a tallith). At a seedy nightclub in Riga, Alice learns that her father might be at a hospital in Poland; but when she gets to the hospital, she finds that he already left.

As Virgil waits to hear from Alice, his mind turns even more insistently to the story of the Iceman—the discovery; the clumsy attempts at extracting the body from the ice ("We tried with a pneumatic chisel but it slipped time and time again—a couple of times it went right through his left thigh"); the press conferences and the battles over ownership; the significance of the objects found with him (a broken stick, strips of leather, fragments of birch bark); and competing theories about how he died (X rays show rib fractures). "He was aged between thirty-five and forty, which, in the Neolithic period, would have made him an old man" (17, 64). What was he doing at that altitude at the beginning of winter?

The threads of the different stories weave and flow in seemingly random ways, and two or three scenes often occur in the same space and time, compelling us to find connections, patterns, resonance among the fragments. The complexity is delightful, engaging. Occasionally breathtaking: when Alice finally telephones Virgil and he hears her voice, the image of her face appears on the skin of his bare chest as she talks to him. Even though we realize that a closed-circuit camera must be capturing her image and there must be a projector somewhere—ah, there it is—still the veracity of the effect is palpable: we are marked by those we love, inside and on the surface of our bodies. In the course of telling him what has happened, Alice mentions the BBC journalist who helped her figure out the significance of her father's belongings. "Did you—" Virgil probes, but cannot finish the question. "No, we didn't," she answers impatiently. "Yes. No. It doesn't matter" (56). When the conversation ends, Virgil is shaken, disturbed by what he suspects, what he imagines. He lies down on the floor, his favorite insomnia sleeping place; suddenly the bed starts to move across the stage right over him, as if not only his thoughts, but his whole world now traverses time and space to be where she is. In its new position, the bed becomes both the one on which Alice and the journalist lie down and Virgil's own bed. In an exquisitely choreographed sequence, Alice and the journalist take off their shirts and lie on the bed together. Virgil crosses to the bed, takes off his pants, and lies down; at the same time, they get up, dress, and repeat the process again. Just as they lie down, Virgil gets up, puts on his pants and crosses to the table, leans against it for a moment, then pushing off, goes back toward the bed. The whole sequence repeats four times. Worlds overlap, bleed through. We live, seem to be, where our affections lie. Or our fears. And watching this sequence, we feel the dynamic relation, how a chance encounter in Poland sets off a turbulence in London. Or is this the way Virgil's mind and body play the imagined scene over and over again? Repetition itself, a tyrant?

The journey we began in our theatre seats, holding our leaf and adjusting to those disorienting little shifts in time, space, and perspective, has plunged us into a kaleidoscope of movement, a world where objects have fluid meanings and multiple uses. The rock from the opening becomes a pillow, a gravestone, a dying place. Objects, losing their utility, become sacred (a broken watch, a folding chair); and sacred objects, colliding with the utilitarian world, risk losing their sacredness and becoming mere things. "What's so special about this body? What's it worth?" demands a reporter (28); "My name is Clare Mulvey. I'm calling from Sydney, Australia, look I'm having IVF treatment at the moment, and I wondered if there's any chance of some of that Neolithic sperm coming my way?" . . . (32). We laugh. Virgil wonders, "How many children did he have? What word did he use to signify summer? . . . or this place? How many songs did he know? Had he yet heard the story of the flood?" (55).

The chair. Remember the chair that collapsed during Simon McBurney's opening monologue? At some point after the apartment first assembled, Virgil picked up the collapsed chair and put it away under his bed. Later, he drags it out from under the bed to fix it and carries it to the table. A stunning image that—a naked man alone in his flat, his arms outstretched, carrying a broken chair with its spindly legs dangling; the chair looks vaguely human, and both figures appear oddly fragile. Just as Virgil gets to the table, a voice calls out, "Herr Professor, can we see the body?" Virgil turns front and a rash of paparazzi flashbulbs go off; the bright white lights burn the image into our retinas: the naked body of Virgil holding the chair in his arms, Pietà fashion. Then Virgil lays the collapsed chair on the table. "Why is the body naked?" yells a journalist. Two scientists cover the chair with a sheet. They examine the body, hovering around the table in their white lab coats. An amusing image this—the seriousness with which the scientists study the broken chair; but the association is made, and it isn't long before the chair plays a central role in our drama—it transforms into the lanky, leathery-brown figure of the Iceman.

Even though we can clearly see the actor-puppeteers manipulating the chair—one moving the right arm and a tall walking stick, another the legs, another the left arm and head (just a wadded pillowcase deftly held in the air), there is something in the rhythm and the angle of movement, something in the precise way the spindly legs ease forward that let's us recognize the withered body of the 5,000-year-old Iceman suddenly animated with life. Virgil's voice recounts the event: "Evidently overtaken by a blizzard or sudden fog, the Iceman was in a state of total exhaustion." Our bodies resonate as step-by-step the figure moves downstage. Where do you feel the impact? Where does it hit you? In the shoulder? The back? Or, like me, deep in the hip where femur nestles at the inmost point—the point of release into momentum when we climb. Yes, yes, that's it—the impulse up and out, the forward flow of movement against the wind. Virgil's voice continues: "In the gully in the rock perhaps familiar to him from previous crossings of the pass, he sought what shelter he could from the bad weather. A terrible fatigue engulfed his limbs. He knew that to fall asleep meant death. He staggered forward a few more steps." A momentary stop, the Iceman tilts his head. It's a pillowcase, I know, still my suboccipital muscles register the shift and lengthen. The figure scans the horizon; my head yields, ever so slightly, in concert with his. And yours? Virgil's voice continues: "He staggered forward a few more steps. He slipped and fell against a rock. The birch-bark container fell from his hand; his cap fell off." The Iceman falls to his knees; his head, that elegantly tilted pillowcase head, falls slowly against the stone. "He only wanted a short rest, but his need for sleep was stronger than his will power. . . . Soon his clothes froze to the ground" (63).

A few last shallow breaths heave slowly through his body, then stillness. The actors slowly back away, upstage. The figure is alone. Feel the hush? The mix of awe and dread. The holding back and leaning forward. We're near the edge, the wind, the hint of vertigo. Virgil sits on his bed on one side of the stage, Alice on the other side of the stage illuminated only by the dim light of a pay phone; the still body of the Iceman lies on its left side downstage center. Virgil, on his cell phone: "That's one theory. We can't know for sure because we can't ask him . . . Alice? Are you there?" . . . "Virg—can you hear me?" . . . "Alice, you're breaking up . . . Alice . . ." (71). Dim, solitary shafts of light isolate each one of our three players. "The separation of beings is limited to the real order," writes Bataille. "It is only if I remain attached to the order of things that the separation is real" (1991a, 192).

The light fades out on Alice, yet we hear her voice continue under the following, an intimate voice that seems not to be coming from outside ourselves, but from inside, not her questions, but our own: "What does nakedness remind us of?" Virgil crosses up to the table. "Dear God, what does nakedness remind us of? Naked, our needs are so clear, our fears so natural. . . . Seeing a naked body of any age, we remember our own. It is how we put our-

selves in someone else's place. In the gully, for example, 5,000 years ago."
Virgil lies down on the table on his left side, facing upstage, his body echoing the taut rigid line of the Iceman's frozen body. "Seeing a naked body of
another person we make an inventory of our own" (71).

The other actors move up behind the table; they hold up a metal frame
and peer through it as though looking through a museum display window—
the Iceman's refrigerated display unit at the museum in Balzano. The voice
continues, "Shoulder blade, ribs, clavicle. We list the sensations we feel in
each part, one by one, all of them indescribable, all of them familiar, all of
them constituting a home" (71). One of the people peering through the window suddenly ducks under the frame and slowly moves in to change places
with Virgil/the Iceman. Slowly, one by one, each of the actors steps in and assumes the place on the table, replacing the one before—the same position,
the same moment of rigid stillness, then a quick turn over and up and off,
only to be replaced by another body, and another, and another, and another.

> ALICE (voice-over): All of them indescribable.
> VIRGIL (voice-over): All of them indescribable.
> ALICE (voice-over): All of them familiar.
> VIRGIL (voice-over): All of them familiar.
> ALICE (voice-over): All of them constituting a home.
> VIRGIL (voice-over): All of them constituting a home. (72)

The rolling continues and grows quicker and quicker. Lights shift to
backlight and the tumbling figures are seen in silhouette. The momentum
accelerates, as does our breathing and the dizzyingly palpable sense of millennia upon millennia of bodies stretching down to us. "A broken stick.
Splinters of wood. Strips of leather. Twisted grass. Fragments of birch bark"
(73). As the last body rolls over the table, all furniture pieces slide quickly
off, and the actors form a line in profile across the front edge of the stage. In
unison, they lean down; each picks up a tall walking stick. They lean back
and scan some distant horizon; suddenly they look to the right. What is it?
Danger? The future? The past? The unfathomable present? A huge projection of the Iceman slowly appears on the distant wall. They turn and move
toward the image. Lights fade to black.

The moment of rupture, of fissure—"the miraculous moment when anticipation dissolves into NOTHING," and we sit, plenum taut, and weep,
peering into that impenetrable abyss, dizzy with horror and joy (1991b,
203). "We draw near to the void," says Bataille, "but not in order to fall into
it. We want to be intoxicated with vertigo, and the image of the fall suffices
for this" (1991b, 109).

NOTES

1. Theatrical "tricks" to simulate emotion were also legendary. One of the most famous was attributed to David Garrick, who in his day was touted as "natural" in comparison to the great, but artificial, Betterton. Critics noted that in performances of *Richard III*, Garrrick's hair actually stood on end when he saw Banquo's ghost. It was later revealed that Garrick had a mechanical wig that he controlled to effect the trick of his hair standing up. No such tricks were ever ascribed to Duse, however.

2. Although official company instructions designated that actors were to take off only as many clothes as locally allowed by law, audience members who participated (there were always a few who joined in) were not bound by the rules; and indeed, actors often impulsively transgressed this restriction.

3. Diderot determined that the actor should not try to feel the emotions that he represents in performance, but should indicate them by means of external signs that are taken for the real thing. For Diderot, the actor's being subject to the passions of the body indicates both faulty technical control and bad art. Rather, the great actor creates an "inner model" of the part from observation and reflection, then "arrange[s] the whole thing in his head" (Roach 1996, 133) so that he is able to perform it the same each time. The great actor controls the unruly sensibility of the body through discipline, technique, and a particular disconnect between the expression of passion and sincerity. For a thorough discussion of Diderot's acting theory, see Roach 1996.

4. Founded in 1983 by Simon McBurney, Annabel Arden, and Marcello Magni, Theatre de Complicite has created more than 30 productions, toured to more than 40 countries, and received more than 25 international awards. Recent theatre productions include: *The Elephant Vanishes* (a co-production with Setagaya Public Theatre of Japan); *Measure for Measure* (Royal National Theatre); *Noises in Time* in collaboration with the Emerson String Quartet (based on the life of Shostakovich); *The Street of Crocodiles* (based on the writings of Bruno Schultz); Ionesco's *The Chairs*; *The Three Lives of Lucie Cabrol* (based on writings of John Berger); and Brecht's *Caucasian Chalk Circle* (Royal National Theatre). *Mnemonic* was conceived and directed by Simon McBurney and devised by the company for the Salzburger Festspiele. *Mnemonic* opened in London at the Riverside Studios in November 1999.

5. Quoted entries for this section are compiled from three sources: the published script, my notes from a live performance of *Mnemonic* in New York (May 2001), and my notes from a London Theatre Museum Video Archive recording of a performance of *Mnemonic* taped at Riverside Studios (January 2000).

WORKS CITED

Bataille, Georges. 1991a. *The Accursed Share: Volume I*. Trans. Robert Hurley. New York: Zone Books.

———. 1991b. *The Accursed Share: Volumes II and III*. Trans. Robert Hurley. New York: Zone Books.

Beck, Julian. 1991. *The Life of the Theatre*. New York: Limelight.

Butler, Judith. 1990. Performative Acts and Gender Constitution: An Essay in Phenomenology and Feminist Theory. In *Performing Feminisms*. Ed. Sue-Ellen Case. Baltimore: Johns Hopkins University Press.

————. 1992. Contingent Foundations: Feminism and the Question of "Postmodernism." In *Feminists Theorize the Political.* Ed. Judith Butler and Joan Scott. New York: Routledge.

————. 1993. *Bodies That Matter: On the Discursive Limits of Sex.* New York: Routledge.

Derrida, Jacques, and Paule Thévenin. 1998. *The Secret Art of Antonin Artaud.* Trans. Mary Ann Caws. Cambridge: MIT Press.

Foucault, Michel. 1998. *Essential Works of Foucault, Volume Two.* Trans. Robert Hurley. New York: New Press.

Grotowski, Jerzy. 1968. *Towards a Poor Theatre.* New York: Simon and Schuster.

Le Gallienne, Eva. 1965. *The Mystic in the Theatre: Eleonora Duse.* New York: Farrar, Straus, and Giroux.

Neff, Renfreu. 1970. *The Living Theatre/USA.* New York: Bobbs-Merrill Company.

Roach, Joseph. 1996. *The Player's Passion: Studies in the Science of Acting.* Ann Arbor: University of Michigan Press.

Rostagno, Aldo. 1970. *We, the Living Theatre.* New York: Ballantine.

Scott, Charles. 2002. *The Lives of Things.* Bloomington: Indiana University Press.

Shaw, Bernard. 1991. *Bernard Shaw,* Vol. 2, *The Drama Observed.* Ed. Bernard F. Dukore. University Park: Pennsylvania State University Press.

Theatre de Complicite. 1999. *Mnemonic.* London: Methuen.

Twain, Mark. 1920. *The Adventures of Tom Sawyer.* New York: P. F. Collier and Sons.

Ubersfeld, Anne. 1999. *Reading Theatre.* Trans. Frank Collins. Toronto: University of Toronto Press.

SOVEREIGN POLITICS

Part Four

TEN

ANDREW CUTROFELLO

The Accursed Share *and* The Merchant of Venice

In the preface to the first volume of *The Accursed Share,* Bataille promises to "overturn" political economy (1988a, 10). Just as Marx criticized the classical bourgeois political economists for failing to unlock the mystery of surplus value, so Bataille criticizes modern economists for considering economic phenomena from a merely "restricted" rather than a "general" point of view. Modern political economy is restricted because it focuses on relatively isolated and recursive systems of the type production-consumption-production, and because in so doing it takes production rather than consumption to be the raison d'être of the entire process. According to Bataille, the restricted point of view is misleading in the first respect and pernicious in the second. An increase of energy in any local system cannot be sustained indefinitely; eventually something must give and the pent-up energy spent. Hence the question is not *whether* but *when and how* sumptuary consumption will take place. When considered from a general point of view that factors in all energy flows within the solar system, the real problem faced by economic systems is not how to extract surplus value for the sake of production, but how to dissipate surplus energy through sheer consumption, that is, without recuperation of the loss sustained (Bataille 1988a, 21).

In showing how various societies have grappled with this problem, Bataille comes up against the phenomenon of the potlatch, which, he says, "has a privileged place in general economy" (1988a, 69). As described by Marcel Mauss in *The Gift: The Form and Reason for Exchange in Archaic Societies,* the potlatch is a ritual practice by which a tribe either gives away or destroys an enormous quantity of its own wealth (1990). As such, it has the appearance of pure expenditure or consumption. But in fact, the potlatch typically functions as a means for acquiring either counter-gifts or prestige, thereby paradoxically serving to increase wealth. In this respect it embodies the elementary form of venture capital.

We can think about the paradox of the potlatch in one of two ways. On the one hand, we can regard its failure to break with the principles of restricted exchange as contingent, as a function, say, of what Kant would call pathological inclinations (whether conscious or unconscious) that happen to (but in principle need not) contaminate the actions by which wealth is destroyed. On the other hand, we can recognize the failure as necessary in the sense of being inseparable from the very happening of consumption. Bataille seems to think about the paradox in both ways. Insofar as he regards it as possible to give away or destroy wealth without any recuperation, he urges us to "make one more effort" at being general economists (as the Marquis de Sade urged his contemporaries to make one more effort at being republicans). Yet he also suggests that an act of pure expenditure can only take place in a vanishing instant when there would no longer be any "taking place" at all. This is the thesis that Derrida takes up in *Given Time: 1. Counterfeit Money,* when he suggests that gift-giving, if there is any, cannot occur within time (1992). For both Bataille and Derrida, abandoning a restricted point of view—that is, abandonment itself—is not just impossible; it is *the* impossible. But unlike Derrida, who expresses reservations on precisely this point,[1] Bataille bids us to confront the impossible by undertaking a *sacrifice* in which the boundaries between self and other disappear.

Bataille's principal objection to capitalism is that of all economic systems it provides the least favorable conditions for sacrifice. The lingering need to dissipate excess wealth, intensified by so-called "crises of overproduction," is met only through periodic world wars (1988a, 119). Bataille, writing in 1947, suggests that the only way to prevent the Cold War from culminating in a third world war is for the United States to direct its excess wealth toward *"raising the global standard of living"* rather than toward "military manufactures" (1988a, 187). Thus he ends the first volume of *The Accursed Share* by calling for a radicalization of the Marshall Plan. The choice that Bataille presents us with is accordingly between two different ways of consuming excess wealth: blindly, by slavishly sleepwalking into world war; or lucidly, through a lavish act of expenditure. What is paradoxical in all this is that the opposition Bataille sees between nuclear escalation and "raising the global standard of living" is not between sacrifice and generosity; on

the contrary, it is between the anti-sacrificial logic of capitalist expansion-
ism, on the one hand, and, on the other, an anti-capitalist communism for
which the difference between sacrifice and generosity disappears. After all,
the only way to ensure that a generalized Marshall Plan does not serve the
telos of increased production is if its giving away of wealth functions as a
genuine sacrifice rather than as a profitable investment. Thus we find Bataille responding to the paradox of the potlatch by longing for a sacrifice
that would be absolutely total.

In what follows, I would like to explore this longing through a reading
of Shakespeare's play *The Merchant of Venice.*[2] As we will see, Shakespeare confronts the paradox of the potlatch in the contrasts that he portrays between
pagan and Christian practices of risk-taking, and between Jewish and Christian practices of money lending.[3] Insofar as Shakespeare seems to be saying
that Shylock the Jew remains stuck within a restricted point of view, in contrast to the general ethic adopted by Antonio the Christian, *The Merchant of
Venice* might be read as an apologia for Christianity on roughly Bataillean
grounds. However, Shakespeare complicates this picture in a number of
ways, notably by calling attention to an obscure melancholia that haunts
both Antonio and Shylock's daughter Jessica, who hopes to forsake her
father's restricted ways by marrying a Christian. Exploring the tensions in
Shakespeare's play will help explain why Bataille finds the sovereignty of "expenditure without reserve" not in Christ but in Nietzsche, the self-professed
antichrist whom Bataille pointedly allies with communism rather than with
(fascist) anti-Semitism. Conversely, reading *The Accursed Share* through the
lens of *The Merchant of Venice* will enable us to question Bataille's identification of generosity and sacrifice.

 I

In *The Merchant of Venice,* Shakespeare brought together two traditional
folktales, one pertaining to a spiteful creditor who seeks to exact a pound
of flesh from his debtor, the other to a maiden whose hand in marriage can
only be attained if the suitor correctly guesses which of three caskets contains her picture.[4] Instead of resulting in a mere pastiche of separate episodes, Shakespeare's play interweaves the two stories so that they form a
coherent whole. Thus we find the debtor—a merchant named Antonio—
impawning himself to the vicious creditor Shylock for the sake of Bassanio,
who by choosing the correct casket becomes the successful wooer of Portia.
Shakespeare does not merely *coordinate* the two stories; by providing Antonio with the motive of assisting Bassanio, he *subordinates* the creditor-

debtor narrative to the story of the three caskets. In so doing, he enables us to see the restricted creditor-debtor relation from a general—or, at least, more general—point of view.

We are alerted to this difference in perspective at the very beginning of the play. Antonio is melancholy, and his friends Salerio and Solanio assume that this is because he is worried about the merchandise that he has consigned to sea. Antonio assures his friends that this is not the case, for by distributing his wealth among several different ships bound for different ports he has greatly reduced the chance of loss. This tells us that Antonio is a shrewd investor who in matters of business takes only calculated risks. It also suggests that the cause of his sadness cannot be discerned from the narrow purview of a profit-oriented restricted economy. No sooner is this conveyed than Bassanio appears, signaling the more general point of view that will be taken on both Antonio's sadness and his eventual contract with Shylock. As Salerio and Solanio (who are just as interchangeable as Rosencrantz and Guildenstern) take their leave, Antonio's parting words to them underscore the fact that they belong entirely to the world of restricted economy: "I take it your own business calls on you, / And you embrace th'occasion to depart" (1.1.63–64).

Before explaining to Antonio that in order to woo Portia he needs to borrow money, Bassanio first apologizes for the fact that he has already squandered an earlier sum that Antonio lent him. Antonio replies impatiently that he does not care about the debt, nor would he, had Bassanio "made waste of all I have" (1.1.157). Right away we see the difference between Antonio the merchant and Antonio the friend. Unlike the "restricted" Antonio, the canny venture capitalist who has wisely diversified his portfolio, the expansive Antonio is willing to give all for love. Yet these two aspects of Antonio's personality are not merely indifferent to each other. Were he not a merchant, Antonio would not possess the great wealth that will enable him to help his friend. Conversely, were he not a merchant, his wealth would not be tied up in capital investments and so he would not have to borrow money from Shylock. Although Shakespeare will repeatedly contrast Antonio's Christian generosity—as a moneylender who does not charge interest—with Shylock's Jewish usury, it is important to remember that Antonio only finds himself contracted to Shylock because of his own restricted profiteering.

After Antonio agrees to assist Bassanio, the scene shifts from Venice to Belmont, where Portia is being courted by a slew of undesirable suitors. We learn of the three caskets: one gold, one silver, and one lead, each bearing a cryptic inscription. Before Bassanio arrives, the Prince of Morocco is enticed by the words inscribed on the gold casket: "Who chooseth me shall gain what many men desire" (2.7.5). Much to his displeasure (and Portia's relief), the prince finds inside the casket not her portrait but a skull. Next, the equally unmarriageable Prince of Arragon tries his luck with the silver casket, which bears the inscription, "Who chooseth me shall get as much as he deserves" (2.9.36). Inside he finds "the portrait of a blinking idiot" (2.9.54). The mistake made by both men is to reason from a restricted point of view. To them, Portia is a valuable commodity, so it seems to follow that her portrait must lie within one of the two caskets that has value as a commodity. When Bassanio finally appears, he exposes his predecessors' shared error by rejecting both "gaudy gold" and the "pale and common drudge / 'Tween man and man" in favor of "meagre lead, / Which rather threaten'st than does promise aught" (3.2.101, 103–105). The threatening inscription on the lead casket reads: "Who chooseth me must give and hazard all he hath" (2.7.9). By accepting this *total* risk—as Antonio did in lending him money—Bassanio seems to leave behind the calculated risk-taking of restricted economy in favor of the unrestricted risk-taking of general economy. However, it is precisely here that we encounter the paradox of the potlatch; for at the very moment when Bassanio makes his choice, he does so in the hope that by *risking* all, he will *win* all: "And here choose I. Joy be the consequence!" (3.2.107).

Just as Antonio's Christian generosity has been contrasted with Shylock's Jewish usury, so Bassanio's Christian risk-taking is contrasted with pagan circumspection. But Christian risk-taking—like Christian generosity—turns out to be the best investment of all. This point is underscored by the fact that Bassanio does not merely "hazard all" in an impulsive, unthinking act; on the contrary, he reasons—*calculates*—that to win Portia he must repudiate calculating rationality. To be sure, he cannot know that his gamble will pay off; at most, he knows that the only gamble worthy of a payoff is one that truly risks everything. But that only makes him a shrewder investor. Of course, one could argue that in winning Portia he seeks not to increase his material wealth (as the princes would have done) but to win her love. Yet when he first described Portia to Antonio, the first thing Bassanio noted about her was that she was "a lady richly left" (1.1.161). Be that as it may, when he does win Portia, Bassanio—like Portia herself—is overcome with an ecstasy that transcends all restricted bounds. Portia is the first to give voice to this feeling: "O love, be moderate, allay thy ecstasy, / In measure rain thy joy, scant this excess!" (3.2.111–12).

The rapture shared by Portia and Bassanio joins them not only to one another but also to Portia's attendant Nerissa and to Bassanio's friend Gratiano, who soon announce that their betrothal also depended on Bassanio's choice of the right casket. The ever-widening circle of love's rapture is hinted at by Bassanio when he likens his "confusion" to the experience of a crowd after a rousing speech by "a beloved prince": "Where every something, being blent together, / Turns to a wild of nothing, save of joy / Express'd and not express'd" (3.2.177, 181–83). These words seem to suggest a specifically Christian experience of communion, and were it not for Shylock, the play could well end here. But Shylock has excluded himself from the community of Christians, a fact we are reminded of when Salerio (himself, as already noted, a representative of restricted economy) arrives to announce that Antonio's bond is forfeit and that the unrelenting Jew demands his "pound of flesh." In contrast to Jessica, who hopes to become Christian by eloping with Lorenzo, Shylock refuses to be assimilated to the Christian community—until, eventually, he will be forced to do so by Antonio and the Duke.

Because Shakespeare treats both Jessica and Shylock as potential Christians who can choose to convert, what we might call the "ethical" anti-Semitism depicted in *The Merchant of Venice*—the equation of Jewishness with "stubbornness"—is markedly different from the racial anti-Semitism of the Nazis, for whom Jews were subhuman animals that had to be excluded from the community in order for the community to exist *as* a community (though Bassanio's description of the crowd "blent together" and turned "to a wild of nothing" by a fiery orator could be said to anticipate the euphoria felt at Nazi rallies) (3.2.181–82). As befitting a play classified with his comedies, Shakespeare suggests that a Christian community need not be based on a principle of exclusion at all. However, it might be argued that without a rebellious Shylock, the community of lovers could not establish its difference in kind from a pagan community of mere sexual partners. For perhaps the only way to distinguish Bassanio's *apparent* act of expenditure without reserve from the calculated risk-taking of the pagan princes is to identify the former with Antonio's perfect generosity, and the latter with Shylock's unrepentant usury. To show that Antonio is different in kind from Shylock and not just a better speculator, Shakespeare depicts Shylock not merely as falling short of the Christian ideal of generosity but as openly rebelling against it. This is conveyed by his refusal to show mercy toward Antonio by freeing him from his bond. However, precisely because he is different in kind from Antonio, Shylock turns out to be different in kind from the pagan princes as well. In refusing any recompense other than his pound of flesh, he reveals a desire or drive that is of a completely different order than that of mere rapacity. It is as if, after the betrayal of the daughter who has stolen his ducats, Shylock has entered a zone "beyond the pleasure principle." As such, he serves as a negative image of Antonio, who is also "beyond the pleasure principle," but as a generous Christian rather than as a spiteful Jew. Only by vilifying Shylock can Shakespeare confirm Antonio's virtue. Thus, unlike his daughter, who is able to throw off her Jewishness by marrying a Christian, Shylock remains an *irreducibly* Jewish figure whose very unassimilability to the Christian community guarantees that the community is Christian and not pagan.

The reading that I have just sketched suggests that Shakespeare displaces the paradox of the potlatch—the theme of the story of the three caskets—by attempting to draw a hard-and-fast distinction between Shylock and Antonio. However, it could just as easily be argued that in the figure of Shylock he has projected what Antonio disavows and what is arguably the true cause of the mysterious melancholy to which he gives voice in the play's opening line ("In sooth, I know not why I am so sad"), namely, the fact that despite his desire for the pure expenditure of the gift, he cannot escape the acquisitive stance of restricted economy. This interpretation can be supported by the fact that just as the play does not end when Bassanio chooses the right casket (because of Antonio's debt to Shylock), so it does not end when Antonio is freed from his bond. Instead, Shakespeare continues the story by introducing the famous episode of the rings.

Portia has given Bassanio a ring that he has promised never to give away. Likewise, Nerissa has given Gratiano a ring with the same proviso. But after Portia, disguised as Balthazar, delivers Antonio from his bond to Shylock, she playfully tricks Bassanio by asking for his ring as recompense. At first, Bassanio refuses, asking her to demand any other gift instead. Chiding him for his ungenerosity, "Balthazar" departs. But then Antonio intercedes, bidding Bassanio to requite the person who has saved his life: "My Lord Bassanio, let him have the ring. / Let his deservings and my love withal / Be valued 'gainst your wive's commandment" (4.1.449–51). Reluctantly, Bassanio consents (as will Gratiano to the disguised Nerissa's request for her ring). Here, an act of restitution takes place, for in asking Bassanio to give up the ring for his sake, Antonio has in effect demanded a counter-gift for his gift to Bassanio. Bassanio is free to refuse this request, but if he does, he will show himself to fall short of his friend's generosity. Thus he finds himself for the second time in the play in the predicament of the potlatch, only this time he expects despair (in the form of Portia's reproaches of his faithlessness) rather than joy to be the consequence of his choice. In acceding to his friend's request, Bassanio truly does risk losing all. But in doing so, he repays the debt that he owes Antonio, thereby closing the circuit of a restricted exchange. Thus, Antonio unwittingly finds himself back in the order of restricted economy after all. In light of his unconscious demand for symbolic restitution, is it not conceivable that Salerio and Solanio were right (or *almost* right) all along—that what made Antonio sad from the first was the thought that his investments—in *Bassanio,* not in the *Andrew* (his ship)—might come to nought?

Just as Antonio gives voice to a melancholia whose origin he cannot fathom, so Jessica confesses to Lorenzo that "I am never merry when I hear sweet music" (5.1.69). Lorenzo suggests that this is because her "spirits are attentive" like those of wild colts tamed by "the sweet power of music" (5.1.70–72, 79). Whereas "the man that hath no music in himself" is not to be "trusted," Jessica's ability to be "moved with concord of sweet sounds" attests to her worthiness of becoming a Christian (5.1.83–84, 88). Thus Lorenzo's interpretation of Jessica's sadness can be read as an implicit rejoinder to Launcelot Gobbo's complaint that "we were Christians enow before" (3.5.21–22). If Shakespeare is suggesting that the capacity for melancholia is an eminently Christian virtue, then Antonio's sadness at the beginning of the play would seem to attest to nothing more than his unbounded love for Bassanio. This (more likely) reading goes against the one I proposed above, since it suggests that Antonio's love is different in kind from an economic investment. There is infinite yearning in his feeling for Bassanio, and it can only be fulfilled by including Antonio in the circuit by which rings are exchanged between Bassanio and Portia.

In the second volume of *The Accursed Share,* Bataille suggests that unlike animal sexuality, which serves the useful end of reproduction, eroticism derives its allure from the fact that animal sexuality is subject to human prohibitions. On this view, marriage is itself a kind of transgression—not insofar as it reverts to animal sexuality, but, on the contrary, because it sustains, while crossing, the boundary between the animal and the human (Bataille 1993, 58). Analogously, Shakespeare could be said to locate true "sovereignty" in the marriages of the three amorous couples who reunite at Belmont at the end of his play. At the beginning of Act 5, Jessica and Lorenzo anticipate their own erotic coupling by comparing—and implicitly contrasting—their union with that of non-Christian pagans whose marriages failed to be consummated for one reason or another. The other two pairs of lovers arrive, and after a brief comedy of errors, Bassanio and Gratiano discover that they have unknowingly given their rings back to Portia and Nerissa. All three marriages can now be successfully consummated, and the play ends with Shakespeare discreetly veiling the couples' ecstatic unions.

 II

Like Shakespeare, Bataille attempts to circumvent the paradox of the potlatch by holding out for the possibility of a sovereign experience of community. However, instead of contrasting Christian love with Jewish miserliness and cruelty, he appeals to a Nietzschean ethic of sovereignty that is different in kind from the false Nietzschean ethic of servility invoked by the Nazis. To experience a sovereign moment is not to triumph over others but to identify with the sovereign moments of "all men." In the experience of sovereignty, intoxicating joy merges with excruciating suffering: "It is a question of marking, in the labyrinth of thought, the paths that lead, through movements of vehement gaiety, to that place of death where excessive beauty begets excessive suffering, where all the cries that will ever be heard are mingled, cries whose powerlessness, in this awakened state, is our *secret* magnificence" (1993, 370). In light of Bataille's seemingly cryptic comment that *"the sexual act is in time what the tiger is in space"* (1988a, 12), it is tempting to compare this vision of commingled cries of suffering with Benjamin's reference to the "tiger's leap . . . in the open air of history," which "Marx understood as revolution" (Benjamin 2003, 395). But Bataille means something different. For Benjamin, the tiger's leap represents an act of redemption for past suffering, and as such, it attests to the vigilance of solidarity. For Bataille, by contrast, the "secret magnificence" of intoxicated suffering reaches its epiphany in the nothingness of a "night" that is, paradoxically, the condition of its *dis*appearance.[5] Just as the tiger is a "luxurious" animal that, when it feeds, consumes enormous quantities of energy, so the sexual act epitomizes "a sudden and frantic squandering of energy resources" (Bataille 1988a, 34–35). As such, both represent favorable occasions for a sacrifice.

Had Bataille devoted a chapter of his book *Literature and Evil* to *The Merchant of Venice,* I suspect he would have regretted the fact that in the end Shylock *shrank back* from claiming his pound of flesh (Bataille 2001). Initially, Shylock declares himself to be absolutely firm in his intention to sacrifice Antonio, scoffing at the disguised Portia's plea that he show Christian mercy to his debtor: "By my soul I swear / There is no power in the tongue of man / To alter me: I stay here on my blood" (4.1.240–42). Yet no sooner is he threatened with the rigor of the law than he abandons his pledge to "torture" Antonio (3.1.117). Bataille would surely have regarded this as a mark of cravenness, not only because he believed that sacrifice was a viable form of useless consumption, but because he regarded it as the *highest* act through which human beings attain genuine sovereignty—and *dignity.*

The eminently Kantian value of human dignity might seem out of place in Bataille's thinking, but one of his explicit aims in *The Accursed Share* is to specify the conditions under which "man in general" is "worthy of respect" (Bataille 1993, 337). In his *Grounding for the Metaphysics of Morals,* Kant claims that man is worthy of respect insofar as he is an "end in itself" who, as such, cannot be assigned a market "price" (Kant 1993, 40). Instead of equating human dignity with sovereignty, however, Kant subordinates human beings—as mere "members" of the kingdom of ends—to a sovereign God. Bataille regarded this as just another way of treating humanity as a means to a higher end. To accept, with Nietzsche, that "God is dead" is to equate full human dignity with sovereignty. Sovereignty, in this sense, cannot be equated with mere autonomy, for "an autonomous decision may have no sovereign quality at all; it may even be servile" (1993, 311).

Acquisitive consciousness is inherently servile, as Hegel showed in his account of the master/slave dialectic. Likewise, for Bataille, obedience to moral principles—even those that one gives oneself—is just another form of servility. To attain genuine sovereignty, one must experience oneself as "the *nothing* of pure expenditure" (1988a, 190). Nietzsche had such an epiphany, and it led him to equate sovereignty—that is, the dignity of man—with the "escape from the reduction of being to thinghood" (Bataille 1993, 385). Thus for Nietzsche, as for Kant, human beings are worthy of respect insofar as they cannot be reduced to the status of mere things. Yet unlike Kant, Nietzsche does not reduce human beings to mere instruments of the moral law. The ethical stance that he adopts is truly sovereign in that it "does not *commit itself*," that is, it "does not place us in the service of some means" (Bataille 1993, 380).

Bataille's critique of an ethics of commitment is directed not only against Kant but also against Sartre, who in *Being and Nothingness* equated the subject with nothingness, but only by defining consciousness as a perpetual—and therefore, in Bataille's eyes, perpetually slavish—negation of things rather than as wholly other than the order of thinghood (Sartre 1993). The Sartrean conception of an existential situation in which consciousness must choose its manner of being remains, for Bataille, within a fundamentally utilitarian construal of the committed subject. In rejecting the existentialist conception of commitment, however, Bataille does not lapse into a solipsistic construal of the sovereign subject. To achieve sovereignty is to be in "*communication . . .* with all the *sovereign moments* of all men" (Bataille 1993, 370). This explains why Bataille *literally* identifies with Nietzsche: "I am the only one who thinks of himself not as a commentator of Nietzsche but as being the same as he" (1993, 367). It also explains why he allies Nietzsche with the communists rather than the fascists. As originally conceived by Marx, communism promised to free humanity *from* its enslavement to things and *for* the sovereignty of consumption by installing a semiautonomous economic system of production (Bataille 1988a, 135). Under Stalin, however, communism only accelerated the tendency to reduce human beings to laborers enslaved to things (Bataille 1988a, 140). According to Bataille, the mistake that Stalin made was to repudiate all forms of sovereignty in an indiscriminate (though paradoxically sovereign) manner instead of rejecting only those traditional forms of pseudo-sovereignty that have been predicated on the degradation of a portion of humanity (Bataille 1993, 323).

Despite the failures of Stalinism, Bataille regards communism as capable of achieving true sovereignty—unlike fascism, which is irremediably servile insofar as it equates sovereignty with domination. Because sovereignty amounts to communion with all other human beings, Nietzsche "could not accept a world in which man—*in which each man*—would be a means and not the end of some common endeavor" (Bataille 1993, 367). Bataille laments the fact that Nietzsche used the expression "will to power," because the conflation of sovereignty with power led the National Socialists to misappropriate his thought (Bataille 1993, 453n1). In contrast to power or dominion, which (in Kantian terms) has an "extensive magnitude" in both time and space, sovereignty has only an "intensive magnitude" in the essentially evanescent instant in which it takes place. That is, unlike power, which garishly installs a utilitarian "concern for the future," sovereignty discreetly vanishes in "the reign of the moment" (Bataille 1993, 379). "In such a night as this"—to quote Lorenzo and Jessica (5.1.1ff.)—no clear distinction can be drawn between love and betrayal, for "sovereignty is NOTHING" (Bataille 1993, 430).

 III

In the first volume of *The Accursed Share,* Bataille characterized the shift from restricted to general economy as a "Copernican transformation" with both speculative and practical consequences (1988a, 25). In *Critique of Pure Reason,* Kant inaugurated *his* Copernican turn by arguing that the world as a whole could not be regarded as a closed system. This is the upshot of his solution to the first antinomy of pure reason. From the fact that the world as a whole has *no* determinate magnitude whatsoever (neither finite nor infinite), Kant concludes that in a certain paradoxical respect, the cosmos as a whole is perpetually unfinished.[6] Strange as it may seem, Bataille agrees with Kant about this. This explains why, paradoxically, he limits the context of general economy to that of the "biosphere" alone rather than to that of the cosmos as a whole. It also explains why he has nothing to say about the first law of thermodynamics, according to which the total sum of energy in the universe remains constant.[7] Bataille's thesis seems to have something to do with the second law, according to which entropy increases over time. But like the first, the second law applies to the universe as a whole only insofar as it is conceived as a closed system, and to view it like this is already to take too restricted a point of view on energy flows. For Kant, the laws of thermodynamics have an empirically unrestricted validity, but only with respect to the nature we encounter from a transcendentally restricted (phenomenal) point of view. The task of advancing from a transcendentally restricted to a general point of view (i.e., to a view of the world as a noumenal totality of things in themselves) remains an ineliminable yet unresolvable problem, one that would require us to transcend the limits of possible human experience, whether through an intellectual intuition, which is denied us, or through (moral) faith.

Instead of thinking of the problematic horizon of human experience in these onto-theological terms, Bataille assumes that human existence only attains a general point of view on the cosmos insofar as it approaches the *impossible.* For Kant, the limiting idea of God is the idea of the sum total of possibilities that we think of as the ground of our own existence. But for Bataille, the non-existence of God is vouchsafed in the idea of the impossible as the true ground of possibility itself. One cannot attain the impossible precisely because it is not possible. But since the possibility of death, as Heidegger famously insisted in *Being and Time,* is the possibility of no longer having possibilities,[8] death itself can be figured as the impossible. In the absence of a categorical imperative that could orient us with respect to what is possible (or rather practically *necessary*) for us—something that Levinas will recover via his para-phenomenological account of the epiphany of the face of the other—Bataille is left with a desire purified of all pathological (i.e., possible) objects and so driven toward the impossible, that is, again, toward death. The great passion that sustains all of his writings is the passion to *be* dead, that is, to experience one's own death as the impossible. To achieve this would require that one be able to encounter oneself as a corpse. Ordinarily, of course, a corpse is something we can encounter only from a second- or third-person point of view. But Bataille invites us to identify with corpses from a first-person point of view, to imagine ourselves capable of saying, "I am dead." Since this is something that none of us can accomplish alone, it requires a strange experience of community, one that Bataille takes to be exemplified in sacrifice, particularly in a sacrifice in which victim and executioner completely identify with each other. This was the impossible ideal to which the group Acéphale aspired in the 1930s. Bataille would not have called it an ideal because he regarded the impossible as wholly other than the order of ideality. Yet one could argue that precisely insofar as it remains unattainable, the impossible can only be represented inadequately as an ideal, even if as a counter-ideal to the Kantian conception of God. In any event, the idea that the impossible could only (or best) be approached through sacrifice explains why Bataille was so fascinated, even obsessed, by a series of photographs (one of which he owned) depicting the slicing to death—the claiming of a pound of flesh—of a Chinese felon (Bataille 1989). Throughout *The Accursed Share,* Bataille urges us to make sovereignty—the experience of the impossible— the sole desideratum of our activity. Yet he cannot appeal to utilitarian considerations, nor can he tell us that we have a duty to consume uselessly, as if such an activity were an end in itself in the Kantian sense. Instead, he adopts the argumentative strategy of the seducer, and like all scrupulous (or unscrupulous) seducers, he allows himself any manner of rhetorical device to bring us to his point of view. In the first volume, we are told that we will be *better off* adopting an ethic oriented toward useless consumption. Toward this end, he introduces the crucial, but ultimately questionable, distinction between usefulness and acceptability, suggesting that we should opt for an ethic of sumptuary expenditure over an ethic of accumulation, not because the former is more *useful* in the long run, but because the loss we would sustain through pure expenditure is more *acceptable* than the loss we would otherwise sustain: "It is only a matter of an acceptable loss, preferable to another that is regarded as unacceptable: a question of *acceptability,* not utility" (Bataille 1988a, 31).

At the beginning of the second volume, Bataille appears to acknowledge the failure of this argument (as a seduction strategy), conceding that "I could not then prevent consumption from being seen as something useful." He now turns to a domain which, he claims, *"cannot serve any purpose,"* namely, eroticism (1993, 16). Bataille's chances with us seem better this time, for what could be more seductive than the erotic? And yet we are being enticed to a very specific form of the erotic, to things that provoke horror, such as incest, sex with corpses, and sacrifice—in a word, to the *morally* impossible. In volume three, Bataille reflects on the ethical stance of the archseducer, Mozart's Don Giovanni. What interests him is not the Don's libertinism but his refusal to relent when faced with the prospect of eternal torment for his villainies. Unlike Shylock, Don Giovanni does not shrink back when faced with the full force of the law. On the contrary, he says no to it at the very moment that it closes its icy grip upon him. Bataille was fascinated with this decision, regarding it as *the* ethical act par excellence.[9] But he thought that Nietzsche went one step further, for whereas Don Giovanni says no to an *external* law, Nietzsche—like a diabolically evil Kant—says no to a law that "never ceased to impress itself on [him] *from within*" (Bataille 1993, 405).

Like the Don, Shylock was challenged by an external law to which he (unlike the Don) ultimately gave in. Thus, even if he had taken his pound of flesh, his act would not have been as great for Bataille as it would have been had he done so against the objections of his own conscience. More capable of diabolical evil would be Portia, who at the end of Shakespeare's play finds herself in a position structurally analogous to that of Shylock. This occurs when Bassanio is faced with the unhappy choice of sacrificing either Portia for Antonio (by giving up the ring) or Antonio for Portia (by refusing to yield it). The fact that Portia only pretends to feel betrayed in the play's final scene should not obscure the lingering need for another symbolic act of restitution, and it comes when Antonio offers his soul as a bond for Bassanio's faithfulness, just as he once offered his body to Shylock: "I dare be bound again, / My soul upon the forfeit, that your lord / Will never more break faith advisedly" (5.1.251–53). Portia accepts this contract, and in so doing she acquires the power of carrying out a Christianized version of the act that Shylock ultimately shrinks back from. Were she to claim her pound of *spirit*—if, say, Bassanio were again to favor Antonio over her—she would be in a position to do what Shylock could not, namely, sacrifice Antonio by saying no to the *internal* law that would command her to show mercy. Here we would have an example of what for Bataille would count as a genuinely sovereign act, an act through which human existence achieves true dignity.

Of course, Shakespeare does not go this route; he ends his play with the retreat of the lovers and Gratiano's warning to himself (with a double entendre): "Well, while I live I'll fear no other thing / So sore, as keeping safe Nerissa's ring" (5.1.306–307). But if Bataille had written the play's sixth act—as the psychoanalyst Nicolas Abraham (1994) provided a sixth act for *Hamlet*—he might have depicted a very different Portia: not the merciful Christian who resembles Sade's virtuous Justine, but a Portia closer in sensibility to the unflinchingly evil Juliette.

Whether this would have made for a better play is another question. Had Bataille ever actually written a sequel to *The Merchant of Venice,* I'm sure it would have been fascinating to read. But it is difficult not to share the concerns of those, like Jean-Luc Nancy (1991), who have wondered whether we should allow ourselves to be seduced by the allure of sacrifice. At the same time, it would be facile to refute Bataille by invoking Kantian bromides about what it really means to treat human beings with dignity. In the face of Kantian theses and Bataillean antitheses, Shakespeare may offer us not so much a solution as a way of being attentive to the nature of such ethical aporias.[10] Consider the moment when Bassanio is called to respond to Antonio's request that he give up the ring. At first Bassanio is torn between two moral impossibilities, namely, sacrificing Portia for the sake of Antonio, and sacrificing Antonio for the sake of Portia. In finally agreeing to Antonio's request, he runs an incalculable risk in a way that he arguably hadn't when choosing among the three caskets. Whether or not he escapes the paradox of the potlatch—which, after all, may be impossible—Bassanio's decision cannot be characterized as either moral in Kant's sense or sovereign in Bataille's sense. It is not moral because it amounts to breaking a promise; and it is not sovereign for the simple reason that Bassanio is desperately trying to avoid a sacrifice of any sort. This would disappoint Bataille. But Shakespeare's point is that it is not always through cowardice that one shrinks back from the abyss; sometimes we do so because we find ourselves claimed by another abyss, namely, the abyss of conscience.[11]

NOTES

1. "Rereading these texts by Bataille today in another way, I wonder whether, despite the difference he indicates between mastery and sovereignty, this latter word does not still maintain an extremely equivocal theologico-political tradition, particularly in the sacrificial logic that Bataille takes up in this context. Later I would use this lexicon in a much more prudent fashion" (Derrida and Roudinesco 2004, 93).

2. For another attempt to read Shakespeare's play through the eyes of Bataille, see Wilson 1996.

3. For another take on Shakespeare and the potlatch, see Jackson 2001.

4. For a brief account of the sources of these two folktales, see Anne Barton's introduction to *The Merchant of Venice* in *The Riverside Shakespeare,* 284. All references to Shakespeare's play will be to this edition.

5. On this thematic of the night, which Bataille associates with Maurice Blanchot's novel *Aminadab,* see Bataille 1988b, 81–82, 84, 104, 106, 108.

6. "The world . . . exists neither as **an in itself infinite** whole nor as **an in itself finite** whole. It is only in the empirical regress of the series of appearances, and by itself it is not to be met with at all. Hence if it is always conditioned, then it is never wholly given, and the world is thus not an unconditional whole, and thus does not exist as such a whole, either with infinite or with finite magnitude" (Kant 1998, 518 [A505/B533]).

7. This point was made to me by Dan Price.

8. "Death is the possibility of the absolute impossibility of Dasein" (Heidegger 1962, 294).

9. In *The Impossible,* Dianus chides himself for failing to live up to this ideal: "Oh bogus Don Juan in his frigid inn, victim of the commander's caretaker!" (1991, 44). Conversely, Monsignor Alpha speaks of "the hope . . . that I would grip the stone hand of the commander" (Bataille 1991, 92). Speaking in his own name, Bataille characterizes himself in *Guilty* as "the Don Juan of the possible" (1988b, 107). And in his early essay "The Sa-

cred Conspiracy" he writes: "More than anything else, the overture to *Don Giovanni* ties my lot in life to a challenge that opens me to a rapturous escape from the self" (1985, 181).

10. This point is underscored in Lukacher 1994.

11. My thanks to Dan Price and, especially, to Shannon Winnubst for their helpful comments on earlier drafts of this paper.

WORKS CITED

Abraham, Nicolas. 1994. "The Phantom of Hamlet *or* The Sixth Act." In Nicolas Abraham and Maria Torok, *The Shell and the Kernel, Volume I.* Ed. and trans. Nicholas T. Rand. Chicago: University of Chicago Press.

Barton, Anne. 1997. Introduction to *The Merchant of Venice.* In *The Riverside Shakespeare,* 2nd ed. New York: Houghton Mifflin Company.

Bataille, Georges. 1985. The Sacred Conspiracy. In *Visions of Excess: Selected Writings, 1927–1939.* Ed. Allan Stoekl. Trans. Allan Stoekl with Carl R. Lovitt and Donald M. Leslie Jr. Minneapolis: University of Minnesota Press.

———. 1988a. *The Accursed Share: Volume I.* Trans. Robert Hurley. New York: Zone Books.

———. 1988b. *Guilty.* Trans. Bruce Boone. San Francisco: Lapis Press.

———. 1989. *Tears of Eros.* Trans. Mary Dalwood. San Francisco: City Lights Books.

———. 1991. *The Impossible.* Trans. Robert Hurley. San Francisco: City Lights Books.

———. 1993. *The Accursed Share: Volumes II & III.* Trans. Robert Hurley. New York: Zone Books.

———. 2001. *Literature and Evil.* Trans. Alastair Hamilton. London: Marion Boyars.

Benjamin, Walter. 2003. On the Concept of History. In *Selected Writings,* Vol. 4: *1938–1940.* Ed. Michael W. Jennings. Cambridge, Mass.: Harvard University Press.

Derrida, Jacques. 1992. *Given Time: I. Counterfeit Money.* Trans. Peggy Kamuf. Chicago: University of Chicago Press.

Derrida, Jacques, and Elisabeth Roudinesco. 2004. *For What Tomorrow . . . : A Dialogue.* Trans. Jeff Fort. Stanford, Calif.: Stanford University Press.

Heidegger, Martin. 1962. *Being and Time.* Trans. John Macquarrie and Edward Robinson. New York: Harper & Row.

Jackson, Ken. 2001. "One Wish" or the Possibility of the Impossible: Derrida, the Gift, and God in *Timon of Athens. Shakespeare Quarterly* 52 (1): 34–66.

Kant, Immanuel. 1993. *Grounding for the Metaphysics of Morals,* 3rd ed. Trans. James W. Ellington. Indianapolis: Hackett.

———. 1998. *Critique of Pure Reason.* Trans. Paul Guyer and Allen W. Wood. New York: Cambridge University Press.

Lukacher, Ned. 1994. *Daemonic Figures: Shakespeare and the Question of Conscience.* Ithaca, N.Y.: Cornell University Press.

Mauss, Marcel. 1990. *The Gift: The Form and Reason for Exchange in Archaic Societies.* Trans. W. D. Halls. New York: W. W. Norton and Company.

Nancy, Jean-Luc. 1991. *The Inoperative Community.* Trans. Peter Connor. Minneapolis: University of Minnesota Press.

Sartre, Jean-Paul. 1993. *Being and Nothingness.* Trans. Hazel E. Barnes. New York: Washington Square Press.

Shakespeare, William. *The Riverside Shakespeare,* 2nd ed. New York: Houghton Mifflin Company, 1997.

Wilson, Scott. 1996. Heterology. In *The Merchant of Venice.* Ed. Nigel Wood. Philadelphia: Open University Press, 124–639

ELEVEN

Richard A. Lee Jr.

Politics and the Thing: Excess as the Matter of Politics

 *Introduction*

We all know by now that metaphysics, which we take as the fundamental philosophical discourse in the West, is, or at the very least, should be, at an end. We began to hear the faint death pangs of its passing in Nietzsche, but by the twentieth century, it was terminal. Heidegger, Adorno, and Derrida all took aim at this philosophical discourse, and all attempted to show that it never really was what it claimed to be. Indeed, there was always something not quite right about metaphysics. For it asks what seems like the oddest of all questions. In the face of things that are, in the face of the plenitude of existence and being, metaphysics questions that very being, as if it were somehow problematic. Or, more properly, it does not ask about that being, but posits that whatever it is we find ourselves among, the being of those things does not show its face immediately. That is, in the face of the seemingly unquestionable givenness of what might be the object of a purported metaphysics, it seems strange to question that very object—to refuse to admit the obviousness of what *is* there, but instead posit something that does not even manifest itself as reality. It is not like looking for your glasses when they are sitting on the top of your head. It is not even like looking for your glasses when you haven't realized they are on your nose. It is like looking for your keys even though you know that they are in your hand. There is something not quite right about this.

Politics and the Thing

How does something that is so common, so factical, so apparent come to be questioned? How does it come to pass that "The answer to the question, 'what is that' brings us to the 'essence' of a thing? 'Table': what is that? Mountain, sea, plant: each time asking 'what is that' we ask after the 'essence of the thing'" (Heidegger 1997, 1). That is, how was it ever possible for metaphysics to turn away from things with which we deal in our everyday lives toward things like "essence," "form," and "substance?" How did it ever happen that the world in which we find ourselves came to be silent and only given a voice by this "higher level essentiality?" (Adorno 1998, 14).

It is the same with the concept/word "thing." We do not meet "things" in the world, but people, tables, chairs, dogs, and jobs. On the one hand, to say that this here before me is a thing is to say almost nothing about it. It indicates the highest level of generality, a level so high that nothing is determined whatsoever when I call this a thing. On the other hand, to say that it is a thing is already to mark it in such a way that it no longer appears as it had before, but now it enters a realm—that of things, of *mere* things, the realm the very questioning has constituted. The questioning creates a kind of space in which what is here before me can become a thing. Once it is designated as a thing, it is no longer what it was; it is removed from its site and brought into a new site opened and delimited by a kind of theoretical gaze.

When I was growing up, my father would often take on projects around our house. Sometimes, these were small: patching a hole in a wall, repainting a room, unclogging a drain. Other times, because of a lack of money to pay someone who actually knew what they were doing, he would take on tasks that were, frankly, beyond his skill. You always knew when these were coming because he would always wear the same work outfit—the flannel shirt, his old army pants, a cap, and work boots. Our basement was filled with all sorts of tools and what I, not being as "manly," would call "notions"—nuts, bolts, drill bits, wires, and things I did not even know. Some of these were highly specialized, being suited for just one task.[1] However, I was almost always disappointed to learn their actual function within the sphere of utility. One can imagine, for example, six pipe wrenches of different sizes hanging side by side on a basement wall, all looking similar, even in their incredibly important differences. Yet these are nothing compared to that weird loopy thing used to grasp, turn, and then remove an oil filter from a car. This thing seems incredibly unique. When it turns out to be useful for removing oil filters and not, say, for cutting tall wild grasses that can be used to make thatched roofs, then its uniqueness turns suddenly boring.[2]

Having dressed suitably for such a project—say rewiring a ceiling fixture—he would then hunt for an assistant. I liked my dad, but I also seemed never to remember that assisting him meant being screamed at, and eventually I would walk off the job in tears.[3] The screaming, of course, did not begin right when we (or rather he) set to work. Rather, as the actual complexity of the task became apparent, and my father's lack of actual ability and knowledge related to the task would become obvious, the level of his anger increased. It is a general rule in such instances that the anger can never be directed to its proper source, for that would amount to admitting that he had no control over the sphere of utility in which he was operating and over which he ought to have been sovereign. One rarely confronts such anger among licensed electricians. My father's anger, then, would become generalized. "Hold the light THERE!" This is how it would always begin. As if the problems of the task were somehow related to improper lighting and not improper training. Next, the demand for tools would become more like rage at the need for tools at all, at the otherwise obvious and nonthreatening fact that our hands cannot cut wires, drive screws, or saw wood. As the level of anger would increase, my father's ability to speak in sentences, and eventually even words, would wane. "Give me . . . get me that . . . HAND ME THE . . . **would you just give me that damned <u>THING</u>!!**"

Certainly the fact that anger makes one lose control of speech is not unusual or peculiar to the context of utility. What is, however, interesting is that before the entire capacity for meaningful (and, I might add, *useful*) language is destroyed by rage, we have recourse to this word "thing." This word still operates, if only at the border of utility, and in two ways. Inasmuch as "thing" is the most general noun, spoken within the realm of tools (things) arrayed around us, it is still useful. To scream, "Hand me that *thing*" is still to utter a command related to an object whose presence has been commanded by the task. Herein lies the second way in which "thing" operates on the border of utility. The task at hand demands and commands *things*. More appropriately, these objects become things only because they function within a sphere of utility.

Heidegger comes close to this situation in his analysis of tools in *Being and Time* (1962; 1993). The important analytic moment is a break in the transactions that tools have with us and with one another, that is, when they become, precisely, unusable. It is only when an assignment is disturbed that the assignment itself can become explicit. That is, when a being resists, for one reason or another, its utility in the pursuit of some project, its assignment in that structure, that is, its character as useful, comes to the fore. In this way, Heidegger recognizes that while beings are caught up in the works of Dasein, in the projects of production, they are not present as things that are grasped in a theoretical way, but are grasped, as it were, by the hand itself and put to work. Heidegger's analysis, therefore, seems to match quite closely my experience of assisting my father. At the moment that my father shouts "thing," the very object seems to have slipped out of utility, or, at the very least, is on the brink of slipping out of utility.

Heidegger offers three modes in which this readiness-to-hand of equipment falls into what I may call "closure" in that it is not "disclosed" (*aufschließen*): conspicuousness, when an entity is unusable; obtrusiveness, when an entity is not able to be picked up and used because it does not offer itself to the hand; and obstinacy, when an entity stands in the way of Dasein's concern (1962, 102–105; 1993, 72–76). In each of these cases of what we may call deficient concern, the entity as it were steps out of the world and presents itself to us, not in its utility, but as a thing that stands outside of the world, that has crossed the border out of utility. But in each case, it is the assignment itself that determines not only the utility but also the nonutility of an entity. In such cases, the readiness-to-hand of an entity discloses itself only in that very readiness-to-hand being closed off. So Dasein grasps the "having been ready-to-hand." The very character that equipment has, such that it belongs to Dasein's being in the world, comes to the fore, then, when equipment stands outside the world and is removed from the sphere of utility.

Heidegger's analysis of how the disclosure of something as having been useful, and therefore, in a way, concealed as what it is leaves aside the crucial element of this kind of situation. As my experience with my father shows, it is not, in fact, the case that we are always already at work. The fact that my father had to don special clothes, the fact that he arranged the tools and ar-ranged me among the tools as well, shows that one "goes to work." This going to work requires the constitution of a sphere of utility as such. That is, neither I nor my father found ourselves within this project. It was consti-tuted by him. This constitution, then, stretches out to all the objects that he arranged within the sphere of the project. When proper names break down because of his anger (and note, here, that it is precisely not the unusability of the equipment at issue, but the contestation of the sovereign authority to constitute the sphere of utility), my father then names each object for what it is: a thing. A being, therefore, becomes a thing, not by a breakdown in its utility, but rather because of a sovereign gesture that deploys some beings and not others. "Thing" and utility, it turns out, are the same, and both are constituted by the gesture of a sovereign. There must be, therefore, a larger "economy" within which the position of a sovereign becomes not only pos-sible, but even necessary.

🌣 *Utility, General Economy, Sacrifice, Becoming a Thing*

"What is before me is never anything less than the universe; the universe is not a thing, and I am not at all mistaken when I see its brilliance in the sun" (Bataille 1991, 57). When we take a step back from the specific economies in which Dasein finds itself in its concernful dealings to the general economy of those concerns taken as a whole, we step back from the world of Dasein to the universe. That is, what allows for one to have concernful dealings such that one is "in-the-world" is the fact that the universe presents the need for such concernful dealings. Why do we engage with entities in this concernful fashion? Certainly a particular answer can be given once a particular concern has been put in play: We are concerned with lasers and computers in order to build bombs. But can we not push the analysis to a general level? Why are we concerned with building bombs? That is, why is there, in general, production, consumption, and work at all, and not just this or that particular form of concern? While one may set to work on this or that project, are there not principles of a general economy that delineate the need to set to work in general? This is the task that Bataille sets for himself in *The Accursed Share.*

While Heidegger's phenomenological analysis is, precisely because it is phenomenological, delimited by the sphere that pertains to the mode of being of Dasein, Bataille's shift to the level of general economy necessarily moves beyond that mode of being to the conditions for the possibility of concern at all. This move "requires thinking on a level with a play of forces that runs counter to ordinary calculations, a play of forces based on the laws that govern us" (Bataille 1991, 12). From the point of view of the general economy, the main principle is that "the living organism, in a situation determined by the play of energy on the surface of the globe, ordinarily receives more energy than is necessary for maintaining life; the excess energy (wealth) can be used for the growth of a system (e.g., an organism); if the system can no longer grow, or if the excess cannot be completely absorbed in its growth, it must necessarily be lost without profit; it must be spent, willingly or not, gloriously or catastrophically" (Bataille 1991, 21).

It may seem strange at first to situate Bataille's concerns within the framework of Heidegger's phenomenological analysis of worldhood. However, it should be clear that the function of utility in both analyses provides the proper link from Heidegger's specific analysis to Bataille's general economic analysis. In other words, Heidegger's account uncovers the worldhood of the world by means of an analysis of Dasein's concern. In this case, Dasein works on the basis of some end, that is, in-order-to. Yet as we saw, Heidegger's analysis must stop short of thinking through the principles of the setting of tasks. For Bataille, however, the setting of tasks is the crucial point of departure: "Humanity exploits given material resources, but by restricting them as it does to a resolution of the immediate difficulties it encounters (a resolution which it has hastily had to define as an ideal), it assigns to the forces it employs an end which they cannot have. Beyond our immediate ends, man's activity in fact pursues the useless and infinite fulfillment of the universe" (Bataille 1991, 21). The exploitation of material resources is tied to a difficulty—one might call this a concern—that requires solution. The difficulty sets a goal, a telos. Yet Bataille goes one step further, toward "useless and infinite fulfillment of the universe." Heidegger's analysis of being-in-the-world rightly sets out the principles of the specific economies that Dasein constructs on the basis of its ends. Bataille, however, inserts these specific economies within the flow of energy on the surface of the earth.

Bataille's principle of general economy is that there is always excess. It is this excess that poses the "economic" problem in that it is what constitutes the wealth that circulates in this most general economy.[4] The excess has to be put to work in growth, or it has to be spent in exuberant squandering, or it threatens the very existence of all beings within the system. So the work that exhibits one's concern in dealing with the world has a utility of its own. If there is always excess, work must either lead to growth or to spending the excess without return—in glorious exuberance. From the point of view of this general economy, then, focus must be placed, not on those operations that lead to growth, but on those operations that allow for expenditure without return. That is, utility now has a dual function. Its proper function is in the operation of growth and reproduction. However, there is a strange kind of utility present in the glorious exuberance, for it allows for life when the limits of growth have been reached. However, this inevitable loss cannot be accounted for as utility except that it is useful for the system as a whole. In other words, the sphere of utility itself presupposes an entire sphere of expenditure without return that makes possible the sphere of utility in which energy is used for productive purposes. Without the sphere of glorious exuberance, utility itself will come to be destructive—un-useful. This is not to indicate that expenditure without return is not destructive. Indeed, much of Bataille's first volume is taken up with historical investigations into the destructive ways in which excess has been outside the system—in ways that are often destructive to things outside.

In this regard, utility and becoming a thing appear in a new light. Recall that for Heidegger the sphere of utility constituted by Dasein's concernful dealings meant that the being of equipment was caught up in its being put to work "in-order-to." So while a thing is ready to be taken up in hand and caught up in order to produce, its being ready for doing is hidden from Dasein. It is when, as we saw, the entity for one reason or another cannot be taken up in hand and put to service in-order-to that its mode of being can come to the fore. That is, utility presents the being of equipment only in its usefulness, but when it stands there before the hand and shows its inability to be taken up into hand and put to work, then its character shines forth. The being of equipment surfaces only in falling away. From the phenomenology of Dasein's worldhood and being-in-the-world, this analysis makes sense. However, from the point of view of general economy, it becomes clear that some entities *must be placed outside the sphere of utility,* that is, there has to be exuberant spending. Far from being a special mode of being that belongs to entities only when they are no longer useful, *Vorhandenheit* is the necessary condition of life and, consequently, of utility. It is utility that makes an entity a *thing,* but it is glorious exuberance that removes entities from the universe of "things" and returns them to another sphere, the sphere of the sacred, for example.

Let me be clear here. Bataille is not arguing that the sacred is a more primordial sphere from which entities are taken up into utility and thus made things. Rather, the sacred is just one possible sphere into which one can cast things so as to squander them without return. In other words, Bataille is not positing a sacred realm that is the realm of excess energy and that forms the basis of the sphere of utility. The sacred functions, particularly in Aztec society, as a way to turn entities, particularly humans to be sacrificed, out of the realm of utility and allows them to be squandered without return. To see how this functions, and to see how an entity becomes a thing and can be turned out of the realm of things, let us look more closely at Bataille's analysis of Aztec sacrifice.

Aztec society is organized around two main poles: warfare and sacrifice. It may seem, on the face of it, that a society based on warfare may entail sacrifice. However, there is a difference between a rationalized military society that is bent on conquest and colonization, and a society in which the wealth brought by conquest is squandered through sacrifice. Bataille depicts a society in which those conquered through battle are brought back as slaves who will ultimately be sacrificed to feed the sun and the earth. It is a society of consumption that wears the violence of consumption on its external visage. The one to be sacrificed was not held prisoner, but was treated as a lord. Festivals surrounding sacrifice were lavish, including banquets, dancing, multiple sexual relations with young women who will also be sacrificed. The one to be sacrificed was brought into the family of the soldier who conquered him and treated as a son. At the moment of sacrifice, his chest was cut open, his beating heart removed and offered to the sun, and his flesh returned to the soldier who conquered him to be consumed in a banquet.

Yet the violence of consumption that is seen in this society is not without its own level of rationalization, for the king remains in his palace while the court participates in the sacrifice and favors the victim. This indicates that the sacrifice is one of substitution. That is, it indicates that the violence of the sacrifice is turned outward rather than spreading inward in the society. The warrior sacrifices by going out into the battlefield. But that sacrifice is paid for by the "sumptuary expenditure" of the sacrificer. This indicates a certain "softening" of the ritual, a softening that is indicated by its insertion into the context of the sacred.

> Sacrifice restores to the sacred world that which servile use has degraded, rendered profane. Servile use has made a *thing* (an *object*) of that which, in a deep sense, is of the same nature as the *subject,* is in a relation of intimate participation with the subject. It is not necessary that the sacrifice actually destroy the animal or plant of which man had to make a *thing* for his use. They must at least be destroyed as things, that is, *insofar as they have become things.* (Bataille 1991, 55–56)

The warrior nature of Aztec society ensured that the society was exposed externally to the riches of other societies. This wealth contributes to the growth of Aztec society. However, this growth has its limits, limits determined ultimately by space. When the limits are reached, the wealth has to be spent without return, without contributing to further growth. The sacrificial violence that circulates in this consumptive society finds an outlet only in the sacrifice that places wealth beyond utility. The consumption that is sacrifice, however, is not consumption "in the same way as a motor uses fuel" (Bataille 1991, 56), but is a consumption without return.

This is how, from the point of view of general economy, the sphere of utility, and consequently, the sphere of things is constituted. In terms of this sacrificial society, the slave, the prisoner of war, is taken up by the master as wealth, as a thing that is bound to labor, just as a work animal is a thing (Bataille 1991, 56). In so doing, the master removes the slave from the world that the master inhabits, for the master makes a thing of the slave. But in making of the slave a thing, the master at the same time estranges itself from its own being because the master has given itself the limits of a thing or a sphere of things. "Once the world of things was posited, man himself becomes one of the things of this world, at least for the time in which he labored. It is this degradation that man has always tried to escape. In his strange myths, in his cruel rites, *man is in search of a lost intimacy* from the first" (Bataille 1991, 57). It is in labor that the intimacy of one's being with the world, with the universe, is first removed. Slavery is a more violent form of this loss of intimacy. But slavery arises only on the basis of a society in which the degradation of labor has been conquered. The sacrificial society of the Aztecs was "just as concerned about *sacrificing* as we are about working" (Bataille 1991, 46).

Sacrifice, then, returns an intimacy that was lost. But how is this intimacy restored? Only in returning what has been placed in the order of things back into the divine order can this intimate communication take place. This intimate communion restores an interior freedom, but a freedom given in destruction, a freedom "whose essence is to consume *profitlessly* whatever might remain in the progression of useful works" (Bataille 1991, 58). In other words, while the sacrifice consumes, it consumes precisely that which has been consecrated and set apart from the world of things, thereby making it impossible for what has been consecrated to be returned to the world of things.

> The victim is a surplus taken from the mass of *useful* wealth. And he can only be withdrawn from it in order to be consumed profitlessly, and therefore be utterly destroyed. Once chosen, he is the *accursed share*, destined for violent consumption. But the curse tears him away from the *order of things;* it gives him a recognizable figure, which now radiates intimacy, anguish, the profundity of living things. (Bataille 1991, 59)

The accursed share, the excess that must be spent gloriously without profit, and for that reason is cursed, is, to speak something like the language of Heidegger, what constitutes the universehood of the universe. The excess of energy on the surface of the globe puts living organisms in the position of having to put that wealth to work or to squander it in glorious exuberance. Consumption takes us only so far. After consumption, even in its most violent form, still leaves an accursed share, other forms must be found to expend without profit. The destructive force of some of these forms over other less destructive forms is the question that wealth poses to us.

The setting of something outside the sphere of things, of utility, does not appear only in sacrificial societies. "At the origin of industrial society, based on the primacy and autonomy of commodities, of *things,* we find a contrary impulse to place what is essential—*what causes one to tremble with fear and delight*—outside the world of activity, the world of *things*" (Bataille 1991, 129). Here too, intimacy, a lost intimacy, is in question. Religion provides what Bataille calls an "external form of intimacy" (129). The question of intimacy can be posed in another register, for what is at stake in intimacy is sovereignty: "But even if the solution of the problems of life—the key to which is a man's not becoming merely *a thing,* but of *being in a sovereign manner*—were the unavoidable consequence of a satisfactory response to material exigencies, it remains radically distinct from that response, with which it is often confused" (131). Sovereignty, now thought in terms of the principles of general economy, arises not from one's concernful dealings with the world of things, but rather from the relation to that which is, which must be, placed outside the world of things.

If being sovereign means being without limiting of its own accord, then sovereignty must mean also being outside the relation of ends and means, the relation of utility, that constitutes the sphere of things (Bataille 2001, 189). Yet to be outside the relation of utility is to prefer death to servitude. This is the political issue, the issue that makes politics, namely, how sovereignty is expressed, not in relation to things—in which case we become mere things—but in relation to what is the opposite of a thing because it stands outside the realm of ends and means that constitutes a thing. Yet in that case, is not sovereignty the move outside the sphere in which decisions take place, the sphere in which the use of energy is the crucial issue? Sovereignty, therefore, does not remove one from the pressure of excess energy, but is one form of glorious exuberance in which energy is given without return. Death and sexual reproduction are the originary forms of spending without return. Sovereignty, with its necessary connection to death, does not provide a sovereign relation to things, but a sovereign withdrawal from things. As such, sovereignty may not be the goal of politics, but its end, its annihilation. While capitalism is the surrender to things, the return to a lost world, to the Catholicism of the Middle Ages, to the lost community of the premodern world is the surrender to an excess that is no longer our own.

Thus Heidegger's privileging of concern in exposing the worldhood of the world on the way toward uncovering Dasein's being-in-the-world exposed the decisive significance of utility. It is, after all, utility that makes of a collection of stuff equipment, an environment, and ultimately, a world. He resists the ancient metaphysical gesture of attempting to push utility into the realm of mere phenomenality, while privileging the sphere of essentiality where utility is removed. Of course, the resistance to metaphysics also entails a resistance to the life of leisure that it entails. Dasein's world is one where each Dasein is working toward something and putting equipment to work in these concernful dealings. Yet the gesture that places Dasein's concernful dealings in the context of being-toward-death also places Dasein always on the horizon of sovereignty.

But how can we resist the question of the actual, concrete content of this concern? How can we resist the move to placing our concern within the concerns of Bataille's general economy? When we move to the concerns of general economy, then we are concerned not only with the worldhood of the world, but about how entities come to be things at all. This is always in relation to the concern for expenditure, a concern that ultimately has to do with the glorious exuberance of excess, of spending without return. In that case, we can no longer afford to focus on the broken hammer, on the missing screwdriver, but must focus our attention on the actual dropping of bombs and occupation of foreign countries. If we fail to concern ourselves with these general economic concerns, the destructive force of our glorious exuberance will be returned a hundredfold back on us.

NOTES

1. One might think here of things like a sparkplug wrench or that weird gadget used to remove oil filters from cars. My ability to provide further examples ends here, again because of the relatively low level of "manliness" that I have achieved. This indicates that the division of labor along the lines of gender is entirely wrapped up with this question of thingliness and utility. While Irigaray's (1985) analysis of woman as commodity certainly would inscribe "woman" into a sphere of utility, at the same time it also prevents women, traditionally, from "sovereignty" in Bataille's sense. That is, it prevents them from constituting a sphere of utility and placing "things" within it or casting them out to be spent without return. Objects that serve only one purpose fascinated me because they each seemed so odd among the rest of the tools.

2. On the other hand, my kitchen is filled with "tools" that serve only one highly specialized purpose, and I have come to enjoy the kind of beauty such tools have. Putting these tools to work is a lot like watching Andre Agassi or Venus Williams play tennis. Surely, if they also were to win the Nobel Prize for physics, their beauty would turn to offensiveness—the way that Greek heroes must have been, if only secretly, offensive to the ancient Greeks.

3. Really, though, it was more like running away sobbing, thus indicating publicly the level of "manliness" I had achieved. I was not sovereign in this sphere of utility, and thus always risked being a useful thing myself.

4. It should be clear that when Bataille speaks of a general economy, he is not referring merely to the production-distribution-consumption of goods and services but also to the most general level of all: the energy (wealth) on the surface of the globe.

WORKS CITED

Adorno, Theodor W. 1998. *Metaphysik: Begriff und Probleme.* Ed. Rolf Tiedemann. Frankfurt: Suhrkamp.

Bataille, Georges. 1991. *The Accursed Share: Volume I.* Trans. Robert Hurley. New York: Zone Books.

————. 2001. *The Unfinished System of Nonknowledge.* Trans. Michelle Kendall and Stuart Kendall. Minneapolis: University of Minnesota Press.

Heidegger, Martin. 1962. *Being and Time.* Trans. John Macquarrie and Edward Robinson. New York: Harper & Row.

————. 1993. *Sein und Zeit,* 17th ed. Tübingen: Max Niemeyer.

————. 1997. *Vom Wesen der Wahrheit.* Ed. Hermann Mörchen. Gesamtausgabe: II. Abteilung: *Vorlesungen 1923–1944,* vol. 34. Frankfurt: Vittorio Klostermann.

Irigaray, Luce. 1985. *This Sex Which Is Not One.* Trans. Catherine Porter and Carolyn Burke. Ithaca, N.Y.: Cornell University Press.

TWELVE

ALLAN STOEKL

Excess and Depletion: Bataille's Surprisingly Ethical Model of Expenditure

In this essay I will examine Georges Bataille's theory of expenditure, most notably as it is worked out in his seminal work, *The Accursed Share* (*La Part maudite*), in light of the ecological as well as economic problem of depletion. Is Bataille's theory obsolete? Does it propose, in counterproductive fashion, the need to burn off excess resources—fundamentally, excess energy—when, in fact, we are facing the imminent depletion of those very resources? I will argue that Bataille's theory is in fact one of both expenditure and depletion. By following Bataille's logic, we will ultimately arrive at another way of thinking about what human survival will mean in the future—how, in other words, *sustainability* can be conceived in relation to the most fundamental human practices.

The Accursed Share, first published in 1949, has had a colorful history on the margins of French intellectual inquiry. Largely ignored when published, it has gone on to have an interesting and subtle influence on much contemporary thought. In the 1960s, fascination with Bataille's theory of economy tended to reconfigure it as a theory of writing: for Derrida, for example, general economy was a general *writing.* The very specific concerns Bataille shows in his work for various economic systems are largely ignored or dismissed as "muddled."[1] Other authors, such as Michel Foucault and Alphonso Lingis, writing in the wake of this version of Bataille, have stressed, following more closely Bataille's lead, the importance of violence, expenditure, and spectacular transgression in social life.[2]

The basis for Bataille's approach can be found in the second chapter, "Laws of General Economy." The theory in itself is quite straightforward: living organisms always, eventually, produce more than they need for simple survival and reproduction. Up to a certain point, their excess energy is channeled into expansion: they fill all available space with versions of themselves. But, inevitably, the expansion of a species comes against limits: pressure will be exerted against insurmountable barriers. At this point a species' explosive force will be limited, and excess members will die. Bataille's theory is an ecological one because he realizes that the limits are internal to a system: the expansion of a species will find its limit not only through a dearth of nourishment, but also through the pressure brought to bear by other species (1976a, 40; 1988, 33–34). As one moves up the food chain, each species destroys more to conserve itself. The amount of energy consumed by simple bacteria is thus much less than that consumed by a tiger. The ultimate consumers of energy are not so much ferocious carnivores, however, as they are the ultimate consumers of other animals and themselves: human beings.

Man's primary function is to waste, or expend, prodigious amounts of energy, not only through the consumption of other animals high on the food chain (including himself), but in rituals that involve the very fundamental forces of useless expenditure: sex and death. Man in that sense is in a doubly privileged position: he not only wastes the most, but alone of all the animals is able to waste *consciously*. He alone incarnates the principle by which excess energy is burned off: the universe, which is nothing other than the production of excess energy (solar brilliance), is doubled by man, who alone is aware of the sun's larger tendency and who therefore wastes consciously, in order to be in accord with the overall tendency of the universe. This, for Bataille, is religion: not the individualistic concern with deliverance and personal salvation, but rather the collective and ritual identification with the cosmic tendency to expend.

Humans waste not only the energy accumulated by other species, but, just as important, their own energy, because humans themselves soon hit the limits to growth. Human society cannot indefinitely reproduce: soon enough what today is called the "carrying capacity" of an environment is reached.[3] Only so many babies can be born, homes built, colonies founded. Then limits are reached. Some excess can be used in the energy and population required for military expansion (the case, according to Bataille, with Islam [1976a, 83–92; 1988, 81–91]), but soon that too screeches to a halt. A steady state can be attained by devoting large numbers of people and huge quantities of wealth and labor to useless activity: thus the large numbers of unproductive Tibetan monks, nuns, and their lavish temples (1976a, 93–108; 1988, 93–110). Or, most notably, one can waste wealth in military buildup and constant warfare. No doubt this solution kept populations stable in the past (one thinks of the constant battles between South American Indian tribes), but in the present (i.e., 1949) the huge amounts of wealth devoted to military armament, worldwide, can only lead to nuclear holocaust (1976a, 159–60; 1988, 169–71).

This final point leads to Bataille's version of a Hegelian "Absolute Knowing," one based not so much on the certainty of a higher knowledge as on the certainty of a higher destruction. The imminence of nuclear holocaust makes it clear that expenditure, improperly conceived, can threaten the very existence of society. Bataille's theory, then, is a profoundly *ethical* one: we must somehow distinguish between versions of excess that are "on the scale of the universe," and whose recognition-implementation guarantees the survival of society (and human expenditure), and other versions that entail blindness to the real role of expenditure and thereby threaten man's, not to mention the planet's, survival.

This, in very rough outline, is the main thrust of Bataille's book. By viewing man as waster rather than conserver, Bataille manages to invert the usual order of economics: the moral imperative, so to speak, is the furthering of a "good" expenditure, which we might lose sight of if we stress an inevitably selfish model of conservation or utility. For if conservation is put first, inevitably the bottled-up forces will break loose, but in unforeseen and in, so to speak, untheorized ways. We should focus our attention, not on conservation, maintenance, and the steady state—which can lead only to mass destruction and the ultimate wasting of the world—but instead on the modes of waste in which we, as human animals, should engage.

But how does one go about privileging waste in an era in which waste seems to be the root of all evil? Over fifty years after the publication of *The Accursed Share,* we live in an era in which nuclear holocaust no longer seems the main threat. But other dangers lurk, ones just as terrifying and definitive: global warming, deforestation, and the depletion of resources—above all, energy resources: oil, coal, even uranium. How can we possibly talk about valorizing waste, when waste seems to be the principal evil threatening the continued existence of the biosphere on which we depend? Wouldn't it make more sense to stress conservation, sustainability, downsizing, rather than glorious excess?

✺ *What Appears to Be Wrong with Bataille's Theory?*

To think about the use-value of Bataille, we must first think about the nature of energy in his presentation. For Bataille, excessive energy is natural:

it is first solar (as it comes to us from the sun), then biological (as it passes from the sun to plants and animals to us), then human (as it is wasted in our monuments, artifacts, and social rituals). The movement from each stage to the next involves an ever-greater wasting: the sun spends its energy without being repaid; plants take the sun's energy, convert it, and throw off the excess in their wild proliferation; and animals burn off the energy conserved by plants (carnivores are much less "efficient" than herbivores), all the way up the food chain. "On the surface of the globe, *for living matter in general,* energy is always in excess, the question can always be posed in terms of extravagance [*luxe*], the choice is limited to how wealth is to be squandered [*le mode de la dilapidation des richesses*]" (1976a, 31; 1988, 23, italics in original). There never is or will be a shortage of energy; it can never be used up by man or anything else because it comes, in endless profusion, from the sun.

Georges Ambrosino, Bataille's friend, a nuclear scientist, is credited in the introduction of *The Accursed Share* (1976a, 23; 1988, 191) as the inspiration for a number of the theses worked out in the book. In some unpublished "notes preliminary to the writing of *The Accursed Share*" (1976a, 465–69), Ambrosino sets out very clearly some of the ideas underlying Bataille's work:

> We affirm that *the appropriated energies produced during a period are superior in quantity to the appropriated energies that are strictly necessary to their production.*
> For the rigor of the thesis, it would be necessary to compare the appropriated energies of the same quality. The system produces all the appropriated energies that are necessary to it, it produces them in greater quantities than are needed, and finally it even produces appropriated energies that its maintenance at the given level does not require.
> In an elliptical form, but more striking, we can say that *the energy produced is superior to the energy necessary for its production.* (1976a, 469)[4]

Most striking here is the rather naïve faith that, indeed, there always will be an abundance of energy, and that spending energy to get energy inevitably results in a surplus of energy. Ambrosino, in other words, projects a perpetual surplus of energy return on energy investment (EROEI).[5] One can perhaps imagine how a nuclear scientist, in the early days of speculation about peaceful applications of atomic energy, might have put it this way. Or a petroleum geologist might have thought the same way, speculating on the productivity of the earth shortly after the discovery of a giant oil field.[6] Over fifty years later it is much harder to think along these lines.

Indeed, these assumptions are among those most contested by current energy theorists and experts. First, we might question the supposition that, since all energy in the biosphere ultimately derives from the sun, and the sun is an inexhaustible source of energy (at least in relation to the limited life spans of organisms), there will always be a surplus of energy. The correctness of this thesis depends on the perspective from which we view the sun's energy. From the perspective of an ecosystem—say, a forest—the thesis is true: there will always be more than enough solar energy so that plants can grow luxuriantly (provided growing conditions are right: soil, rainfall, etc.) and in that way supply an abundance of biomass, the excess of which will support a plethora of animals and, ultimately, humans. All living creatures will in this way always absorb more energy than is necessary for their strict survival and reproduction; the excess energy they (re)produce will inevitably, somehow, have to be burned off.

If we shift perspective slightly, however, we will see that an excess of the sun's energy is not always available. It is (and will continue to be) extremely difficult to achieve a positive energy return directly from solar energy.[7] As an energy form, solar energy has proven to be accessible primarily through organic (and fossilized) concentration: wood, coal, and oil. In human society, at least as it has developed over the last few millennia, these energy sources have been tapped and have allowed the development of human culture and the proliferation of human population. It has often been argued that this development/proliferation is not due solely to technological developments and the input of human labor; instead, it is the ability to utilize highly concentrated energy sources that has made society's progress possible. Especially in the last two hundred years, human population has expanded mightily, as has the production of human wealth. This has been made possible by the energy contributed to the production and consumption processes by the combustion of fuels in ever more sophisticated mechanical devices: first wood and then coal in steam engines, and then oil and its derivatives (including hydrogen, via natural gas) in internal combustion engines. Wealth, in other words, has its origins not just in the productivity of human labor and its ever more sophisticated technological refinements, as both the bourgeois and Marxist traditions would argue, but in the energy released from (primarily) fossil fuels through the use of innovative devices. In the progress from wood to coal, and from coal to oil, there is a constant progression in the amount of energy produced from a certain mass of material. Always more energy, not necessarily efficiently used: always more goods produced, consumers to consume them, and energy-based fertilizers to produce the food needed to feed them. The rise of civilization as we know it, then, is tied directly to the type of fuels used to power and feed it.[8]

Certainly Bataille, following Ambrosino, would see in this ever-increasing energy use a continuation—but on a much grander scale—of the tendency of animals to expend energy conserved in plant matter. Indeed, burning wood is nothing more than that. But the fact remains that by tapping into the concentrated energy of fossil fuels, humans have at their disposal (ancient) solar energy—derived from fossil plants (coal) and algae (oil)—in such a concentrated form that equivalent amounts of energy could never be derived from solar energy alone.[9]

In a limited sense, then, Bataille and Ambrosino are right: all the energy we use ultimately derives from the sun. They are wrong in ignoring the fact that for society as we know it to function, with our attendant leisure made possible by "energy slaves," energy derived from fossil fuels, with their high EROEI, will be necessary for the indefinite future.[10] There is simply no other equally rich source of energy available to us; moreover, no other source will likely be available to us in the future. Bataille's theory, on the other hand, ultimately rests on the assumption that energy is completely renewable, that there will always be a high EROEI, and that, for that reason, we need not worry about our dependence on finite (depletable) energy sources. *The Accursed Share* for this reason presents us with a strange amalgam of awareness of the central role energy plays in relation to economics (not to mention life in general) and a willful ignorance concerning the social-technological modes of energy delivery and use, which are far more than mere technical details. We might posit that the origin of this oversight in Bataille's thought is to be found in the economic theory, and ultimately philosophy, both bourgeois and Marxist, of the modern period, where energy resources and raw materials do not enter into economic (or philosophical) calculations, since they are taken for granted: the earth makes human activity possible, and in a sense we give the earth meaning, dignity, by using resources that otherwise would remain inert, unknown, insignificant (one thinks of Sartre's "in-itself" here). Value has its origin, in this view, not in the "natural" raw materials or energy used to produce things, but in human activity itself. Bataille merely revises this model by characterizing human activity—in other words, production—as primarily involving gift giving and wasting, rather than production and accumulation.

We can argue, then, that solar energy is indeed always produced, always in excess (at least in relation to the limited life spans of individuals, and even species); but it is fossil fuels that best conserve this energy and deliver it in a rich form that we humans can effectively use. Unfortunately, these fuels can be depleted, indeed, are in the process of being depleted.

Why is this important in the context of Bataille? For a very simple reason: if Bataille does not worry about energy cost and depletion, he need not worry about energy conservation. Virtually every contemporary commentator on energy use sees only one short-term solution: conservation. Since fossil fuels are not easily replaceable by renewable sources of energy, our only option is to institute radical plans for energy conservation—or risk the complete collapse of our civilization when, in the near future, oil, coal, and natural gas production declines, and the price of fuel necessarily skyrockets.[11] Indeed, some commentators, foreseeing the eventual complete depletion of fossil energy stores, predict a return to feudalism (Perelman 1981), or simply a quasi-Neolithic state of human culture, with a radically reduced global population (Price 1995).

Without a theory of depletion, then, Bataille can afford to ignore conservation in all senses: not only of resources and energy, but also in labor, wealth, and so on. He can also ignore (perhaps alarmist) models of cultural decline. In Bataille's view, energy will always reproduce itself with a surplus; thus, the core problem of our civilization is how we waste this excess. We need never question the existence of the "energy slaves" that make this squandering of the products of human labor, and of our own time and effort, possible. Nor will there need to be any consideration of the fact that these virtual energy slaves may very well, in the not-so-distant future, have to be replaced by real human slaves. (Who or what else would do the work?)

🌐 Bataille, Depletion, and Carrying Capacity

Steven A. LeBlanc's book *Constant Battles: The Myth of the Peaceful, Noble Savage* would seem, at least at first, to pose an insuperable challenge to Bataille's view of wealth, expenditure, excess, and the social mechanisms that turn around them.

LeBlanc's larger argument is that warfare in all societies—hunters and gatherers, farmers, as well as industrialized "modern" societies—arises from competition for increasingly scarce resources as the carrying capacity of the land decreases. It should be stressed that carrying capacity[12] is linked to population growth: the latter is never stable, and, up to a point, the land can support an increasing number of individuals. There is, however, an inverse relation between population and carrying capacity: the limits of the latter are rapidly reached through a burgeoning population, and a higher population depletes the productive capacity of the environment, thereby making the revised carrying capacity inadequate even for a smaller population. But as carrying capacity is threatened, many societies choose warfare, or human sacrifice, rather than extinction (LeBlanc 2003, 177–78, 195).

I stress the importance of LeBlanc's thesis—that violent conflict arising out of ever-growing population pressures and diminishing carrying capacity of the environment characterizes all developmental levels of human society—because it highlights another apparent weakness of Bataille's theory. LeBlanc would argue that there is no model of what we held so dear in the 1960s: a noble savage—Native American, Tibetan, or whoever—who is or was "in harmony with the environment." Bataille's theory, at first, at least, would seem to posit just such a harmony, albeit one that involves the violence of sacrifice rather than the contentment of the lotus-eater. Man in his primitive state was in harmony, not with the supposed peace of Eden, but with the violence of the universe, with the solar force of blinding energy:

> The naïve man was not a stranger in the universe. Even with the dread it confronted him with, he saw its spectacle as a festival to which he had been invited. He perceived its glory, and believed himself to be responsible for his own glory as well. (Bataille 1976a, 192)

While LeBlanc's theory of sacrifice is functional—he is concerned mainly with how people use sacrifice, in conjunction with warfare, to maximize their own, or their group's, success—Bataille's theory is religious in that he is concerned with the ways in which people commune with a larger, unlimited, transcendent reality. But in order to do so, they must enjoy an unlimited carrying capacity.

And yet, if we think a bit more deeply about these two approaches to human expenditure (both LeBlanc and Bataille are, ultimately, theorists of human violence), we start to see notable points in common. Despite appearing to be a theorist of human and ecological scarcity, LeBlanc nevertheless presupposes one basic fact: there is always a tendency for there to be *too many* humans in a given population. Certainly populations grow at different rates for different reasons, but they always seem to outstrip their environments: there is, in essence, always an excess of humans that has to be burned off. Conversely, Bataille is a thinker of limits to growth, precisely because he always presupposes a limit—if there were no limit, after all, there could be no excess of anything (yet the limit would be meaningless if there were not always already an excess, for the excess opens the possibility of the limit). As we know, for Bataille too there is never a steady state: energy (wealth) can be reinvested, which results in growth; when growth is no longer possible, when the limits to growth have been reached, the excess must be destroyed. If it is not, it will only return to cause us to destroy ourselves: war.

> For if we aren't strong enough to destroy, on our own, excessive energy, it cannot be used; and, like a healthy animal that cannot be trained, it will

come back to destroy us, and we will be the ones who pay the costs of the inevitable explosion. (Bataille 1976a, 31; 1988, 24)

In fact, Bataille sounds a lot like LeBlanc when he notes, in *The Accursed Share,* that the peoples of the "barbarian plateaus" of central Asia, mired in poverty and technologically inferior, could no longer move outward and conquer other adjacent, richer areas. They were, in effect, trapped; their only solution was the one that LeBlanc notes in similar cases: radical infertility. This, in effect, was the solution of the Tibetans, who supported an enormous population of infertile and unproductive monks (1976a, 106; 1988, 108).

Bataille does, then, implicitly face the question of carrying capacity. Perhaps the ultimate example of this is nuclear war. The modern economy, according to Bataille, does not recognize the possibility of excess—and therefore limits; the Protestant, and then Marxist, ideal is to reinvest all excess back into the productive process, always augmenting output in this way. "Utility," in this model, ends up being perfectly impractical: only so much output, finally, can be reabsorbed into the ever-more-efficient productive process. As in the case with Tibet, ultimately the excess will have to be burned off. This can happen either peacefully, through various postcapitalist mechanisms that Bataille recommends, such as the Marshall Plan, which will shift growth to other parts of the world, or violently and apocalyptically, through the ultimate in war: nuclear holocaust. One can see that, ultimately, the world itself will be *en vase clos,* fully developed, with no place for the excess to go. The bad alternative—nuclear holocaust—will result in the ultimate reduction in carrying capacity: a burned-out, depopulated earth.

> Humanity is, at the same time, through industry, which uses energy for the development of the forces of production, both a multiple opening of the possibilities of growth, and the infinite faculty for burnoff in pure waste [*facilité infine de consumation en pure perte*]. (Bataille 1976a, 170; 1988, 181)

Modern war is first of all a renunciation: one produces and amasses wealth in order to overcome a foe. War is an adjunct to economic expansion; it is a practical use of excessive forces. And this perhaps is the ultimate danger of the present-day (1949) buildup of nuclear arms: armament, seemingly a practical way of defending one's own country or spreading one's own values, of growing, in other words, ultimately leads to the risk of a "pure destruction" of excess—and even of carrying capacity. In the case of warfare, destructiveness is masked, made unrecognizable, by the appearance of an ultimate utility: in this case the spread of the American economy, and the American way of life, around the globe. Paradoxically, there is a kind of self-consciousness concerning excess, *dépense,* in the "naïve" society—which recognizes waste for what it is (in the form of unproductive "glory")—and a thorough ignorance in the modern one, which would always attempt to put waste to work, even at the cost of apocalypse.

Bataille, then, like LeBlanc, can be characterized as a thinker of society who situates his theory in the context of ecological limits. From Bataille's perspective, however, there is always too much rather than too little, given the existence of ecological ("natural") and social ("cultural") limits. The "end" of humankind, its ultimate goal, is thus the destruction of this surplus. While LeBlanc stresses war and sacrifice as means of obtaining or maintaining what is essential to human (personal, social) survival, Bataille emphasizes the maintenance of limits, and survival, as mere preconditions for engaging in the glorious destruction of excess. By seeing warfare as a mere (group) survival mechanism, LeBlanc makes the same mistake as that made by the supporters of a nuclear buildup; he, like they, sees warfare as practical, serving a purpose.

If, however, our most fundamental gesture is the burning off of a surplus, the production of that surplus must be seen as subsidiary. Once we recognize that everything cannot be saved and reinvested, the ultimate end (and most crucial problem) of our existence becomes the disposal of a surplus. All other activity "leads" to something else, is a means to some other end; the only end that leads nowhere is the act of destruction by which we may—or may not—assure our (personal) survival (there is nothing to guarantee that radical destruction—*consumation*—does not turn on its author). We work in order to spend, in other words. Survival and reproduction alone are not the ultimate ends of human existence. We could characterize Bataille, for this reason, as a thinker of ecology who nevertheless emphasizes the primacy of an ecstatic social act (destruction). By characterizing survival as a means, not an end (the most fundamental idea in "general economy"), expenditure for Bataille becomes a limitless insubordinate act—a real *end* (that which does not lead outside itself). I follow Bataille in this primacy of the delirium of expenditure over the simple exigency of personal or even social survival (which we can associate with LeBlanc). This does not preclude, however, a kind of ethical aftereffect of Bataille's expenditure: *survival for this reason can be read as the fundamentally unintentional consequence of expenditure, rather than its purpose.* Seeing a nuclear buildup as the wrong kind of waste—because it is seen as a means, not an end—can lead, in Bataille's view, to a rethinking of the role of expenditure in the modern world, and hence, perhaps, to the world's (but not modernity's) preservation.

🏵 *The Idea of Limits*

Carrying capacity poses a limit to growth: a society can destroy the excess through sacrifice, infanticide, ritual, festival; or excess can be put to work through the waging of war, in which case carrying capacity may be expanded through the appropriation of another society's land. War too, however, shows some elements of religious, purely wasteful expenditure in that it entails, as does sacrifice, glory. Especially in modern times, war also brings with it the possibility of defeat: in that case, there is no glory, and certainly no possibility of the expansion of carrying capacity. Indeed, as in the case of nuclear holocaust, societies run the risk of completely obliterating—wasting —the carrying capacity of their land.

In accord with Bataille's implicit ethical model, one can argue that the limits imposed by carrying capacity evoke two possible responses from societies. First, a society can recognize limits. Here, paradoxically, one violates limits, consciously transgresses them, so to speak, by recognizing them. Through various forms of ritual expenditure, one ultimately respects limits by symbolically defying the very principle of conservation and measured growth—of, in other words, limits. "Spending without reserve" is the spending of that which cannot be reinvested because of the limit, and yet the very act of destruction is the transgression of the logic of the limit, which would require, in its recognition, a sage and conservative attentiveness to the dangers of waste. If there is a limit to the production of goods and resources, however, we best respect and recognize that limit through its transgression—through, in other words, the destruction of precious energy resources. To attempt to reinvest, or put to use, the totality of those resources, to guarantee maximum productivity and growth, would only ignore the limit (rather than transgressing it), thereby eventually lowering the limit, if not eliminating it entirely (reduction of carrying capacity, ecological destruction, desertification).[13]

Such an affirmation—of limits and expenditure—entails a *general* view of economy, and, we might add, ecology. In positing such a respect for limits through their transgression, we forego an individual concern, which would customarily be seen as the human one (but which is not, in Bataille's view): a concern with personal survival, enrichment, and advancement. This approach, that of self-interest, is for Bataille (and for LeBlanc as well) ultimately tied to the simple ignorance of limits: not their transgression, but their violation. In the case of transgression of limits, we risk what might be personally comfortable or advantageous in order to attain a larger "glory," which is tied to unproductive expenditure and entails a possible dissolution of the self. From a general perspective, this expenditure is (as Bataille would say) on the scale of the universe; it must be, in principle, on the scale of the carrying capacity of a given landscape or ecology (else the expenditure would very quickly cancel itself out).

This version of limits and their transgression is identical with Bataille's conception of eroticism. What separates man from the animals, according to Bataille, is the interdiction of "immediate, unreserved, animal pleasure [*jouissance*]" (1976b, 47). Decency, the rules against sexual expression, incest, and intense pleasure that characterize human society, is fundamental to an organized society. But the human is not exclusively to be found in the interdiction: its ultimate "self-consciousness" is derived through the ecstatic transgression of that interdiction. Interdiction is an aftereffect of transgression, just as conservation is an aftereffect of expenditure (we produce and conserve in order to expend). What ultimately counts for us as humans (for us to be human) is an awareness of the necessity of expenditure (including that of our own death)—an awareness that animals lack.

> Of course, respect is only the detour of violence. On the one hand, respect orders the humanized world, where violence is forbidden; on the other, respect opens to violence the possibility of a breakout into the domain where it is inadmissible. The interdiction does not change the violence of sexual activity, but, by founding the *human* milieu, it makes possible what animality ignored: the transgression of the rule. . . .
> What matters is essentially that a milieu exists, no matter how limited, in which the erotic aspect is unthinkable, and moments of transgression in which eroticism attains the value of the greatest overthrow [*renversement*]. (Bataille 1976b, 47–48)

Eroticism, the general or collective experience of transgression, is impossible without the knowledge of human limits, interdictions. In the same way, we can say that the destruction of excess in an economy is only "on the scale of the universe" if it maintains and respects limits. We could even go beyond this and say that the maintenance of those limits, the carrying capacity in today's terminology, is only possible through the ritual, emotionally charged destruction of excess wealth (and not its indefinite, seemingly useful but indifferent reproduction), just as interdictions are only meaningful, and therefore maintainable, when they are periodically transgressed.

The only other approach to limits, as I've indicated, is to ignore them: the consumption of scarce resources can go on forever. In the realm of eroticism, this would be either to be entirely unaware of moral limits (interdictions)—as are animals—or, on the other hand, to see limits as so absolute that no meaningful transgression can take place; in this case, all eroticism would be so minor, so secondary, that no intimate relation between interdiction and eroticism could be imagined, and no dependence of interdiction on the transgressive expression of eroticism could be conceived. In this case, limits would be so overwhelming that they would not even be limits: one in effect could not violate them, since they would be omnipresent, omnipotent. Their transgression would be inconceivable (to try to violate them would simply manifest one's own degeneracy or evil, one's status outside the community, in an asylum or hell). Not coincidentally, this position is that of a religious-social orientation in which flamboyant expenditure—sexual, religious, phantasmatic—is inconceivable, or unworthy of conception, and in which all excess must therefore be reinvested in material productive processes (even eroticism is subordinated to the production of more people): Calvinism, the "Protestant ethic," and so on. This is the narrow view, that of the restricted economy, the economy of the "individual":

> Each investor demands interest from his capital: that presupposes an unlimited development of investment, in other words the unlimited growth of the forces of production. Blindly denied in the principle of these essentially productive operations is the not unlimited but considerable sum of products consumed in pure loss [*en pure perte*]. (Bataille 1976a, 170; 1988, 182)

This restricted economy, which hypostatizes limits (moral, personal) only ultimately to ignore them or degrade them, is the economy that values war as a mode of expansion (typified, for Bataille at least, by Islam) and as utility (self-defense, deterrence, mutually assured destruction). The limit is ignored in the restricted economy only at the risk of reimposition of an absolute limit, cataclysmic destruction (nuclear holocaust, the simple elimination of carrying capacity: ecological catastrophe).

Bataille's ethics, then, entails a choice between these two alternatives: recognition of limits through the affirmation of expenditure in a general economy, and ignoring of limits through a denial of expenditure in a closed or restricted economy. The first entails the affirmation of pleasure, ritual, glory, and anguish before death; while the latter entails the ego-driven affirmation of utility and unlimited growth, with all the attendant dangers.

The irony in all this is that in the first, transgressive and "human" ethics will inevitably be sensitive to ecological questions—respectful of carrying capacity—through its very affirmation of waste. The second, attempting to limit severely or do away with waste and thereby affirm the particular interests of an individual or a closed social group, will only universalize the wasting—the ultimate destruction—of the carrying capacity that serves as the basis of life. Conservation is therefore a logical aftereffect of expenditure; we conserve in order to expend. In other words, we conserve, not to perpetuate our small, monadic existences, but rather to make possible a larger generosity, a larger general economy that entails the transgression (in *angoisse*) of our narrow, selfish "practicality," our limitedness (i.e., the inevitable postponement of pleasure).

By expending we conserve. Bataille's utopian ethics foresees a society that creates, builds, and grows in order to waste, but by doing so, maintains the indefinite continuation of a human culture whose very humanity is inseparable from that general—collective and ecstatic—expenditure. The raison d'être of the society, so to speak, will lie in the very unreasoned logic of its excessive and transgressive expenditure. This highest value will be maintained and known through recognition of limits, which is ultimately reasonable, but to which the act of expenditure cannot be reduced.

The Duality of Expenditure, and the Object

Bataille's model in *The Accursed Share* ultimately depends on a distinction between types of expenditure and what we might call the modes of being associated with each type. This is significant because much of Bataille's analysis entails a critique of the confusion between different types of expenditure and economy: the "restrained" and the "general." Indeed, Bataille would argue that many of our current ills under capitalism derive from the confusion between the two realms; a Bataillean ethics would work to separate them.

First, "good" expenditure. Bataille associates it with an uncontrollable "élan": "riches prolong the burst of the sun and invoke passion"; "it's the return of the breadth of living to the truth of exuberance" (1976a, 78; 1988, 76). Here again, we have the passions unleashed by a naïve intimacy with the sun and the profound workings of the universe. But this intimacy is inseparable from the violence of enthusiasm.

Contrary to the world of work, the world of expenditure entails spending without regard for the future, affirmation of ecstasy now, and the refusal of things (*choses*) that only serve a purpose and that contribute only to one's own personal security and satisfaction (profit). Thus, Bataille's theory is not only an economic one but an ethical one that criticizes the affirmation of *self*.

As we've seen, however, this affirmation does not serve to deny what is usually, and perhaps wrongly, associated with the self: pleasure. For this reason, Bataille proposes a subject that, in its habitation of an intimate world, refuses the stable and reasonable order of things in order to enter into a profound communication with others and with the universe. This communication, this intimacy, entails a kind of relation that is radically different from the use of a seemingly stable thing to achieve a purpose. In *The Accursed Share,* Bataille writes:

> The *intimate* world is opposed to the *real* as the measureless is to measure, as madness is to reason, as drunkenness is to lucidity. There is only measure in the object, reason in the identity of the object with itself, lucidity in the direct knowledge of objects. The world of the subject is night: this moving, infinitely suspect night, which, in the sleep of reason, *engenders monsters. I propose, concerning the free subject, which is not at all subordinate to the "real" order and which is occupied only in the present, that in principle madness itself can give us only an adulterated idea.* (1976a, 63; 1988, 58: Bataille's italics)

In spite of this emphasis on the subject, it should be stressed that Bataille is nevertheless attempting to put forward a concept of the instant, and of experience—if those words have any meaning at all—which exits from the personal, individual realm; indeed, the very notion of a "general" economy means that individual, isolated interest is in principle left behind, and that instead, a larger perspective is embraced, one in which the individual's concerns and worries are no longer paramount. Replacing them are the larger energy flows of the subject, of society, and of the universe.

Having said all this, one should stress that this Bataillean ideal—for that's what it is, really—is itself already double, mixed with a recognition of the other reality. The *angoisse*—anguish, dread—before this "inner experience" is a human cut of sense, meaning, and purpose with which one engages when one comes to "face death." "Joy before death" is not separable from a dread that serves to install a human meaning in an otherwise cosmic, but limitless and hence non-human, event. Without dread, in other words, the "subject" merely melds with the ambient surroundings, like an animal. It is dread—which includes the very human knowledge of death—that serves to limit, demarcate, the event and give it meaning.

Meaning? Does that mean it's "significant"? For what? For some useful purpose?

Not entirely. Dread entails a recognition of limits, of course, but also their defiant overcoming. Much like the Stone Guest in Mozart and Da Ponte's *Don Giovanni,* the "subject" recognizes and affirms the limit only to overcome it in defiance. In the same way, transgression inevitably entails an affirmation, along with an overcoming, of interdiction. Sacrifice entails dread: it is "communication"—but communication *of* dread (Bataille 1976a, 518).

Bataille also makes it clear that dread is intimately tied to sense, even to reason. In some unpublished notes to *La Limite de l'utile* (written shortly before *The Accursed Share*), he wrote:

> To anyone who wants glory, the inevitable dread must first be shown. Dread distances only impertinence [*outrecuidance*]. The danger of "strong feelings" is that one will speak of them before experiencing them: one tries to provoke them by verbal violence, but one only ends up introducing violence without force. (1976a, 512)

Bataille goes on to speak of the ancient Mexicans, but their "reality" only underscores the need for an "anguished [*angoissé*] and down to earth [*terre à terre*] research." A "slow rigor" is required to "change our notion of ourselves and of the Universe" (1976a, 512).

All this is ultimately important because it shows us the *double* nature of Bataille's project. Not just an affirmation of death, madness, wild destruction, and the leap into the void, these terms, associable with excess, *dépense,* are nevertheless always moved toward—they can never simply be grasped, attained—through and against what would seem to be their contrary: interdiction, the limit, "down-to-earth research." Transgression would not be transgression without the human limit of meaning—of interdiction—against which it incessantly moves. Bataille's method is not that of the raving madman, but of the patient economist, writing against a "closed" economy, and of the Hegelian, writing against a narrow consciousness that would close off ecstasy, expenditure, and loss. Indeed, the final point Bataille wishes to reach is a higher "self-consciousness," not of a stable and smug awareness, but of a knowledge facing, and impossibly grasping, a general economy of loss—in dread. Thus Bataille can write of a self-consciousness that "humanity will finally achieve in the lucid vision of a linkage of its historical forms" (1976a, 47; 1988, 41).

A very particular self-consciousness, then, linked to a very peculiar concept of history. A self-consciousness, through a "slow rigor," that grasps man, not as a stable or even dynamic presence, but as a principle of loss and destruction. A history, not of peak moments of empire, democracy, or class struggle, but as exemplary instances of expenditure. And a future, not in absolute knowing, but in a finally utopian "not-knowing," "following the mystics of all periods," as Bataille puts it in the final footnote to *The Accursed Share* (1976a, 179; 1988, 197). But he then goes on to add, about himself: "But he is no less foreign to all the presuppositions of various mysticisms, to which he opposes only the lucidity of *self-consciousness.*"

So there is, then, what we might call a good duality in Bataille. In fact, the "accursed share" is itself, for want of a better term, doubled: it entails and presupposes limits, dread, self-consciousness, language (1976a, 596–98), along with madness, "pure loss," death.

But the same thing could be said, again for want of a better term, of the various ways this "part" is diluted or betrayed: what we might call, to differentiate it, "bad duality" (in contradistinction to the "good" duality of the transgression, in *angoisse,* of the recognized limits of self, body, and world).

"Bad duality," as I crudely put it, is the indulgence in expenditure out of personal motives: to gain something for oneself (glory, social status) or for one's social group or nation (booty, territory, security). From the chief who engages in potlatch, all the way to the modern military planners of nuclear war—all conceive of a brilliant, radical destruction of things as a *useful* contribution: to one's own social standing, to the position or long-term survival of one's own society.

And yet, for all that, Bataille recognizes a kind of devolution in warfare: earlier (sacrificial) war and destructive gift-giving still placed the emphasis on a spectacular and spectacularly useless destruction, carried out on a human scale. Later warfare, culminating in nuclear war, heightens the intensity of destructiveness while at the same time reducing it to the status of simple implement: one carries out destructive acts (e.g., Hiroshima) to accomplish certain useful policy goals.

Implicit in Bataille's discussion of war, from the Aztecs to the Americans, is the loss of intimacy. Aztec war was thoroughly subordinated, on the part of both victor and vanquished, to the exigencies of passion; as time went on, it seems that martial glory came to be associated more and more with mere rank. Self-interest replaced the "intimate," exciting destruction of goods and life. Modern nuclear war is completely devoid of any element of transgression or dread; it is simply mechanized murder, linked to some vague political or economic conception of necessity. Ultimately, for this reason, war in Bataille's view must be replaced by a modern version of potlatch, in which one nation-state (the United States) gives without counting to others (the Europeans, primarily).

Modern war remains, for all that, an example of mankind's tendency to expend. It is merely an extreme example of an inability to recognize *dépense* for what it is. It thereby constitutes a massive failure of self-consciousness: "bad duality" as the melding of the "tendency to expend" with the demand for utility and self-interest.

Something, however, is missing in Bataille's analysis. This steady progression in types of warfare, while signaling the difference between what we might call "intimate" war (the Aztecs) and utilitarian war (the world wars), nevertheless does tend to conflate them in a very specific way. They are all seen as moments in which humanity plays the role of the most efficient destroyer, the being at the top of the food chain that consumes—in both senses of the word—the greatest concentrations and the greatest quantities of energy. Ultimately, the difference between Aztec war and American war is exclusively one of self-consciousness; ironically, it was the Aztecs who, in their sacrificial/militaristic orgies, were in closer touch with, and had greater awareness of, the nature of war. The Americans might be the greater consumers, but their knowledge of what they are doing is minimal (only the Marshall Plan, augmented through a reading of Bataille, would solve that problem).[14]

What isn't discussed is the nature of the destruction itself. Bataille never considers that contemporary *dépense* is not only greater in *quantity,* but is different in *quality.* How is it that mankind has gone from the relatively mild forms of destruction practiced by the Aztecs—mountains of skulls, to be sure, but still, relatively speaking, fairly harmless—to the prospect of the total devastation of the earth? Why has destruction been amplified to such a degree? Does it change the very nature of the expenditure carried out by modern societies?

The answer, I think, is to be found in the nature of the consumption itself. Bataille in effect makes the same mistake that traditional economists make concerning the origin of value: that it is to be found primarily in human labor. If, however, we see the skyrocketing of the creation of value in the last two centuries to be attributable not solely to inputs of labor, but to the energy derived from fossil fuels (Beaudreau), we will come to understand that the massive increase in mankind's capacity to waste is attributable not only to, say, technical innovation, the more efficient application of human labor, and so forth, but to the very energy source itself. The Aztecs, like many other traditional societies, derived their energy from muscle power: that of animals, slaves, and, in warfare, nobles. Destruction, like production, entailed an expenditure of energy derived from very modest sources: calories, derived from food, transformed by muscle, and applied to a task. We might call this energy (to modify a Bataillean usage), and its destruction, *intimate:* that is, its production and expenditure are on a human scale and are directly tied to a close relation with things. Just as intimacy for Bataille implies a passionate involvement with the thing—primarily its *consumation,* the intense relation with a thing that is not a thing—so in this case, having to do with the production and destruction of value, my muscle power assures that my relation to what I make or destroy will be passionate.

A hand tool's use will entail physical effort, pain, pleasure, satisfaction, or anguish. It will be up close and personal. The same will go for the destruction of the utility of that tool; there will be a profound connection between "me" and the destruction of the thing-ness of the tool.[15] By extension, the utility, "permanence," of my self will be put in question through an intimate connection with the universe via the destroyed object or tool.

Just as there are two sources of economic value—muscle power and inanimate fuel power—there are two kinds of expenditure. The energy derived from fossil or inanimate fuel expenditure, for production or destruction, is different in quality, not merely in quantity, from muscular energy. No intimacy (in the Bataillean sense) can be envisaged through the expenditure of fossil fuels. The very use of nonorganic fuels—coal, oil, nuclear—implies the effort to maximize production through quantification, the augmentation of sheer quantity of things. Raw material becomes, as Heidegger put it, a standing reserve, a measurable mass whose sole function is to be processed, and ultimately discarded.[16] It is useful, nothing more (or less), at least for the moment before it is discarded; it is related to the self only as a way of aggrandizing the latter's stability and position. There is no internal limit, no *angoisse* or pain before which we shudder; we deplete the earth's energy reserves as blandly and indifferently as the French revolutionaries (according to Hegel) chopped off heads: as if one were cutting off a head of cabbage. "Good" duality has completely given way to "bad."

As energy sources become more efficiently usable—oil produces a lot more energy than does coal in relation to the amount of energy needed to extract it, transport it, dispose of waste (ash and slag)—more material can be treated, more things produced and dumped. Consequently, more food can be produced, more humans will be born to eat it, and so on. And yet, under this inanimate fuels regime, the very nature of production—and above all, of destruction—changes. Even when things today are wasted, they are wasted under the sign of efficiency, of utility. This very abstract quantification is inseparable from the demand of an efficiency that bolsters the position of a closed and demanding subjectivity. We "need" cars and SUVs; we "need" to use up gas, waste landscapes, forests: it is all done in the name of the personal "lifestyle" we cannot live without, that is clearly the best ever developed in human history, the one everyone necessarily wants. We no longer destroy objects, render them intimate, in a very personal, confrontational potlatch; we simply leave items out for the trash haulers to pick up or have them hauled to the junkyard. There can hardly be any intimacy in the contemporary cycle of production-consumption-destruction. As Bataille put it, concerning intimacy:

Intimacy is expressed only under one condition by the *thing* [*la chose*]: that this *thing* fundamentally be the opposite of a thing, the opposite of a product, of merchandise: a burning-off [*consumation*] and a sacrifice. Since intimate feeling is a burning-off, it is burning-off that expresses it, not the *thing*, which is its negation. (1976a, 126; 1988 132: Bataille's italics)

War, too, reflects this non-intimacy of the thing: fossil-fuel- and nuclear-powered explosives and delivery systems make possible the impersonal destruction of human life in great numbers and at a great distance. Human lives are now simply quantities of material to be processed and destroyed. This killing is different in kind from that carried out by the Aztecs. All the sacrificial elements, the elements by which the person has been transformed in death, have disappeared.

Bataille, then, should have distinguished clearly between intimate and impersonal varieties of wasteful expenditure. It is not merely a question of our attitude toward waste, our "self-consciousness": also fundamental is *how* the wastage is carried out. Waste based on the consumption of fossil or inanimate (nuclear) fuels cannot entail intimacy because it is dependent on the thing *as* thing, as

[w]hat we know from the outside, which is given to us as physical reality (at the limit of the commodity, available without reserve). We cannot penetrate the *thing* and its only meaning is its material qualities, appropriated or not for some use [*utilité*], understood in the productive sense of the term. (1976a, 126; 1988, 132: Bataille's italics)

The origin of this destruction is therefore to be found in the maximization of the efficiency of production; modern, industrialized waste is fundamentally only the most efficient way to eliminate what has been overproduced. "Growth" is the ever-increasing rhythm and quantity of the treatment of matter for some purported human purpose and that matter's subsequent disposal/destruction. One could never "self-consciously" reconnect with intimacy through the affirmation of some form of industrial production-destruction. To see consumer culture as in some way the fulfillment of Bataille's dream of a modern-day potlatch is for this reason a fundamental misreading of *The Accursed Share*.[17] Bataille's critique is always an ethics; it entails the affirmation of a "general economy" in which the particular claims of subjectivity are left behind. To affirm a consumption that, in spite of its seeming delirium of waste, is simply a treatment of matter and expenditure of fossil energy in immense quantities, lacking any sense of internal limits (*angoisse*), and always with a particular and efficacious end in view ("growth," "comfort," "personal satisfaction," "consumer freedom"), is to misrepresent the main thrust of Bataille's work. The point, after all, is to enable us to attain a greater "self-consciousness," based on the ability to choose between modes of expenditure. Which entails the greatest intimacy? Certainly not nuclear devastation (1949) or the simple universal depletion of the earth's resources and the wholesale destruction of ecosystems (2006).

🌼 *Duality Today*

This is not to say, however, that contemporary (mechanized) modes of waste are entirely lacking in what made "primitive" expenditure so seductive: displays of prestige. We often hear that people cannot give up car culture and other forms of hyper-waste because they are "exciting," delivery systems for "freedom," and so on. Life without the combustion of inconceivable quantities of fossil fuels and the consumption of objects derived from those fuels would be mournful, gray, a hopeless existence under the rule of an intellectual theocracy, a tiny group of censorious liberal neo-puritans. Al Gore's "defeat" in the presidential election of 2000 is taken as proof that a candidate for major office who intimates in the most subtle way concerns for the environment is destined for oblivion. Pleasure, speed, and the profligate waste of natural resources are seen to be inseparable: undeniable freedoms. "Real men don't conserve."

To a large extent, we need not engage in debate around the question of car culture at all; the imminent decline in world oil production within the next twenty or thirty years (if that long) will put paid to the car culture, and eventually even most manifestations of "global culture" (since "globalization"—world trade and emigration/immigration—is wholly dependent on the mass consumption of fossil fuels) without any intervention on the part of ecological terrorists—or critics.[18] But mankind will still be around, of course, after oil becomes prohibitively expensive; the "tendency to expend" will always be there. What utopian future can we attempt to think, then, on the basis of Bataille's theory?

First, we should note that any future must take into account—indeed, even posit as fundamental—the thirst for sacrifice and glorious expenditure. To attempt to deny the passion associated with these activities will doom any future scenario to irrelevance. And the excitement of car culture, devoid as it may be of any real "intimacy" in the Bataillean sense, at least allows people to feel that there is more to their lives than simple production and reproduction. The smell of fine Corinthian leather, the excitement of using a radar-detector and outsmarting the highway patrolman, the gleam of desire in your neighbor's eye when he ogles your new car—these are all pleasures that are not to be denied. So too, is the sense of freedom one derives from accelerating down an open road. And, undoubtedly, they are based in some way on expenditure: leather, speed, chrome—none of it is necessary, all of it indicates a waste not only of fossil-fuel-based resources but of labor-time as well. Moreover, part of the excitement of car culture is based on the amount of my own time and effort I waste on my auto-centric project. I like the rush, the force pressing my body back against the seat, the heedlessness concerning the amount of my time spent exclusively to procure the joy of acceleration.[19]

Here, however, we might recall Bataille's critique of potlatch. The problem there was the hijacking, so to speak, of sacrificial destruction, its subordination to personal interests: the rank, or prestige, of the chief, affirmed, not as explosiveness,[20] but as a thing. "Bad duality," as I dubbed it, but one that still entails some vestiges of spectacular expenditure. We can say that some form of this occurs today, although it only accounts for a tiny portion of the mechanized waste of the industrial world. Resources still are wasted in an effort to establish permanent prestige: the individual who spends over $600,000 on a new Ferrari Enzo is flamboyantly consuming his wealth in order to impress, but also intimidate and outclass, others.[21] Behind the wheel of an Enzo, the freedom of mind-boggling speed is inseparable from the pleasure of invincibility of monumental standing: the ownership of, or even the association with, such a car. Here we have once again a form of the "bad duality" I discussed above, but now yoked to a hyper-consumption quite foreign to the fundamental tendency of sacrifice (*la pure dépense*) that one would find in, say, potlatch.

Despite the relatively minor frequency of this type of enthusiastic expenditure in the industrialized world, it nevertheless has cast its glamour over the overall consumption of mass-merchandized goods. One no longer buys shoes just to be shod; one buys a certain model, no doubt popularized by certain sports figures, in order to be "cool." Even the most humble four-door family sedan must somehow remind its owner of the Ferrari Enzo. That glow of excitement, of object-mediated freedom, is what was supposedly missing from the old Communist world, marked as it was by a sheer closed economy of consumption geared to production.[22]

So there is an ersatz intimacy—the joy of the reckless struggle for the freedom associated with prestige—remaining in the hyper-consuming world today, apparently enough to justify its continued existence, on the rare occasions when it is not being justified through utility alone (we "need" more highways, etc.). But that's the problem: if we attempt to discuss any regime of energy consumption other than the current one of hyper-waste, we will inevitably be dismissed as killjoys.

The "freedom" of the car is, however, derived from a double prestige: either status prestige, elevation over others or over one's earlier (poorer) self, or the prestige of elevation above space and time: an absolute speed that negates landscape and the time of self-propelled travel and cynically negates others who do not have access to, or who are not captivated by, that speed.

If, on the other hand, we dissociate the "tendency to expend" characterizing humanity from the selfish consumption of huge amounts of fossil-fuel-based energy—if, in other words, we posit a "good" duality in contradistinction to the current regime of the "bad"—we can then continue to affirm excess, but excess, the destruction of the *thing,* as a movement of intimacy. Energy now will be wasted on an intimate level, that of the human body, against the imperious demands of the self. The expenditure analyzed by Bataille is always on the level of corporeality: the arousal of sexual organs, the movement of muscles, the distortions of words spewing from mouths.

The problem, then, entailing a task never fully undertaken by Bataille, is to conceive of a "good" duality, the affirmation of sheer expenditure in the face of dread and the recognition of limits (interdiction, human sense), on the scale of human muscle power and the mortality of the body. A return to the past? Not really, since the imminent depletion of fossil fuel resources will push us in that direction anyway: muscle power, body power, will be a, if not the, major component in the energy mix of the future.[23] But certainly what's imperative is a recognition that an economy *not* based on the profligate waste of resources nevertheless must recognize the "tendency to expend," must, indeed, be based upon it. And inseparable from that tendency, as we know, are the passions, as Bataille would call them: glory, but also delirium, madness, sexual obsession. Or, perhaps closer to home, a word rarely if ever used by Bataille: freedom. The freedom of the instant, freedom from the task, from the subordination of pleasure to a long-term, ever-receding, and largely unjustified goal. The freedom of sovereignty, perhaps. But not the freedom of prestige, rank.

"Expenditure without return" is a floating concept, defined in opposition to the restrained economy whose possibility it opens, but which it defies. As an end not leading outside itself, it could be anything; but what's most important is that with it there is a movement of "communication," of the breaking of the narrow limits of the (ultimately illusory) self-interested individual. And no doubt as well some form of personal or collective *transport,* or enthusiasm. This concern with a *mouvement hors de soi* can no doubt be traced to Sade, but it also derives from the French sociological tradition of

Durkheim, where collective enthusiasm was seen to animate public life and give personal life a larger meaning.[24] As Bataille puts it in *L'Économie à la mesure de l'univers:*

> You are only, and you must know it, an explosion of energy. You can't change it. All these human works around you are only an overflow of vital energy. . . . You can't deny it: the desire is in you, it's intense; you could never separate it from mankind. Essentially, the human being has the responsibility here [*a la charge ici*] to spend, in glory, what is accumulated on the earth, what is scattered by the sun. Essentially, he's a laugher, a dancer, a giver of festivals. This is clearly the only serious language. (1976a, 15–16)

Bataille's utopia thus entails a community united through common enthusiasm, effervescence; and in this sense, there is some good "glory"—it's not a term that should be associated exclusively with rank or prestige. Certainly, the Durkheimian model, much more orthodox and (French) Republican, favored an egalitarianism that would prevent, through its collective enthusiasm, the appearance of major social inequality. Bataille's community would continue that tradition, while arguing for a "communication" much more radical in that it puts in question the very limits of stable human individuality. On this score, at least, it's a radical Durkheimianism: the fusion envisaged is so complete that the very limits of the individual, not only of his or her personal interests but of the body as well, are ruptured in a community that would communicate through "sexual wounds."

Yet there's nothing that is *inherently* excessive. Because waste can very easily contribute to a sense of rank or can be subsumed as necessary investment/consumption, no empirical verification could ever take place. This is the paradox of Bataille's project: the very empiricism we would like to *guarantee* a "self-consciousness" and a *pure dépense* is itself a function of a closed economy of utility and conservation (the study of a stable object for the benefit and contentment of mankind, etc.). Waste, *dépense,* intimacy (the terms are always sliding; they are inherently unstable, for good reason) are instead a function of difference, of the unassimilable, but also, as we've seen, of ethical judgment. It's a Bataillean ethics that valorizes the Marshall Plan over nuclear war, that determines that one is linked to sacrifice in all its forms, whereas the other is not. We can go so far as to say that expenditure is the determination of the social and energetic element that does not lead outside itself, to some higher good or utility. Paradoxically, this determination itself is ethical, because an insubordinate expenditure is an affirmation of a certain conception of the human, beyond the closed economy of the personal, or the social as guarantor of the personal. But such a determination does not depend on an "in-itself," on a definitive set of classifications, on a taxonomy that will guarantee the status of a certain act or a certain politics.

Expenditure, then, may be affirmed—not through *ressentiment,* but through a willed difference with the closed economy of use and the cult of personal satisfaction. If we return to the model of hyper-expenditure with which we are familiar to the point of its invisibility, we can say that loss can be framed as an inefficiency in relation to the efficiency of the inanimate fuels regime. Thus, for example, walking or cycling is a gross waste of time and effort when one could drive. The expenditure of blood sugar instead fossil fuel in "transport" is one instance of a larger expenditure of the logic of fossil fuel use, of obesity, of the passive regime of spectator sports, of the segregation of society by physical space (according to race and social class), of the degradation of the environment in support of the production, use, and disposal of cars, and of the economy of "growth" that is dependent on the use of ever greater quantities of depletable resources.[25] This difference with the closed global economy, this affirmation of physical pleasure and "self-consciousness" in a Bataillean sense, is what we might call one version of a contemporary affirmation of the general economy—no matter on how intimate a level.

Walking or riding a bike a ridiculous distance each day in order to get somewhere, at least if judged by contemporary standards of comfort and well-being, is literally *senseless.*[26] It is only if we see it in and as an economy of difference and knowledge—impossible knowledge—that this act can be put in perspective. Physical movement as transportation, display, dance, exhaustion, passion, *all together,* in an urban space made dense and polysemous by the different modalities of bodily expenditure—all this makes possible the reinscription of "freedom," its reassignment from the sociotechnical frame[27] previously associated with the regime of hyper-consumption, social standing, and inanimate fuel-based energy depletion.

All of this is important if we consider that a regime of "sustainability" will offer only austerity. Recent books devoted to "managing the decline"— that is, surviving the end of the era of cheap fossil fuels—have presented visions of a future in which life will be made more sensible, "small," because the wasteful habits of current consumers will, necessarily, be curtailed. Cooperatives, sensible (slower) transportation alternatives, smaller houses, less travel, rigorous recycling, all will be practiced, will have to be practiced, if there is to be any future at all.[28] This is commendable futurology, but notably lacking from all these models of the future is the one element that might give them some appeal: excitement, passion, freedom, glory, the sense of transgressing limits—even orgiastic sexuality and madness.[29] The excesses of a consumer society will be curtailed in this sane future, to be sure, but the "ends" of society, the passion or delirium, collective or individual, that (according to Bataille at least) will inevitably drive it (if there is to be any human self-consciousness) seem to be lacking. Ivan Illich, perhaps the most lucid of social analysts, likes the term "conviviality," a notion that implies nonhierarchical institutions, close deinstitutionalized personal relations in what now might be considered a rather austere economic setting.

This is a laudable ideal, but one can only imagine along with it, and against it, another economy, another ecology: one in which nature is not necessarily to be preserved (conserved) primarily for the comfort and perpetuity of man; one in which the violence of expenditure, on the part of mankind and of "nature," is put forward, and in which *sustainability will be a logical aftereffect.* A future, in other words, that will celebrate expenditure on a human, physical scale, a scale that will preclude the hyper-expenditure that recognizes no limits and that delivers only a secondary, selfish freedom. This expenditure on the part of the body, in violent contact and contrast with other bodies, maneuvering in the city, over mountains and through valleys, will come to usurp, in its practices of freedom and obsession, the actions through which mountains and valleys are mere things to be processed and discarded. It will not be "beautiful" in its "smallness," its "slowness"; it will not assume that the angelic or brutish ecstasy of which we are capable and destined is a cause or aftereffect of the current regime of expenditure, either its hyper-waste or its relentless commodification. It will not entail a quasi-religion with man, living in sustainable comfort, as its chief deity. Conservation, austerity, these terms only have meaning if they are practiced in the name of something else; a hermetically sealed, that is, closed economy, as Bataille shows, is unthinkable. There will always be a rupture in the system that both opens its possibility and is unthinkable within it. Waste logically precedes conservation, then; but its practice entails conservation as an aftereffect. For without some form of conservation, there can be no consistent carrying capacity, and without the latter, no notion of expenditure.

Our first question, which is inseparable from an ethical approach to economy, will be: How and what do we waste? What model of waste will condition the practice of maintaining or modifying a carrying capacity? And we will inevitably think within a horizon, a series of limits, as Bataille himself does when he elaborates the ethics of expenditure; no thought can be elaborated in and as a realm of limitless, sheer waste. But from within the ethics of limits, we have no choice but to work out a theory of excess in an era of radical shortage,[30] a practice of human-powered velocity in an era of gas lines, a theory of glory in and against an epoch of seemingly relentless constraint. "Good" duality, in effect: the incessant transgression of all-too-human limits.

ALLAN STOEKL

NOTES

1. Derrida (1978) characterizes the crucial fifth section of *The Accursed Share,* in which nuclear destruction and the Marshall Plan are discussed, as "most often muddled by conjectural approximations" (1978, 337n33).

2. See, for example, Foucault's *Discipline and Punish*—especially the importance he places on the (constitutive) role of violent spectacle in society—and Lingis's emphasis, for example, in *Trust* (2004), on transgression and excess in interpersonal relations.

3. "Carrying capacity" refers to the population (of any given species) that a region can be reasonably expected to sustain. It is defined by LeBlanc in this way: "The idea [of carrying capacity] in its simplest form is that the territory or region available to any group contains only a finite amount of usable food for that group. Different environments can carry or support different numbers of people: deserts can support fewer people than woodlands, the Arctic can support very few, and so on" (2003, 39).

4. My translation. Ambrosino's text is not included in the English translation of *The Accursed Share.* Many of Ambrosino's texts of the late 1940s and early 1950s published in *Critique,* the review edited by Bataille, display the same assumption, that energy is available in infinite supply—not only in the universe as a whole, but in modern fossil-fuel-based economies. This is a most peculiar position for a trained physicist to take. See, for example, his review of Norbert Wiener's *Cybernetics,* in *Critique:* "Energy, in a physical sense, is everywhere (the least gram of matter, etc. . . .), [and] the sources of negative entropy, with which man furnishes himself, and his industry, are practically inexhaustible [*intarissable*]" (1950, 80).

5. On EROEI and its implications for any energy retrieval, distribution, or consumption system, see Heinberg 2003, 138.

6. The last really massive oil field found by petroleum geologists was the Al-Ghawar, discovered in Saudi Arabia in 1948 (one year before the publication of *The Accursed Share*).

7. See Heinberg 2003, 142–46.

8. See Beaudreau 1999, for whom value in industrial economies is ultimately derived from the expenditure of inanimate energy, not labor power (7–35). Conversely, "[human] labor in modern production processes is more appropriately viewed as a form of lower-level organization (i.e., supervisor)" (18).

9. It has taken millions of years of concentration in the fossilization process to produce the amazingly high-energy yields of fossil fuels: tapping into sunlight alone cannot come close. F. E. Trainer, for example, sees enormous problems with the use of solar energy to fuel human society, even the most parsimonious: the difficulty of collecting the energy in climates that have little direct sunlight (1995, 118); the inefficiency of converting it to electricity and storing it, where at least 80 percent of the energy will be lost in the process (118–24); and even the expense of building a solar collection plant, where, in Trainer's estimation, "it would take eight years' energy output from the plant just to repay the energy it would take to produce the steel needed to build it!" (124)—all these facts indicate that solar energy in relation to human civilization is, well, too diluted.

10. The "energy slave" is based on the estimate of mechanical work a person can do: an annual energy output of 37.2 million foot-pounds. "In the USA, daily use per capita of energy is around 1000 MJ, that is, each person has the equivalent of 100 energy slaves working 24 hours a day for him or her" (Boyden 1987, 196).

11. See Odum and Odum 2001, "Policies for Transition and Descent," 131–286.

12. See note 2, above.

13. See the prime example cited by LeBlanc: an area of Turkey where he did research as a young anthropologist. "Almost 10,000 years of farming and herding have denuded an original oak-pistachio woodland, and today [in a photograph of the area] only a few trees can be seen in the distance" (2003, 140).

14. Perhaps complimentary copies of *The Accursed Share* could be distributed in the Department of Defense and the Pentagon.

15. Heidegger's analysis of the defamiliarization, so to speak, of the useful but unremarked object in *Being and Time* clearly anticipates Bataille's take on the object, the "thing," both useful (and hence largely invisible) and, in another, "general" context, not. (For Bataille, the object is not just broken, wrenched out of its familiar context: it is rendered orgiastic, insubordinate, "cursed matter," etc., and here following the tradition of reading the "sacred" in the French anthropological tradition [Durkheim, Mauss]).

16. In, of course, Heidegger's famous postwar essay, "The Question Concerning Technology" (1977).

17. This is the legacy of a well-known article by Jean-Joseph Goux on Bataille: "General Economics and Postmodern Capitalism" (1990). See also Blood 2002, an informative and useful article on Bataille and Derrida in this context.

18. See Deffeyes 2001, and Heinberg 2003. The "Hubbert's Peak" argument is that the extraction of oil has followed a classic bell curve; both for American oil reserves, which reached the top of the peak around 1970—perfectly following M. King Hubbert's prediction of the 1950s—and world reserves, which will probably reach their peak no later than some time between 2010 and 2020. Hubbert's theory, applied globally, does not predict complete oil exhaustion after the peak has been reached, but merely indicates the point after which the quantity of oil being extracted worldwide will start to decline. At that moment—not of the total disappearance of oil, but of the beginning of the decline of oil production—a staggering realization will sweep the world's oil markets: oil production is declining, at a time of rising demand, *and there is nothing to remedy the situation.* The effect on oil prices is easily imagined. Obviously, rising oil prices will cut demand; the complete exhaustion of oil resources may very well not come for centuries. It's a question of accelerating shortfalls, not of simply "running out" of oil. Heinberg's is probably the best overall book on the social implications of the imminent decline of the fossil fuel economy. For a mordant consideration of the prospects of American society in light of "Hubbert's Peak," see Kunstler (perhaps the most brilliant urbanist writing today).

19. With all the time spent working to pay for the car, commuting in it, waiting for repairs, sitting in traffic jams, and so forth, the average American spends 1,600 hours a year in or on his car. As Illich puts it, "The model American puts in 1,600 hours to get 7,500 miles; less than five miles per hour" (1973, 31).

20. "[Rank] is an explosive charge. The man of high rank is originally only an explosive individual (all men are explosive, but he is explosive in a privileged way). Doubtless he tries to prevent, or at least delay the explosion. Thus he lies to himself by derisively taking his wealth and his power for something they are not" (Bataille 1976a, 77; 1988, 75).

21. Although it is true that the "super-rich" who would buy cars like the Enzo are likely spending a smaller portion of their income on automotive transport than are the "middle-class" individuals killing themselves to pay off minivans and SUVs.

22. The irony, of course, lies in the fact that when the Iron Curtain fell, the eastern bloc countries were revealed to be, in terms of natural resources and conservation, among the most wasteful and polluting on earth.

23. When oil hits $150 a barrel (a modest estimate for, say, 2015—see note 18, above),

car culture will very quickly become a distant, albeit fond, memory. The notion of globalization, celebrated or excoriated by so many postmodern critics, will seem equally arcane, since the quick and cheap transport of people and things and even information will come to an end. For further considerations on the end of the fossil fuel era, see Heinberg 2003, as well as the articles and polemics on the rather sobering Web site www.dieoff.org.

24. See Strenski on Durkheim as a thinker of sacrifice, and Richman on Bataille's connection to the tradition of Durkheim and on both Durkheim and Bataille as latter-day avatars of the French intellectual tradition that conceives society to be grounded in sacrificial expenditure.

25. For a systematic and thorough indictment of the official American automobile culture, in all its social and ecological ramifications, see Alvord 2000.

26. These standards are more and more associated with the mass propagation and maintenance of obesity. The universalization of car culture has resulted in an epidemic of obesity: the energy one would otherwise spend on transporting oneself (walking, cycling) comes to be accumulated on the body in the form of fat (see Alvord 2000, 89–90). One of the forms of wealth (hoarded energy) expended in future acts of post-car-culture potlatch will therefore be the wattles of fat that adorn the bodies of so many modern individuals.

27. On the sociotechnical frame—a regime entailing both a given technology and the social implementation from which it is inseparable—see Rosen 2002, 174–78. The sociotechnical frame on which Rosen focuses is that of the bicycle. Rosen makes this trenchant observation: "A sustainability-centered sociotechnical frame of the bicycle will have to wrest the values of freedom and autonomy back from the sociotechnology of the automobile and re-integrate them within a wider conception of sustainable mobility. The sheer difficulty of this task can be demonstrated by trying to imagine a car-dependent relative, friend or colleague attaching the same sense of freedom he or she identifies with their automobile to public transportation, car-sharing, or multi-modal trips. One cause for optimism is that for cyclists these values are intrinsic to their modal choice" (Rosen 2002, 175). Rosen is an unusual author in that he recognizes the importance of emotional, even ecstatic experience ("freedom," "autonomy") in the choice or development of a sociotechnical frame. In other words, mere grim sustainability is not enough; some "inner experience," to borrow Bataille's term, will, in the future, have to come into play. See notes 28 and 29, below.

28. There is a virtual library of books arguing for a "sustainable" development that frame their arguments in the mode of self-sacrifice, downsizing, lowered expectations, sanity, slowness, refusal of the excitement of consumption, conservation in a rigorously closed economy. See, e.g., Odum and Odum 2001; Brown 2001; Schumacher 1989; Illich 1978; Trainer 1995.

29. "The supreme value in conserver society must be living as simply as possible—consuming as few non-renewable resources as is compatible with comfortable material living standards. The focal criterion must be what is *sufficient*. Is this house, this coat, etc. good enough to do the job? Instead of finding luxury attractive we must value recycled and repaired items. We must in other words undergo a complete reversal in our thinking about luxuries" (Trainer 1995, 133; Trainer's italics).

30. This is what Bataille himself did; the late 1940s and early 1950s were an era of seemingly insuperable shortage and gray constraint: food rationing, housing shortages, cities in ruins, accompanied by the perceived need for a communism that would restrain or eliminate the inequalities of society and its attendant waste and therefore do away with *shortage*. Sartre was the hero of the day, the setter of the intellectual agenda, certainly not Bataille—

and Sartre's existentialist theory was based on a theory of *lack* (lack remedied, of course, by human intervention, labor). Bataille's gesture—to proclaim that the central problem of the postwar era was not shortage but the glut of wealth (energy) with which humans were destroying themselves—was magnificently perverse. And right on the money.

WORKS CITED

Alvord, Katie. 2000. *Divorce Your Car! Ending the Love Affair with the Automobile.* Gabriola Island, B.C., Canada: New Society.

Ambrosino, Georges. La Machine Savante et la vie: Norbert Wiener, *Cybernetics. Critique* 41 (October 1950): 70–82.

Bataille, Georges. 1976a. *Oeuvres Complètes,* Vol. VII. Paris: Gallimard.

———. 1976b. *Oeuvres Complètes,* Vol. VIII. Paris: Gallimard.

———. 1985. *Visions of Excess: Selected Writings, 1927–1939.* Ed. Allan Stoekl. Minneapolis: University of Minnesota Press.

———. 1988. *The Accursed Share, Volume I.* Trans. Robert Hurley. New York: Zone Books.

Beaudreau, Bernard C. 1999. *Energy and the Rise and Fall of Political Economy.* Westport, Conn.: Greenwood Press.

Blood, Susan. The Poetics of Expenditure. *MLN* 117 (4) (2002): 836–57.

Boyden, Stephen. 1987. *Western Civilization in Biological Perspective.* Oxford: Clarendon Press.

Brown, Lester. 2001. *Eco-Economy: Building an Economy for the Earth.* New York: Norton.

Deffeyes, Kenneth S. 2001. *Hubbert's Peak: The Impending World Oil Shortage.* Princeton, N.J.: Princeton University Press.

Derrida, Jacques. 1978. From Restricted to General Economy: A Hegelianism without Reserve. In *Writing and Difference.* Trans. Allan Bass. Chicago: University of Chicago Press.

Foucault, Michel. 1977. *Discipline and Punish: The Birth of the Prison.* Trans. Alan Sheridan. New York: Vintage.

Goux, Jean-Joseph. 1990. General Economics and Postmodern Capitalism. In *Yale French Studies* 78: 206–24.

Heidegger, Martin. 1977. *The Question Concerning Technology, and Other Essays.* Trans. William Lovitt. New York: Harper Torchbooks.

———. 1996. *Being and Time.* Trans. Joan Stambaugh. Albany: State University of New York Press.

Heinberg, Richard. 2003. *The Party's Over: Oil, War, and the Fate of Industrial Societies.* Gabriola Island, B.C., Canada: New Society.

Illich, Ivan. 1973. *Tools for Conviviality.* New York: Harper & Row.

———. 1978. Energy and Equity. In *Toward a History of Needs.* Berkeley, Calif.: Heyday.

Kunstler, James Howard. 2001–. The Clusterfuck Chronicle. http://www.kunstler.com

LeBlanc, Steven A. 2003. *Constant Battles: The Myth of the Peaceful, Noble Savage.* New York: St. Martin's Press.

Lingis, Alphonso. 2004. *Trust.* Minneapolis: University of Minnesota Press.

Odum, Howard T., and Elizabeth C. Odum. 2001. *A Prosperous Way Down: Principles and Policies.* Boulder: University Press of Colorado.

Perelman, Lewis J. 1981. Speculations on the Transition to Sustainable Energy. In *Energy Transitions: Long-Term Perspectives*. Ed. L. J. Perelman, A. W. Giebelhaus, and M. D. Yokell. Boulder, Colo.: Westview Press, 185–216.

Price, David. 1995. Energy and Human Evolution. *Population and Environment: A Journal of Interdisciplinary Studies* 16 (4) (March 1995): 301–19.

Richman, Michele. 2002. *Sacred Revolutions: Durkheim and the Collège de Sociologie.* Minneapolis: University of Minnesota Press.

Rosen, Paul. 2002. *Framing Production: Technology, Culture and Change in the British Bicycle Industry.* Cambridge, Mass.: MIT Press.

Schumacher, E. F. 1989. *Small is Beautiful: Economics as if People Mattered.* New York: Perennial Library.

Strenski, Ivan. 2002. *Contesting Sacrifice: Religion, Nationalism, and Social Thought in France.* Chicago: University of Chicago Press.

Trainer, F. E. 1995. *Consumer Society: Alternatives for Sustainability.* Sydney, Australia: Zed.

Contributors

Alison Leigh Brown is Professor of Philosophy in the Department of Humanities, Arts, and Religion at Northern Arizona University. She is author of *Fear, Truth and Writing* and *Subjects of Deceit*.

Andrew Cutrofello is Professor and Graduate Program Director in the Department of Philosophy at Loyola University Chicago. He has written four books, including *Continental Philosophy: A Contemporary Introduction* and *The Owl at Dawn: A Sequel to Hegel's Phenomenology of Spirit*.

Zeynep Direk was born in Istanbul, Turkey, and received her Ph.D. from University of Memphis. She is Associate Professor of Philosophy in Galatasaray University, Istanbul, Turkey. She is author of *Dünyanın Teni* [The Flesh of the World] and *Başkalık Deneyimi* [Experience of Alterity], and co-editor (with Leanord Lawlor) of *Derrida: Critical Assessments*.

Jesse Goldhammer received his Ph.D. in political science from the University of California, Berkeley. He was a visiting scholar at U.C. Berkeley's Institute of Governmental Studies and at the University of Texas at Austin's Department of Government. He is author of *The Headless Republic*.

Dorothy Holland is Associate Professor of Theatre at the University of Richmond where she also serves as co-coordinator of the Women, Gender and Sexuality Studies Program. A contributor to *Theatre Survey* and *Theatre Symposium*, she is currently working on a study of the performance of time.

Pierre Lamarche is Assistant Professor in the Department of Philosophy, Utah Valley State College. He is currently completing two manuscripts: an anthology on the work of Antonio Negri entitled *Reading Negri*, co-edited with Max Rosenkrantz and David Sherman, and his own *Ontology of Boredom*.

Richard A. Lee Jr. is Associate Professor and Chair in the Philosophy Department at DePaul University. He is author of *Science, the Singular, and the Question of Theology* and *The Force of Reason and the Logic of Force.*

Alphonso Lingis is the author of thirteen books, including *The Community of Those Who have Nothing in Common; Dangerous Emotions; Trust; Body Transformations: Evolutions and Atavism in Culture;* and *The First Person Singular.*

Ladelle McWhorter is the James Thomas Chair of Philosophy and also Professor of Women, Gender, and Sexuality Studies at the University of Richmond in Richmond, Virginia. She is author of *Bodies and Pleasures: Foucault and the Politics of Sexual Normalization* (Indiana University Press, 1999) and more than two dozen articles on Foucault, Bataille, Irigaray, and race theory.

Lucio Angelo Privitello is Assistant Professor of Philosophy and Religion at the Richard Stockton College of New Jersey. He is author of "Introducing the Philosophy of Education and Pedagogy of Chauncey Wright," in *Transactions of the Charles S. Peirce Society,* and "The Incompossible Language of Natural Aristocracy: Deleuze's Misreading of Visconti's *The Leopard,*" in *Senses of Cinema.*

Allan Stoekl is Professor of French and Comparative Literature at Penn State University, University Park. He is currently completing a book-length study of Bataille's theories of religion and expenditure from the perspective of fundamentalist religious revival and imminent resource depletion in the twenty-first century.

Amy E. Wendling is Assistant Professor of Philosophy at Creighton University. She is currently working on the importance of labor to modern political philosophy and on rehabilitating Marxist feminism.

Shannon Winnubst is Professor of Philosophy at Southwestern University. In addition to essays on vampires, Kafka, feminist theory, race theory, and a number of twentieth-century French philosophers, she is author of *Queering Freedom* (Indiana University Press, 2006).

Index